Service Science for Socio-Economical and Information Systems Advancement:
Holistic Methodologies

Adamantios Koumpis
ALTEC Information & Communication Systems S.A., Greece

INFORMATION SCIENCE REFERENCE

Hershey · New York

Director of Editorial Content: Kristin Klinger
Senior Managing Editor: Jamie Snavely
Assistant Managing Editor: Michael Brehm
Publishing Assistant: Sean Woznicki
Typesetter: Sean Woznicki
Cover Design: Lisa Tosheff
Printed at: Yurchak Printing Inc.

Published in the United States of America by
        Information Science Reference (an imprint of IGI Global)
        701 E. Chocolate Avenue,
        Hershey PA 17033
        Tel: 717-533-8845
        Fax: 717-533-8661
        E-mail: cust@igi-global.com
        Web site: http://www.igi-global.com/reference

Library of Congress Cataloging-in-Publication Data

Koumpis, Adamantios, 1969-
 Service science for socio-economical and information systems advancement : holistic methodologies
/ by Adamantios Koumpis.

        p. cm.

 Includes bibliographical references and index.
 Summary: "This book studies numerous human factors, aspects of conceptual modeling, and economics
of a new service as they apply to the service culture"--Provided by publisher.
 ISBN 978-1-60566-683-9 (hardcover) -- ISBN 978-1-60566-684-6 (ebook) 1. Service industries.
2. Information technology. 3. Corporate culture. I. Title.

 HD9980.5.K68 2010
 338.7'61--dc22
                                2009004394

British Cataloguing in Publication Data
A Cataloguing in Publication record for this book is available from the British Library.

Advances in E-Collaboration (AECOB) Series

ISBN: 1935-2883

Editor-in-Chief: Ned Kock, Texas A&M International University, USA

Virtual Team Leadership and Collaborative Engineering Advancements: Contemporary Issues and Implications

Edited By: Ned Kock, Texas A&M International University, USA
Information Science Reference • copyright 2009 • 396PP • H/C (ISBN: 978-1-60566-110-0) • $195.00

Virtual team leadership and collaborative engineering bring teams, product engineering, and processes into the 21st century through the use of e-collaboration technologies. These powerful tools accomplish work efficiently and effectively, whether communication takes place only through e-collaboration technologies or in combination with face-to-face interaction. Virtual Team Leadership and Collaborative Engineering Advancements: Contemporary Issues and Implications addresses a range of e-collaboration topics, with emphasis on two particularly challenging ones: virtual team leadership and collaborative engineering. With contributing authors among the most accomplished e-collaboration, virtual team leadership, and collaborative engineering researchers in the world today, this book presents a blend of conceptual, theoretical, and applied chapters creating a publication that will serve both academics and practitioners.

E-Collaboration in Modern Organizations: Initiating and Managing Distributed Projects

Edited By: Ned Kock, Texas A&M International University, USA
Information Science Reference • copyright 2008 • 320PP • H/C (ISBN: 978-1-59904-825-3) • $180.00

E-Collaboration in Modern Organizations: Initiating and Managing Distributed Projects combines comprehensive research related to e-collaboration in modern organizations, emphasizing topics relevant to those involved in initiating and managing distributed projects. Providing authoritative content to scholars, researchers, and practitioners, this book specifically describes conceptual and theoretical issues that have implications for distributed project management, implications surrounding the use of e-collaborative environments for distributed projects, and emerging issues and debate related directly and indirectly to e-collaboration support for distributed project management.

The Advances in E-Collaboration (AECOB) Book Series publishes books that address the design and implementation of e-collaboration technologies, assess the behavioral impacts of e-collaboration technologies on individuals and groups, and present theoretical considerations on links between the use of e-collaboration technologies and behavioral patterns. Examples of such technologies are web-based chat tools, web-based asynchronous conferencing tools, e-mail, listservs, collaborative writing tools, group decision support systems, teleconferencing suites, workflow automation systems, and document management technologies. Considering the aforementioned areas of focus, the Advances in E-Collaboration (AECOB) Book Series seeks to fulfill the need for a platform to address the emerging principles of e-collaboration technologies. This book series aspires to supply researchers, practitioners and academicians, a high-quality and prestigious channel of publication for these areas of immediate social implication. The ongoing efforts of the series to bridge the gaps of existing literature within e-collaboration and its surrounding disciplines will foster further growth and influence the knowledge society in whole.

IGI GLOBAL
DISSEMINATOR OF KNOWLEDGE

Hershey • New York

Order online at www.igi-global.com or call 717-533-8845 x100–
Mon-Fri 8:30 am - 5:00 pm (est) or fax 24 hours a day 717-533-7115

Dedication

To Callisto and a hopefully bright future

Table of Contents

Preface

The area of services (e-services, Internet or Web services, etc.) becomes more and more populated with literature of almost all types. Several prestigious business, IT and computer science publications signified the momentum by dedicating special issue promoting terms such as "Services Science".

This book aspires to shed light on the phenomenon of services from different perspectives, thus linking several matters that we tend to think as of belonging to different disciplines though there is a unifying element in all of them. It is in this respect that the aim of the book is to provide food for thought and inspire different audiences spanning from the business analyst or key decision maker in an organization operating within a structured corporate environment to the independent free lance IT consultant that needs a companion to formulate questions that are not to be found in any conventional e-service programming manual or reference title.

Services both as a science and as a practice in today's corporate environments are seriously suffering from many different suboptimalities. Some of these suboptimalities are structural (lack of a coherent framework to apply the service), other metaphysical (lack of a supporting culture that would increase the demand and strengthen the market for the service) or of transcendal (lack of capacities in the humans that are implementing the services to the customers) and ephemeral nature (lack of an appropriate technology to support the service idiosyncracies – can you imagine amazon.com without any Internet?). For some others a framework that would comprise both organisational and technology aspects could be an answer to certain pitfalls and shortcomings currently faced.

As we today live in a "post manufacturing" world, we all face an important challenge in establishing lasting changes of culture and values in our organisations – even the ones that we are simple customers or consumers of their services. This makes it a must that organized learning processes are anchored within the organisation either for the design of a new service, or for the improvement of existing and operational ones.

Traditional service management courses and training are considered suboptimal as it often seems that the long-term effect is missing. Furthermore, traditional courses are often used by the organisations to train their employees so they can perform better, but in the same ways as they always have done.

There are several positive aspects to both approaches, but if the goal of the learning is to gain new knowledge about a service and to establish changes in service-related behaviour as well as further learning in the service-based organisation, it is important to use a strategy based on service-related theories and methods that take individual as well as organizational aspects into consideration.

There is a saying: 'have hammers, will see only nails', just because you have a hammer in your hand. In the greater scheme of things, corporate service practicing includes more than scientific approaches and methods.

Hence, the results (observations, conclusions and theories) of one scientific discipline cannot be intelligently applied or implemented in disregard of other scientific theory. The scientific communities have organised themselves in disciplines (e.g. economics, computer science, business administration, law, etc.). These might in turn be organised – or thought of – as some 'blocks' of sciences such as natural science, social science, human science etc. This internal organisation is especially visible in the academic community.

There, a holistic understanding of service science as such runs the risk of being overlooked. This risk appears despite that theory of service science may be part of the academic training in each of the disciplines. A student may learn about the very specifics of service theories and approaches developed, approved of, or otherwise adopted in the discipline he or she studies. When making the transition to the job market, the student then needs to develop into an intra-disciplinary service practitioner.

This is an example of intra-disciplinary approach, which should be carefully distinguished from inter-disciplinary approaches. We could also say that intra-disciplinary approaches, including the theory and methods implied, constitute the service toolbox that we equip the readers of the proposed book with.

My own experience working in the service industry dates back to the beginning of 1990. I have been closely involved with a wide range of different organisations in the research, the business software and the IT consultancy in general, and different types and levels of service practicing styles and cultures. In all these settings, I have been exposed to different learning strategies based on problem-based and project-organised approaches, and have experienced that they provided quite another learning outcome. I consider such a service-centred approach an effective and motivating way to organise the kind of processes and practices needed in today's turbulent environment.

For a book to attain the recognition of academics, researchers and practitioners as a useful primer in the field of services and e-services, similar to what *The Mythical Manmonth* did in the area of software engineering (and) project management several years before is an extremely ambitious goal. Especially nowadays that the shelf time for a book or similarly the Web-shop window of opportunity is extremely short, there is no time left to look back.

I firmly believe that the market does need a book on this topic and this book has been planned to cover lots of topics. What I also know (and now much better than when starting the project) is that a book of this kind is extremely difficult to write. So independently of the individual views of the readers, my intention was to help open an era in the market for similar books that shall treat the addressed subject of services and e-services in a holistic way and not only from a technical or managerial standpoint.

We all at least experience how a variety of problems and shortcomings of our service-based economy affects our lives, our careers and our beings by means of analyzing situations and presenting modern practices that can improve the way researchers, field practitioners and ICT professionals account for their core business service-related activities and improve their service design, management and optimization skills. To achieve this, throughout the book we present a mixture of position and concept themes followed by case study and application-oriented experiences. The aim is to provide a holistic view to the reader and most importantly open the door to novel practical implementations.

The book is expected to be used by academics, researchers and students possibly to support an introductory course on services or e-Services, or to complement needs for bibliography in the field of e-commerce applications and systems or CRM applications and systems.

As much of the content included in the two aforementioned areas (e-commerce and CRM) deals with services and e-services, the book may offer an interesting alternative to a plethora of similar and me-too books which fail to attract a critical mass of readers as well as in facing a second edition.

Except from the academic audience that this book aims to address (my experiences in recruiting people from academia in my Division and my many years involvement in European research projects have convinced me that the students are not given a holistic perspective on what they learn in their schools), it also aims to address audience from the computer applications industry, software engineers, IT and business consultants, accountants, technology solution providers, (e-)service developers, enterprise managers and decision makers (including top level managers). In this respect the book may facilitate its use as a guide for ICT professionals from academia, research institutions and industry, providing them with a broader perspective of how to improve their service creation, production and management assets.

As it will become obvious from the structure of the book chapters, the reader is helped to develop a holistic understanding of the service field that is currently lacking both in the academia and the industry. Service ethics or the culture that a particular service may foster is *not* independent on the functionality offered or the user interface provided to its users and the overall interactivity provided to the customers. Additionally, the reader will benefit from real world analyses and insight to success and failure stories while also analogies will be drawn that could help both academic and industry readers to find a utility path that will work for each reader individually.

ORGANISATION OF THE BOOK

It is time to go briefly through the contents of each chapter. Though many things changed several times during the planning and the writing of this book, I demonstrated all my stubbornness that people who live with me (like my wife) or work with me (like my colleagues at ALTEC Research Division) tell not to change the set or the sequence of the chapters.

Chapter 1: Service Science and Practice

This introductory chapter aims to make clear the holistic nature of services to our lives linking the science part to the practice matters. Bringing examples for service successes and failures, this chapter shall help the reader position him or herself with the field under examination. We present and discuss the collaborative approach towards service design and the contextualisation of services as leverage for attaining competitive advantage. Critical factors are listed that concern relationship management in business service contexts and which are considered in terms of the collaboration dimension. The chapter closes with an examination of power dependencies and trust in collaborative service arrangements.

Chapter 2: About the Nature of Services

Here we elaborate on the intangible nature of services – and how it materializes to tangible commodities and results. The aim of this chapter is to increase the awareness of the reader regarding the complexities related to even simple forms of services that we regard as trivial.

Five propositions are presented upon which the proposed service development framework and the underlying processes are built; all five of them are also related with corresponding problem areas in the real world and the markets. Two sections are devoted respectively to the nowadays more increasingly and intensively faced step changes in the conceptualisation of services and the e-services iceberg.

Chapter 3: Typology of services

Classes and taxonomies of services – how can they be categorized, with respect to different parameters, factors, dimensions. Why some of them matter and some other don't? How can they be organized to serve specific purposes, etc. The major part of the chapter is justly devoted to the presentation of the Service Analysis Model (SAM).

With its four constituent building blocks, SAM provides an insight to the analysis of services and is followed by a section devoted to the synthesis of service and the composition of new ones. The chapter closes with the presentation of a real test case implemented for a manufacturing company to improve their service supply chain.

Chapter 4: Services and the Humans

We examine the various aspects of influence and impact that services have on the humans and vice versa. How an interactive space is created to link both entities – and most importantly – how humans interact with each other through services of all kinds.

We examine the starting points of a real world service design and implementation case that is representative of the difficulties that one faces when trying to make practice out of theory. Designing a service that would help people offer and get a better service in the European technology transfer domain is the starting point.

We continue examining the users and their particular needs, then looking inside the service mediation process and the various user service scenarios. And conclude with a description of system deployment issues.

Chapter 5: Services and the Computers

In symmetry with Chapter 4, here the core subject in this Chapter is the relationships between services and their implementations in computer applications and information systems. Again, the interactive space is examined that is created to link both entities – and most importantly – how computers interact to each other through services.

A theoretical part of the service development framework is presented related with Information Supply Chains and is followed by an implemented test case for a manufacturing enterprise. Important part is devoted to practical concerns like configurability of a service in other or new contexts and de novo construction of a service supply chain.

Chapter 6: Services and the Workplace

How our workplaces are formed and shaped with respect to our conceptualization and understanding of services? How organisations can be characterized, affected and marked through their idea of services?

Workplaces are considered as open learning factory – open to the communities they belong to, to the markets they operate for and to the employees, customers and contractors of all types they interact with. How can all the new learning items be capitalised and transformed into knowledge assets for the companies and the employees? How can the use of a Learning Assets Management system like the CARAMBOLA concept we present be used for improvement of all aspects of service planning, implementation and operation?

Chapter 7: Service Economics

Here we examine the economies of services as well as matters related to service economics. Do the same or similar laws that drive the other fields of the non-services economy also govern the service-based economy as well? How can wealth matters be addressed in the services field with application of well-know economics patterns?

An improved accounting method for project management accounting is presented based on the idea of value centres next to the well-known concepts of cost centres and profit centres. The method can be of direct use for value based management purposes that is of central importance for all service-related activities (improvement / optimisation, planning, deployment, etc.).

Chapter 8: Service Physics

When aiming towards user-centred service design, a core issue to the design of "ergonomically correct" service interfaces is their appropriateness with respect to the particular human user behaviour attributes, as they evolve during the utilisation of an interactive service and its constituent applications.

The exploitation of human behaviour aspects in the service interaction techniques design process is of significant interest and is presented in this Chapter. Though it has been tempting to synthesize many of the presented service design guidelines we prefer to adopt a laundry list-like approach as the materialisation of a service interface design technique heavily depends on a plethora of parameters. In many cases, for the same audience a service implementation needs to be differentiated from other similar services, while in certain other cases this is not part of the recommended actions.

Chapter 9: Service Metaphysics

Transcendal matters of services: communities of users, service idealism, theological and existentialist perspectives on services – this chapter (in contrast to the previous one) is the most philosophical part of the entire book though it is of straight utility for its linkage to many service business and management topics. Furthermore, in this Chapter we present a methodology (PACE) that helps for the valuation of intangible assets like (what else?) services.

PACE is presented with practical examples and contextually linked with project and other service related activities. Services unequivocally constitute an area where increasing interest of experts from the areas of intellectual capital management and valuation will be concentrated, as they on their own possess qualities and characteristics of intangible assets because of their immaterial nature.

Chapter 10: Culture of Services

How do all different types of services affect the reality and routine of the service consumer / user? What cultural effects can we recognize to the community or the individuals? What are the cultural aspects of any newly introduced service? And how these can positively or negatively affect the society at large?

In this chapter we present results of a research exercise related with the building of services for a collaborative community environment for experiential learning in medical emergencies. Extensive use of the Living Labs methodology has been made and is reported and related with the presented framework. The final part of this chapter is devoted to configuration aspects of the collaborative service environment.

Chapter 11: Future of Services

The dominance of services in our world and the challenges that the society and the individuals are facing. About the emergence of *the* Service Science as an independent discipline that will be taught, studied, researched and applied. Formulation of the scientific foundations of *a* Service Science.

Spirituality and transcendal elements in the service discipline. Novel concepts and knowledge areas: service terrorism, service anarchy, service activism, service tyrannies. The role of history and arts and the inrush of humanities in the service domain.

Acknowledgment

I would like to thank family, friends and colleagues for their support during the long process of this project. Their advice, comfort and encouragement helped me to bring to completion what seemed at times a very distant and vague deliverable.

Particular thanks to my wife, Maria, without her support over the years this book would never have been completed.

I would also like to acknowledge all the editing assistants, supervisors and managers of IGI Global, a long chain of names and Christine Bufton is the last one and the first here for me to express my thanks; her patience and persuasion urged me on to complete the last mile of this book.

This work would not have been possible without access to the research material and the case studies that have been now for more than twelve years carried out in the Research Division of Unisoft and later ALTEC - my particular thanks go to all the people that had been with us all these years.

In particular, I would like to thank Dimitris Tektonidis, Apostolos Vontas and Androklis Mavridis, good people and good colleagues for many years now. Androklis especially is co-creator of PACE and continues his work in intangible assets valuation for his (soon-to-get) PhD. Also, certain parts of work reported here regarding the service supply platform had been realised as part of a successful European project that I had been part of, namely the IST Agent Academy project coordinated by Professor Pericles Mitkas. The project, besides being a research success story, gave the opportunity for four new researchers to unfold their creativity, namely Ioannis Athanasiadis, Dionysis Kechagias, Andreas Symeonidis and Kyriakos Chatzidimitriou. Especially the latter two had been heavily involved in what we used to call the ALTEC test case. To both I owe my gratitude.

Chapter 1
Service Science and Practice

This introductory chapter aims to make clear the holistic nature of services to our lives linking the science part to the practice matters. Bringing examples for service successes and failures, this chapter shall help the reader position him or herself with the field under examination. We present and discuss the collaborative approach towards service design and the contextualisation of services as leverage for attaining competitive advantage. Critical factors are listed that concern relationship management in business service contexts and which are considered in terms of the collaboration dimension. The chapter closes with an examination of power dependencies and trust in collaborative service arrangements.

The idea behind this book is extremely simple. And the title of this book, that was designed with the help of the editors from the publisher is totally descriptive and does not contain any dose of deliberate marketing mislead. Having graduated as a computer scientist and having worked in the industry for a long period, I have accumulated an extremely great amount of experiences all of which relate to suboptimalities in service related issues: not only how one provides a service but also how

DOI: 10.4018/978-1-60566-683-9.ch001

one designs this particular service, and most importantly how this specific service has been conceived and conceptualised. And – to not leave out further important parts of the service supply chain – how the recipient of the service relates him or herself with the provided service.

In a simplified world where for each service there is a provider and a supplier, both of which have consensually agreed on what exactly shall be the subject and the conditions of the interaction between them. But this simplified world does not exist at all – or it may exist under some very specific circumstances and also not for long as disruptions from the 'outside' world shall sooner or later emerge and will bring back the system to its usual suboptimal levels.

However, in all my encounterings with the academic community as a student or reader of scientific publications as well as in my experiences with the industry or the research communities, it seemed to me that all agreements and decisions for any type of services were made under the assumption of a smooth and friction-free operational environment. Of course this assumption had all times been proven wrong – and a great puzzlement for me was why are all steps regarding the lifecycle of a service characterised by an entire lack of common sense and an absolute stubbornness to improve aspects that are usual points of expected pitfalls? Why for a big number of easy-to-fix and obvious matters do we need a special appeal for an epiphany?

The reason is simple and relates with the title of this book: unfortunately we all have been educated to think according to clichés or templates: *this* is a problem of physics and *that* is a problem of mathematics; *this* is my problem and *that* is your problem; *this* is my service and *that* is your service. For *this* aspect of the service I am the responsible and for *that* aspect I am not.

The term holistic may make some readers raise their eyebrow: whatever relates with the term *holistic* or related terms like *multi-disciplinary* or *cross-disciplinary* or *inter-disciplinary* may look like an attempt for the scientification of astrology. However, similar to the medicine that we all agree it is not an exact science like we tend to think for mathematics, we can see the de facto existence of service science. The most important issue in this exploration of service science fundamentals is to have an open mind that seeks questions – old ones and new ones. The answers may easily follow or may simply be difficult to find yet. At least, one common denominator for the majority of the service failure stories that I have experiences in all these years related to a simple fact: people denied to address the problem (the service as well) as a whole and tended to fragment it into non-sense making pieces, some of which they had fanatically ignored (e.g. as supposedly non relevant), some other they characterised as not of their responsibility, and finally selectively chose to address some parts that they thought of as being of their responsibility and – very important … - possible to solve and manage in their own mystic scale of computational capabilities.

The above way, it is only His invisible hand that makes our world go round, the economy moving, sectors of the economy produce and other sectors consume. I am tempted to give a rough estimation that perhaps the suboptimality level that our economies operate at may lie at the level of 80% (of suboptimality) or else 20% (of optimality). Fortunately even this low level of optimality still proves helpful and gives us some basic levels of prosperity – but *not all of us*. With declining physical resources and increasing concerns for the implications of an international crisis in socio-economic relationships, capture of a competency to improve our service infrastructures shall have a huge impact in our lives and may be the key issue for the achievement of sustainability.

Many people design a service without linking it with other services or processes and without positioning it within a grid of related services or processes. This of course leads us to the inauguration of the era of interoperability (once you have at least two services, you have to make them interoperable – usually through the creation of a third service to serve the interoperability of the previous two). And how sure can one be that the ones, who had mistakenly designed two non-interoperable services, will now improve their understanding for the services, their business domain and the world in general so that the third service that they will now design to facilitate the interoperability of the previous two services shall exhibit an improved behaviour?

We tend to take assignments from our boss, from our customers, from another department within our company with a closed mind – trying to deliberately minimise the conceptualisation efforts regarding how we shall treat the assigned problem or issue, trying to find the closest match with a previous case or a pattern we are used to manage and solve. This is not bad and for some cases it is what people should do. I don't expect an IRS auditor to unfold all his hidden creativity for the processing of all the tax declaration applications he receives. Or the reception desk clerk of an insurance company or a librarian who perform deliberate abstractions regarding their services (though in many cases this is what exactly is needed). But for a great number of cases there is a need for people to use their brains in both an efficient and an effective way, combining information they have with other information they should ask from other people, discussing their concerns with others who may help – or may be part of the future problem recipients.

Even the simplest information system does not exist *in vacui*: it is part of a complex chain of relationships and many of its parts need to be thought as subject of a continuous advancement. It is not my aim to use hype words and buzz terms like ecosystem, but the simple reality is affirmative: even the simplest system exhibits characteristics of a living system – wherever we may draw the guiding defining principles for it i.e. biology, agent theory or sociology. In our case, life is not related with properties or qualities that we usually attribute to human systems or agent-based systems but to the simple fact that such a system interacts with several other entities (human ones or other non-humans like some other information systems) and is therefore acting as the recipient and the provider of services.

For the design of a service, what has been described as the Scandinavian approach in the past was the participatory design, namely the design of the service together with its future users so that the requirements will not be subject of the service designer's magnanimity or the service programmer's creative intellectual assets. This needs to be elaborated to include aspects like: who is going to support and maintain the service? How is the service going to evolve? At least some parts of such a service evolution are obvious to think and proactively take care of like when dealing with children that grow and need bigger size shoes for the next year.

Most of us are nowadays used with the convention that the term services and their implementation through the electronic medium as e-services is defined here as not just a single technology but a combination of technologies, applications, processes, business strategies and practices necessary to do business electronically.

Electronic services have been in existence for over 25 years and many of the large organisations in sectors such as retail, electronics and automotive have made extensive use of e-services of different types for facilitation of their business requirements. Other variants of such operational and hands-on approaches for defining e-services do not specify the requirement for a service to be inter-enterprise but different definitions share the emphasis on computer application to computer application using an agreed standard and without human intervention.

The ubiquitous presence of the Internet, associated low cost network access and improved human to application interface via more advanced web browsers has now facilitated wider penetration and Internet services are touted as a key enabler for collaborative relationships. Internet tools, application programs, and open protocols provide opportunities to lower transaction costs, facilitate close ties, the sharing of resources and the transformation of value chains through collaborative relationships. However, the underlying organisational and management issues tend not to be given as much attention as the actual technical linkage and systems integration issues. One question that is interesting to explore is whether previous adopters of e-services may be able to use their experience of traditional services based on conventional inter-organisational systems to implement new Internet based e-service systems more effectively. This may be in terms of the technical understanding of the importance of standards and integration with IT systems through to an understanding of the need to manage the organisational and management issues.

COLLABORATIVE VERSUS COMPETITIVE PARADIGM: BUSINESS DRIVERS AND THEORETICAL CONTEXT FOR COLLABORATIVE SERVICE ACTIVITIES

The corporate community pursues collaboration in order to share risks, share costs, gain economies of scale, gain technical and market knowledge, conduct research and jointly develop standards. This implies that collaboration can also be seen as a strategy to improve the flexibility and responsiveness of organisations to emerging opportunities and that through collaborative relationships a company can absorb knowledge from partners and thus increase its organisational competencies.

Such a type of intelligent collaboration through the introduction of advanced service infrastructures for relationship management with suppliers, customers and partners in ways that add value to product and services is of extreme importance and should be regarded by companies and in general all types of organisations as a natural place for long-term investments even in periods of financial – and social structures and values – crises. Such organisational learning is concerned with all processes in the organisation that lead to the assimilation of new knowledge and its application to a service setting.

We all see that the standard model of innovation as a linear process, from research through to design, development and then manufacturing, is often now carried out concurrently and collaboratively through networks of organisations exchanging information through e-service technologies. Collaboration may also be tactical and may change with time and firms can adopt positions in networks, rather than 'monogamous' collaborations. There is one way, for example, to differentiate between value networks and dynamic markets where the former is characterised by a limited number of long term relationships while the latter involves many relationships over shorter time scales in order to maximise product, price or delivery configurations by selecting appropriate business partners.

One path to follow is to try find advice and recommendations or even guidelines to follow for collaborative service design and implementation projects to succeed. Such guidelines should include the need for all partners to perceive themselves to be benefiting from the collaboration and for a participative ethos with wide consultation among participants and within partner organisations. This emphasis on equal bargaining power, consultation and power sharing also needs to be supplemented with a learning and change orientation.

Trial and error learning appears to be a prominent feature of most collaborative projects involving small and medium-sized enterprises (SMEs) because many lack expertise in emergent technologies and their applications. However, trust, a common culture between participants and the stability of the participating organisations combined with their continuing commitment, plays an important part in the success of such collaborative projects.

In general it is easy to see that networks that turn their suppliers, subcontractors and even competitors into close collaborators share common characteristics, including successful uniform standards for exchange of information, rigorous performance standards, sharing of benefits with all partners, an on-line presence for all key business processes and the development and testing of new opportunities with network partners. and though no clear theory of collaboration has emerged (at least till now…), the theories and dominant themes identified with collaboration as approached by different schools of thought and researchers include several approaches which would not have been regarded as parts of the same Weltanschauung – at least in traditional non holistic terms – such as new institutional economics, strategic competitive analysis, innovation networks and organisational learning.

And though we have found no single theoretical perspective that provides the foundation for a general theory of collaboration there is plenty of room to suggest a range of theories that may fit together to form the basis of such a theory. For example, strategic management theory in relation to how partners regulate their behaviours for collective gains, economic theory concerned with overcoming impediments to efficiencies in transactions, political theory in terms of who has access to power and resources and also resource dependency theory concerned with circumstances under which stakeholders will adopt collaborative alliances are elements of such an approach that would aim to set the foundations for a new service science discipline.

The real world and the market put a lot of increasing competitive pressures on companies exacerbating the need for greater flexibility, efficiency, responsiveness and innovation. Firms may therefore seek to collaborate in order to compete more effectively in their chosen markets. Using (common, if possible) e-services and e-service infrastructures provides a potential enabler to allow firms to react to the strong pressures, emanating from an ever more complex environment, by transcending organisational boundaries and creating privileged relationships with trading partners.

Collaborations may take different forms, have varying lifecycles and involve different scope and depth of relationships. However, real world experiences indicate that a number of factors contribute to implementing e-services to support collaborative business relationships. These include the sharing of benefits, the need for agreed information interchange standards, a consultative approach based on mutual trust together with willingness to learn and adapt processes and practices. These factors are critical to relationship management in business contexts and are now further considered in terms of the competitive collaborative continuum.

USING SERVICES FOR COMPETITIVE ADVANTAGE

Though we are close to the end of the first decade of the (still) new millennium, it is easy for a researcher or a practitioner to recognise that the origin of much of the contemporary work in IT strategy lies with Porter's framework regarding competitive forces (Porter 1980, Porter, 1985) and power relationships are commonly analysed using this framework. Historically speaking, Porter developed the five forces model to consider strategic choices in competitive environments.

The basis of this model is that a firm exists within an industry and to succeed it must effectively deal with the competitive forces which exist within the particular industry. Porter outlines five threats that may impact on a firm and these include the bargaining power of suppliers and buyers, the threat of new entrants and substitute products and rivalry within the industry. Buyers or suppliers may be powerful enough to bargain away much of the profitability available to the firm and increasing buyer and supplier switching costs can reduce that power by making a change of relationship expensive. Porter suggested that firms could deal with these threats by following one of the three generic strategies of cost leadership, product/service differentiation or focusing on a particular niche. Of course, and as expected, numerous other researchers have built on Porter's work to develop hybrid approaches for competitive advantage.

Porter also considered the concept of the value chain with primary activities forming a linear flow from suppliers through to customers. Each activity must be carried out and linked effectively to achieve optimum overall performance. A recurring theme in the corpus of research work related with business interoperable systems is the role of IT systems as a key enabler for competitive advantage through cementing relationships with customers, enabling integration forwards or backwards in the industry value chain or in establishing a technological lead.

Of course there is no disagreement that through e-service networks firms can achieve an integration effect by tightly coupling processes at the interface between stages of the value chain. Once a firm decides to subcontract then it starts to share its value chain management with a partner then this is in effect collaboration. However, the view that subcontracting can somehow be done without close co-operation misses the importance of the concepts of the value chain and the complementarities of assets. With the evolution of standards and protocols for information exchange, services were seen as having an increasingly important part to play in the strategic use of IT for competitive advantage. However, quite apart from the general scepticism that has developed with regard to sustainable advantage, gaining competitive advantage from Web based service applications proved to be particularly elusive. It is not uncommon for an IT company to find out that of e.g. ten different applications in customer companies studied only one shows the potential for giving significant competitive advantage by locking out other suppliers through proprietary technology, while most of the supplied systems may have been driven only by competitive necessity. Furthermore, and as the technology matures companies do not perceive e-services as providing any special advantage vis-à-vis their competitors as in certain industries it has become the standard way of doing business.

This does not mean that there is no available space for exploring and identifying business value proponents that can be associated with the deployment of e-services that can be also mapped to Porter's framework to demonstrate the link with the competitive advantage that could be derived. The key point remains and has to do with the fact that building any kind of an e-service system requires a strategy which should include an understanding of the impact of e-services on the given industry *and* corporate structure, the potential for new business models and the opportunities for competitive advantage.

Value generation, competitive distinction and profitability should be regarded as the three essentials of successful e-business strategy, design and execution. In the constant turbulence of the Internet dominated environment the value chain will deconstruct and reconfigure to reflect its changing role and suggest a reversed version of Porter's value chain structure that is customer driven.

And it is not accidental or by chance that in a review of strategy and the Internet, Porter himself (2001) had confirmed the continuing imperative of competitive advantage through building on the proven principles of effective strategy. There Porter argued that as all companies embrace Internet technology, the Internet will be neutralised as a source of advantage.

Competitive advantage will arise instead from traditional strengths such as unique products, proprietary content and distinctive physical activities. It is at this point that e-services may be able to fortify those advantages but are unlikely to supplant them if they are not reflecting a true service culture and dedication to values and codes that have their roots in traditional service design. How can a company claim high quality e-service deployment when they lack on the all times classic trio of ingredients, recipes and a master cook to give life to a superb service?

Moving beyond the narrow competitive perspective of individual organisations, the potential of e-services to facilitate business and create new opportunities is recognised by communities of common interest at industrial and scientific levels. Early examples of trading communities in areas such as insurance and chemicals testify to the advantage of collaboration between competing companies in the same industry sector in improving information flow to provide cost benefits and improved customer service levels.

However, the biggest and most serious challenges for an inter-organisational system to evolve into more sophisticated levels of integration lie, as expected, outside the corporate environment. Especially as far as collaboration is concerned, this may evolve from a data-based system to providing partners direct access to information and then expanding information sharing beyond business transactions to other areas of co-operation. This implies that a strategy can result only when a company's internal business services and processes are fully aligned around its intended service flows and the supporting service structures and process engagements with its partners.

Our experiences are mainly concentrated in the area of interfirm collaboration, usually centred on IT initiatives, and it is true that this might be a possible route to competitive success. However, collaboration should be regarded as competition in a different form – all people and organisations who failed to see this they run a serious risk that might have set them out of their market, their business or their job.

The tragedy is that several people I talked to after such an incident has taken place, denied to see the point and thus failed in exploiting their case as a learning exercise to protect them from future failures. Having personally gone through the transformation of a family business to a part of an impersonal (and sometimes) arrogant corporate structure I was able to experience the need for firms to reconfigure themselves and to develop their core competencies, by learning from partners. Shorter product life cycles, more intensive competition, faster technological change and more specialised markets have led to various kinds of interfirm agreements, collaborations and partnerships as large firms join together to create strategic partnerships and also incorporate small firms in recognition of their capability for flexibility, responsiveness and innovation. On the other hand be it that your company is a small mouse or a lion, a minnow or a whale, or even a happily and fortunately dinosaur survivor, they all share same processes (eating, sleeping, hunting, protecting their living space, copulating, etc.) and thus there is a lot common to discuss and share thoughts about as far as services are concerned.

The concept of the extended enterprise appears in various guises and has been a recurring theme in the minds of people dealing with services from the academia and the industry. A common theme there is the role of inter-organisational IT systems in supporting physically discrete business partners working closely together to manage the flow of goods and services along an entire value chain. How can for instance a Value Added Partnership (VAP) in the health industry value chain facilitate the involved parties to share information and coordinate value added activities among manufacturers, distributors, retailers and third party insurance suppliers? And how can Japanese automobile manufacturers where the keiretsus of tightly knit companies have to some extent set the example for VAPs by sharing out the value added work among trusted partners? Information partnering can be one solution, where shared investments in hardware and software enable all involved parties to pass large volumes of intellectual capital and not only data or information for joint e.g. marketing programs, cross selling and to take advantage of new channels of distribution.

Of course, and as expected, the principle that businesses operate within a larger network, or extended enterprise, which may include intermediaries, regulatory bodies and competitors as well as suppliers and customers is not new. On the other hand, it is another story to view this reality from a service perspective and try to configure the organisation of a co-operation based framework for e.g. organising economic activity to create international competitiveness for globally oriented firms like the Deutsche Bahn or Deutsche Telekom or Siemens, to name only three German firms that got rid of the national level of developing their markets and exporting their 'goods' elsewhere abroad and now rather create global markets on their go.

However, all three again adopt a relationship based, collaborative paradigm for network activities entailing close co-operation and the sharing of resources and information. This concept of the extended enterprise implies a shifting of the boundary of the organisation out to include elements of other organisations. It therefore offers an alternative to the strategic options of vertical or horizontal integration in that information exchange and sharing enables greater efficiency, flexibility and innovation to respond to market requirements. Be it that someone names his or her corporate intangible assets a Value Chain or prefers the term Strategic Network, it is all about longer-term, purposeful arrangements amongst distinct but related (usually for-profit) organisations that allow those firms to sustain competitive advantage with respect to their competitors outside the chain or the network. The most important aspect is how one can take a proactive attitude in care of it. Although the key aspects for success depend on collaboration and trust, IT can play a key role in facilitating these aspects through service sharing and deployment of common service infrastructures.

In recent years there has also been a general trend towards partnership sourcing together with a reduction and consolidation of the supply base in order to have better relationships with fewer companies. Such a partnering approach to suppliers is characterised by longer term contracts, integrated key processes and a commitment to collaborative relationships compared to the more traditional approach which reflects an adversarial stance, reactive suppliers and an emphasis on cost reduction. The ethos of this modern trading practice is for buyers to view their suppliers as part of their extended enterprise that covers the whole value chain of corporate activities.

The application of the concept of organisational networks in the real world lacks consistent terminology with terms such as virtual networks, strategic networks, dynamic networks, extended networks and value networks. These different terms are often used as synonyms but sometimes also indicate different characteristics related to longevity, purpose and culture. However, the common theme is one of traditional external boundaries of organisations beginning to blur, often with e-services as a key enabler of such change. The separation between internal and external processes becomes less clear as inter-organisational systems facilitate more co-ordinated exchange and sharing of information and this may involve the innovative use of e-service technologies for new organisational arrangements, value acceleration and new value added processes.

This 'virtualisation' of companies to form an extended enterprise means that if one partner improvises and fails a whole service or only a service process execution, then the whole network may break down because all partners are taking part in the same overall logical business process. However, the corporate world generally lacks a holistic perspective on the difficulties and risks of interdependence inherent in these models. And in addition to this, the valuation of the effectiveness of collaboration and the trade-off involved also requires consideration. Collaborative arrangements, for example, may eliminate competition within a supply chain, effectively keeping out suppliers who possess superior services, goods or processes but who are not party to the collaboration.

POWER DEPENDENCIES AND TRUST IN COLLABORATIVE SERVICE ARRANGEMENTS

The concept of the extended enterprise with the emphasis on collaboration, mutual benefits and long-term relationships does need to be treated with some scepticism. There is evidence of a gap between the language used to articulate the desire to partner and the commercial reality of how power is exercised in implementing the practice. We all know by experience how information asymmetries may give rise to opportunistic behaviour, where one party uses information available only to them to their own advantage, while mechanisms for controlling such behaviour has been discussed in the context of 'the prisoner's dilemma'. Even where vertical desegregation takes place there are dangers of over-dependence where a core firm can find itself managing the assets of its partners and in effect converting the network into a vertically integrated organisation.

These dangers link to my experiences of all the wrong advice I had given to people who (fortunately for both me and them) were capable to separate the relative value of my advice to them from the wrongness of a potential application – something that seems difficult to theoritise as most of us do it intuitively and not by following some type of an algorithm. To cut the long story short, and supported also by my experiences from working in European projects as member of industrial and academic consortia, where companies claim that they are collaborating, more often than not this was a euphemism for cutting costs and reducing investments rather than designing more superb products or more effective relationships.

When talking of services trust is an important concept because it is a key enabler of co-operative human actions (and this forms another good candidate synonym for defining a service). The term trust is interpreted in many different ways though usage within the computer science discipline tends to be narrow and mechanistic, focusing on aspects such as encryption standards.

However, in the wider business sense of confident reliance by one party on the behaviour of another party or parties, a trader may be dependent not only on the other party to the trade but also on the e-market operator and any intermediaries and service providers. It is therefore the 'people side' of the transactions that many players have begun to question and suggest that social exchange theory is useful for explaining the importance of trust and the role it plays in cementing and expanding the relationship of trading partners.

In a B2B service deployment scenario trusting behaviours are initiated in the face of uncertainty and make both parties vulnerable to risk as both parties do not know if their actions will be reciprocated. In the context of social exchange theory, suppliers and their clients may provide favours having no way to assure an appropriate return but trusting others to discharge their obligations. If a firm reciprocates another's trust in them then they prove themselves worthy of being accorded continued and extended favours, hence social exchange generate trust in social relations through their recurrent and gradually expanding character.

Of course there is a need to differentiate between trading partner trust, concerned with aspects such as keeping commitments and negotiating honestly, and electronic trust concerned with issues such as the confidentiality, integrity and authenticity of service related data. The adoption of B2B e-services may thus depend as much on the reliability of trading partners as on the reliability of the technology. Trust is therefore one of the important elements that make service related partnerships and service networks successful, especially where risk, uncertainty and interdependence exist.

However trust does not exist in a vacuum and there is a need for an appropriate context where trust between internal partners can be built, managed, and maintained. Such a context would include a suitable legal and contractual framework, reliable technology to support communication and information exchange as well as a shared understanding of the entire underpinning service environment, such as an innovative environment or a sense of order and stability. This last point brings us to the issue of the service culture for which a separate Chapter in this book is dedicated.

REFERENCES

Porter, M. E. (1980). *Competitive Strategy: Techniques For Analysing Industries And Competitors*. New York: Free Press.

Porter, M. E. (1985). *Competitive Advantage: Creating And Sustaining Superior Performance*, New York: Free Press.

Porter, M.E. (2001). Strategy and the Internet. *Harvard Business Review*, March.

Chapter 2
About the Nature of Services

Here the author elaborates on the intangible nature of services – and how it mate-rializes to tangible commodities and results. The aim of this chapter is to increase the awareness of the reader regarding the complexities related to even simple forms of services that we regard as trivial. Five propositions are presented upon which the proposed service development framework and the underlying processes are built; all five of them are also related with corresponding problem areas in the real world and the markets. Two sections are devoted respectively to the nowadays more increasingly and intensively faced step changes in the conceptualisation of services and the e-services iceberg.

Though both the results and the outcomes of services are in many cases tangible and visible to us, and the same holds for their 'ingredients', services themselves are rather of an intangible and immaterial nature. There are many interesting definitions that try to organise knowledge in the area of services with aspects of the service delivery process.

At a great extent we are used in operational definitions that relate a service with

DOI: 10.4018/978-1-60566-683-9.ch002

the time that has been necessary for its delivery. However, this is not necessarily academically correct: in many cases, the human provider of a service carries years of experience and previous education which is not counted by us – what we see only is how much time he or she spent *for* us or on our case.

However, we can all accept that if we want a celebrity lawyer to work for us we shall pay him or her more money than a young graduate who has not yet proven any professional excellence.

On the other hand, we tend to forget that the celebrity lawyer is too busy polishing his image and fostering his public relationships and administering his numerous clients and managing his own people, therefore we shall actually not get a service by him or herself and rather end up being serviced by one of his or her team members – not necessarily the brightest or more ambitious one. While in case we had chosen the young but still unknown one, we would get personal service. It is up to us to choose of course, but it is good to know what we pay for and match this with what we get in return. The most exciting thing with the service industry is that there exist huge margins for profit and charlatanism and that it is not always easy to distinguish between what shall end up in a good customer relationship or in a bad one. In a great extent, these borders are unknown even to the ones who provide the services.

Many services can be designed by someone for delivery or provision by others. However, many services are difficult or impossible and not sense-making to try to abstract or conceptualise: simply they are a mix of the individuality of their provider and this cannot be subject of any rational description.

The possible options are countless: we can consider the case of an extremely well designed service (to avoid using the term optimal) that has been implemented in an unlucky way. In a similar fashion, even a less well designed service can have a good or even optimal implementation that can grant it a commercial success. To choose which of the two is best is highly subjective – personally I prefer the second case: optimising something than decreasing the level of optimality the more we leave the downy field of theories to enter the coarse fields of practice.

In a 2003 Conference of the Association for Computing Machinery (ACM), two outstanding members of the profession expressed the following thought: 'An appealing vision of the evolution of computing is that the computer disappears – with the task and experience dominating, and the tools receding into the background' (Pingali and Sukaviriya 2003).

Further to this, Professor Thomas Davenport concludes in his book that "*It is difficult to impose a new process on a large group of knowledge workers who don't want to work that way*". He continues by recognising that "*Too much of the work is invisible or is carried out in a way that can't easily be assessed or measured*" and concludes noting that "*A process orientation implies design – we are not just accepting work the way it is, but trying to find better ways to perform it*" (Davenport, 2005).

In my opinion, both of the above profile the evolution and what we should expect from the field of services in the years to come. While over the past 75 years, workplaces have changed dramatically, noisy mechanical adding machines and typewriters have been replaced by silent PCs, global electronic communication now occurs round-the-clock without any physical transfer of paper documents.

Unfortunately, in many collaborative situations – and service design, implementation and delivery constitutes an essential part of them – what we can afford to call a typical worker is more concerned with his or her task at hand and would rather use collaborative tools only to the extent they do not interfere with their work. Furthermore, collaborative tasks and design processes often involve the physical environment and physical objects as well as access to the information being stored in electronic form and delivered through electronic devices or display tools.

In this respect, we experience the following paradox cutting across today's information greedy and knowledge intensive society:

- Workers are using extremely advanced technology services and (potentially) content-rich applications in their personal lives.
- While their working environments remain obsolete and monolithic, both in terms of supporting tools, applications and media and of underlying metaphors.

The metaphors and the various conceptual schemes and mental representations that people use for carrying out most types of service related tasks and job assignments, spanning from what we call 'simple' and 'everyday' to those we tend to regard as more abstract or sophisticated, and which work and the learning process in general are part of, have a great significance to the way tasks are carried out and work practices are developed for carrying out these tasks. By the use of such a non-material or intangible culture (it is extremely important to mention here the work of Lakoff and Johnson (1980), which is inherent to any specific job assignment, being able to 'serve' it and to sufficiently express its characteristics, it is often possible to improve substantially the way a task is executed, no matter how abstract, complex, detailed or sophisticated may this be. That same nonmaterial or intangible culture also consists of all ideas, values, norms, interaction styles, beliefs and practices that are used by the members of a collaborative service environment.

Continuing the above thread of syllogism, the metaphors and the various types of conceptual schemas and mental representations that people use for carrying out most types of service and service related tasks and activities, spanning from what we call 'simple' and 'everyday' to those we tend to regard as more abstract or sophisticated, have an increased significance to the ways these tasks are carried out, to the practices that are developed for carrying out these services, as well as to the overall 'culture' that characterizes them. With the use of such appropriate metaphors, conceptual schemas and mental representations, which appertain to a particular task, being able to 'serve' it and sufficiently express its characteristics, it is possible to improve substantially the way such a service is performed.

In several parts of this book I shall refer to what I call Situation Room (SR) which deals with a concept I aspire to employ as a central metaphor of the collaborative service environment of the future, supporting customer and corporate requirements, work and management practices, organizational issues, and emerging enabling technologies.

The usage of concepts and metaphors used in the context of military applications, as it is the case with the proposed *Situation Room*, is likely to prove extremely useful and rewarding for application in the field of services and service related processes. An important element, which marks not only the usefulness and utility but also the value of this particular concept of the Situation Room, is the facilitation of the corporate learning process. Both the use of the concept of Situation Room and its accompanying framework for application in the corporate services and process grid and service-related decision making activities, as well as the contribution they make to the increase of the corporate service knowledge capital, can be regarded as essential intangible assets of a company (or an organization), and as such they can be assessed and valuated by means of quantitative and qualitative approaches.

Table 1 sets the stage for what shall be the subject of five propositions I make which reflect my view on the nature of services.

Below I present each of the five propositions and briefly comment on them.

FIRST PROPOSITION

The metaphors and the various types of conceptual schemas and mental representations that people – either as individuals or as members of a team – use for carrying out most types of service development tasks, spanning from relatively 'simple' and 'straightforward' ones to those we tend to regard as more abstract, sophisticated or complex, have an increased significance to the ways these tasks are carried out, to the practices that are developed for carrying out these services, as well as to the overall 'culture' that characterizes them.

I use three different terms interchangeably – and the aim is to exploit the semantic 'additivity' caused by joining their notions. What I support here is that:

Table 1. The five propositions on the nature of services

	What is it about?
Existence proposition	The metaphors and the various types of conceptual schemas and mental representations that people – either as individuals or as members of a team – use for carrying out most types of service development tasks, spanning from relatively 'simple' and 'straightforward' ones to those we tend to regard as more abstract, sophisticated or complex, have an increased significance to the ways these tasks are carried out, to the practices that are developed for carrying out these services, as well as to the overall 'culture' that characterizes them.
Improvement proposition	With the use of such appropriate metaphors, conceptual schemas and mental representations, which appertain to a particular service or service related task, being able to 'serve' it and sufficiently express its characteristics and idiosyncrasies, it is possible to improve substantially the way service development is executed.
Business-as-War proposition	The usage of concepts and metaphors used in the context of military applications, as it is the case with the notion of a Situation Room, is likely to prove extremely useful and rewarding for application in the area of service development in the IT sector, as well as in the wider area of related business and commercial services.
Learning proposition	An important element, which marks not only the usefulness and utility but also the value of this particular concept of the Situation Room for support of the service development process, is the facilitation of the corporate learning process.
Corporate capital proposition	Both the use of the concept of Situation Room and its accompanying framework for application in the corporate service development process grid and decision making activities, as well as the contribution they make to the increase of the corporate service knowledge capital, can be regarded as essential intangible assets of a company (or an organization), and as such they can be assessed and valuated by means of quantitative and qualitative approaches.

What we tend to call or recognize as:

- Either metaphors
- Or conceptual schemas
- Or mental representations

and which people use for practicing service development tasks which again span:

- From 'simple' and 'straightforward'
- To 'more abstract, sophisticated or complex'

are forming an important part of the (relative) success that people have in performing these tasks.

This success, again, may refer:

- Either to the actual level of e.g. physical performance of an action as part of

a service development process
- Or to some practice that is developed for performing that particular action
- Or, finally, to the 'culture' that underlies this particular service related activity.

I call this first proposition *Existence proposition*, as it makes the assumption that there exists this linkage between mental abstractions and people's tasks as an organic part of a service development process. Causality or dependency relationships are of further interest, as the main point to be examined here is whether this claim is holding in actual – or not.

Regarding this aspect, a researcher has stated more than 10 years ago that since (the now regarded as legendary) *"Visicalc's metaphorical ledger and the Xerox Star's desktop metaphor, interface designers have been incorporating metaphors into user interfaces. User interface (UI) guidelines for most of the popular operating systems encourage the use of metaphors in interface design. They suggest that applications should build on the user's real-world experience by exploiting concrete metaphors thereby making applications easier to use. Surprisingly little research supports the popular belief that metaphors in user interfaces facilitate performance."* (Smilowitz, 1996)

In her research, Smilowitz explored the use of metaphors in interface design, concentrating on the case of World Wide Web and the Web browsers at a time that much of what we nowadays consider as cliché did not even exist at all. This tremendously increases the value of her work in regard to the future implications in what we tend to call as digital economy. Having conducted a series of experiments, she came up with the conclusion that though User Interface metaphors can facilitate users' interactions, however, various metaphors are not equally effective, some are no better than non-metaphoric interfaces.

Again I think it is important to emphasise that having in mind the time that her research appeared (late 1996) and how the Zeitgeist was at that time, her investigation on issues such as the integrality of a particular metaphor are important and support the appropriateness of the posed research questions.

SECOND PROPOSITION

With the use of such appropriate metaphors, conceptual schemas and mental representations, which appertain to a particular service or service related task, being able to 'serve' it and sufficiently express its characteristics and idiosyncrasies, it is possible to improve substantially the way service development is executed, no matter how abstract, complex, complicated, sophisticated or detailed this is.

This second proposition – I call it *Improvement proposition* as its central meaning is that:

People / companies can significantly improve the way they perform service development tasks, independently on their complexity, difficulty or other related characteristics, if they have access to or are driven by:

- Either an appropriate metaphor
- Or an appropriate conceptual schema
- Or an appropriate mental representation

Reversing the way I stated this above – but not changing the logical order, this reads like:

- If people / companies have access to an appropriate metaphor, then they can improve the way they perform a service development task (that the metaphor relates to or explains or describes)

In case this statement is true, it holds also the (conditional only) validity of the complementary statement, like:

- If people / companies do not perform successfully a service development task, then this is possibly because they have not had access till now to an appropriate metaphor

It is obvious that the main argument here relates to the facilitating ('enabling') nature of an appropriate metaphor. And because 'appropriate' as a term may make people feel uncertain about its meaning, I actually mean *good* metaphors.

Donald Norman, an internationally established and legendary figure in the area of human factors and design has been touching this issue in his 1988 now classic reading and in its later (1990) revised appearance. (Norman's books are a must for connoisseurs in many different areas and disciplines - not only computer programmers as one would expect). At a final level of analysis, any modern consumer of consumer electronics applications and services has good reasons for reading Norman.) There, on exploring the matter of usage of metaphors and adoption of conceptual models, amongst others he states that metaphor is both useful and harmful, providing the explanation that the problem with metaphor is that not all users may understand the point. Worse, they may take the metaphor too literally and try to do actions that were not intended. Still, this is one way of training users. It is for this, according to Norman, that coherent conceptual models are valuable and, in his opinion, necessary, but there still remains the bootstrapping problem; how does one learn the model in the first place? - why by conventions, words, and metaphors.

On this topic, several years later in (Norman, 1999) he defines the 'design space' with the following constituents:

- The Conceptual Model
- Real Affordances
- Perceived Affordances
- Constraints
- Conventions

Norman recognizes that we should neither confuse *affordance* with *perceived affordances* nor confuse *affordances* with *conventions*. According to Norman, *affordances* reflect the possible relationships among actors and objects: they are properties of the world, while *conventions*, on the other hand, are arbitrary, artificial and learned. Once learned, they help us master the intricacies of daily life, whether they be *conventions* for courtesy, for writing style, or for operating a word processor. Designers can invent new real and *perceived affordances*, but they cannot so readily change established social *conventions*. Know the difference and exploit that knowledge. Skilled design makes use of all.

Later in Chapter 5 (Services and the computer) I open the discussion with a hypothetical 'Boolean' service, namely a case of a simple and unsophisticated service instance, that if we look closer we recognize a growing complexity that may attack initially the designers or the service and finally its future customers and users. Norman's views are invaluable in this respect; at the end what counts is not the fuzzy arguments that one used to convinced his or her boss for financing a new service development project, nor the buzzwords that marketing people used for convincing innocent people to become customers of this brand new service. The common denominator comes to the above constituents as these are mentioned by Norman. It is therefore that the value and utility of Norman's work is immense – both when you are designing a new $ 19.95 coffee machine or a new multi-million Euros service infrastructure (try to think: why should it be any different?).

THIRD PROPOSITION

The usage of concepts and metaphors used in the context of military intelligence applications, as it is the case with the notion of the Situation Room, is likely to prove extremely useful and rewarding for application in the area of service development in the IT sector, as well as in the wider area of related business and commercial services.

This forms the third proposition – I can call it the ***'Business-as-War' proposition***.

What it is about here may lie at the level of intuitive interpretations of the business field related to the preparation for the launch of the new service, the market intelligence exercises performed, the investigation for finding the final way to address the market and customers, etc., and analogies that can be drawn between this field and war-making activities. (We tend to think of war as a primitive process that reflects lower levels of the human intellectual process but this is an extremely dangerous mistake. A war is always an extremely complex and multi-leveled conglomerate and shares many commons with enterprise ventures and services.)

For instance, according to one approach I would look at the *similarities only*:

One starts a war for achieving certain goals and benefits, but he has to:

- Pay some costs for this
- Set priorities
- Organize plans of attack to the enemy
- Also define the enemy (this rather happens at a different, more intellectually-driven level)
- Ensure his position
- Hopefully end the war or start a new one

It is obvious that a war in this example can be regarded as an *economy*[1] – in the same way also that it is viable to regard a service as an economy too (more on this in Chapter 7).

Last but not least, it is always tempting to find differences even between different wars or different businesses; and what we use to say is that 'this war is different from some other', or 'this is a different business', but in all cases we agree that they both share some common characteristics which help them to belong in the same class of war or business.

This hypothesis is not new and is not an innovation to refer to this. It has appeared several times in the literature, and there is an interesting corpus of information and research in this field. For instance, central gravity to this issue is given by Smith in a work published back in 2002. There the author recognizes that adaptation to the Information Age will require changes in the following four dimensions:

- Mission space (what the military will be called upon to do)
- Environment (the conditions, constraints, and values that govern military operations)
- Concepts (the military business model or the way we do what we do)
- The business side of the DoD (the way the organization supports value creation) (Smith, 2002).

Effects-based Operations (EBO) is about the first two of these four dimensions while Network Centric Warfare (NCW) addresses the last two. Hence, EBO and NCW form a synergistic treatment of military transformation. They deal with the why, what, how, and support of military operations. While the author who comes from the military discipline continues with extensive coverage of the addressed application area and provides further evidence on this, it is interesting to compare with the claim that is made in the article of another author, namely Fuller back in 1993 who comes from the business world and where it is recognized that it is no secret why companies fail: the failure starts at the top. *"CEOs and their senior executives know the problems; in fact, in the privacy of their offices, they'll volunteer them to you:*

- *'We have the information in the company. But we don't seem to get it to the right place',*
- *'We get the information to the right place. But then we can't seem to make the choices we should',*
- *'We're okay at choosing what to do, but we're too damned slow. By the time we pull the trigger, the target's moved',*
- *'We know what needs to happen. But we never seem to execute. I never see action.'*

For some companies, the list of symptoms includes bad habits that slowly erode performance: rivalries in the executive suite, endless turf consciousness, resource struggles between business units. In short, functional boundaries drive a wedge between managers who should be on the same side but who act like the Army, Navy, and Marines competing to see who leads the invasion. In these cases you hear sentiments like, 'We can't pull together, we're always pulling separately. There's too much internal friction around here.' (Fuller, 1993)

I still remember the impression that was made to me when reading Fuller's views – and though the place that his thoughts were published was not a widely known one, it is indicative that you may find value everywhere – you only need trained eyes and nose and ears to recognize it.

In every struggling large company, according to the same author, the symptoms are the same. *'It's all just a matter of where it hurts worse'*. And the author concludes identifying that in the life-or-death quest for strategic change, business has much to learn from war. Both are about the same thing: succeeding in competition. Even more basic, both can be distilled to four words: informed choice / timely action. The key objective in competition - whether business or war - is to improve your organization's performance along these dimensions:

- To generate better information than your rivals do
- To analyze that information and make sound choices
- To make those choices quickly
- To convert strategic choices into decisive action

Together they represent informed choice / timely action.

Independently on whether we agree or not to the core matter (i.e. how much are these two activities of business and war close to each other), we can comfortably agree that we can use the metaphor of war to approach the field of service development. This, in turn, may trigger two questions which we should by now have expected to appear, concerning the holding or not of the two first propositions namely of the *Improvement* and the *Existence*. Supporting evidence for both can only be given using indirect means:

- Regarding the linkage to the second proposition, given the above analysis, we could come to the idea that the third proposition is a special case of the second, namely that the business-as-war concept is a facilitator for performing better a service development task. Namely this of doing business, by means of using material and food for thought and analysis and examples and past cases from a different field, namely this of war making.
- Regarding the linkage to the first proposition, simply by backtracking, we can judge that the *Existence Proposition* holds, as the result of the 'existence' and the holding of the *Improvement Proposition*.
  - ○ Even if the approach I use seems iconoclastic or unorthodox, there is no doubt that there is sequence of steps that has been built and thoughts where the third one appears as a product of specialization of the previous two.

FOURTH PROPOSITION

An important element, which marks not only the usefulness and utility but also the value of this particular concept of the Situation Room for support of the service development process, is the facilitation of the corporate learning process.

What I left totally out from the analysis in the previous proposition was the reference I make to '*the notion of the Situation Room*', which I regard as an '*extremely useful and rewarding* [metaphor] *for application in the field of corporate service development processes'*.

Now, as part of the fourth proposition I need to support that:

The metaphor of a Situation Room, as a special case of a business-as-war conceptualization:

- Except from being useful in general, bringing utility and (helping a company) creating value with respect to service development tasks, it also
- Facilitates the overall corporate learning process.

In the literature in this area, several authors such as the path setting research of Argyris (1977), have used different definitions or models of organizational learning or have not rigorously defined their terms.

From this perspective, our view regarding learning in service intensive industries by means of using the Situation Room concept is dedicated to helping organizations become better *learning systems* – which shall also hopefully affect their service development capabilities as well. In this respect, I adopt the definition of the Society for Organizational Learning www.solonline.org according to which organizational learning is regarded as "the capacity or processes within an organization to maintain or improve performance based on experience".

It is not a novelty to recognize that:

- All organizations engage in some form of collective learning as part of their development; and that
- The creation of 'culture' and the 'socialization' of the corporate members and employees in this culture rely on learning processes to ensure an institutionalized reality.

Nevis firstly mentions this in a book that appeared back in 1987[2]. In this sense, Nevis recognizes that it may be redundant to talk of 'learning organizations', and concludes that all learning is not the same; some learning is dysfunctional, and some insights or skills that might lead to useful new actions are often hard to attain. The current concern with the learning organization focuses on the gaps in organizational learning capacity and does not negate the usefulness of those learning processes that organizations may do well, even though they have a learning disability.

It is in this context that I propose the use of Situation Room as a medium to accommodate and as a vehicle to host successfully the learning needs of a company, and hence I aspire to provide enough evidence of the claim made in this fourth proposition which I shall call the ***Learning Proposition***.

FIFTH PROPOSITION

Both the use of the concept of Situation Room and its accompanying framework for application in the corporate service development process grid and decision making activities, as well as the contribution they make to the increase of the corporate service knowledge capital, can be regarded as essential intangible assets of a company (or an organization), and as such they can be assessed and valuated by means of quantitative and qualitative approaches.

According to Quinn (1992) *"there is little question that the 'intangibles' of databases, peronal know-how, technological understanding, communication networks, market knowledge, brand acceptance, distribution capabilities, organizational flexibility and effective motivation are the true assets of most companies and the primary sources of their future income streams"*.

The organizational learning perspective on the approach to the Situation Room pays attention on the learning process as a central function. As defined by several sources, learning consists of constructing new knowledge (understanding) through taking in and processing information through the cognitive structures of the brain.

According to more recent work by Argyris together with Schön, this time of 1996, *'learning' is correcting errors (including surprises, and wrong predictions)... One corrects them by adjusting the data or revising the cognitive structures that produced the failed expectations... Knowledge, produced through learning, flows through organizations to become output, usually combined with physical product, and it is a part of every process... Knowledge, therefore, makes up a significant part of the fabric of the organization.* (Argyris and Schön, 1996)

And last but not least, most of us are familiar with the work of Nonaka and Takeuchi published back in 1995 which continues to be a reference attractor for academics and researchers in the fields of knowledge management. The two authors have developed and proposed a theory of the successful Japanese company that centers on the processes of creating knowledge, especially new product ideas and designs. Their theory of organization included a theory of knowledge, to make a compelling case. More specifically, they recognized that people do not just receive new knowledge passively; they interpret it actively. Thus what makes sense in one context can lose meaning when communicated to people in a different context. The major job of managers is to direct this confusion toward purposeful knowledge creation. Both senior and middle managers do this by providing employees with a conceptual framework. Middle managers serve as a bridge between the visionary ideals of the top and the often chaotic reality of those on the front line of business. (Nonaka and Takeuchi, 1995)

I call this fifth hypothesis the ***Corporate Capital Hypothesis***.

Table 2. Propositions related with the search items and the investigation procedures

	Focus aspects
Existence proposition	• General. Validity - True or false? • Examination of conditions related to its application in the field of services (sector-, context- or other parameters-specific) • Distinction between people as individuals and as members of a team • Single metaphor or groups / sets of metaphors • Metaphor nature and connotations • Sharing of metaphor qualities • Imposed or enforced vs voluntarily adopted metaphor • Simple vs complex metaphors • Simple vs complex tasks • Development of practices for service and task accomplishment
Improvement proposition	• Metaphor fits to a service development task or not • Metaphor affordance matters for service development • Improvement of service development through metaphor • Verification in different settings: abstract, complex, complicated, sophisticated or detailed ones • Choice of improvement indicators – qualitative and / or quantitative • Cost – benefit matters
Business-as-War proposition	• Analogy drawing between 'war' and 'service development' • Orchestration of service development activities in a war-like fashion • The long view: Corporate mission and strategy, market geopolitics, the corporate economy • The short view: Resources utilisation and coordination, increase of corporate service development capacity
Learning proposition	• Does the concept of Situation Room facilitate corporate learning at large? • Does the concept of Situation Room facilitate learning regarding service development? • Returns of the learning curve • Learning fit to corporate context and culture • Learning fit to specifics of the area addressed by the service or the addressed market
Corporate capital proposition	• Is the corporate Situation Room an intangible asset of the company? • Or simply a 'tool' to support service development? • How can the valuation of this asset take place? • Can it support the valuation of the corporate service development process? • Can it support the valuation of each service itself?

I present in Table 2 for each of the five research propositions a set of focus aspects which are worth in our opinion to consider when trying to make the transition from theory to a reality check.

I present in Table 3 some representative elements of relationship between the five propositions and the problem areas.

STEP CHANGES IN SERVICE CONCEPTUALISATION

Market pressures increasingly mean that companies move away from the model where they hold responsibility for every single stage of the processes required to bring their services to market. The trend in modern business is to gain economies by forming an alliance with trading partners whose core competencies complement

Table 3. The five propositions on the nature of services and the identified problem areas

Problem areas / Propositions	Reducing barriers to corporate intelligence	Improving industrial competitiveness	Supporting emerging industrial practices	Developing new ways of undertaking research	Delivering improved education / training to workforce	Assisting technology integration	Involving all levels of the workforce in product R&D
Existence proposition			Is a service under consideration in a position to support novel and 'emerging' practices of work?			Does the application of service apply to complex business process grids? And/or to the creation of new realistic service user / usage environments?	
Improvement proposition	Will the service application exhibit the potential to be a vital tool in the corporate intelligence process?		And also improve the productivity, the efficiency and the monetary gains?		Workers better equipped for the roles of developers and users of corporate intelligence		
Business-as-War proposition				Are multi- and interdisciplinarity positively affecting the corporate service development 'wars'?			The service regarded as a support instrument for concentrating the commitment and engagement of the entire workforce
Learning proposition		Does user involvement for service operation lead to learning?			Learning is now part of the core business process of the workers		
Corporate capital proposition		Does service operation help increase the corporate intellectual capital? In a business sense-making way?					Service as an aggregator for the corporate *human* capital

the overall process. Competitive forces, in the automobile industry for example, now oblige companies to focus upon their core competencies in order to create and maintain a successful edge and to partner with other companies for support in areas outside those competencies, for example in engine, gearbox or instrumentation sub-assemblies.

However, for this approach to yield the maximum benefits when transferred in the area of services, the interacting partners must be able to coordinate their activities in some way, ideally through a forum capable of promoting communications between the diverse partners. In the case of an insurance company or a bank it is not about tangible products that are manufactured and shipped from the supplier to the customer as semi-final or final products; all trading elements are of intangible nature and deal mostly with information. If, for example, the supplier relationship framework provided a means to consider how e-services could support the different types of supplier relationships involving different levels of collaboration, then it should be taken as an obvious step that the company to be involved in such a transaction should also be capable to recognise the need to build closer relationships with their suppliers, competitors and all kinds of e-service third party intermediaries in order to enhance the efficiency and effectiveness of their value chain.

Today's typical value chain is often complex, as it comprises multiple networks of customers, trading partners and distributors, each with their own set of requirements. It is also characterised by fragmentation made up of a geographical spread with a mixture of proprietary systems and manual processes. Unfortunately, in such a configuration a value chain is only as good as its *weakest* link. Inter-organisational business process automation and technical integration represent significant challenges that are obviously greater than those faced internally within organisations. However, the links are not only made up of the enabling technology. With increasing depth of collaboration, interpersonal and inter-organisational relationships, trust and communication also become critical factors in ensuring the exchanging and sharing of information. And the role of services is eminent to achieve this.

One can argue that there is always an element of artificiality in segmenting developments but there is undoubtedly a step change that can be clearly identified in almost all cases of service implementation within a corporate environment and the take up of Internet based e-service connectivity (i.e. how one connects existing service infrastructures with new e-services, how one links existing IT systems to support new (types of) services, how to create service and e-service aggregates out of existing infrastructures, etc.). However, when considering the wider picture to include the additional organisational dimensions of using e-services for collaboration then it appears to be more a question of evolution rather than discontinuous change.

Operational service infrastructures we experience in our everyday lives have proliferated and take different forms although multidisciplinary research into the implementation and change management issues is still thin on the ground. Appropriate infrastructure with secure and integrated systems, compatible technologies, common data bases, file formats and user interfaces are one aspect of the challenge.

THE E-SERVICE ICEBERG

A number of efficiencies are claimed for e-services but cost savings coming from margin compression may not be sustainable, especially where a longer term and collaborative relationship is deemed to be advantageous for all involved parties. The smooth transition to electronic processes associated with e.g. the service procurement process, together with the change in culture, is the hidden and (usually) underestimated part of the e-service 'iceberg'. The lower cost of the Internet and opportunities for ubiquitous connectivity can create an enthusiasm that greatly underestimates the real cost and effort in bringing the benefits of collaborative relationships to fruition.

From our experience in implementation projects, the Internet was seen as the means of enabling closer service relationships but the organisational setting and entrenched cultures of the organisations proved to be the main stumbling block rather than the applications and technologies. The failure to engage the main stakeholders, particularly the suppliers and the buyers, dramatically limits the scope and success of such projects.

Amongst other parameters, the e-service 'iceberg' includes the underestimation of investment of management time in building closer relationships, in the planning of joint processes with suppliers, in reviewing internal processes and managing the transition to new roles for buyers. More fundamentally, the process of collective learning is also undermined by difficulties of moving to the mindset of the extended organisation where a participative and consultative approach with partners is required to bring about long term benefits for all parties.

Lack of consultation and the alienation of buyers who tend to see the new system and the IT department in particular, as an unnecessary interpolation between themselves and the suppliers further exacerbate existing internal tensions. The experience I usually draw from implementation projects underlines the need to modulate the appeal of the Internet in easing interconnection with trading partners with a consideration of the organisational and cultural context of implementation. But I am afraid this sounds trivial though it is quite not.

It is still early days in the evolution of e-services and realisation of the business benefits will require systemic understanding within a business and between businesses. Technical issues need careful consideration in implementing commercial level e-service infrastructures. These include issues such as integration (both internally with legacy systems, and externally with suppliers), service data management, the development and adoption of service standards, technical support, service reliability, security and privacy. However, these technology aspects are a necessary but not sufficient prerequisite for successful working of e-service systems.

There does appear to be in most implementations I studied a disturbingly high element of using inappropriate technology just because it exists. There are limits to the use of information technology in supporting collaborative processes in the service environment. Additionally, most implementations, for different reasons, tend to underestimate or ignore the fundamental contribution made by human expertise to the service conceptualisation process. Personal contact and interpersonal face to face communication continue to be required in solving information and communication problems and such interpersonal communications can also foster trust and facilitate creative solutions with mutual benefits.

It is questionable whether organisations have genuinely recognised and learnt from the contribution that a robust service infrastructure can make to their business. The role of senior managers is key in developing an integrated and strategic approach and in providing understanding, vision and leadership. A holistic and systemic view prevails in the framework with recognition that implementing e-services has implications for the effective management of change concerning organisation structures, working practices, roles and job content. Evidence from our experience indicates a gap between actual and good practice and an inability among stakeholders to adjust their thinking to a network perspective that reflects the difficulties organisations have in unlearning older practices and adopting new ones.

The framework developed and presented in later Chapters of this book may be viewed from the perspective of collaborative relationships as the pivotal focus. Business, information technology and organisational aspects affect collaborative relationships but these also have interdependent relationships. These mutually reinforcing aspects have similarity to the duality of action and structure inherent in any type of enterprise constituent. This duality refers to the structure of social institutions being created by human action. Through human interaction structures are reproduced but may also change. On the other hand, human action is constrained by the way in which humans utilise institutional structure as a resource in interpreting their own and other people's actions. Thus social structure both informs and constrains human action and, in turn, human action both produces and reproduces social action. Integrating service technologies into the business, changes the business, and consequently changes the very potential of the business. Collaborative relationships and the mutual interactions are themselves to some extent mediated by the structure and conditions of the interorganisational environment. However this environment can be changed if an organisation is powerful enough within the industry or because organisations within the industry take on a more 'network' perspective through a process of collective learning.

Politics, power and influence are important to consider in the context of e-services and collaborative relationships. Lack of commonality and congruence of objectives may create major barriers. There are examples that show that some companies may prefer to continue using existing manual processes that they know will work with a minimum of problems, rather than radically overhaul existing business practices and systems to implement electronic service links. Another key source of frustration for many companies seems to be that their trading partners are often not on the same level in terms of IT skills, budget, staff availability etc. In addition to important political and vested interests within the organisations there are also differences in perception between the constituents of the extended enterprise. Building relationships is a difficult process but having an intermediary in the position of the e-service platform provider may also be perceived as intervening in established relationships. Although contracts provide a legal framework to define the obligations of partners, they can be costly to write and enforce and also cannot cover for all contingencies.

It is clear that where e-service technology provides the enabling infrastructure to support collaborative relationships then lack of trust may be a key inhibitory factor. Lack of consultation or perceived failure to live up to the expectations of partners for example, will result in participants adopting a negative posture characterised by reluctance to share information and a lack of willingness to review their processes. There can be no doubt that business structure both reflects the degree of trust that exists between participants and influences its future development. Our experience from implementation projects indicates the importance of cultural factors in establishing a suitable environment in which collaboration and information exchange may take place and flourish. This requires a social environment based on consultation both internally and externally with suppliers and partners. Creating such a background appears to be a case of cultural evolution but the role of management vision and commitment through clear leadership in setting the general climate is critically important. Implementation difficulties from the case studies indicate the need for a top-down organisational drive for change management to overcome any internal cultural barriers. It also underlines the need for senior management to communicate a cohesive business vision for e-services to internal stakeholders in the firm and the need to instil a collaborative, knowledge-sharing culture within the firms in the extended enterprise.

REFERENCES

Argyris, C. (1977). Double loop learning in organizations. Harvard Business Review, (September-October): 115–124.

Argyris, C., & Schön, D. A. (1996). *Organizational Learning II*. Reading, MA: Addison Wesley.

Davenport, T. H. (2005) *Thinking for a Living: How to get better performance and results from knowledge workers*, Boston: Harvard Business School Press.

Fuller, M. B. (1993). Business as war. *FastCompany, 00* (November).

Lakoff, G., & Johnson, M. (1980). *Metaphors We Live By*. Chicago: Univ. of Chicago Press.

Nonaka, I., & Takeuchi, H. (1995). *The knowledge-creating company. How Japanese companies create the dynamics of innovation.* New York: Oxford University Press.

Norman, D. A. (1988). *The psychology of everyday things*. New York: Basic Books.

Norman, D. A. (1990). *The design of everyday things*. New York: Doubleday.

Norman, D. A. (1999). Affordance, conventions, and design. *interactions*, 6(3), May/June, 38 – 43. New York: ACM Press.

Pingali, G., & Sukaviriya, N. (2003) Augmented Collaborative Spaces. In *Proceedings of ACM Conference '03, November 2nd – 8th*.

Quinn, J. B. (1992) *The Intelligent Enterprise: A Knowledge and Service Based Paradigm for Industry*. New York: Free Press.

Smilowitz, E. D. (1996, October). Do Metaphors Make Web Browsers Easier to Use? In the *Proceedings of the 2nd Microsoft Usability Conference 'Designing for the Web: Empirical Studies'*, Microsoft Campus.

Smith, E. A. (2002) *Effects Based Operations: Applying Network Centric Warfare in Peace, Crisis, and War.* Washington, DC: DoD Command and Control Research Program.

ENDNOTES

[1]   Webster's On-line dictionary provides, though as third option, the following definition for the word economy: "The system of rules and regulations by which anything is managed; orderly system of regulating the distribution and uses of parts, conceived as the result of wise and economical adaptation in the author, whether human or divine; as, the animal or vegetable economy; the economy of a poem; the Jewish economy" (http://www.webster-dictionary.org/definition/economy).

[2]   It is quite a pity how much we focus mainly if not only on recently published research work. Of course there is an obvious utility in relating someone's work with other recent outcomes. But many fundamental aspects of the research in the service field – I regret to say – have been said much time ago. Of course the people did not use terms we now use but it is worth to look back and explore research that had a significant impact to the field of services.

Chapter 3
Typology of Services

Classes and taxonomies of services – how can they be categorized, with respect to different parameters, factors, dimensions. Why some of them matter and some other don't? How can they be organized to serve specific purposes, etc. The major part of the chapter is justly devoted to the presentation of the Service Analysis Model (SAM). With its four constituent building blocks, SAM provides an insight to the analysis of services and is followed by a section devoted to the synthesis of service and the composition of new ones. The chapter closes with the presentation of a real test case implemented for a manufacturing company to improve their service supply chain.

What has become obvious to us as result of our exposure to several service deployment and usage pitfalls, is that we are not facing a lack on enabling technologies but on paradigms for successfully conceptualizing, profiling, designing, implementing and, finally, deploying them.

In this context, the main aim of our investigation had been centered around the provision of a new open paradigm on how on the one hand service customer and users,

DOI: 10.4018/978-1-60566-683-9.ch003

and on the other hand service development communities can coexist and co-work for the definition of new service concepts and service delivery environments.

At a second level, what is important is to help all the involved parties (i.e. service suppliers and service users) on the requirements elicitation processes, the compliance validation and quality checking processes *in a synergetic way* with both users' and developers' communities forming essential part of the intellectual service engineering processes.

It is highly important to understand how to capitalise on the interactions between users and developers as part of a value chain that creates new intellectual capital for new service types by exploring problem-solving principles in computer science and other disciplines. This necessitates the existence and fostering of closer links between the sides of the users and the developers, both of which need to share a space for expressing as well as exploring their own modes of thought and help improve their problem-solving paradigm.

Better understanding and communication with the future users of the services requires the software creation to be placed at the level of abstraction the users can understand. Better communication between IT- and application field specialists will lead to avoidance of misunderstanding, loss of time and resources and in the effect to systems that better address the needs of the service end users. This refers to the creation of *policies, processes* and *practices* that will enrich the *people* in both communities of users and developers to coexist smoothly and gain from their interactions.

I support an interactive approach in modelling new forms of jointly defined service modeling processes.

As shown in Figure 1, except from the formal and structured interactions (in many cases of transactional nature) between members of the two communities or within each of the two communities, there is a great number of informal and unstructured (or better: ill-structured) interactions which people tend to leave outside of their agenda of items-to-think-about.

The French philosopher Luis Althusser (1918 – 1990) defined a practice as any process of transformation of a determinate product, affected by a determinate human labour, using determinate means (of production). Nowadays that we talk a lot about practices on the Net, in services or e-services, it is tragically timely how much we lack on intellectuals that will be able to transform and process technology problems into societal or political ones and vice versa.

Any service modeling environment must take into account emerging approaches from the software and services engineering disciplines, adopt a cross- and inter-disciplinary research agenda and adhere to best research results internationally, best practices and standards to avoid any rework and to assure future adoption. Furthermore, better understanding and communication with the future users of the

Figure 1. Besides the formal and structured interactions, there are much more important and densely organised informal and unstructured ones

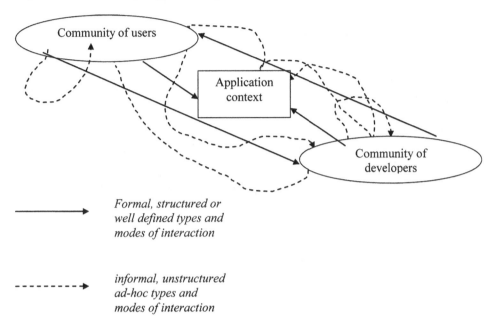

particular services requires the service software creation to be placed at the level of abstraction the users can understand.

Better communication between IT- and application field-specialists will lead to avoidance of misunderstanding, loss of time and resources and in the effect to systems that better address the needs of the end users. This refers to the creation of *policies, processes* and *practices* that will enrich the *people* in both communities of users and developers to coexist smoothly and gain from their interactions (see Figure 2).

Having several first and second hand experiences in the success and failure faced from the more demanding and relatively complicated projects or tasks, to less complex and simple ones, the story has to do usually with the same ingredients:

- *People*, and
- *How these interact to each other* or with each other, and
- *How they perceive and analyse the world they live in*, the events that are taking place and to which they have or need to respond at, and
- *How they document their knowledge*, their wants, their goals, their history of what they did or they aimed to do, and,

Figure 2. Impact and influence patterns amongst people – processes – practices and policies.

- *How they access and make use of the documented knowledge* – be it theirs or someone else's, and finally,
- *How they manage to improve their behavior* either at the individual level or at the collective one, or – sometimes – at both through learning processes or other optimization processes.

However, to manage a coordinated behavior of individuals is a difficult – if not unachievable task at all. Even if people are working together for the same goal, and have all unanimously agreed to the same objective and target, it is in the human nature that they shall develop differentiations in regard to the means that each individual shall employ for meeting any specified end. Or, even in the case that there is agreement regarding the means, there will be different opinions on the instrumentations of these very specific means, the orchestration of all individuals around them, etc. This helps us come to the conclusion that the main difficulty concerns the synthesis of all these different 'resources'.

Though the starting point for us has been problems that appear in the corporate world, any type of 'problem' that involves most of the above components can be regarded as subject to the same need for being approached with a preferably simple and consistent method for modeling the problem and, secondly, trying to 'tackle' or 'solve' this in the most easy or straightforward and - if possible - unique way.

An important challenge in establishing lasting changes of culture and values in an organisation involves ensuring that organized learning processes are anchored within the particular service grids of the organisation. Traditional courses and training are considered efficient, but it often seems as the long-term effect is missing. Furthermore, traditional courses are often used by the organisations to train their employees so they can perform better, but in the same ways as they always have done. There are several positive aspects to both tactics, but if the goal of the learning is to gain new knowledge and to establish changes in behaviour as well as further learning in the organisation, it is important to use a strategy based on pedagogical theories and methods that take individual as well as organizational learning into consideration.

There is a saying: 'have hammers, will see only nails', just because you have a hammer in your hand. In the greater scheme of things, collaborative service modeling processes include more than scientific approaches and methods. Hence, the results (observations, conclusions and theories) of one scientific discipline cannot be intelligently applied or implemented in disregard of other scientific theory. The scientific communities have organised themselves in disciplines (e.g. economics, political science, legal science or law, etc.). These might in turn be organised – or thought of – as some 'blocks' of sciences such as natural science, social science, human science etc. This internal organisation is especially visible in the academic training.

In such academic training, however, holistic understanding of science as just science runs the risk of being overlooked. This risk appears despite that theory of science may be part of the academic training in each of the disciplines. A student may learn about the very specifics of sub-theories and approaches developed, approved of, or otherwise adopted in the discipline he or she studies. When making the transition to the labor market, the student then develops into an intra-disciplinary practitioner.

This is an example of intra-disciplinary approach, which should be carefully distinguished from inter-disciplinary approaches. I could also dare to say that intra-disciplinary approaches, including the theory and methods implied, constitute the toolbox that we equip the students with. Because of their training, the disciplinary students might later – more or less automatically and thus probably unreflectedly – bring their intra-disciplinary approaches into their future research. Our own experience working with service modeling processes dates back to the beginning of 1990.

I have been closely involved with a wide range of different organisations in the research, the business software and the IT industry in general and different types and levels of decision-making styles and cultures. In all these settings, I have been

Figure 3. The four building blocks of the Service Analysis Model (SAM)

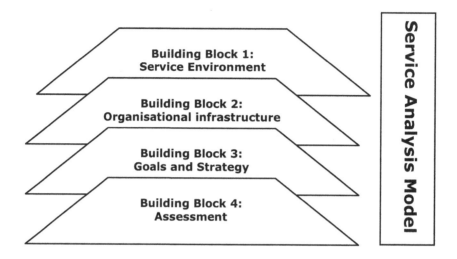

exposed to different learning strategies based on problem-based and project-organised approaches, and have experienced that they provided quite another learning outcome. I consider such a community-based learning approach an effective and motivating way to organise the kind of learning situations needed when working with changes in behaviour, strategies, and innovative processes in companies and organizations, as it is for the case of service development.

THE SERVICE ANALYSIS MODEL (SAM)

This model is critical for the market application of services within real world environments and demanding contexts of use. While several models are generic and support for the application of services in a given context only, the Service Analysis Model is providing the expressive power and means for applying in the given market context.

It builds on four building blocks (see Figure 3), which directly relate with the wider notion and semantic attributes of a service. More specifically, these are:

Building Block 1: Service Environment

The aim of this first building block of the Service Analysis Model concerns environmental (external) analysis. This aims to facilitate transparency about the specific chances and risks of a particular product's market or any other context that is the subject of a particular service analysis session.

However, environment as such implies also further aspects related e.g. to science, technology and society as well as the relative positioning of the particular company to each of these. This implies also the need for identification, analysis, and assessment of relevant parameters. Such an analysis can be reactive (e.g. after a product has been launched in the market, after a product prototype has been handed to the Marketing people, after …) or proactive (before a product has been launched in the market, before a product prototype has been handed to the Marketing people, before …).

Forecasting of future developments regarding a particular product and its environment may only be based on historical data and is generally regarded as risky because of dynamics in the environment. Trends and their analysis must therefore form an integral part of the environmental analysis. Based on the results of the analysis, scenarios for future development can be developed. The results of the environmental analysis are used for the strategic product lifecycle management process.

The methodology to be devised has to describe the procedure of how to carry out an environmental analysis according to the specific scope and needs of a particular company and product combination[1].

I provide in Table 1 some more items that would be useful to form the basis of the space of semantics for this first building block of SAM.

Building Block 2: Organisational Infrastructure

The aim of the organisation analysis is to achieve transparency about the company specific strengths and weaknesses as much this can have a direct impact to the particular situation under consideration.

Similarly to the environmental analysis, there is first of all the identification, analysis, and assessment of relevant parameters. The scope depends from the overall objective. The analysis again can be retrospective based on historical data or perspective. The forecasting of future developments is risky because of dynamics in the environment. Trends and their analysis must be an integrated part of the organisational analysis too.

Based on the results of the organisational analysis, scenarios for future development can be developed. The results of the organisational analysis are to be used for the strategic product lifecycle management process in combination with the results of the environmental analysis. The organisation analysis provides a performance evaluation for the company so that they can better assess their potential with respect to the situation under consideration.

Table 1. Requirement summary for the analysis of environmental aspects of a particular situation

Items and parameters	Market
	Suppliers (number, USPs, costs, price, turnover, stability, etc.)
	Products and services (USPs, price, etc.)
	Customers (number, groups, importance, demands, etc.)
	Competitors (number, market share, target markets, strategy, etc.)
	Markets (segments, strengths, etc.)
	Technology (innovation steps, functionalities, costs, etc.)
	e.t.c.
	Politics
	Current and planned international (e.g. European Union), national (country) and regional (federals state) legislations
	Regulatory framework (product sector tariffing or protection aspects, e.t.c.)
	e.t.c.
	Culture
	National cultural specifics
	Individual histories
	Market ethics, practices and customs (if possible with a quantification and linkage of them to the product under consideration)
	e.t.c.
	Extended Enterprise partners and Value Chain member
	Profiles
	Assessment of positive intakes and spillover effects
	e.t.c.
Analysis methods and instruments	Segmentation, clustering, portfolios
	Benchmarking
	Chance/risk, SWOT, potential, trend, scenario
	Road mapping (technology, products)
	e.t.c.
Approach	Top-down: processing of existing and new qualitative and quantitative data for product analysis and planning purposes
	Bottom-up: processing of existing mainly quantitative data for product analysis purposes

To provide an analogy, if the environmental analysis provides an overview of the market in which a product is going to penetrate, the organisational analysis is focused to those intra-enterprise aspects (most of them of infrastructural nature) which will interactively affect the future of this specific action. A further analogy from the war domain is that while the environmental analysis provides data and information on the territory where a battle is going to take place, the other actors to be involved and possibly affect the operation, the organisational analysis is putting emphasis to aspects related to the type of men our army is having, the type of skills and competencies with respect to those of the opponent, the knowledge they have or that which they have to acquire, etc.

What the case studies I will be examining in the next paragraphs aim to highlight is that before applying SRA by companies as a tool for practical employment, these companies have to create transparency about the business goals, the organisational and technological starting point, and capacity for assessing (many different aspects of) the environment they are operating at.

In this process, the following questions must be answered by them:

- Do the company's processes and information add sufficient value to differentiate it from the competitors?
- In which value activity/ies, value to the company's information and/or processes can be added? How to support this with e-business?
- What is the appropriate e-business support for each value activity interaction, bearing in mind the organisational and technological capability of suppliers and customers and the likely direction of the own value chain in the future?
- Can the company add sufficient value to processes/information on its own, or should it consider taking part in an Extended Enterprise?
- What is the company's most appropriate role in the Extended Enterprise?
- Which distinctive competencies does the company need to strengthen its position in the Extended Enterprise?
- What level of e-business does the company need to sustain its participation in an Extended Enterprise?

The organisation analysis finally has to identify the potentials of using SRA as a leverage by targeting the audience to populate the Situation Room of the company. For instance, while for company A decisions regarding a specific issue for a product need to be addressed by a team consisting of the Commercial Director and a set of Regional Directors, which will decide on a policy and demand or command its implementation to the Technical Dept or the Product Manager, for some other company (with a different – and rather much better... - culture and value system) they would ask for Technical Dept and / or the Product Manager to drive the discussion or at least have a leading role therein, while also representatives from the Marketing Dept might participate.

Conclusively, we can see that the results of the organisational analysis are critical because they help us to solve the problem by better defining it. (For many corporate failure stories, the main reason comes back to an erroneous or inconsiderate definition of "what is the problem").

Our methodology will describe the procedure of how to carry out an organisation analysis according to the specific scope and needs of a company (see Table 2).

Building Block 3: Goals and Strategy

Strategy[3] is based on market requirements on the one hand and a company's abilities on the other hand. Strategy is a complex and multi-layered matter. The market requirements might change rapidly and the own abilities have to be developed and adapted in goal-oriented way. A strategy has to close the gap between market demands and company abilities. Strategy has to provide the mid- and long-term orientation for a company and forms the basis for definition of operative short-term goals.

Goals should be regarded as the result of the combination of strengths and weaknesses with respect to opportunities and threats. There are quantitative and qualitative goals. In order to use goals as guidelines that drive decision-making within the Situation Room, dependencies between individual goals must be made transparent and have to be put into a goal hierarchy. A potential analysis needs to also assess the plausibility of goals.

Another aspect that is of importance here is that the particular organisational structure interacts with the strategy. More specifically, the structure of the Information Supply Chain – independently of whether it concerns the internal corporate environment i.e. within departments, or the interfacing with external ones, is representative of the overall strategy that a particular company follows in its business activities, its positioning with respect to competitors, suppliers and customers, etc.

Thus, interactions between structure and strategy on the one hand concern adaptations at the structure level to better serve a devised strategy (i.e. the top down approach), while on the other hand bottom-up modifications to a previously defined strategy may be needed to facilitate good or optimal practices within a specific structure.

Of particular interest in my research has been the employment of the concept of a Situation Room for revisiting the notion of strategy; instead of keeping the strategy as a distant high level ("strategic") issue, I tended to reconsider it as a tightly coupled entity to that of a practical tool namely this of the SRA.

What is obvious and will become more apparent is that in addition to the strategy (associated to a great extent with the corresponding structure), the actual implementation of the particular structure also plays a significant role.

From our experiences in the software business, a specific strategy mapped to a specific scheme, may be considered as under-performing, being based not on strategy-specific criteria but mainly on implementation-related ones.

Table 2. Requirement summary for the analysis of organisational items

Items and parameters	**Human resources**
	staff number
	qualification
	(core) competencies
	e.t.c.
	Structure
	hierarchy
	allocation to products and services (also related with financial figures as variants, costs, turnover, profit, e.t.c.)
	e.t.c.
	Processes
	in-/outputs, activities, resources, constraints, objectives, interfaces
	e.t.c.
	Control aspects
	process key figures
	e.t.c.
	Technology
	production facilities (automation degree in development, e.t.c.)
	employed know-how
	ICT infrastructure
	e.t.c.
Analysis methods and instruments	Efficiency, pay-off
	ABC/XYZ, process cost, failure possibility and impact
	Core competences
	Technology portfolio
	Quality Function Deployment (QFD)
	chance/risk, PEST[2], SWOT, sensitivity, potential, benchmarking
	trends, scenarios
	road mapping (products)
	e.t.c.
Approach	top-down: processing of existing and new qualitative and quantitative data for organisational analysis and planning purposes
	bottom-up: processing of existing mainly quantitative data for organisational analysis purposes
Critical points and risks	information needed for strategic decisions is mostly not available in operative systems
	interactions with building block 1 for environmental impact

Figure 4. How a client's request causes change within the corporate environment and services: Case A

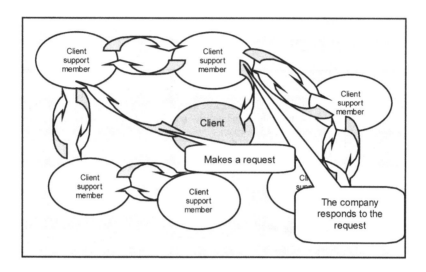

For example, in the case of forming the info chain structure for communication with clients, the scheme to which a company might have converged represents at a great extent the philosophy and the overall approach of the particular company with its clients.

For instance, I consider two specific cases:

- Case A, representing a strategy for keeping low communications overheads with clients.
- Case B, representing a strategy for serving the client according to "the client is king" principle and by embodying the latter within the company's grid of operations.

According to Case A, I consider the following structure as depicted in Figure 4.

Here, I have the client communicating with only a single contact point in the company, who may be a sales person, a secretary, a help desk worker, e.t.c. Of course it does make a difference who that single contact person is, as:

- In case he is considered as an "intelligent human agent", he will be able to develop a good idea of the client's request and thus be able to draft a plan

Figure 5. How a client's request causes change within the corporate environment and services: Case B

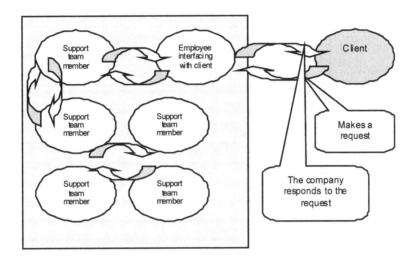

which he will subsequently communicate to the other people in the company. Or alternatively, he will be able to delegate the task to the appropriate person or department. Furthermore, he may be the one who will communicate with the client for informing him about the satisfaction of his request, e.g. in terms of providing him with the sought solution / result.

- In case he is not considered as an "intelligent human agent" (e.g. in the case of a blond secretary), he will have to either "post" the request to a department that seems to him as more appropriate, and without filtering in or out anything from the original request.

Companies that are positioned in the service sector, as well as administration departments that are interfacing with clients or suppliers, have accumulated experiences and the majority of them has somehow converged to schemes and structures that are considered as well-balanced with respect to the costs and benefits related to their operation.

What is relatively easy to see from the above, and will become more apparent from the description of the second Case (see Figure 5), is that except from the strategy (that is recognisable at a great extent to the corresponding structure), it is also the implementation of the particular structure that does play a significant role.

From experiences that I have from the software business sector, it follows that a specific strategy that has been mapped to a specific scheme, may be considered

Table 3. Requirement summary for the definition of goals and strategy

Items and activities	**Strategy**
	Formulation
	Review
	Update
	e.t.c.
	Goals
	Definition
	Consistency check
	Ranking (goal system)
	Calculus (synthesis and decomposition)
	Communication
	Adaptation
	e.t.c.
Approach	Top-down: strategy definition
	Bottom-up: goal agreements
Critical points and risks	Incompatibility of goals and strategies amongst the participating entities of the Situation Room

as under-performing, based not on strategy-specific criteria but mainly on implementation-related ones[4].

According to Case B, the client is not kept "outside" the company value chain; he is rather embodied in the people's network, being (perhaps) able to monitor (parts of) the ongoing interactions, and thus may add (his personal) value by means of experiences and expertise, in the service provision process (see Table 3).

Building Block 4: Assessment

The strategy assessment determines the benefit of a particular business decision options by quantitative and qualitative assessments. In literature there are well-established scenario techniques which allow the impact analysis of different assumptions with regard to (any particular) value adding benefits. A result of this is the creation of preferential roadmaps. This part of the model has to describe the procedure of how to develop different scenarios and carry out an environmental analysis according to the specific scope and needs of a company.

What is to be taken for sure is that working in and with networks together with the mastery of key processes enables change in enterprises through evolutionary processes of which an instance is this of the Situation Room Analysis.

In the current context, change should be regarded as an enabling factor for enabling adaptation of a corporate structure, so that the latter better responds to external conditions and the given context.

Actually, the idea of introducing change as the result of evolutionary processes is not new at all. Furthermore, it can be regarded as one of the most important consequences of game theory in that it can be used to determine situations where one behavior is more fit than all known alternatives, or alternately, a specific mix of behaviors where no one behavior is more fit than any other (Friedman, 1991).

In both cases, the result is considered as an *evolutionary stasis* with respect to the behaviors being considered - there is no *change* in relative frequency of the employed strategies over time. These situations are named, according to the game theoretical terminology as Evolutionarily Stable Strategies (henceforth: ESSs). More specifically, in the literature of game theory we identify two types of ESS:

- "Pure" ESS is where one strategy totally out-competes all others. In our case, this should be read as follows: mastery of a key process by a specific corporate environment, or alternatively, by a specific corporate scheme, should out-compete any other scheme. That means that regardless of its frequency, it is always more fit than any known alternative. A strategy that is a pure ESSs is considered as immune to invasion by other known strategies. In the old paradigm of doing business in a controlled environment, such a strategy might be sought and considered as ideal.
- "Mixed" ESS is where two strategies permanently coexist, thus increasing the complexity of the implementation, as in a real world application any actor should distribute its resources for achieving a certain / acceptable level of "mastery" in several key processes. From a computational perspective, in contexts where three or more strategies to play, it is possible to have a situation where there is no devisable ESS.

It is at this stage that ad hoc or heuristic approaches are employed that may either attempt to simplify the complexity of the given context, or alternate the actual problem to be addressed.

A further implication of this is that all business relations in an enterprise (internal and external) actually and potentially may take the form of a co-operative game. Working groups (comprised either by intra- or inter-enterprise personnel) seem to play an increasingly important role in business activities, both at the low "operational" level and at the high "strategic" one. The importance of this phenomenon is reflected in the emergence of endogenous policy models.

The latter concentrate on the interaction between working groups while the corporate Management tends to keep for itself the role of the policymaker (or the arbiter?). Of course, in the case of inter-enterprise working groups, where people are involved in a cross-enterprise Situation Room, representatives from the Management boards of the participating companies are included.

These models are typically focussing on Nash equilibriae of a properly defined game with complete information, where the various working groups (parts of a Situation Room) and the corporate Management are the (fully rational) players.

These issues are of obvious empirical relevance, since neither the set of working groups (and of the respective Situation Rooms which they are populating) nor their cardinality appear to be constant over time. In fact, organisational maintenance and attracting of new members (or getting rid of old ones that show sub-performances) is a continuing concern for such groups.

Moreover, the realism of assuming complete information and (any type of) sophisticated strategic behaviour can be seriously questioned given the complexity of the business environment being dealt with.

Taking into account that game theory is, after all, the part of economic theory that focuses not merely on the strategic behavior of individuals in economic environments, but also on other issues that will be critical in the design of economic institutions, such as;

- How information is distributed (Harsanyi, 1968),
- The influence of players' expectations and beliefs and
- The tension between equilibrium and efficiency (Myerson & Satterthwaite, 1983).

In general, game theory has already achieved important insights into issues such as the design of business contracts and resource allocation mechanisms which take into account the sometimes counterintuitive ways in which individual incentives operate in complex environments having decision makers with different information and objectives.

There have been two means for "confronting" game theory with evidence: in the laboratory and in the field. More specifically, in laboratory studies, expected utility theory (as originally formulated by von Neumann and Morgenstern (1944) was one of the first subjects to attract the sustained attention of experimenters.

From the very beginning this effort has both provided indications of the extent to which the predictions of the theory are approximate guides to individual choice behavior, and identified particular situations in which a significant proportion of subjects consistently violate the predictions of the theory. Using procedures of this kind, experimental methods allow investigators to measure some of the parameters on which the predictions of a theory may depend, and which would be unobservable in non-experimental situations[5].

Experimental data can also provide insights into field data. More specifically, field studies, as opposed to laboratory studies, are what economists traditionally do, in terms of concentrating their research efforts in studying behaviour of existing (operational) systems or of ad hoc developed, in order to check the validity of assumptions and of any hypotheses made.

SERVICE SYNTHESIS AND COMPOSITION OF NEW SERVICES

Conclusively, I note that any interactions between Situation Room participant, as these are described in the Situation Room model according to a generic process classification scheme, may built on the notion of a co-operative game and according to various modelling perspectives. In thinking about coalitions, these may be for instance formed between:

- A working group, which is considered as a single part of a Situation Room, and the corporate Management for achieving a particular business objective. In this case, the basis for the formation of the coalition would be related to the achievement of a mutually wished management of corporate resources (e.g. minimisation of new product deployment times, which would be combined with an increase in the monetary returns for the workers).
- Two working groups representing parts of two distinct Situation Room, both involved in the same decision-making process. In this case, the involved groups may identify a window of opportunity for forming a coalition for achieving their (perhaps common) goal. In any case, even when considering the case of two competitive working groups, formation of a coalition might be justified in terms of minimising the overall uncertainty that might exist when no communication and joint planning had existed, which would imply bigger operational costs (see Table 4).

It is easy to see that an SRA implementation should encompass features expected to dominate in distributed service provision environments, which will adopt a decentralized approach in all aspects related to the service design, the provision and the lifecycle management.

The starting point for the design of the access to service environment relates to the following:

- An SRA **e-service is regarded as an aggregate formed by fundamental service elements**, which are implemented by means of corresponding components.

Table 4. Requirement summary for the strategy assessment

Items and activities	Strategy assessment
	qualitative and quantitative scoring
	risk and sensitivity analysis
	etc.
	Strategy road mapping
	agreement
	visualisation
	etc.
	Strategy selection
	communication
	translation into / from operative goals
	etc.
Approach	top-down: by the management (centralised / centrally coordinated)
	bottom-up: by the individual workers or groups of them (decentralised / anarchic)
Critical points and risks	data quality
	availability of qualitative and quantitative assessment criteria
	environmental dynamics

- The IT-realisation of a generic SRA e-service is platform independent and uses common components. A service agent infrastructure may be used to "route" SRA e-service elements intelligently, and carry out other key information supply-related operations.
- The SRA e-service agent infrastructure thus supports the decentralised process execution that is so essential to the dynamic character of an efficiently networked inter-organisational infrastructure like the SRA implementation.
- In the context of the above, the e-service agent "navigation" aspect deals with the interconnection of the various service flow scenarios of the SRA implementation that involve the static, or structural characteristics of the service pathway elements amongst the particularly involved entities (i.e. the SR participants and the various systems connected to).

More specifically, e-services are described as combined work- and information flows, which I call in the context of the book *service flows*. An indicative service flow is depicted in Figure 6, according to which:

- The overall service flow involves inclusion of several info supply chain "nodes".

Figure 6. Implementing alternative service flows with use of the agent concept

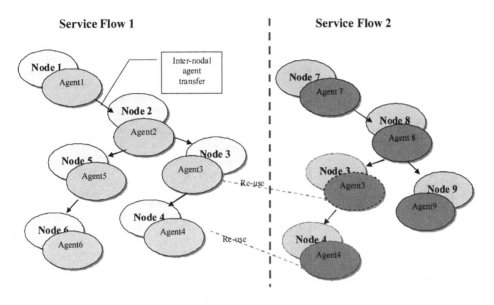

- The service agents are enabling the service flow between the various nodes by means of transferring both data and metadata information amongst them.

Upon the reception of an e-service, then given the particular scenario under execution as well as specifics related to service agent permissions and access rights, as these are specified by the relevant service data elements, the SRA agent execution may commence according to three alternative modes:

1. Immediate scenario execution, which forms the case of an *Executor*
2. By means of presenting a user interface entity informing the particular node / user about the event, and delegating the latter for choosing whether to e.g. resume execution at that moment, to redirect the execution to another user or to decide inclusion into a waiting list. This forms the case of a *Controller*.
3. No information is communicated to the particular node user and the service agent is immediately included in a waiting list; this forms the case of a *Coordinator*, where the user's decision is expected for enabling the scenario execution or whether the service agent may be relocated elsewhere for execution (i.e. moved further to another node).

Information describing the services in terms of service flows, service elements and service pages is depicted in the service database (see Figure 7).

Figure 7. Service database: Design of primary schemes and structures

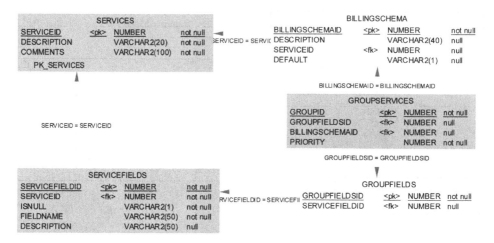

As seen in the figure, the scheme can be augmented for inclusion of billing information. Even in the case that the SRA is given for free to corporate management, it is essential that an assessment of the particular **utility**[6] and valuation that someone may attribute to a particular Situation Information Exchange Matrix.

Implementation conventions that have been followed concern the following:

- Each *e-Service* consists from fields that exist at the "AllFields" tables. A set of those fields are described by a unique e-Service which will be then instantiated as a *service flow*. This Set of fields are stored on the "servicefields" table.

- Especially in regard to the billing aspect, care has been taken so that every *e-Service* can support multiple billing schemas. Each billing schema consists from groups that include different fields.

- Registration of a new service is realised in the respective e-Services tables (Services, ServiceFields, GroupSrvices) by selecting the fields from table AllFields that are appropriate to it.

- To start with, we add a new record in the Services table.

- For every field of AllFields table that is selected (must belong to the service), a new record in ServiceFields is added with the name of the field, if it is mandatory or not for this service and its relationship with GroupServices table.

- The GroupServices table provides extra information for every service like access rights, execution priorities, e.t.c., and shlould be connected with the billing subsystem. By the end of this process, the new entries in the ServiceFields table will be as many as the fields of the service that has been created.

Figure 8. Modeling service related entities: primary investigation

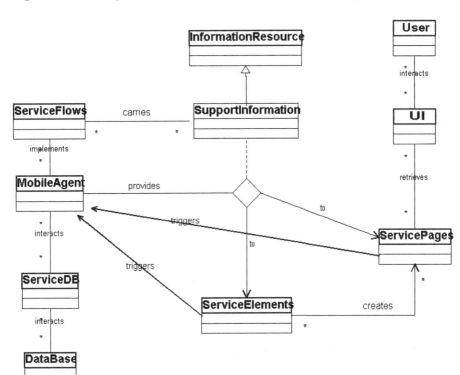

For the actual model of operation UML was employed in two different and distinct roles:

- The UML as Modeling Language and as a standard to design and customise the Dilemma model of "Service flows – Service elements – Service pages". This usage of the language focuses on the UML notation.

- The UML as a Core Model of the Dilemma Model of "Service flows – Service elements – Service pages" from which other submodels may inherit concepts (e.g. for domain-specific SRA specialisations, or for reflecting variations in the underlying business models of the inter-organisational service provision aspects. The usage of UML intended to minimise the complexity of the "Service flows – Service elements – Service pages" model by re-using via inheritance and therefore reducing the number of modelling concepts. This usage of the language focuses on the UML metamodel.

Figure 9. Modeling service related entities: going one step deeper

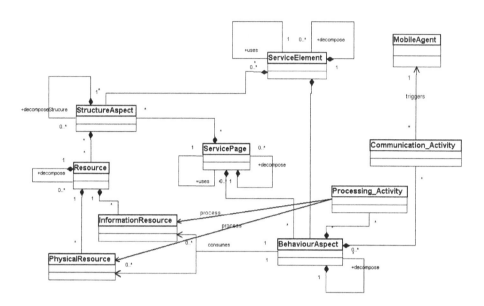

In Figure 8, the semantical aspects of the concepts to be demonstrated from within an SRA implementation are depicted which concern the relative positioning of the service agent as a facilitator of the service flow by means of being triggered either by a SR participant (the latter using the interaction means provided by the e-Service pages) or by an application, which is related to some particular Service element(s).

It is also easy to see that between the service agent and the physical resources of a particular SRA implementation, "intervenes" the service flow aspect (as generator of the various e-services), while the Service database is independent on the physical resources of the particular SRA implementation.

Furthermore, in Figure 9 it is easy to denote the following important properties of the system:

- Both Service elements and Service pages are enabled to share structural and/ or bahavioural "aspects" in terms of accessibility to the SRA Resources and the Communication activities respectively.
- The linkage between the two "aspects" (i.e. the bahavioural and the structural) is facilitated by the notion of the Processing Activity, which shows an innovative idiosyncracy in terms of indirectly affecting the particular SRA Resources.

Conclusively, the SRA access-to-service environment should enable the SR participants to:

- Establish an overall Service flow Direction, by means of providing linkage to a set of pre-programmed SRA resources that are executed in the distributed (Internet) environment.
- Acquire SRA Resources for a particular service property which may be either a Service flow, a Service element, or a Service page).
- Provide "Capabilities" to a Service flow by means of integrates both structural and behavioural aspects from within a single perspective, which will be utilised to instantiate the actual service delivery at the end user's point.
- Execute the Service flow by means of utilising resources to accomplish the particularly assigned service scenario.

The last may also be regarded also the "bottom-line" for the actual e-Service delivery by a particular Service flow to support the purpose of the latter's establishment (i.e. the reason for existence of that particular Service flow in the overall info supply chain value chain).

TEST CASE FOR SERVICE SUPPLY CHAIN MANAGEMENT

The operational framework for the test case I present in the following paragraphs concerns the specification of communication, coordination and information management procedures for each entity within a service supply chain – actually this is usually realised rather as a network. It employs a decision support system, implemented using a multi-agent system (MAS) architecture and aimed to enhance the functional capacities of the ATLANTIS ERP system of ALTEC S.A. ALTEC is one of the biggest ERP vendors in Greece with an installed base of 40.000 companies from all business sectors and with activities on software, system integration, services and products and telecommunications, in several branches all over Greece, while also operating subsidiary companies in Romania and Bulgaria. Of course, this same approach can be replicated in any other enterprise context and with use of any existing or operational information systems infrastructure as well as business processes available.

The constraints for the design of the considered service framework are composed of the characteristics in a given business environment, including the human operation (processes to be triggered or adapted, decisions to be made, etc.) and the other design decisions such as the specified technical architecture. In this respect, the addressed field can be regarded as the other principal-level design phase in conjunction with architectural design and before the technical-level design.

The design aspects of our test case are linked bi-directionally to the architecture design via design constraints; in this respect the entire design process can be considered as iterative.

Service Application Domain

The business environment is changing rapidly every day; henceforth, enterprise information systems must be able to adapt to changes in markets quickly and flexibly while also being able to control large amounts of software resources and these software resources must be integrated.

One solution that is attracting a great deal of attention is the concept of Enterprise Application Integration (EAI). EAI can adapt to changes in markets quickly and flexibly. In this respect, our test cases forms a representative "example" for achieving application integration at the shop-floor with the office level of an industry and how we enable an innovative integration environment with increased adaptability and flexibility from the ATLANTIS ERP System to the single logical entities within the corporate environment such as the customer, a service order, a service supply request, all of them modelled in a way that reflects the current practices of the company and the domain that it belongs to. In this respect we can afford to classify the test case as being in the field of service supply chain management.

The operation design for the ALTEC test case takes into account the specification of communication, coordination and information management procedures for the entities in the entire service supply chain network and for each sub-function of the overall coordination task. The constraints for the design are composed of the given business environment, including the human operation and the other aspects, i.e. the specified architecture.

For operation four layers are of interest. The levels are from bottom to top: communication, information management, coordination, and learning and adaptation. The lower layers can be regarded as the bases for higher layers.

On communication level the basic principles of how the communication takes place have to be defined. The information management has to define the information operations performed by the entities. Also the type of information handled has its meaning. Information management types define the roles of local data management and information exchange as parts of the overall information management approach across the service supply chain. Furthermore, these operations pose requirements on the communication layer of the service supply chain.

The coordination defines the coordination operations performed by the entities. The basic features of a coordination scheme include the objective of coordination, planning horizon and coordination type. The more detailed features of a coordination scheme may be outlined by specifying entities decision procedures and their behaviour in different situations or operational phases of the service supply chain.

The decision procedures define the characteristics of the decision processes inside the entities. The decision procedures utilise data provided by information management operations and indicate communication needs. The decision procedures can be described by defining the data used in decision making, decision methods and criteria.

Decision making is in many cases done in cooperation of human and supporting technology. Decomposition and allocation of the production task are important coordination functions. It is a combination of process-planning and job-scheduling functions. The purpose of the coordination is to assure the coherence of all task decomposition and allocation decisions in respect of the global goals of the service production.

Another important coordination phase is the execution phase. This phase corresponds to the combination of service production process execution and monitoring. The distribution of this task means that units supervise their local operations that can be dependent on the operations of other agents. The purpose of the coordination is to ensure that production is performed according to a predefined schedule and to indicate the need for replanning when needed.

The learning and adaptation level covers aspects like enhancing coordination and adjusting it to changing situations. These are often longer-term tasks, like assessment of performance, goal-setting and operation reconfiguration. The distribution of learning means learning among the units in which the learned results of individual entities can be combined and distributed to the others to become global knowledge.

This last aspect of the learning, as it is easy to assess, is the most critical and difficult level to achieve, for which any type of progress and input is highly useful and contributing.

Service Design Considerations

The goals of the service supply chain operation design originate mainly from (quantitative) performance objectives. The constraints of the design are set by the "outer" systems of the overall business environment, including human organisation and other parts of the system design, especially the chosen architecture model.

Aspects to take into consideration are:

- The performance and flexibility of the business enabled by the particular service management task,

Table 5. Primary service design alternatives in inter-enterprise operation

Design aspect	Possible value set
Communication level	
Synchronicity	Asynchronous
Paradigm	Messages
Language scope	Compact
Information-type	Structured, unstructured

- The characteristics of the overall business task, its subtasks and constraints placed on them,
- The goal information distribution between the involved service delivery units,
- characteristics of the managed business system and the distribution architecture adopted for its control,
- The availability and completeness of the state of information,
- The particular policy used, e. g. Lean Management, Just-in-Time, e.t.c.
- The restriction on service production flexibility, e.g. by specialisation of human agents, 'machines' and other facilities needed for the successful service completion.

Inter-Enterprise Aspects of the Service Supply Chain Operation

In inter-enterprise service supply chain operation, the architectural communication restrictions disable some types of information management and coordination. The focus of operation is (more) in local procedures with (more) limited communication than in the intra-enterprise case (see Table 5).

Intra-Enterprise Aspects of the Service Supply Chain Operation

The design of a communication scheme for intra-enterprise service supply chain operation is influenced by the coordination and information management schemes and the communication restrictions imposed by the obtained architecture model. Communication is orientated towards the demand for information and it has to make sure that the requested information will be transmitted goal-directed.

The reduction of unnecessary communication is an important design goal. A looser connection is regarded as better with respect to the reliability and maintainability of the system. A looser connection is also associated with a greater autonomy of entities and more abstract content in communication. The information management

Table 6. Primary service design alternatives in intra-enterprise operation

Design aspect	Possible value set
Communication level	
Synchronicity	Synchronous, asynchronous
Paradigm	Messages, shared memory
Language scope	Compact, moderate, extensive
Information-type	Structured, unstructured

is heavily effected by the coordination structure. Information access varies with information-type, ranging from purely locally orientation to global access.

Probably the most characteristic features of the decision procedures are the coordination type and the amount of global coordination information. These properties are considerably determined by the overall control architecture of the particular service framework we intend to employ – in our case it was the ATLANTIS ERP system but this may of course vary amongst organisations. The command type coordination approach with global information is used in centralised and hierarchical architectures. In architectures with horizontal peer-to-peer communication channels, the nature of coordination must become increasingly co-operative with a decreasing amount of global coordination information.

Another important property of decision procedures is the amount of iterative problem solving needed between the agents. For iterative, predictive methods substantial communication is required. The learning and adaptation ability depends on the extent of group behaviour and target of adaptation. Learning is primarily individual for each agent (type) or it may be group learning for certain classes of agents. Adaptation changes the applied communication, information management or coordination schemes, or learning and adaptation scheme itself (see Table 6).

On the Class of Supported Applications

For supporting the desired class of service supply chain management business applications in ALTEC's ATLANTIS ERP system, two different types of agents have been identified as those ones that are needed to build and maintain in the platform. These are:

- **Pattern identification agents,** which are responsible for identifying service patterns related to a specific service *scheme* according to a set which will be initially provided and which has to be dynamically fine-tuned and improved (also change in the cardinality and granularity aspects).

- **Recommendation agents,** which provide customised suggestions to different types of enterprise users from various departments such as Sales, Supplies, Accounting etc. related to proposed alterations of the existing service policies for the different service *schemes* under consideration.

From the above, one can see that the main medium that is used for building the service agents is this of a service *scheme*.

A service scheme can be regarded as the placeholder of information entities, which will be used and shared by the different categories of service agents. In our first attempt we have come to identify two first service *schemes*, namely the service sales scheme and the service supplies scheme for which the following holds:

- *Service sales schemes* concern how a specific customer or customer type behaves in terms of requests for specific services or service types.
- *Service supplies schemes* concern how a specific service supply or service supply type behaves (i.e. how it is demanded) in terms of requests for:
  - Specific services or service types
  - Specific customers or customer types

Of course the latter service recommendation agent type can be further specialised to come up with different specialisations of service recommendation agents related to the above roles, while a further possibility might be to enhance the different recommendation agents types to negotiate amongst them for coming up with suggestions that are satisfying more than one parameters.

This satisfies also the original lack on representing semantics that was a shortcoming of the first test case, and which are now to be faced by:

- The aforementioned service schemes for Sales, Supplies
- The affected entity *types* (customer, service, supply) as these are represented / managed by the ERP ATLANTIS.

A further point that is satisfied – taking also into account the feedback we received in the early implementation phases from end users and customers of the system on this – relates to the tracking of user activities in regard to providing improvements for:

- Better recognising patterns with respect to the adoption of recommendations given to the users (this concerns the operation of the pattern identification agents);

- Reduction of the recommendations that are not undertaken by the users (this concerns the operation of both the pattern identification and the recommendation agents);
- Discovery and identification of the number of the most suitable recipients on corresponding recommendations (this concerns the operation of the recommendation agents).

Finally, there we needed to introduce two system agents, namely:

- An ATLANTIS Agent which is responsible for the handling of communications such as queries and data retrieval with the ATLANTIS ERP system, and
- A DM Agent (Data Mining Agent) responsible for performing communications related with the supply of DM results, management of DM representations / expressions, assignment of tasks triggered by the DM module, etc.

As far as state-of-the-art approach in this area are concerned, there is no mystic path or transcended way for re-inventing the wheel; quite in contrast, we tried to build on top of existing approaches. During the past few years ERP systems have opened up their tightly interwoven modules and created application programming interfaces (APIs) to connect to 3rd-party best-of-breed systems.

ERP systems are offering a broad range of open integration schemes, including extensible mark-up language (XML) messaging and proprietary connectors or open APIs, since easy integration to 3rd-party applications has become a key point for them.

Nowadays, the industry faces significant interoperability issues as it seeks to provide solutions for distributed systems consisting of clients and servers of heterogeneous hosts to enable joint service operations. XML and related technologies offer promise for applying data management technology to documents and, also, for providing a neutral syntax for interoperability among disparate systems. The adoption of XML and of other leading edge software technologies in order to enable interoperability among dissimilar databases and message formats seems to be an efficient and effective solution approach.

The work on this task has additionally been inspired by the vision that an industrial manager (is able to) monitors the entire plant having on his desk only an front end to both the ERP system and any other 3rd party Supply Chain Management applications. That is why through the beginning of the project we did insist and suggest for adding functionality such as the status of the current configuration: service agents are thus enabled to send to the ERP the new configuration each time a change occurs, and the ERP stores the information and displays it in "real-time".

This will enable industry demands to minimize time and expenditure related with the setting up of new business processes, setting up new (clusters of) activities, reengineering of existing ABC (: Activity-based costing) classifications, or due to other changes either in the technical production or business environment.

A future service supply unit will consist of systems which have their own de-central intelligence: By using plug-and-participate-concepts, these systems will be able to connect by their own means to a wider service supply chain control network, while the required product dependent intelligence is supported by intelligent agents.

A highly flexible and adaptable plant as a technical reaction on today's highly turbulent surroundings is designed, where there will be the least amount of centralised control as possible and the only supervision to the service supply operations will happen from within an ERP system. Service agents will do all the other work. In this respect service supply chain management can be seen as managing of the entire order service delivery process from immaterial suppliers of know-how, expertise or structured information to the final service delivery to the end customer.

The service supply chain may contain many tasks involved in the customer service order-delivery process, such as reception of 'raw' materials which on the case of a service may constitute of structured or unstructured information, creation of new information or knowledge, distribution of information or knowledge, warehousing of information or knowledge and finally, as expected, sales operations. Similar to the conventional supply chain management systems for tangible goods, service supply systems are for planning, control, and optimisation of immaterial flow in service supply chains, embracing all steps from the extraction of intangible 'raw' materials (as it is the case I mentioned above of expertise, know-how, information or knowledge) to service logistics and distribution.

The service supply chain is often very complex because a large number of resources, operations, and functions put together make the service chain very complex. The most important flows in the service supply chain are information and other immaterial entities flows.

In general, the information flow advances backwards in the service supply chain whereas the immaterial service flow advances forward. In this model, customer demand is the driving impulse for the service supply chain. Companies in the service supply chain exist for customer service. They want to produce services efficiently with low cost structure. Customer demand service is information for the whole service supply chain and this information flow usually advances backward. The immaterial service flow advances forward because the customer has a need for something that the service supply chain produces and "pushes" ahead in the service chain.

The idea of is to work between customer demand and the service supply chain supply. With the help of efficient planning and optimisation functionality the main company can forecast customer service demand and plan the service operation of the whole service supply chain and companies in it. When all IT-systems of the companies in the service supply chain are integrated, information of the customer service demand can be accessed in all the companies at the same time. That kind of operations enables efficient customer response at the right time required.

The presented test case is representative for the type of needs that one faces as an ERP vendor when considering solutions to be provided for commercial service supply systems. With regard to the levels of planning it is helpful to distinguish between:

- Strategic planning systems for optimisation and modelling of the configuration of service logistics frameworks;
- Optimisation tools for the local optimisation with service operative systems;
- Extended ERP-systems with service management functionality to offer an integrated, sustainable solution.

For our test case, we consider the third case i.e. extended ERP-systems with service management functionality.

Service Development Approach

Regarding the system functionality we have worked on two main ways, one where the ERP system sends an invoice e.g. for a service order for execution and a second where the ERP controls the current status of the various service subsystems and of the particular service order.

Different XML files for each request, each time, are to be delivered to the service supply chain members (through the service agents of course) based on agents that will inform that the previous one has ended. These requests can be agents that were generated and follow through the entire service request lifecycle until there are completed.

Such an application integration system that can communicate with ALTEC's ATLANTIS ERP system or any other ERP system has been developed, consisting of an XML Server that has the ability to communicate from one side with XML (Receive XML requests and Response with XML Responses) and the other side with SQL for getting data from a relational database management system (RDBMS).

From our analysis, the application data that are communicated for a medium-level installation on a daily basis are ca 6-7.000 in terms of new service data entries, update of existing service data records, revisions of issued service invoices and (less) for configuring service data streams from the related service units.

The basic business driver had to do with the increase of the corporate ability to support better (: faster, easier and more resource-efficient) development of applications that facilitate ALTEC's software development tasks for custom applications on top of ATLANTIS or as extensions of functionality already provided by ATLANTIS ERP in terms of supporting EAI scenarios. In compliance to this, our expectation from the test case had concentrated on the employment of the service delivery platform for the creation of customisable and highly adaptive and "expert" end user shells on top of the ATLANTIS ERP.

The migration of companies towards Enterprise Resource Planning (ERP) systems was emphasised in the mid-1990s in order to integrate and automate all of a company's business processes and enable them to minimise time and expenditure related to daily business. Industries necessity to integrate their ERP systems with their automation control systems drove software vendors to provide integration solutions to Manufacturing Execution Systems (MES) and to Supervisory Control and Data Acquisition (SCADA) systems, creating a situation in plant automation that can be described as oriented towards centralization with inefficiencies to cope with time, quality and cost stresses of the global economy.

ERP systems interfaces cannot be seen as a reliable solution to integration problems. The reason for this is that ERP modules co-exist with other applications (e.g. legacy, supply chain management etc). Therefore, there is a need to integrate the "integrated suites" with the rest applications. Application Integration technology may address this integration need. In Application Integration technology the integration of ERP systems with other inter-organisational applications can be done with XML, Java Beans and Middleware technologies, which are more efficient and flexible than traditional EDI technologies and can be used to integrate best-of-breed modules as well as other applications (e.g. legacy systems).

Enterprise Application Integration (EAI) includes approaches and mechanisms to allow sharing of information on support of "common business events". This is maybe a very short definition to what the EAI stands for. The variety and the complexity of the Enterprise Application have created a new issue for research since the available technology does not support EAI to a satisfactory level.

EAI is not data interchange between applications. The higher structures and the logic of the Enterprise applications such as ERP or CRM systems cannot be described in the data layer. An effective integration is defined to the entities layer where information has characteristics and semantic. EAI is responsible for information interchange between the world of data and the world of entities without the loss of any characteristics or semantics between different types of applications.

Different models of integration have emerged as the complexity of integration has shifted to a software-oriented view. Primarily integration was accomplished through the customisation of software to produce the desired outcome but it requires significant effort to handcraft each particular integration. A large part of this effort is related to the distributed processing aspects of the integration that must be custom

Table 7. Comparison of existing and the adopted approach for Application Integration Approaches

	DATA-BASED (EXISTING)	AGENT-BASED (ADOPTED)	OTHER (COMPONENT INTEGRATION)
Degree of Integration	Loosely coupled[7] integration	Tightly coupled integration	Tightly coupled integration
Communication Type	Asynchronous dominates	Asynchronous	Synchronous dominates
Communication direction	One-way	One-way and request/reply	Request/reply
Abstraction of business rules	Naive	Simple	Complex

developed as well. These custom integrations also were difficult to reuse, requiring a duplication of effort for each integration task.

Our main focus area is this of functional integration which is based on integration of software at the code level or at the level of an object (: in our case, it concerns ATLANTIS Business Objects). It could also be done through an application-programming interface (API) for the software if one exists. It allows the integration of software for the purpose of invoking existing functionality from other new or existing applications. The integration is done through interfaces to the software. Access is customised to each application, including the semantics and behaviour of the application. Another approach would use a connector that hides the internals of the application. A connector is software whose purpose is to provide access into the software and its functionality while hiding the complexity of creating the actual connections into the software. It makes the software appear to have been designed with the original intention of providing easy access and integration.

In the considered test case we used a functional integration and more specifically an interface that can support the workflow, processes and data manipulation of the system.

In Table 7, I describe the anticipated differences between the approach currently employed (1st column) with the adopted one (2nd column) in the test case, while as a separate alternative I provide (3rd column) a competing / competitive approach namely this of component based integration.

Below I present 4 representative use cases dealing with aspects of the service supply platform construction.

Use Case 1: Service Supply Platform Installation Use Case

The service supply platform installation process can be thought as formed by the following activities:

1. *Current enterprise architecture assessment.* The ATLANTIS ERP consultant talks to the corporate system manager in order to verify the current configuration of the software systems and network. If the current systems configuration is not adequate for the service supply platform, some installation will be performed.
2. *Service supply modules installation.* Involved service supply server installation made by the ATLANTIS consultant.
3. *Web server updating* (to access related pages). Web server updating, it may be included in the service supply platform installation.
4. *Firewall updating* (to enable access to related pages). Only for extra-company visibility.
5. *Functional test.*

Actors

*   *System manager* is the person in charge of modification of the access permissions of all the servers having some services or data needed by the service supply platform.
*   *Service management consultant* is the expert of the service supply platform and of the solutions space of it with respect to ATLANTIS. Thus, as background he needs to be an ATLANTIS consultant. In this phase the main job of the service management consultant is the correct installation of all the service supply platform modules in order to see the current services and data source already functioning in the enterprise network.

Use Case 2: Service Supply Platform Start-Up (Boot-Strapping)

This phase is devoted to the insertion of the particular ontology and the interfaces to the service domain data needed for the management of the test case process. I refer below the involved activities.

Business Process Assessment

The service management consultant together with a company business process expert draws a detailed model of the current processes involved in the service supply chain management activities that are to be supported.

Business Process Analysis and Mapping

As well as the previous phase, some investigations about the business process need to be done by the service management consultant together with the company responsible so that concept and functionality mapping is carried out with respect to the concepts and functionality of the service supply platform. After this phase, the service management consultant should check if the data gathered in the previous phase (Business process assessment) are sufficient. If not, a further iteration is necessary.

Ontology Insertion

As ontology I approach the partial representation of the concepts related to the service supply chain management process and the specific business problem to tackle with. Involved persons are for this step the Business process experts under the coordination of the Business process manager.

External Data Connection / Import

Some data that will be used during the process mapping and implementation are already present. They are accessible by using some applications developed in other contexts, or – in general – related modules of ATLANTIS.

The service management consultant should understand how to manage these data, which interface must be adopted and set. Besides, some critical and bandwidth consuming data should be imported into the platform and updated. The entire ideal service supply structure may be substantially affected by this issue as well.

At the end of this phase a generic service supply platform user should be able to view and access to the ontology entities without knowing if an entity is inside or outside the ATLANTIS environment. The last formed also a requirement for the developer team from the side of ALTEC: the tighter the end system would be to the ATLANTIS ERP, the easier it will be promoted and marketed.

Templates Insertion

The last activity related to the start-up / bootstrapping use case reflects a major need: the application of the service supply platform should be easy-to-use as much as possible.

The service management consultant should insert all the templates (service sales "schemes", service supplies "schemes", etc. as per the terminology described in previous paragraphs) ready to be provided to the Business process experts at the right time. Moreover, according to the needs of the platform users (service experts and service process manager) some automated procedures and wizards should be created in order to reduce the service process mapping duration.

Actors

- *Service manager*. See the previous use case.
- *Service management consultant*. See the previous use case.
- *Service process analyst* is the person (internal or external) who knows all the process or sub-processes involved in the service process that we aim to solve through employment of the platform. The service management consultant needs the help of the business process analyst in order to grasp the business process data structure and reproduce it as ontology.
- *Service process manager* is the person who knows the current process and all the data that can be used in order to get the solution of problems related with it. Usually, the Business process manager knows all the experts that can be consulted.
- *Service expert* is the person asked to contribute by the Business process manager*.

Use Case 3: Process Mapping Use Case

According to the interviewed people the service process mapping is one of the most time consuming problems when regarding a new service request. Some causes have been detected like the lack of a centralised knowledge repository or the reluctance of the Business process analysts to document their own knowledge about a particular service.

Service Process Creation

The service manager needs to study the documentation and decides whether to open a new service process or simply to adapt an existing one. This seems a trivial task but it is not and in many cases the success or failure of a new service platform implementation depends on the management of a whole setting of such "trivial" issues.

Service Problem Evaluation

The Business process manager, with the help of some similarity searching features provided by ATLANTIS preselected scenarios, looks for any suggestion that could provide a starting point for the next service mapping step. Some possible suggestions could be:

- A similar service process
- A similar service problem
- A group of service process experts which know how to proceed

Depending on the results obtained, the Business process manager decides if a final solution has been reached, in such a case, a final report is emitted and then the process is closed.

Experts Selection and Notification

If the service process manager judges the current situation not sufficient for a final solution, a new solving step has to be open and a new group of service process experts is to be selected. After the selection, the service process experts are notified about the problem and the previous solving steps.

Service Problem Evaluation (by the Service Process Experts)

During this phase, each Business process expert involved in the current solving step, studies the problem. It is important to highlight some service supply platform features that are very important in this phase:

- Ability to find other cases that can help the Business process expert to find a solution
- Ability to find similar cases related to processes about different models (implicit knowledge)
- Ability to find similar processes in order to determine which steps can be avoided.

Obviously, the possibility to work offline is fundamental. Most of the time, a Business process expert is out of office (usually dealing with customers) and needs to work to the service supply platform without connecting to the server.

Service Experts Contribution Evaluation

At any moment, the Business process manager can decide to close the current solving step with notification to the involved Business process experts.

Actors

- *Service management consultant.* See the previous use case.
- *Service manager.* See the previous use case.
- *Service process expert.* See the previous use case.

Use Case 4: Service Supply Platform Management Use Case

The data instances held by the system are not static; each time a new case is instantiated a large amount of new data should be imported or simply viewed by the service supply platform. Two cases may be analysed:

- *Automatic synchronisation.* The service supply platform should be able to view by a customised interface the external data.
- *Guided import.* When a new case has been realized, the service supply platform should be able to import all the data related to this new case into its own repository.

Obviously, all the standard management facilities should be available (ex. Backup and restore control, user management, etc.).

Actors

- *System manager.* See the previous use cases.
- *Service management consultant.* See the previous use cases.

DEVELOPMENT OF THE SUPPLY CHAIN TEST CASE

As already mentioned, the operational framework for our test case was a decision support system, implemented using a multi-agent system (MAS) architecture and aimed to enhance the functional capacities of the ATLANTIS ERP system of ALTEC S.A., one of the biggest ERP vendors in Greece with an installed base of 40.000 companies from all business sectors and with activities on software, system integration, services and products and telecommunications, in several branches all over

Greece, while also operating subsidiary companies in Romania and Bulgaria.

The main goal of the new service was to generate specific recommendations about the way a specific order will be transacted in order to satisfy requests posted by customers. The specification of communication, coordination and information management procedures for each entity within a Supply Chain has been realized as a network of coordinating service agents.

As we all know, Enterprise Resource Planning (ERP) systems are business management tools that automate and integrate all company facets, including real-time planning, manufacturing, sales, and marketing. These processes produce large amounts of enterprise data that are, in turn, used by managers and employees to handle all sorts of business tasks such as inventory control, order tracking, customer service, financing and human resources.

Despite the support current ERP systems provide on process coordination and data organization, most of them – especially legacy ones – lack advanced Decision Support (DS) capabilities, resulting therefore in decreased company competitiveness. In addition, from a functionality perspective, most ERP systems are deprecated to mere transactional IT systems, capable of acquiring, processing and communicating raw or unsophisticated processed data on the company's past and present supply chain operations. In order to optimize business processes in the tactical supply chain management level, the need for analytical IT systems that will work in close cooperation with the already installed ERP systems has already been identified, and DS-enabled systems stand out as the most successful gateway towards the development of more efficient and more profitable solutions. Probing even further, some suggest that decision-making capabilities should act as an extension of the human ability to process knowledge and proposes the unification of knowledge management systems with the classical transaction-based systems, while others claim that the integration of smart add-on modules to the already established ERP systems could make standard software more effective and productive for the end-users.

The benefits of incorporating such sophisticated DS-enabled systems inside the corporate IT infrastructure are:

- Enhancement of the decision maker's ability to process knowledge,
- Improvement of reliability of the decision support processes,
- Provision of evidence in support of a decision,
- Improvement or sustainability of organizational competitiveness,
- Reduction of effort and time associated with decision-making, and
- Augmentation of the decision makers' abilities to tackle large-scale, complex problems.

Within the context of Small and Medium sized Enterprises (SMEs) however, applying analytical and mathematical methods as the means for optimization of the supply chain management tasks is highly impractical, being both money- and time-consuming. This is why alternative technologies, such as Data Mining (DM) and Agent Technology (AT) have already been employed, in order to provide efficient DS-enabled solutions. The increased flexibility of multi-agent applications, which provide multiple-loci of control can lead to less development effort, while the cooperation primitives that AT adopts, define Multi-Agent Systems (MAS) as the best-fitted choice for addressing complex tasks in systems that require synergy of multiple entities.

On the other hand, DM has repeatedly been used for Market Trend Analysis, User Segmentation and Forecasting. Knowledge derived from the application of DM techniques on existing ERP historical data can provide managers with information non-trivial, implicit, previously unknown and potentially useful, which can be used as an advisor to their decision-making capabilities.

During the past few years ERP systems have opened up their tightly interwoven modules and created application-programming interfaces (APIs) to connect to 3rd-party best-of-breed systems. ERP systems are offering a broad range of open integration schemes, including extensible mark-up language (XML) messaging and proprietary connectors or open APIs, since easy integration to 3rd-party applications has become a key point for them.

In addition, we see that DM and MAS have been used separately for efficient enterprise management and decision support. (Rygielski et. al., 2002) have exploited DM techniques for Customer Relationship Management (CRM), while (Choy et. al., 2002) have used a hybrid machine learning methodology for performing Supplier Relationship Management (SRM). On the other hand, MAS integrated with ERP systems have been used for production planning (Peng et. al., 1999), and for the identification and maintenance of oversights and malfunctions inside the ERP systems (Kwon and Lee, 2001).

Elaborating on further work, we have integrated AT and DM advantages into a versatile and adaptive multi-agent system that acts as an add-on to established ERP systems. Our approach employs Soft Computing (SC), DM, Expert Systems (ES), standard Supply Chain Management (SCM) and AT primitives, in order to provide intelligent recommendations on customer, supplier and inventory issues. It is addressed not only to the managers of a company - "Managing by wire" approach (Haeckel and Nolan, 1994)-, but also the lower-level, distributed decision makers - "Cowboys" approach (Malone, 1998). Our framework utilizes the vast amount of corporate data stored inside ERP systems to produce knowledge, by applying data mining techniques on them. The extracted knowledge is diffused to all interested parties via the multi-agent architecture, while domain knowledge and business rules are incorporated into the system by the use of rule-based agents. It merges the, already proven capabilities of data mining with the advantages of multi-agent systems in terms of autonomy and flexibility, and therefore promises a great likelihood of success.

Test Case Architecture

Regarding the system functionality we have worked on two main ways, one where the ERP system sends an invoice e.g. for a service order for execution and a second where the ERP controls the current status of the various subsystems and of the service order.

The Multi-Agent System (MAS) add-on is composed of 6 different agent-types, working in close cooperation with each other. The agent types along with the human agents and other objects are depicted in Figure 10.

The developed Intelligent Recommendation Framework(IRF) has six different types of agents:

1.   The Customer Order Agent type (COA)
2.   The Recommendation Agent type (RA)
3.   The Customer Profile Identification Agent type (CPIA)
4.   The Supplier Profile Identification Agent type (SPIA)
5.   The Inventory Profile Identification Agent type (IPIA)
6.   The Enterprise Resource Planning Agent type (ERPA)

Customer Order Agent Type (COA)

COA is a Graphical User Interface (GUI) agent that could be found at the distributed stores, or at the telephone center of an enterprise. COA enables the system operator (either manager or lower-level employee) to: (a) transfer information in and out the rest of the system, (b) input order preferences into the system and (c) explain by means of visualization the proposed recommendations.

When an order comes into the system, COA provides the human agent with basic functionalities for inserting information on customer id, ordered products along with their corresponding quantities, payment terms (cash, check, credit etc.), backorder policies and, finally, the party (client or company) that will undertake transportation costs.

COA also offers an explanatory unit that employs bar charts, percentages and simple text descriptions of the final recommendation. COA is closely related to the Recommendation Agent.

Figure 10. Intelligent Recommendation Framework(IRF) functional diagram

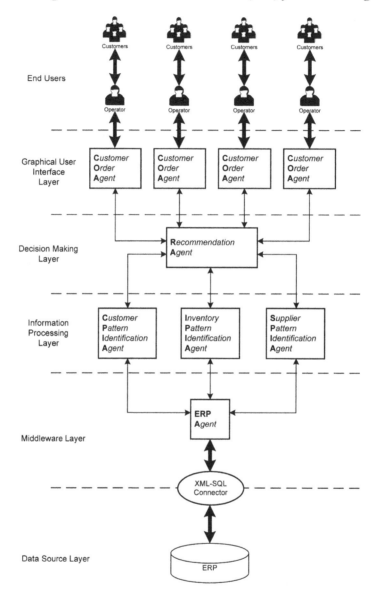

Recommendation Agent Type (RA)

RA is responsible for gathering the profiles of the related to the current order entities. By requesting from the Information Processing Layer agents (CPIA, SPIA and IPIA - each one of them operating on its own control thread) the corresponding profiles, and by taking into account concurrency issues, RA diminishes the cycle-time of the recommendation process. RA has been implemented as a rule-based agent implemented using the Java Expert Shell System, and static business rules can be incorporated into it, by writing the latter into a document that RA reads during its execution phase.

In this way, business rules can be changed on-the-fly, without the need of recompiling, or even restarting the application. RA is responsible for the final formatting of the recommendation that is forwarded to COA.

Customer Profile Identification Agent Type (CPIA)

CPIA is designed to identify service customer profiles, according to historical data found in the ERP system's records. The customer profile identification process can be at a glance described as: Initially, managers and application developers produce a model for generating the profiles of customers.

They select the appropriate customer attributes that can be mapped from the data residing in the ERP database; these are the attributes that are considered as valuable assets for reasoning on customer value. Then, they decide on the desired classification of customers, i.e. added-value to the company, discount due to past transactions etc. CPIA, by the use of clustering techniques, analyzes customer profiles periodically, and stores the outcome of this analysis into a profile repository for posterior retrieval.

When a CPIA is asked to provide the profile of a customer, the current attributes of the specific customer are requested from the ERP database and are matched with those inside the profile repository, resulting into the identification of the group the specific customer belongs. During the development phase, one or more CPIA agents can be instantiated, and the distinction of CPIAs into training and recommendation ones, results to quicker response times when learning and inference procedures overlap.

Supplier Pattern Identification Agent Type (SPIA)

SPIA is responsible for identifying supplier profiles according to their historical records found in the ERP database. In a similar to CPIA manner, managers identify the valuable attributes for generating the supplier profiles. Such profiles can be consisted of value of a supplier for the company and his/her credibility.

In the case there is a pool of service suppliers responsible for procuring a service constituent requested in the current processed service order, SPIA as requested by RA, can retrieve all the current records of the suppliers, match them with the classified ones found inside the profile repository and return all corresponding supplier profiles, characterized on the classification attribute (i.e. credibility).

Then RA can select the most appropriate one (according to its rule engine), and recommend it to the human operator of the system. Apart from this information, SPIA is responsible for fetching to RA information about a specific supplier, such as statistical data on lead-times, expedient for forecasting quantities to be procured etc.

Inventory Profile Identification Agent Type (IPIA)

IPIA is responsible for identifying service profiles. Service profiles consist of raw data found inside the ERP (i.e. service price, related store, remaining quantities), unsophisticated processed data (for example statistical data on product demand) and intelligent recommendations on services (such as related services that the customer may be willing to purchase). Once more, managers and application developers have to identify the requirements of the company and map the profile with the data found inside the ERP. Besides the directly derived data, IPIA is responsible for identifying buying patterns Market Basket Analysis (MBA) by the use of Association Rule Extraction techniques. In order to reduce run-times and due to the fact that MBA has high analysis-time, two or more IPIAs can be instantiated to separate the recommendation from the learning procedure.

Enterprise Resource Planning Agent Type (ERPA)

ERP Agents provide the middleware between the MAS application and the ERP system. These agents can be resembled to transducers (Genesereth and Ketchpel, 1994), because they are responsible for transforming data from heterogeneous applications into agent comprehensible message formats. ERPA handles all queries posted by CPIAs, IPIAs, and SPIAs by connecting to the ERP database and fetching all the required data. It works in close cooperation with an XML connector used for sending XML-SQL queries to the ERP and receiving data in XML format. ERPAs are the only agent types that need to be configured properly, in order to meet the connection requirements of different ERP systems.

Technologies Adopted

The IRF framework has been developed by the use of Agent Academy. All the agents were developed over the Java Agent Development Framework (JADE), while the required ontologies have been developed within the service supply chain management platform. Data mining has been performed on ERP data that are imported to the platform in XML format, and are forwarded to the Data Miner module.

The extracted knowledge structures have been represented in PMML (Predictive Model Markup Language), a language that efficiently describes clustering, classification and association rule knowledge models. The resulting knowledge has been incorporated into the agents by the use of the Agent Training Module of the platform. Agents can be periodically recalled for retraining, since appropriate agent tracking tools have been incorporated into the platform, in order to monitor agent activity after their deployment.

Test Case Parameters

The spirit of ERP and service supply chain management requirements is comparable: the development of small and flexible systems which are structured and co-ordinated from the higher hierarchical levels, but at the same time are subject of continuous optimisation from the lower hierarchical levels.

From the industrial exploitation point of view, the posed requirements has as follows: Companies are working more and more in networks, that means their is an increasing demand for coordination of its value and supply chain. There is trend towards outsourcing and decentralisation of task fulfilment, which means delegation of responsibilities and competencies to autonomous organisation entities, that practice self-organisation and self-optimisation. Furthermore, the challenge exists in design and management of decentralised organisations and in the vertical and horizontal information flow design across department and company boundaries.

The majority of business systems still follows a centralised approach, i.e. central databases, centralised process design and centralised coordination of activities. Heterogeneous information systems, even in one enterprise, make it difficult to co-operate and co-ordinate activities in a network efficiently.

So there is a huge industrial demand for solutions on the implementation level with regard to dynamic organisation concepts and innovative service supply chain management solution suites stemming from the particular service context. The decentralisation of business processes and their autonomous execution independent from rigid central management, is regarded as the key innovation issue for the ALTEC test case. In the same way as done with the general organisational test case requirements, corresponding requirements for the parameters according to which testing will be performed.

Intelligence

The application of the test case should make all requested information available to the right persons (Sales, Accounting, Supplies), on time and at the right place. It will have to combine simple data into complex evaluations and therefore helps the organisations to follow and achieve their goals.

Transparency

Transparency is regarded as availability of all needed information in a defined format for users requiring it, always and everywhere. Transparency enables the reflection of the conditions within the service supply chain without any restrictive preconditions e.g. alteration of a Sales or a Supply scheme, e.t.c. The test case application should not hinder the autonomy and self-organisation of the ATLANTIS entities through restrictive preconditions regarding the sequence of tasks, how it is in general the case in ERP-systems. It has to provide continuously updated information about the system status, that should be made available to the involved human users and inform them in case of a deviation from a planned state.

Therefore qualitative and quantitative key indicators must be defined, enabling the co-ordinator, executor and controller to monitor the network status.

Easy of Use

The test case application should be usable with a minimum of skills and knowledge. User-oriented graphical interfaces will thus make it easier for the user to work for defining user-tailored scenarios.

All information, which a human user needs for the fulfilment of the assigned tasks and activities, has to be available in a simple, easy intelligible form. This is the basis for enabling goal-orientation and basis flexibility, and cause the realisation of transparency and congruence.

Interactivity

This covers both interactivity between different systems (e.g. ATLANTIS ERP and the respective service supply chain management application) and the User-System interaction.

Speed Up of Information Exchange

Speed up of information exchange requires the close to real time provision of information. Because of the speed in which the system status may change within a turbulent business environment and the quantity in which data are generated it is necessary to link the supporting application via a network with the production for network-wide, directed information exchange.

Availability

This relates to the fast provision of general and accurate specific information to support the various categories of employees in creating and developing their own information profile. Availability covers also the information (what type of content the various agents are communicating to each other and to the human user) as well as application functionality (type of supported functionality / function breadth issues).

Flexibility

The term flexibility covers a wide range of requirements that can be reduced to it.

The service supply chain environment is characterised by a high level of turbulence, on which the test case has to react by its own flexibility and dynamic. The underlying agent technology should not be the restraining fact or even an obstacle in that context. This means, that it has to be easy adaptable to changes within the process. Furthermore it should be guaranteed that bigger "interventions" in the application are not necessary and thus the application represents itself to be changeable (at least to some degree).

Taking also into account the fact that the ALTEC test case should facilitate for its implementation in a heterogeneous network that has to be conceived to be used universally also in different ERP system environments with different working expedients and should be feasible to be integrated into the system in a plug-and-play way. This presupposes a high degree of standardisation regarding the recalled data of the single working expedients, as well as the flexibility of the network, that makes these data available.

It must be possible to enhance an application with new services or to customise it to particular user needs. The IT environment must be designed in a modular way so that modules can be assembled together in a way that satisfies the user requirements for the application considered. The system must be designed in such a way that addition of new modules is possible and easy to do.

Concerning the plug-and-play aspect, it is meant that corresponding applications of the AltEC test case are designed in a way that they only have to be adapted, switched on and possibly parameterised. This is especially important for an application that is used in a heterogeneous IT environment. Normally the existing technical resources represent strong limitations in the development and implementation of flexible and adaptable organisational structures and in this way contribute to the segmentation of the existing structures.

Table 8. Test case parameters and corresponding description

Parameter	Description
Intelligence	Subject to sequential use with varying data sets
	Subject to sequential use by different users
Transparency	Amongst the defined user groups
	Amongst the defined user tasks
	Avoidance of *noise* and *silence* effects in the communicated information
Easy of use	Subject to concurrent employment of a basic set of usage scenarios by different users
Interactivity	Amount of interactions and ratio of decisions made (: decision proposals) and successful decisions made (: adopted decisions)
Speed up of information exchange	Amount of entities (both human and agents) to which data is communicated
	Timeliness of data communication
	Ratio of data communicated to the quantity in which data is generated
Availability	Timely info provision amongst the defined user groups
	Timely info provision amongst the defined user tasks
Flexibility	Adaptation capability to different implementations of the same "basic" process
	Customisability for introducing new "thin" agents with user defined tasks (mainly for reporting and info clustering responsibilities)
Data consistency	Application behaviour with varying data sets

Data Consistency

The need for data consistency and integrity is one of the most important requirements for manufacturing applications (see Table 8).

REFERENCES

Choy, K. L., Lee, W. B., & Lo, V. (2002). Development of a case based intelligent customer–supplier relationship management system. *Expert Systems with Applications, 23*(3), 281–297. doi:10.1016/S0957-4174(02)00048-9

Friedman, J. W. (1991). *Game Theory with Applications to Economics*. Oxford, UK: Oxford University Press.

Genesereth M. & Ketchpel S. (1994). Software Agents. *CACM - Special Issue on Intelligent Agents 37*(7).

Haeckel, S. H., & Nolan, R. (1994). Managing by wire. *Harvard Business Review*, (September – October): 122–132.

Harsanyi, J. C. (1968). Games with incomplete information played by 'Bayesian' players. *Management Science, 14*.

Kwon, O. B., & Lee, J. J. (2001). A multi agent intelligent system for efficient ERP maintenance. *Expert Systems with Applications, 21*, 191–202. doi:10.1016/S0957-4174(01)00039-2

Malone, T. W. (1998). Inventing the organizations of the twentieth first century: control, empowerment and information technology. In S. P. Bradley &R. L. Nolan (eds.), *Sense and Respond: Capturing Value in the Network Era* (pp. 263-284). Boston: Harvard Business School Press.

Myerson, R. B., & Satterthwaite, M. A. (1983). Efficient mechanisms for bilateral trading. *Journal of Economic Theory, 29*, 265–281. doi:10.1016/0022-0531(83)90048-0

Peng, Y., Finin, T., Labrou, Y., Chu, B., Long, J., Tolone, W., & Boughannam, A. (1999). A multi agent system for enterprise integration. *Applied Artificial Intelligence, 13*(1-2), 39–63. doi:10.1080/088395199117487

Rygielski, C., Wang, J. C., & Yen, D. C. (2002). Data mining techniques for customer relationship management. *Technology in Society, 24*(4), 483–502. doi:10.1016/S0160-791X(02)00038-6

von Neumann, J., & Morgenstern, O. (1944). *Theory of Games and Economic Behavior*. Princeton, NJ: Princeton University Press.

ENDNOTES

[*]   In many cases, there is no redundancy of expertise that would end up in many different people being able to contribute with their expert opinion. In this respect, the Business Process manager is usually the "proprietor" of a particular service process; e.g. in the case of a Sales related issue, it is the Sales Manager or the Commercial Director.

[1]   We should stick to this: neither with respect to the product only nor to the company only. The reason is rather straightforward: it is different to have FIAT bringing a smart-like vehicle in the market than Daimler Chrysler (that actually did). For the former, it is a move compatible with their corporate history and tradition, which if realised should also be accompanied by an related pricing

strategy (cheaper than the adjacent model). To not do so should be justified to themselves and then to the market. This interactive game forms also part, as it is easy to understand, of an SRA live experiment.

2   A scan of the external macro-environment in which the firm operates can be expressed in terms of the following factors: political, economic, social, and technological. The acronym PEST (or sometimes rearranged as "STEP") is used to describe a framework for the analysis of these macro-environmental factors. A PEST analysis fits into an overall environmental scan. The PEST factors combined with external microenvironmental factors can be classified as opportunities and threats in a SWOT analysis. However, and despite the fact that the concept of the PEST analysis is to look at external factors which influence the business, just as in the SWOT analysis, the focus that a PEST analysis produces is that it shows which external factors are influencing the business; therefore, there is often confusion between a SWOT analysis which looks at internal to business and external to business within the same market factors.

3   I use the term strategy at this level rather with the notion of company policy, i.e. for axiomatically validating the inclusion of some activity to those that can be regarded as valid for the company. Their implementation, of course, forms part of the tactical and operational levels.

4   This again relates to the fact that in many cases criticism for a strategy should be rather addressed to its implementation. However, because decision making is treated as a practice, no distinction between the laboratory-based decision design and its real-world implementation has been made. It is therefore that there exists a need for SR and SRA.

5   For example, the classical game theoretic models of bargaining which date from the work of Nash were unusually resistant to tests with field data because their predictions depend on difficult to observe elements of the bargainers' preferences. But laboratory experimentation presents the opportunity to measure or control these factors, and thus permits bargaining to be observed in environments for which the predictions of these theories can be known, and therefore tested. And when examined in this way, the evidence supports some of the qualitative predictions of these models, for example concerning the effect of risk aversion on the outcome of bargaining, while contradicting others, concerning, for example, what constitutes "complete" information about a bargaining problem.

6   We may refer to the classic concept of *utility* (the capacity to satisfy a demand) as a proxy for value. The definition of utility has been progressively widened in the literature to include all sorts of things from which a human derives satisfaction. Some types of satisfaction are more objective and comparable

than others, but everything that is a "good", by its own nature, will generate utility of one sort or another. Economists use utility as a way to construct equivalents between two goods. In theory, different combinations of two given goods can produce the same level of satisfaction (or utility), thus describing a curve of equivalence. A higher level of utility will require different quantities of the goods. When one of those goods is money, the curve will show the equivalences between money and different quantities of the good for a given level of satisfaction (utility). This is the basis for price formation: the prices of a given good will be theoretically determined by the highest relative utility among the buyers who can afford the trade: the person for whom the good generates a higher relative utility compared with money will be the highest bidder, all other things equal. (Of course, some goods are harder to compare than others, and some don't have a relevant equivalent in money: they have very low relative utility.)

[7] Coupling measures the level of interdependencies between the two components and the impact that changes in one component will have on the other.

Chapter 4
Services and the Humans

The author examines the various aspects of influence and impact that services have on the humans and vice versa. How an interactive space is created to link both entities – and most importantly – how humans interact with each other through services of all kinds. He examines the starting points of a real world service design and implementation case that is representative of the difficulties that one faces when trying to make practice out of theory. Designing a service that would help people offer and get a better service in the European technology transfer domain is the starting point. He continues examining the users and their particular needs, then looking inside the service mediation process and the various user service scenarios. And concludes with a description of system deployment issues.

It is in the nature of humans to provide services – as it is also in the very nature of humans to consume services. The most primitive service is provided by mothers in terms of nursing their young born children. The latter are happy to receive milk for free – though they have to do something from their side too as they need to suck. Same as it is in the nature of humans to both provide (and get) services, it is also

DOI: 10.4018/978-1-60566-683-9.ch004

to provide (and get) bad services.

Bad is a generic term – may be used for *anything* that carries a negative connotation. However, this is what I mean in our case: any service that is unsuccessfully matching the expectations, wants, preferences, capacities, capabilities and needs of its customer or consumer can be simply denounced as bad.

Humans provide services for different reasons: either for fun when they sing in company of their friends, or for earning their life when they sing professionally in front of an audience and are paid for this. In the first case, people's attitude in case of a cacophonous hobby singer is much more tolerant than in the case of a professional singer – especially in case they had paid to listen to him or her. Of course, any successful professional singer has started as hobby singer and has advanced to earn money for this.

But this simple case does not constitute the basis of the service establishment for humans: professional accountants did not evolve from hobby ones; and secretaries did not follow a secretarial path dating back to their school or preschool activities. Same holds for bankers, prime ministers and police men. And most importantly: the same holds also for mothers who suckle and new born babies who suck.

The idea in a great majority of cases in the area of professional services is that someone starts his life as an insurance broker or her life as teacher, and that there is a learning curve and an incremental process that makes them better in hat they do. This is unfortunately a totally incorrect assumption that leads to many (otherwise avoidable) pitfalls and suboptimalities that make many of us find ourselves in unfortunate situations. An ideal world is nothing else than a universe of optimal service providers and customers. Just a brief notice: the customer side is essential to our analysis. A bad service customer damages a service same much as does a bad service provider. Or as we use to say: it takes to tango.

In an ideal world, all people would choose what best suits themselves for executing as a profession – or it would be God's invisible hand that would dictate who would become a teacher and who an internal auditor. Unfortunately people have not shown at least collectively a superb capacity in optimally assigning themselves with service-related professions, and as far as divine intervention is concerned either it is in default or not optimal at all.

Let us examine the case of telephone support personnel. It is in all aspects a demanding task: it needs people that are capable to unfold a multitude of skills many of which lie in the area of what we tend to characterise as 'soft skills'. And for sure, there is a demand for excellent capture of specialised knowledge in the core business domain. Now, think of all the incidents that happened to you during the last week or within the last month and which involved one or more incompetent people. It may depend on many parameters like the number of transactions you have with institutions and other entities, but in general the picture is well known to all of us:

people who seem to fail all adequacy tests staff businesses and organisations. They are assigned tasks or asked to perform tasks that they are unable to cope with and this results in several possibilities:

- A process that was never meant to become complex and / or complicated has become such;
- Time for completion of a task has been extended to unbelievable and unexpected levels;
- The quality of the requested service has deteriorated and in some cases the service has terminated with severe or lethal implications.

The human factor is the common denominator in all the above analysis. Failure to address the human factor in a holistic manner drives sooner or later to service failures.

The main issue with humans and the human factor in general is that it is an extremely costly and idiosyncratic factor that we tend to downgrade in many cases, thinking that this way we make our life simpler … and our business more efficient … and our costs lower, usually finding ourselves facing quite the opposite situation.

The most obvious factor is the one we tend to forget in most cases. Services that are ill-provided or ill-consumed are usually the result of a wrongly formulated conceptualisation regarding the supply or the demand of the particular service. Though elementary, this is the most usual mistake when designing a new service or maintaining an existing and operational one.

A usual fault we make is that when we recruit people to staff a department or a unit of our business we are still capable to effectively influence them through some pieces of on the job training or capacity building exercises. This is not wrong as such – for sure it needs some training so that a person gets all the necessary knowledge and information for operating a help desk application or control room software. But despite what many misinformed optimists think, companies and organisations in general are unfortunately in the mercy of their employees. Actually, they are staffed with final products of the education and the surrounding societal system. How can you expect that your people will act like self-motivated individuals when they have learned (from the school, their family or their previous employer) to not do so? You have higher chances of finding such a person if you look in the local prisons than in the local universities. Of course this cannot be applied as a general law – but it can be applied at least as a rule (of thumb).

In all my years in the IT profession, I have been watching people: my supervisors and my bosses, my colleagues and the members of my group. In general I can cluster them into two general categories: the ones who knew their boundaries and wanted to keep themselves within them, and the ones who always wanted to expand their boundaries or not have any at all. If you ask a person of category A to do the job that demands someone from category B, then it is only your fault that you made this mistaken assignment.

The service world is full of such mis-assignments or mal-assignments: people who should have been banned for their entire life to pick up a phone and address a customer request are mainly staffing the hot line centers. People who have an overdose of irony or sarcasm enough for granting them the role of a CEO of a giga-corporation are found in key positions in companies where exactly these two qualities are capable to cause havoc and ruin the business. People who have no interest at all to serve someone or something, are out there in a service company, providing their own generous contribution for the overall suboptimality of the service field.

The easiest mistake that a service company can make is to forget that much of the wealth that is enjoying it owes to factors that are not part of themselves: they owe much to their customers that have a need they can address, they owe much to the market that has left some place for them to position themselves and address that particular need of their customers, they also owe much to their competition that defines rules and practices that enable their daily operation, finally they owe much to the education system and the society that has provided them with a team of people capable to address the market and the customers and the competition. At the end, it is not risky to talk about service Darwinism: like when considering a particular species that exists because of many different parameters than its own will for existence.

It is definitely not New Age thinking when we recognise the organic relation-ships between an individual and its organisation. Unfortunately, and mainly due to the dominance of engineering blinkers, we tend to ignore them – with the usual implications.

In the rest of this chapter I present the practicalities of designing a service that builds on the real world case of a project that I have been actively involved and which has been implemented under the Research Programme Framework of the European Commission. It is the Dilemma project that aimed to design and develop an integrated system that would provide the basis for the efficient technology transfer between European individuals, enterprises and organizations.

One of the early readers of the manuscript commented to me that 'there is hardly any evidence of the efficacy of the DILEMMA Service'. Information on DILEMMA can be found on the Internet. And as the project has been completed since long ago, I afford to look back and see with a calmer regard what went wrong – and for sure much went wrong. One can argue that since 2002 that the project was completed, technology advanced very much. I agree. But what I strongly believe is that the mistakes that humans make in designing a system or a service don't advance at all: they remain much the same and are usually of elementary type and of same elementary nature.

A key point relates to the usefulness of the service – and the utility it ultimately brought to all stakeholders. The paragraphs you will be able to read offer two levels of reading: one level relates to what the service should ideally offer or at least according to the conceptualization capabilities of the users of the Dilemma service was expected to perform. But there is a further level that deals with the *process* as such, namely the service design and development process and how this leads finally to a system. We all criticize systems and services in the same way that we criticize, as consumers, products. What we tend to forget is that all these final "outputs" are the result of respective processes. And that all the virtues and merits, same as the weaknesses and the demerits of products, services or systems directly relate with the processes that were (or were not) followed and, of course, the humans who followed them.

In this respect, to discuss the DILEMMA experience offers an example of a service development process. And the presentation of the several application forms that had been used in various stages of the project is indicative and also representative of a simple truth that all IT people live in our professional lives: it is not only the experts that tend to think in the box but also and mainly the plain users and consumers.

The reality we faced in DILEMMA was that we found ourselves in front of users that wanted to express their own idea about how the computer screens should look like. This is not service design – when I am approaching the Lufthansa check-in desk I am not concerned about the clerk's screen – I only want to express my preferences (aisle seat in the front part of the airplane). How the person in charge will interact with the computer is not my concern at all. Users of all types and levels tend to expose a wish for intervening in the design of computer screens. This is a natural, 'bestial' behaviour as the screen is regarded as the incarnation of the system or the service. But it is damned wrong. The problem starts when the other side, namely the computer industry, agrees to play this game and offers to the customers options for the design of screens. The matter is more serious than aesthetics (which of course is serious and important as well). A service is not sum of the screens that are used for its delivery. In the same way that a human is not the sum of all its pictures or video shots that are taken by cameras during his or her life.

Innovation Relay Centers (IRCs) are the organizations that have been set up by the European Union as intermediaries for technology transfer mediation. In Europe about 70 IRCs have been operating in about 30 European Union member and associated countries and they all operated more or less in ad hoc ways, with their own custom or home made systems. This lack of a common system hinders capitalization on their various (currently disintegrated) data and information repositories as well as their ability to design individual services that may employ service elements of the other IRCs.

The Dilemma project aimed in developing a system that would allow:

- The IRCs to handle all relevant technology transfer and innovation information, promote the interoperation of the IRCs and open the door to new advanced services, apply and adapt billing to their services,
- The end users (be them private persons or business organizations) a consistent tool for the promoting of their ideas and technologies, finding partners and searching for information thought out Europe.

In the following sections a more practical and detailed overview of the Dilemma project work is given, putting emphasis on the achievements both conceptual and technical ones and aiming to bring on the surface several issues that appear when dealing with the introduction of a real service and not approaching a service as a theoretical construct or a conceptual artefact.

Specifically, a top-down approach is followed in the development of the Dilemma system, as this was experienced during its lifetime. The presentation follows almost the same flow as the evolution of the work in the project.

The first section is devoted to the definition of the target users of the Dilemma system and namely the brokers and end-users. The next section deals with the description of the target mediation process, based on today's mediation process for technology transfer, and the description of the usage scenarios. Once the usage scenarios are defined, the user and functional requirements are specified each one analysed in a separate section, for both classes of users and for the target mediation processes.

The next step is the definition of the required Dilemma services and functionalities for the realization of the target mediation process and fulfilment of the requirements. In parallel we describe the testing and evaluation methodology, as well as the evaluation metrics for the Dilemma system. We also present the definition of the technological solutions that will allow the implementation of the Dilemma system and the fulfilment of the requirement. Same as in the Service supply chain management test case presented in Chapter 3, the agent-programming paradigm has been chosen as the most promising approach for the development of network applications. An important aspect of the Dilemma project is the employment of the system that will be produced. An ongoing work is the definition of the commercialization and marketing process of the system, as well as the business cases where the Dilemma system will provide a commercial advantage to the brokers adopting it. In the final section of this Chapter we summarize the added value that the Dilemma system offers to both brokers and end-users.

TARGET USERS OF DILEMMA SERVICE
AND THEIR INFORMATION NEEDS

The Dilemma system targets two different classes of users:

- The technology brokers and
- The various types of end-users like individual or corporate users, professionals, students, etc.

More specifically the brokers are those who are able to design and operate a full intermediation (i.e. brokerage) service in the technology transfer and innovation exploitation domain, or who can effectively provide the life-cycle management of the service. Within the framework of DILEMMA, *technology brokers* are represented by IRCs which will act as operators of their system, as well as users (privileged) of remote IRCs or other kind of technology brokers (i.e. consultants). The end-users on the other hand are all other entities that wish to offer technology innovations, search for technology solutions, invest in technology ideas etc.

Recognizing the vital importance to Europe of innovation, technology transfer and Europe-wide collaboration, the European Community has provided extensive funding over many years to set up a strong co-operating network of IRCs to strengthen Europe's performance in these critical areas. Europe's future prosperity depends on how well it succeeds in this task. And yet, from the perspective of most end-users, this huge investment has under-performed – for a number of reasons not totally within the control of the IRCs themselves. The Dilemma project was set up principally as a response to the main weaknesses in the system by providing a major tool based on the IRC's own knowledge of the weak points and how these could be addressed. It ensures effective access to data, information and knowledge and supports easy, secure collaboration work across the entire network. The consortium's aim is to have, at the end of the project, a really effective tool that will be in demand by the majority or all of the IRCs due to its powerful and easy access to resources and its strong support for inter-IRC networking. The end result of the Dilemma project is therefore to secure and underpin the existing enormous Community investment in the IRC system and, equally important, to ensure that investment achieves its original aims.

For the Dilemma project the end users are divided into two categories: the *core users* and the *other users*. The *core end-users* are individuals and companies that either offer or request technology information. All other potential (types of) users are considered to be *other end-users* that provide or search for enabling services, like funding, statistical information on technology directions, technology events, such as:

- Consulting agencies and companies may use the Dilemma as a source of knowledge in the implementation of their clients' projects as they can find information on the recent trends in a given technological area;
- Entrepreneurs, the system will help them disseminate and collect information on new technologies and technology trends. Using the system they can find suitable financial resources in order to implement their ideas for new products and technologies or to acquire such technologies in their production;
- Researchers will use the Dilemma to search for partners for joint projects, for opportunities to finance the pilot stage of new products and processes, or for companies where they can introduce new technologies, etc.
- Financial institutions will find broad information on different investment opportunities in existing enterprises or in development of new perspective technologies. The Dilemma will be be of use for the venture capitalists (VCs), since these kind of companies are interested in investing in new technology based firms, or innovators are usually seeking for them for funding.

The above can be public organizations and funding agents; public organizations might for example monitor the evolution of the technology in the country/region and propose actions accordingly (encouragement laws, creation of specialized parks, new education directions etc). Investor agents, be they private persons, private organizations (e.g. banks) or even public organizations (e.g. central or regional development authorities or ministries) might look for information for possible investment in new ideas.

From the aforementioned three categories (technology brokers, core users and other users), brokers and core end-users, constitute the target users of the DILEMMA system, with a special emphasis to the brokers.

The target users have distinct requirements and needs from the Dilemma system. IRCs will use the Dilemma as their everyday tool for their operations. Dilemma will allow IRCs to manage all information related to innovation and technology transfer (like for example, technology offers and requests, funding information, advertisement of events, etc) and serve as a tool enabling them to capitalize on their know-how as well as other intangible assets such as their individual network of expert contact points.

On the other hand the core-end users will use the Dilemma system as a medium for promoting and finding technologies and ideas, contacting partners, following evolution of events and as a first point of contact for a tighter collaborations with the IRCs.

Individuals using the Dilemma system will do so either as:

- Individuals that offer their expertise and know-how in a specific area

- Individuals that possess innovative technologies and/or ideas but do not have the means or knowledge to put them in the market. These latter can be active or passive:
    1. The active ones will look via the Dilemma system for funding, technology requests, events where they can present their ideas etc., while
    2. The passive ones will use the Dilemma system as an advertisement medium where they will place a description of their ideas and will wait for someone who is interested to contact them.

Private companies, independently of their size, such as small start-ups, established SMEs or large enterprises will use Dilemma for promoting, in a European level, their products/solutions/know-how to interested parties, finding potential funding for their products/ideas or even establish collaborations, in the form of projects, joint product development etc. with other companies providing complementary technologies or know-how.

The latter is of utmost importance as it will enable the creation of well-formed (based on needs and opportunities assessment) synergies in the market amongst companies independently on their size.

We expect that companies will also use the Dilemma services for finding other companies to subcontract specific research and technology development parts, or even having companies that will simply orchestrate major development projects by outsourcing and subcontracting all parts of the project.

Information Needs & Categories

Proposals for Co-Operation

These are the data forms, submitted by clients searching partnerships for various reasons either wanting to sell or buy an innovative product. The form is normally an electronic form and its submission is the first act of a client of IRC, sometimes called the profile.

Four types of proposals for co-operation are supported:

- **Business or technological co-operation partner search.** It is submitted by a client seeking for a co-operative agreement towards joint business or technological development matching between two client's proposals can result to a successful co-operation.
- **Technology Offer.** A client specifies a technology, an innovative technology product that might be within the interest of another client, issuing a technology request in the future.

- **Technology Request.** A client seeks for a specific technology and information about the owner of the technology who should in advance have submitted a technology offer
- **Research and Development Partner Search.** It is submitted by client intending to launch R&D activity, seeking for partners with common R&D objective and/or supplementary expertise

One could argue that though different proposals might answer the same question of a client. However, different specification for each proposal might facilitate better fitting of his needs.

Funding Opportunities

These are the data, available to clients searching for funding opportunities, either in order to carry out research (applied or basic) or in order to exploit an idea / product of research commercially (i.e. create a company). Three general sets of information are necessary in order to match information about funding to client data.

- **People searching for funding** - they may submit a funding request form in order to find funding sources)
- **Funding sources information** - these are programmes for research and technological development, etc. or investors looking for specific projects or sector of research in order to fund a start – up company).
- Sources of general advice and information (dowloadable documents, contact details of NCPs for a specific programme etc.

Experts

Information on Experts can be classified according to two sub-categories: That which applies to a firm and that which applies to individuals employed within the firm (see next figure). The more specific a search is, the more information can be gained about the required expert (and the more will be charged!). It is therefore beneficial to include the specific characteristics of each of the levels shown in Table 1.

Figure 1 illustrates the information levels about expertise centers and experts.

Events

Dilemma users need to be aware of a range of information and knowledge events and the system must be able to readily produce a complete coverage of useful events for any individual client. The following sections describe the various event

Table 1. Categorisation of experts in the Dilemma system

Firm Info 1	Firm name (Free text entry; Max XXX characters.)
	Home Country (Selection box entry)
	Countries (or regions) in which it operates (Selection box entry)
	Primary Fields of expertise of firm (e.g. patenting, exploitation agreements, business consulting, etc.): Tick boxes used to categorise these fields.
Firm Info 2	Size (Number of experts employed)
	Size (Turnover)
	Secondary fields of expertise
	Major Client list
	Member of professional bodies
Firm Info 3	Contact Details
	Company History
Individual Info 1	Name of Individual expert
	Member of Professional Bodies (Chamber of Commerce, Trade cooperation etc.)
Individual Info 2	Role in Firm (Partner, employee, sub-contractor, etc.)
	Languages he/she speaks
	Countries in which professional experience exists
	Specific Area of expertise
	Professional Accreditation (e.g. Chartered Management Consultant, Certified Accountant, etc.)
	Customer/Project list
	Previous experience of the DILEMMA host (i.e. the IRC) with him/her (e.g. this lawyer was used for three previous TT negotiations and proved very knowledgeable)
Individual Info 3	Complete CV
	Contact Details (personal)

types that are catered for and this is followed by the formal specification for how Dilemma will handle the relevant information. Table 2 depicts the various types of events that the users are interested in.

Investment for an event where potential investors meet companies with funding needs, can have a general or a sectoral character, e.g. inoformation technologies. The objective is to agree or initiate discussions towards agreement on funding partnerships.

Figure 1. Layering the people, the organizational entities and the information entities

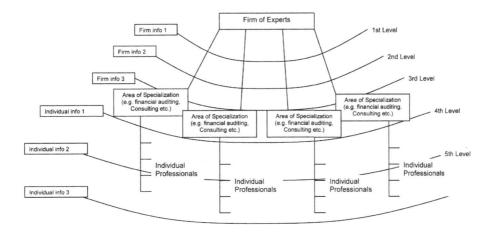

Monitoring and Reporting

In the case of monitoring, it is desired for the DILEMMA system operator to be informed of all major transactions being carried out in the DILEMMA system, without of course being overloaded with by a large amount of messages (i.e. a message to be posted in the customer file each time a customer makes a transaction and perhaps a monthly or weekly report to be posted with all transactions of the customer - or a report each time a critical number of transactions is reached). Monitoring is also important for following the progress of on on-going projects and to provide the opportunity of interfering intervening when something is going wrong (perhaps when an on on-going project seems becomes static stagnant for a long time or when a customer requests it (via the system). Some messages must be posted directly to the DILEMMA system operator such as a new customer registering or a specialized (tailor-made) service is requested (possibility to request via free text query, for a new service).

Monitoring can be done on any transaction, which and might be simply a matter of activating a button. All specifications in the DILEMMA system will be "searchable" so a "matching field for matching" can be established (Client specifications, Information categories (TO, TR, RTD PS and Business PS, Publications, Experts, Events, Funding opportunities) and Charging. The system should allow for the addition of extra queries as each DILEMMA operator might have different needs.

Good reporting depends on good monitoring as it is mainly composed by of the information put together from different monitoring queries. Reporting is the listing

Table 2. Logical organization for the Events concept

Type of event	Description and Objective
Congress	Events with international guests and speakers with political and/or thematic background and mission. The congress is open to a wide public. The objective is the awareness and discussion of state of the art of technology or of special themes
Brokerage	These are one or two day event with international partners and participants organised by one or more IRCs and regional partners for companies and research institutes. Most often organised within the framework of a major sectoral exhibition (e.g. ENTSORGA environmental fair in Köln, Germany) or in the framework of a major technical / scientific conference (e.g. the Internationsl Conference on Cement Chemistry). Event contents include presentation of innovative technologies and/or EC funded research results. Interested parties submit profile or TO/TR/RTD PS into catalogue, catalogue circulates electronic and/or paper form (also posted in organiser IRCs web site), bi-lateral meetings organised based on clients request. The objective is to support transnational technology transfer, initiation of co-operations
Information days	These are one day events, informing about European research programmes, new calls for proposals as well as presenting changes in the work program and changes in priorities. These events can be combined with individual consultations or first contact meetings to form consortia for EU projects . The objective is to provide information and facilitate promotion of EU programmes and partner search for joint projects.
Exhibition (inland)	It could be combined with brokerage events. IRCs normally have a stand with a poster presentation giving away information on their services and improving peoples awareness of the network. The objective is to support transnational co-operations.
Exhibition (abroad)	Participation in international brokerage events abroad or in international fairs. Frequently, if no brokerage event is organised, the host IRC arranges for a common IRC stand so each member can bring their technology portofolio and apart from matching their TOs, TRs and PSs with fellow IRC members, they can visit the exhibition and do a technology watch on the sector and/or collect information for specific clients. The objective is to support transnational co-operations and technology watch.
Seminars / Workshops	Depending on the organisation(s) behind each IRC, these seminars / workshops have different content and take care of various learning needs. What is maybe common to all is the training period (normally 1-3 days) and the number of participants (normally less than 25-30). The objective is to provide training and professional education, support in managing and solving companies internal needs and problems.
Meetings	Meetings are mostly events with internal and thematical relevance such as meetings of the thematic groups (offering the opportunity to IRC members to match their technology portfolio with other members of the thematic group, e.g. ENVIRONMENT) or meetings of national contact points. Some will be of relevance to the client, most will be for internal - intranet (!) use by the DILEMMA operators. The objective it provide training, exchange of know-how and stabilisation of networking, transational technology transfer and business collaboration.
Trade missions	These missions can have outward or inward character. Inward means that companies from abroad visit the IRC of a country or region (e.g. visit Steinbeis Europa Zentrum at Baden-Württemberg): During their visit they get in contact with local companies, organisations and research institutes. Outward missions mean that companies from a given IRC are accompanied by an IRC member, visit the regional companies of one partner region abroad (normally of a sectoral character e.g. Cheese manufacturing). The objective is to provide support of transnational co-operations.
Presentation by the IRC or partner/host organization	Presentation by IRC members of their IRC - host - partner organization and of their services to an audience of companies / organizations / research organizations. Could have a sectoral or regional character and be done in collaboration with local Chambers of Commerce, Technology Parks and Centers, Euro Info Centres and so on. The objective is the Promotion of the IRC Services and of European programmes. Acquisition of clients coming from local companies. Establishing and maintaining links to regional experts who can offer their know-how at events arranged by the local IRC.

of one or a group of monitored parameters for a certain length of time. A simple form of reporting is finding all companies from "city X" interested in technologies from Germany, or finding companies with specific capabilities.

Reporting can be mean totaling the statistics on a certain query: e.g. search on organizations interested in collaborations based on a certain code and date of the expression of interest. Or alternatively, it could be a search on clients who requested services based on a code and the date of the expression of interest. Reporting could be the total of the new "foreign" technologies in the system for a given period, either for entire all of Europe, for a few countries or by country. Of course the system should be able to sort by main subject as well as for country and carry out all sorts of complex queries.

Basically, it should be possible to report on just about everything in the system as well as for ason many parameters at the same time.

The system should perhaps allow every DILEMMA system operator to set their personalized "monitoring profile screen", which will set exactly the parameters, the operator wishes to monitor. The system should also allow the operator to make changes (add or remove parameters). This screen could be divided into major headings such as "new user registration" and "existing users transactions" and under each title a set of parameters can be allocated such as region, new registrations with a specific profile....etc.

Another parameter to take into account is the capability of the system to "remember" the bulk of all the transactions carried out since the beginning of the operation so as to have the ability to implement reporting functions:

A rough Schematic diagram showing the monitoring function of monitoring is shown in Figure 2.

Fields for Matching

The fields of matching will include all the information on each category, all the client information and all the possible charging schemes. Matching, in the form of queries will be includeing all combinations, which are 1. useful and 2. feasible. All specifications in the DILEMMA system will be available for matching (Client specifications, Information categories (TO, TR, RTD PS and Business PS, Publications, Experts, Events, Funding opportunities) and Charging. The system should allow for the addition of extra queries as each DILEMMA operator might have different needs.

Figure 2. Getting the Dilemma user right

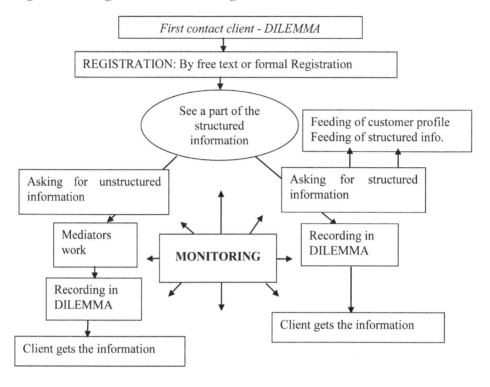

Matching Methodology

Matching should be done in two ways, either by FREE TEXT or by using CODES.

In the case of the free text, the system should allow for the entry of 10 - 15 key words (or more - to be agreed with the technical partners) or the entry of dates (e.g. a client might be interested in a particular period - the technical partners should allow for the mixing of "numbers" and "text"). Numbers should be allowed as they will be needed for a free text search on the number of employees, the turnover and other numerical specifications.

In case of matching by CODES, all available codes can be used as well as a mixture of them. Although most organizations use standard codes, allowance should be made for the entry of other, not-so-common codes that might be used in a certain country. Codes could be CERIF codes, NACE codes, venture economic / market / subject codes, country codes, turnover codes etc.. However, common CODES are really important in order to insure the compatibility of the DILEMMA systems (at leastand of the 6 end user partners to begin withinitially).

Matching Examples

Two types of matching exist will be provided, a simple matching and a more complicated and multi-criteria matching.

Examples of simple matching can be the following:

- A TR, matched to a possible partner through the Subject of interest (cerif code etc.).
- A client looking for a business partner in a specific area, with less than 10 employees.
- A client looking for a technology from a specific country.

Examples of complicated matching can be the following:

- A TO based on a patent, matched to the subject, matched to patent lawyers, matched to lawyers with expertise in the sector, matched to business plan investment fora for the presentation of a business plan, matched to business plan investment fora for the presentation of a business plan on the particular sector.
- A PS for RTD, matched to the subject, matched to info days on the subject of interest, matched directly with potential partners.
- A client looking for a business partner in a specific area with a specific expertise, in order to make set up a joint venture. The client can be matched with local lawyer firms, a financial consultant, investment funds (for example on biotechnology) and a TT event on biotechnology organized by the IRC network.

Charging Aspects

Charging DILEMMA services is based upon the type of service offered, the level of detail of the information supplied, the media (personalised versus generic, multimedia formats, etc). Table 3 depicts some examples of elementary services charged to a possible client.

When the client is on the second level, he can stop at this step or if he wants a more focused answer, we suggest re-running "my DILEMMA" with a more focused profile.

A graphical representation of the charging process, is also shown in Figure 3.

Table 3. Charging aspects: analysis for different types

Level	Type of services	Type of fee	Type of profile used	Media (where?)
Manual search by the customer in the system (without entering any profile)	"test"	Free	Keywords	General DILEMMA interface
Basic information sent back by e-mail after submitting the (customer's) profile. If query for more information on a specific entry	"push"	Free pay per view	Company profile	My DILEMMA[1]
Basic information diffused on "my DILEMMA" after submitting a profile: my DILEMMA, More information (activated by dynamic links on the portal with original documents)*	"push"	Subscription, either included in subscription or pay per view	Company profile, Contact profile	My DILEMMA
Targeted (topic AND sources), Information diffused (by "My DILEMMA") after an audit	"on demand"	(Higher) Subscription	Company profile, Contact profile, Contact requirements	My DILEMMA, Virtual Meeting Space
Negotiation Assistance	Exit of DILEMMA or submitting inquiry in the system			

THE SERVICE MEDIATION PROCESS AND THE USER SERVICE SCENARIOS

The target mediation process is the most essential sequence of stages in the whole series of stages of innovation exploitation and technology transfer activity. All stages of IETT are described in the Section below. This will lead to a set of user requirements described in later Sections.

Stages in the Technology Transfer Activity

The stages in TT can be described as follows:

• **Preparatory actions:** Creating awareness is a constant process, identifying the innovation strategy of the client or assisting the client in defining their innovation strategy, identifying the needs in terms of technical information, identifying the most relevant sources of information, providing assistance and support to companies in the initial recognition of market opportunities or technological needs.

- ***Provide/ get information:*** Provide/ get information (disseminate) on: the company, the project, TOs, TRs, company profiles, registration procedures,

Figure 3. The charging process

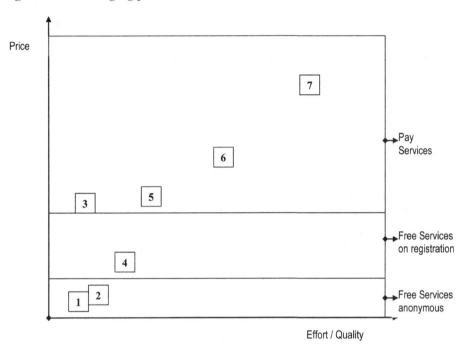

1 | Manual search by the customer in the system

2 | Basic information sent back by e-mail after submitting the (customer´s) profile

3 | Basic information sent back if query for more information on a specific entry

4 | Basic information diffused on "my Dilemma" after submitting a profile

5 | + more information (activated by dynamic links on the portal with original documents)

6 | Targeted (topic AND sources) information diffused

7 | Full Technology Watch Service with Checking, Validating, Reviewing

commercial, financial and tax legislation, international trade law, companies' contact information, contact information for various intermediaries, list on suitable solutions Europe-wide. The information should be provided to the client in the most adapted form (ADDED VALUE!). The IPR status of the TOs should also be checked.

- *Assessment - side actions:* Identification of the target group, evaluation - validation of the project/profile (technical & commercial aspect), matching - selection of partners, provision of support and advice during the phases of comparison of the different alternatives and the selection of the best solution, defining the position of the technology provider/receiver on the market, technical feasibility study and economic feasibility study.
- *Contact:* Provide assistance for Contact (e.g. further information on potential partner, undertaking the task to contact the partner on behalf of the client, ironing out misunderstandings through different language, culture and mentality, help with understanding text - reports), etc. Contact can take very long - up to 2 years, depending on the commitment of the partners. In parallel to the contact, other actions such as ensuring the financing, ensuring the business and legal support etc should take place.
- *Ensuring the financing:* Search for all possible funding opportunities, identification of the best financing schemes, help with drafting of the proposal, assistance with the business plan (often through sign-posting), finding out of any investment for a on the sector, etc.
- *Ensure the business, legal, negotiations support:* Also assuring confidentiality. This is normally done through sign posting to professionals providing business, legal and negotiation support
- *Signposting:* Everything can be signposted if the needed / desired expertise is not available in house. Signposting is not really a step in the whole process, like follow-up and monitoring / reporting, it is to be used during all steps if needed.
- *Negotiations:* Provide assistance and support or signpost to relevant legal consultants for negotiation support.
- *Agreement:* Provision through signposting or direct advice of support during the redaction (drafting) of the TT agreement. (*the information contained in the signing of an agreement is extremely sensitive. Therefore, this will be the last step to be added to the DILEMMA services)
- *Follow-up:* Follow-up should be assured over the whole life time of the IE / TT project. - very important management help).
- *Other:* Monitoring and reporting of the whole process.

There exist different types of TT depending on the nature of the technology transferred, the way etc. These are listed below:

1. Licensing agreements (License agreement (trademarks, models), License agreement (Patents))
2. Creation of start-up companies
3. Creation of spin-off companies
4. Technological co-operation (Research and Development, Technology Transfer, Patent or know-how License, Exchange of Know-how / Know-how and soft-ware, Technological
5. Support / Technical Assistance, co-contracting, R&D costs).
6. Subcontracting (subcontracting capacity, subcontracting specialities)
7. Joint venture (Taking over / Merger / Acquisition of parts of companies, Supply / Demand of Capital (Equity), Company Formation / Incorporation, Financing of Supply).
8. Joint research and development
9. Trade Collaboration (Marketing Agreement, Distribution Support, Franchising / Industrial Franchise)
10. Production Collaboration (Production Agreement / manufacturing agreement, Production
11. Rights, Subcontracting, co-contracting)
12. Commercial agreement with technical assistance (Assistance with starting up an installation, advice on the use of a new process, quality control, technical training, maintenance & machine repair)
13. Related Services (Customer Service, Logistics)

The different natures of TT are listed below:

1. Hitech-lowtech
2. Breakthrough-incremental
3. Complementary know-how
4. Adoption of state-of-the-art technology
5. Other: Localisation (adoption) of existing technologies, New process methods and new equipment / machinery, modernisation of industries / companies.

The nature of the TT can sometimes be unclear. However, it heavily depends on the individual country, its needs and its culture (in some countries, the mentality of the businesses especially SMEs is to adopt existing technology, mostly medium, rather than to opt for state of the art technologies).

A general analysis can be the following:

- Technological innovation, which emphasises the development of new knowledge, products or processes, through the collaboration between companies and R&D organisations;
- Pure technology transfer, which shifts advanced technology out of laboratories into commercial use, mainly but not only through the creation of spin-off companies;
- Diffusion of technologies neither new nor necessarily advanced (although they are often new to the user). In that case technologies may be acquired from a variety of sources, including private vendors, customers, consultants, and peer firms, as well as public technology centres, government laboratories, and universities;
- Technology also diffuses through the transfer and mobility of skilled labour, the activities of professional societies and varied forms of informal knowledge circulation.

Target Mediation Process

Technology brokerage is the core process within which DILEMMA is expected to play its role, based on specific requirements of the two user groups considered in the context of project. Using schematic diagrams, a description of all phases of the mediation process, is given.

The following notes are describing the notation of the diagrams:

- Each phase has a unique reference number
- The main actors in the process description are a) the broker and b) the client (could be a company)
- Within a network of cooperating brokers, each broker has an identification number i.e. Broker 1, Broker 2
- Each client is also assigned an identification code based on two numbers a) the number of the broker to whom he has issued the inquiry (Example: usually it is the number of the national IRC to whom he has made a technology request and b) a code number. So, Client 7.2 is the client 2 of the broker 7.)
- Each step in the process is validated by a transition (in bold italic) establishing that a set of conditions is fulfilled to go to the next step.

For simplicity reasons, the description of the target process is focusing on the Technology Request service as a specific information supply service among the various categories of information services provided by the technology brokers. These information categories are thoroughly analyzed in terms of content in the sections of D.1.1, describing:

a) Technology requests and offer forms, R& D and business partner search forms
b) Event forms
c) Expert forms
d) Funding request/offer forms
e) Public information request forms

Processing of service requests in all categories is similarly realized as in the following schematic description, where the indicative phases of the mediation process are given. Further mediation procedures are occasionally invoked – based upon user or request or broker's initiative – in order to provide relevant information and/or consulting.

Description of Usage Scenarios and Usage Cases

The objective of this subsection is to focus on the factors affecting the quality of brokers' services and not to cover all possible usage scenarios falling in the framework of the target mediation process. For each scenario, a description is given along with key factors, which affect the scenario and also indicating the main requirements of both brokers and end-users.

Usage Scenario A: Inter-IRC Collaboration for Joint Service Provision

Innovation exploitation may start from a technology request that might find a matching for a specific technology offer. However, technology is not forming the sole requirement of the innovation exploitation macro-process. Other "ingredients" concern funding, investments and in house or external expertise. A "turn-key" answer of the mediation process explores all these elements, in an ad-hoc manner, many times based on human communication and slow in overall response times procedures. It is very typical that not all "ingredients" are easily found within the data and information available at national level (i.e. within the geographical region of activity of a specific IRC). Three key examples revealing the need to cover cross-border information are following below:

1. Technological innovation in Greece might not find a willing to invest market at home.
2. Advanced know-how in Bulgaria may not be exploited adequately by the Bulgarian industry.

3. Investments interest in Cyprus is not finding enough and sufficient technological innovation within the country

Representative service cases encountered in today technology brokers' business environment are:

a. The broker is initiating multiple individual processes of communication with other brokers by forwarding the specific technology request to them (see phase - 3 - in the description of the target process). It is the typical scenario for IRC as they are operating today. The broker is initiating a centralized process thread of communication with all other brokers where outcoming information is channeled once while feedback is received using individualized communication threads.

b. The broker establishes a permanent business agreement with broker X in order to ask for funding and broker Y in order to ask for expertise. The reason is to establish business-level relation with brokers, mainly to use efficiently the specialized and high-quality resources of other brokers or other brokers clients in order to combine higher-quality services to the end-user.

c. The end-broker receiving a request from another IRC is pricing the answer he is issuing to the broker who was initially asked by the user. Though not realized today, it is the basic mean for a broker to commercialize some of his services in the brokers' market (consultants, individuals, IRCs, etc).

An example is given below:

During the last two years (1999-2000), the legal framework has been created in Cyprus for the creation of new high technology based firms, through a scheme for incubators subsidized by the Cypriot government. Four such incubators (mostly from the private sector) have been selected to date through a call for proposals, and the process is now in place for the selection of suitable candidates to occupy the incubators.

A client of the Cypriot IRC approaches the Cypriot broker in order to discuss the possibility of the set up of a tele-medicine network in Cyprus. The idea is good and so are the omens. Cyprus has available venture capital funding and through its geographical position offers the possibility of being a centre for tele-medicine in the Middle East. The Cypriot broker, together with the client, concludes that two important parameters are missing: the state of the art tele-medicine technology as well as additional expertise on networks and related software. Together they prepare a technology request, which the Cypriot broker disseminates to the IRC network. A lot of interesting expressions of interests flow back to the Cypriot broker. The broker discusses all the possibilities with the client and they both decide on the technology offered by the Greek broker (on behalf of a research institute specializing on tele-medicine and with tele-medicine centres already in place) and the networks and related software expertise offered by the Bulgarian broker (on behalf of a Bulgarian company specializing in networks and related software).

This step leads to the creation of a new technology based firm, which moves into one of the incubators in Nicosia having gained financial support from Cypriot investors and leads to the signing of a collaboration agreement between the three countries in order to build on their success. This agreement introduces the idea of charging, not only the client but also inter-IRC for the given services.

Having the aforementioned categorization in mind, the following services may be composed:

- Case a fits both the communication with the other two brokers (the Greek and the Bulgarian IRCs) as well as with the network of potential partners operated by the Cypriot IRC.
- Case b concerns potential permanent business collaboration between the Cypriot broker and the Greek and Bulgarian brokers).
- Case c is quite obvious to assess as it introduces the idea per conducted service (see Table 4).

Usage Scenario B: Dealing with Detailed Technological Profiles and Confidential Data

Focusing on phases (5) to (9) in the schematic description of the target mediation process, we see the case where a specific technology request has raised interest (a technology was offered) and a process towards getting more detailed data up to confidential information - and possibly an agreement – has commenced.

The technology provider is usually:

1. Hesitant to provide confidential information to the broker
2. Having in his mind a specific path of information disclosure towards approaching a new customer (technology buyer)
3. Wants to use as many means as possible in order to describe his offering in the best way.

The case is that following the Expression of Interest (EoI) the broker is mediating in the information exchange process between the two parties until a meeting is organized and initiating a path towards non-disclosure agreement. Successive requests for information is a time-consuming process which has currently a success-rate of less than 20%, where success is defined to be the continuation to the next phase

Table 4. Analysis for Usage scenario A: Inter-IRC collaboration for joint service provision

Key factors affecting the quality and efficiency of invoked processes under this scenario	*The main factors of quality in the above mentioned case*
	Speed. With the existing lack on a scalable information infrastructure, as the number of brokers involved is increasing it is more difficult to maintain efficient communication channels with all of them, without also increasing response times and losing in quality of service.
	Efficiency of maintaining and operating business models and various combination of services within the technology brokers business "territory"
	The quality of the technology request
	The time frame of the request (whether the request is valid for 1 month or one year for instance), and the response time, which on its behalf depends on the geographical location of the clients and the time and the format (phone, fax, e-mail) in which they respond to additional requests.
Broker Requirement Addressed[2]	Population of the information repositories Commercialization of the service
	Services adaptability
	Open channels of communication between brokers
End User Requirement addressed[3]	Quality of service
	Integrated services (obtain integrated service from one broker rather than obtaining several minor services from several brokers)
	On time delivery of service
	Value for money
	Sole contact point
Added Value, Functionality, Target Performance	*Benefits for both user categories*
	Direct contact with the client, which provides a hands-on approach, and tailor-made decisions.
	Intra-IRC, business agreements, services design, more data available to the end-user, billing

which is a confidentiality agreement or a direct contact.

The technological profiles, though improved by the technology audit process (see phases –6-7- in mediation process might not be proved adequate to bring the whole picture about the technical feasibility of an agreement. Elaboration on this data, as it is realized today, is highly dependent on human interaction through the broker with not any measurable indicator of how close the information exchange has reached to the direct contact phase.

Human "agents" as a medium for facilitating parts of the mediation process – especially those necessitating interaction – are by no means replaced in the Dilemma system. In contrast to this, their role is repositioned from the current responsibility of executing the mediation process to this of being responsible for the control and coordination aspects of it.

The above may be viewed as task assignments to be accomplished by each human node of a Dilemma Info Supply service, and – using the service flow "algebra" we described in Deliverable 2.1 – to each intra-broker component. In this respect, a first attempt to distinguish (types of) roles for this part of the mediation process can be defined with the "triangle" of executor – controller – coordinator, by means of rating its particular characteristics to which emphasis is given:

- Executor, which is responsible for carrying out "basic" activities on the various mediation steps involved, and has the ability to implement the assigned jobs;
- Controller, which is responsible for applying performance measurements (set by the coordinator) on the executor. and "represents" the ability of the particular broker instance to be kept in the boundaries that are defined by the coordinator ;
- Coordinator, which is responsible for interfacing with other brokers or services provided by other brokers and "rrepresents" the ability of the broker to organize and regulate the assigned jobs (see Table 5).

Usage Scenario C: Combination of Services

An end-user is asking for a specific technology, waiting for the broker to give him information about technology suppliers who might fulfill his request. At the same time, a new public measure is valid and is announcing funding opportunities for all those who want to adopt this specific innovation into their business.

The following cases are encountered today:

- The broker is aware of this measure and he informs the end-user
- The broker is not informing the user, acting in an ad-hoc way dependent upon human-related factors i.e. workload, *extent of knowledge,* "freshness" of information, importance or size of the customer

A similar case might happen when an end user issues a technology offer. Typically the service ends at this point, being in phase (1) of the mediation process. However, it might be the case that an event is organized, inviting key players and new actors to meet and exchange ideas in the area of interest within which the technology offer lies. High interest to participate might be missed if the technology provider does not get the information about the event from the broker.

In both of the above cases, combination of services refer to implementation of a

Table 5. Analysis for Usage scenario B: Dealing with detailed technological profiles and confidential data

Key factors affecting the quality and efficiency of invoked processes under this scenario	*Critical factors within this case*
	Trusting the mediation procedure so that the client can provide more details about his technology
	Rationalization of the time-slots necessary to accomplish the successive communication activities in order to elaborate on the technological information
	Reliability. Reaching contacts and meetings having mature and substantial information exchange, so that to minimize the risk of having useless direct contacts and confidentiality agreements. The worst thing to happen, is that information missing from the technological profile, proves to be very critical, and finally a meeting proves to be loss of time for the client.
	Having complete information available about technological innovation
	The right timing for the brokers to start charging for their services
Broker requirements addressed	Data privacy for the end users
	Relevance of information – Improved quality of service
	Facilitation of the provision of details of technological offers and possible combination with pricing policies and business models for broker's business
	Reliability of the information and data privacy of the end-users
End-User requirements addressed	Personalization for the technology offer
	Data privacy
	Speed, price, reliability, relevance and quality
	Possibility to pay only in the cases that they get something "useful" to them
Added value, functionality, target performance	High level of personalization. The technology provider is the one who customizes his offer according to his knowledge on the product. He is the one who knows what information is more critical in order to keep it under deeper levels (or even priced levels or confidential levels if accepts to put confidential data in the system)
	Pricing. Services and information can be commercialized and charged at all levels of the mediation process.
	Security. The information regarding technology innovation is presented only to the persons/organizations that need to see it, excluding all other intermediaries.
	Reduced time for arranging of direct contacts and increased efficiency of the meetings by bringing the two parties
	Measurable indicators of the success of DILEMMA intervention in this case would be: time savings, and the distribution of levels of detail reached

new service based on the coupling of an existing service thread with either:

- An existing one independently of temporal properties (such as in the case of exploiting funding by the new public measure), or
- A new service that shows explicit temporal characteristics such as in the second case of organizing an event that has a certain launching date, is related with certain deadlines for expression of interest to participate, etc.

The new composed services (have to) show characteristics of all services they come from; inheritance aspects come not as realizations of strictly defined rules but may enable looser connections (especially at the semantic levels) with logical operators e.g. for describing pre- and post-conditions for any of the time-related service components (e.g. the events), while they may use similar schemes for expressing composition with time-independent service properties (as it is the first case).

For example: The company X from the country B is looking for a new technology and the corresponding equipment for the production of plastic bottles for mineral water through an IRC. The investment costs cannot be higher than EUR 100,000. The company can provide only EUR 40,000 out of its own funds and will look for a credit for the remaining amount of EUR 60,000. The broker A disseminates the technology request to the IRCs but cannot advise the client on the relevant financial instruments. Currently most of the IRCs do not provide information on the available financial instruments for TT projects and normally work case-by-case. In such a case the service of the IRC will have to be combined (complemented) with the services of another broker or a financing institution to provide the requested service to the client.

The current set of standard IRC services does not include provision of information and advice on financial schemes, legal issues, IPR issues, etc. which limits the services of the IRCs (see Table 6).

Usage Scenario D: Technology Watch

There is a high need for getting and maintaining technologically aware in terms of innovation and emerging products in a specific domain. Such a request is expressed by means of:

- Provision of thematic / domain-specific keywords
- Indication of the preferred (types of) sources to which the technology watch service should be "plugged" for acquiring data/information

Today, such kind of service is provided based on human resources. It is not pos-

Table 6. Analysis for Usage scenario C: Combination of services

Key factors affecting the quality and efficiency of invoked processes under this scenario	Reliability – Keeping a consistent process towards applying the combined service adequately and at all times, achieves high level of reliability
	Easiness and time consumption in the process of combining services
	Timing
	Relevance of new service
Broker requirement addressed	Service adaptability in order to adapt efficiently to market needs.
	Ability to market more than one services per time
	Independence from staff variation
	Easy access to a variety of information
End-User requirement addressed	Ability to support personalization of the combined services by the user
	Ability to take various kinds of information at once, integrated services
	Relevance of returned information
Added Value	Life-cycle management

sible today to know if there is and to have access to any new relevant information when it is updated without doing another manual query on a periodic and repetitive basis. It is thus a worry to make this service feasible under heavy loads and increased demands (see Table 7).

Table 7. Analysis for Usage scenario D: Technology watch

Key factors affecting the quality and efficiency of invoked processes under this scenario	Pricing of the service
	Balancing of the actual service costs related to payments made to the various data/information sources
	Speed
	Relevance
Broker requirement addressed	Quality of service
	Accuracy in regard to timeliness, in terms of providing awareness on when a new relevant information has been introduced in the system for a selected technology.
End-User requirement addressed	Same as above plus consistency of service
Added Value	Benefit for End-User categories
	More data available to the end-user

FORMALISING THE USER REQUIREMENTS

The user requirements of the DILEMMA system differ depending on the target users. For the technology brokers the requirement concentrate on how the system will provide the tools and services that will allow them to achieve their goals in providing and managing brokerage services. For the core end-users the requirements concentrate on how they will be able to obtain technology contacts and establish collaborations with or without personal mediation from the brokers. These requirements are different, but they complement each other and therefore are not contradictory.

Broker Requirements

Increasing Population of Broker Information Repositories

The most basic requirement for the brokers (the IRCs) is the creation of a common platform that will allow them to collaborate and exchange information and data (phases 3, 6, 8 of the target mediation process) as part of their daily service-related procedures. The data of the brokers come from different sources which can be

a)   Their direct clients which provide technology related information (requests, offers etc)
b)   The corresponding information from other brokers
c)   External information sources (phase 12 of the mediation process) which is part of the know-how of the brokers, like offers for patent sales, funding opportunities, information events etc. These might exist on WWW sites, private or public databases, etc.

Therefore the first requirement from the brokers is a system on which they will be able to "open" their existing data without the need for conducting physical transfer operations, so that they are able to support the transparent access to remote broker data and integrate any external information sources (that is integrate part of their internal know-how into the system). *The DILEMMA system should thus provide services that will allow them migrate their existing databases to a common format, integrate external, non-IRC information sources, add new information categories and manage them according to their evolution.*

Mediation and Usage Behavior Monitoring

A second requirement is the ability to monitor the state of the mediations and extract information that will allow them to improve their services. Nevertheless this monitoring does not need to be interactive, but rather batch. What the brokers require is to be able to collect statistical data, process them according to different criteria and produce reports and graphs of the results. The required results will include, for example, duration of the mediation process, most requested or offered technology domains, requests coming from a specific customer etc. This way the brokers will be able to identify areas of interest and add new information and links, propose assistance to their clients etc. This way another part of the know-how of the brokers will be able to be integrated to the system.

This requirement requires, in addition to a logging service, a set of configurable tools that will allow the extraction of the required information from the log files in the required format.

Security

The third requirement of the brokers is a certain level of security that will

a)   Provide protection against intruders, and
b)   Assure the clients of the authoritativeness and confidentiality of the information they receive and provide to the brokers at some cases of the phase (7) of the target mediation process.

Intruder protection security will require different elements, starting from firewalls, up to authentication processes for access control. *On the other hand authoritativeness and confidentiality will require encryption and document signing services that the Dilemma system will need to integrate or provide access to.*

Commercialization

A fourth requirement is the ability of the brokers to create revenue streams from their services. Clients will be required to pay for accessing the information, and the brokers will need to be able to define pricing policies for different user categories and different services (at phase 7 of target mediation process), including broker-to-broker services (phases 3,6,8 of the mediation process). *The Dilemma system will thus need to link to a billing system that will be able to handle not only the pricing policies, but also to create invoices, verify and charge credit card paid services etc.*

For this the brokers will require flexibility to design pricing schemes in both levels:

•   A first affecting the involved brokers in the supply of a service, and
•   A second affecting the end user level.

The Dilemma system will thus need to link to a billing system that will be able to handle not only the pricing policies, but also to create invoices, verify and charge credit card paid services etc.

Services Adaptability

A fifth requirement of the brokers is the ability to adapt their services and create new ones based upon the services pool they are having (see phases 2 and 10 of target mediation process). The brokers should be able to:

a)   Recombine existing functions and introduce new services,
b)   Modify existing functions in order to enhance existing services, and
c)   Obtain from software producers (either in-house or external) new software packages providing new or upgraded functionality which will be used to improve existing or introduce new services.

This requirement dictates that the Dilemma system should provide a level of modularity and openness allowing the introduction of new functionality and the creation of new services.

Quality of Service

A final, and maybe most important, requirement concerns the quality of the results that the IT system will provide the brokers with. In the context of the brokers high quality translates into relevance of information returned by the system. The information is considered to be more accurate when:

a)   It is given in the correct time frame and
b)   It is relevant to the inquiry.

Specifically, due to the dynamic nature of the technology information managed by the brokers the reply to a query should come within certain time limits, risking otherwise being obsolete and thus inaccurate. To be noted however that the information is not as time critical as stock market prices, but rather as newspaper articles. Relevant information signifies that the reply to query, at one hand, should not contain an excess of items that are not related (in some way) to the expected results, and on the other hand it should contain nearly the totality of the related information items.

It is of course clear that the two quality requirements of timed reply and relevancy of reply are not orthogonal. Given more time, the relevancy should increase and vice-versa. The Dilemma system should thus provide a basic level of quality and allow the brokers to parameterize according to their needs, between timing and relevancy. Other factors of quality that are essential is speed, efficiency and costs of the various procedures in the mediation process.

End User Requirements

The requirements of the core end-users differ somehow to those of the brokers, though all requirements – including those of the brokers – are aiming at the end to improve the level of service that the end user is getting. For the end-user, the broker may be regarded as the one-stop-shop of the various services and his virtual linkage to the various external sources or other brokers. Thus, any requirement of the broker, is affecting directly the final service of the end-user.

Treating Detailed Information and Confidentiality of Data: Personalized Offers

The first requirement is the preservation of their privacy in contacting business with the brokers (phase 1 and 7 of the mediation process). When working with new and innovative technologies even the knowledge that a competitor is interested or offers a certain new technology can provide a major competitive advantage. It is thus important to the end-users that some parts of the technology information are not visible by the brokers, but can be disclosed to interested parties pending authorization of the information provider.

The Dilemma system will thus need to provide the means to support different protection levels of the available information and ways to allow its disclosure in incremental way, according to the access rights of the users. Incremental levels could be associated to advanced detailing of the information and maybe also different pricing schemes starting up from free levels.

Personalization

The second requirement is the ability of the users to personalize the services they receive (phases 1 and 2) from the brokers. The users should not only be able to exit the automated services and ask for active broker assistance at any point of the mediation, but also to be able to parameterize the service details according to their needs.

That means that the Dilemma system should allow the parameterization of the functions out of which a service is composed, by the users providing the adequate tools. Obviously it will be up to the brokers to define the level of parameterization and personalization of the functionalities that is accessible to the end-users.

Quality of Service

Similarly to the broker requirements, quality of the provided services is a need from the end user point of view too. In the context of the users the notion of high quality translates in the acquisition of relevant information with

a) A minimal level of transaction with the system and
b) Timed and correct intervention of the broker.

More specifically a user should be able to obtain the required information by spending as less as possible time with the system. In the same context the use would be expecting that the broker will intervene, at his request, proposing his services at critical points of the mediation.

The Dilemma system should thus offer the efficient user tools for queries and mediation, as well as methods for the user to ask the mediation of the broker passing him as much information as possible. Within this requirement, it is the ability of the users to be actively informed on specific events. That is to establish watchdog queries waiting for a specific event. The Dilemma system should thus provide the means to the users to "program" watchdogs based on their queries.

Other requirements that are the same as with the brokers are the simplicity of the user interface and the ability of the user to know in advance the cost of the services and the different options for payment.

Integrated Services

The end-user dislikes the fact that useful information and useful services are distributed to several service-providers and can only be obtained in a very tiring uncertain and time-consuming manner. The end users prefer to obtain as much information as possible by just one service-provider.

MEETING THE USER REQUIREMENTS

The user requirements – for both end-users and brokers – were outlined in the previous sections. We consider the requirements with respect to the broker users and end-users in turn.

Broker Requirements

Increasing Population of Information Repositories

The main requirement here is to have the broker databases connected, to allow them to collaborate and to exchange data. Data exchanged in Dilemma is handled by the mobile agent platform. Another feature is tool support for the conversion of a broker's native data format to the Dilemma format. Conversion can be handled on-line by placing the conversion code within an agent that interpose between the requesting agent and the broker information repository.

Mediation and Usage Monitoring

This requirement is directly satisfied by the agent platform. Each broker is handed a programmed broker agent that interposes on requests between requesting agents and the data repository. This agent is programmed to store statistics on behalf of the brokers.

Security

There are two security aspects defined in the user requirements: *protection against intrusion*, and *information believability and confidentiality*. The measures that protect broker sites against intrusion are the following. First, each agent that arrives on a broker agent platform is completely isolated from other agents and from other programs on the site. That is, an agent shares no code or data with other programs. Any communication with an agent must go through JavaSeal provided channels that are controlled by a security policy. However, no intrusion prevention mechanism is fully secure. In the case of Dilemma, if an attacker manages to start a corrupted Java environment, then the security measures of the JavaSeal platform can be bypassed.

Regarding information believability and confidentiality, the information in the Secure Space can be encrypted whenever it is stored on disk. The main security property of Secure Spaces is that each item of information in the Space is *locked* with a key. The implementation of Secure Spaces guarantees that an item may not be removed from the space unless the requesting agent possesses the matching key. In this way, the information provider is sure that only agents granted keys to his information may read that information (confidentiality). Further, information consumers can be sure that any information returned by the Space in response to a request on a key K, is information that was locked with K (believability).

Service Adaptability

This is the requirement that new services can be added to the platform, perhaps by reusing existing services. By "service" in the user requirement we mean broker service. In Dilemma, each service is implemented by a set of co-operating agents. For instance, an agent that visits the database of each broker on the network to query its database implements the basic technology search service. New services in Dilemma are added simply by programming and deploying new agents. Recall that program deployment is one of the main advantages of the agent paradigm.

Quality of Service

The two qualities of service mentioned in the user requirements are responsiveness and relevancy. This basically requires that a broker query be serviced with a satisfactory hit-rate in the quickest time possible. In general, relevancy increases as the time taken to search for the offers (and the complexity of algorithms used increases). The advantage of the agent platform is that the search algorithm can be placed inside of a notification agent that resides at a broker site. After a pre-specified time, this agent returns home if it has not already found the information that it is looking for.

End-User Requirements

Confidentiality of Information: Personalized Offers

This is the requirement that the Dilemma system support different levels of access control, meaning that information can be disclosed in an incremental way. As mentioned, the Secure Space model supports this multi-level disclosure model. That is, the first level of information is obtained after negotiation of a key. This second level may have further locked objects that contain more sensitive information. This information can only be accessed by the acquisition of a second key – which depending on the particular payment model of the broker, is only disclosed after new payment.

Personalisation

This requirement is related to the generation of agents that are have user-specific parameters. Users and brokers in Dilemma with the aid of their Web browser will generate agents. The direct interaction between users and agent generation is crucial for the user being able to specify personalized parameters.

On the Role of the Dilemma System

The Dilemma system was envisaged to (i) **fulfil the information needs** of technology transfer, (ii) provide the IRC clientele with comprehensive information concerning TT opportunities and (iii) reduce the costs for search of information on available TT opportunities.

As the Dilemma will provide the end-users with a consistent tool for promoting their ideas and technologies it will open up unique opportunities before the **less-developed regions**, too. The Dilemma will help such regions to overcome the regional disparities and the divide with the more advanced regions of the European countries as the geographical location will stop to be a hurdle before their economic development.

The target mediation process and the requirements of the two user groups for this process, is opening the case for the role of DILEMMA. According to these, the role of DILEMMA in the mediation process is dual:

- To realize the communication channels invoked in the various stages of the mediation processes by:
    1. Implementing the communication and data exchange based on electronic means (Internet and WWW means) and automated replication or forwarding techniques (all phases of target mediation diagram)
    2. Enhancing data exchange and sensitive information provision with secure encapsulation and privacy (phases 1,3,7 of target mediation diagram)
    3. Adding pricing and priced levels of services and information within the various broker-to-end-user transactions and/or broker-to-broker transactions (phases 3,5,6,7,8)
    4. Personalizing the technology offerings based upon the technology provider's knowledge on the levels of criticality of the various data (phase 1)
    5. Enhancing relevance of answers to requests, reliability of brokers, reducing risks (phases 4,5,6,7,8)

The first part of the role is strongly supported by digital design techniques for the various services, based on services flow concept (see D.2.1), elementary priced elements and monitored usage elements.

- To provide a working environment for the brokers by which they will be able to manage the mediation process. It is DILEMMA's role to:
    1. Enable the design of a new service based on information elements and elementary services already available in their services pool or adapt an

already existing service. The service flow concept and the services data model are the key architecture choice towards realising this role.

2. Apply services adaptation based upon usage criteria, given by accounting mechanisms of DILEMMA system. Invoking logging of usage data records (called Service Detail Records) of various usage actions is a key element to provide usage reports, useful before applying any operational policy.

Moving our focus to the use-cases as these were described in the previous Chapter, the role of DILEMMA is as follows.

Usage scenario A: Inter-IRC collaboration for joint service provision

*   DILEMMA Role:
    ○   DILEMMA is automatically forwarding the requests to the entire brokers' network and also collects the various responses
    ○   The broker can use DILEMMA in order to combine a new service based on other services and also define a business agreement between the various providers involved so that some of them might offer parts of their information on a commercial basis. DILEMMA will provide the environment to define the combined service and the pricing schemes

Usage scenario B: Dealing with detailed technological profiles and confidential data

*   DILEMMA Role:
    ○   DILEMMA provides a secure environment – based on the provision of secure encapsulation of multiparted information components – for visualizing over the network technology data (a part of it could confidential)
    ○   DILEMMA offers a scheme for the technology offer that enables multiple levels of information parts of various – incremental – detail, starting from free non-critical information, moving smoothly to more important details which might be priced and/or confidential. DILEMMA role is i. to provide the means to the end-user to customize his offer according to his knowledge and his business objectives and ii. to visualize an offer, level-by-level, so as to reveal the incremental interest of the asking user.

Usage scenario C: Combination of services

- DILEMMA Role:
- The broker has defined specific services to be accompanied and combined with other information sources and services. The definition has been made using the DILEMMA administration services and the DILEMMA system is responsible to implement the service every time it is invoked.
- Both the broker and the end user are able to combine service elements so that new services are created fitting highly individualized needs and addressing in an optimal way existing opportunities in the market.

Usage scenario D: Technology watch

- DILEMMA Role:
  - DILEMMA is providing improved quality of service based upon timeliness of information supply services realized within the implementation of technology watch services
  - Dilemma is able to retrieve automatically and on a dynamic way (means continuous in time) any new relevant information (means matching a specific query) during a given period of time. It is then:
    - Sending this information to the end-user
    - Making the broker aware of the existance of the new information and of the transaction with the end-user

Value for Emerging Technology Markets

The added value of DILEMMA should be examined in terms of the contributions that the project is making to certain aspects of:

1. The aimed IT infrastructure and the underlying technology approaches and organisational concepts that support an integrated approach concerning the design and the lifecycle management of intangible goods and services which in the context of the project concern services in the thematic area of IETT.
2. The innovation exploitation and the technology transfer (IETT) process, which has been chosen as the application domain for the IT developments

As both of the above form the main pillars of the project, the added value is assessed with respect to both of them individually with a concluding statement of the added value of the integrated project outcome.

The adopted technical approach for structuring the Dilemma services (both in terms of design and lifecycle management) using the **service flow concept** exhibits an unequivocal value-addedness of the project and a contribution at the scientific and technology level.

Furthermore the building of the Dilemma services based on:

- **Service elements** that are regarded from the service designer's perspective as these concern reusable elements that may be used for developing new services or enhancing / changing the functionality of existing (operational) ones, and
- **Service pages** that are entities upon which the broker and / or the end user may regard services either for carrying out customization activities such as personalization of the accesses-to-service interface forms a further value-added point of the project.

Having in mind that some of the most essential problems that users, administrators, developers and vendors of information supply services face today may be viewed under the common denominator of "interoperability" problems, the Dilemma approach illustrates possible ways to address these problems. A design goal of the project is to provide a cohesive technological infrastructure independent of any specific implementation pathway and to contain features that are effective and easy to use in a broad range of representative networked service environments which may be subject to variable configurations.

Users of Dilemma Technologies

The Dilemma IT infrastructure is targeted at six categories of users[4]:

1. Dilemma platform and service vendors (may concern IT companies, content providers or - in case they exhibit competencies in any of them - as a specialization of the broker category)
2. Professional Dilemma service providers (as a specialization of the broker category)
3. Dilemma service developers (as a specialization of the broker category)
4. Dilemma service administrators (as a specialization of the broker category)
5. Dilemma service End users
6. Information technology managers (as a specialization of the previous End user category)

These users participate in one or more of the following four stages in the development and usage of the Dilemma-based service infrastructures:

- **Establishment:** Implementing and deploying the Dilemma service approach across the IETT information "supply chain".

- **Build:** Exercising the Dilemma service elements to define a baseline service flow configuration (establishing the exchange paths between known service sources and targets as well as the various filtering mechanisms involved).
- **Operation:** Operating the Dilemma-based service flow infrastructures.
- **Maintenance:** Exercising the introduced concepts to define changes in the distributed service configuration (e.g. to cover changes as "small" as the addition of new service elements in the overall Dilemma service configuration and as "large" as merger with or replacement by another configuration such as in the case of replacing a service flow with a group of supplying service flows loosely linked and using a new distributed management scheme[5]).

In Table 8 we present some usage scenarios that illustrate activities in the Build and Maintenance steps that clearly demonstrate the value addedness of the project.

In regard to positioning the added value of the project in terms of linkage with the business opportunity for the project within a supportive market environment that would favorably sustain business development in that specific area, we note that there is certain potential in coupling the project work with developments in the Application Service Provider[7] (ASP) market segment. Our work in the project helps a revisit to the topic of ASPs for two main reasons (see Figure 4):

- We now see that there is a strong future for ASP related businesses; and
- A great deal has changed on the ASP competitive landscape.

Over the past years multiple variations on the basic ASP model have emerged which warrant review and analysis. In addition, the ASP business model is beginning to face serious challenges regarding its viability and broader market acceptance, linking those models to the potential of providing through ASPs the means for operating into a networked enterprise environment.

In its "purest" sense, the ASP model invokes the delivery of software as a service. In exchange for accessing the application, the client renders rental-like payments; in this respect, an ASP facilitates a remote, centrally-managed "rent-an-application" service for the client. The emphasis is placed on the *use and not on the ownership* of the application. The client no longer owns the application or the responsibilities associated with initial and ongoing maintenance. The client, through an Internet browser, accesses remote, centralized computer servers hosting the application. Only the results from the application are managed locally by the client.

Currently the ability of an ASP to sell "mission-critical" solutions to early ASP adopters hinges to a large degree on whether the application being hosted was designed specifically for delivery over the Internet. In point of fact, many of the

Table 8. Analysis of usage scenarios

		Foreseen Added Value of Dilemma to Users[6]		
User category	**Stage**	**Problem or need**	**Tools and repositories**	**How Dilemma promotes better service utilization**
Dilemma Platform and Service vendors	Build	Must subscribe to standards for inter-vendor interconnect	Dilemma mobile agent infrastructure	Dilemma provides a common "backplane" for pluggable subsystems.
			OMG Repository Common Facility	It may be exploited as a globally usable notation for meta-service exchange protocols which enables flexible distribution of distributed services over a heterogeneous collection of information systems.
			Tools for modeling, development, deployment and service management	
Professional Dilemma Service Providers	Build	Must accumulate and reuse elements from service engagement	Third party and in-house Tools that apply meta-services to concrete service-base catalogues and vice versa	Reusable, editable, and extensible meta-service should provide a first-level "asset base" that builds (new) value. This base of reusable elements starts a self-reinforcing feedback loop with continually increasing returns improved by engagement productivity for the Dilemma user partners (i.e. the IRCs).
Professional Dilemma Service Providers	Maintenance	Must modify Service process configuration: knowing what and where to modify; knowing dependency closure	Third party or in-house tools to manage reconfiguration editing of a service flow	Dilemma exposes the information required to modify a service flow model. Service context definition and self-describing features for the service flows are used to isolate dependency relationships.
Professional Dilemma Service Providers, Dilemma Service Administrators	Maintenance	Must integrate existing tools and data which adhere to standards other than Dilemma's service flow model into a distributed service configuration environment.	Tools based on Dilemma 's ability to incorporate meta-models of services and alternate service definition practices and standards.	Dilemma does or can subsume non- Dilemma service representations. For example, Dilemma may be elaborated in the future to contain any XML-based service model with a focus to domain-specific characteristics.
Dielemma Service Administrators	Build	Must establish and manage expressions, relationships, and lineage over multiple service-base schemata.	Tools that use built-in facilities of Dilemma to define schema content, relationships, and lineage.	Dilemma design is based on need to manage such information at multiple levels. The basic Mobile Agent "packages" will have to be designed to allow navigation of meta-services correlated to schemata.
Dielemma Service Administrators	Maintenance	Must add, subtract, re- partition, reallocate, or merge service resources in deployment configuration.	Service management tools.	Dilemma consists of models of meta-services that assist in making such changes and allow impact of these changes to be assessed.

Figure 4. Acquiring the identity of a prospective service in Dilemma

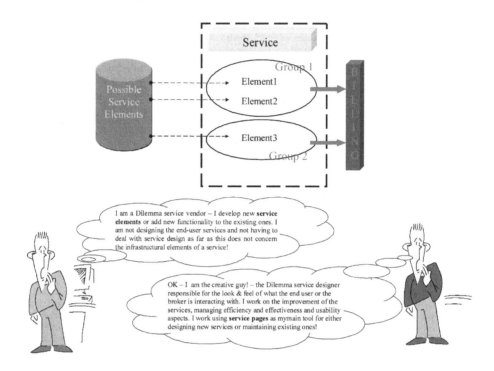

"mission-critical" packages sold by highly respected vendors were ***not*** developed for a hosted / services delivery methodology.

Where the added value of Dilemma comes to the stage relates to the fact that our approach for design and management of services is implemented in a distributed service infrastructure according to planned (actually: envisaged) usage of a multiple actors scheme. The term distributed service infrastructure is used for description of an environment with the following characteristics:

1. It consists of a number of service flows that are executed using resources of several sites simultaneously and
2. The service flows communicate with each other by exchanging messages over a commonly agreed network of participants (in our case it is the network of the IRCs).

In this respect our efforts in the project may be viewed from within the perspective of building the service flow execution kernel for mobile agent applications that may regarded as the high-end of the foreseen ASP market in terms of ***aggregat-***

ing functionality requested by the particular differentiated users of the distributed service environment.

Value of the Dilemma System

The following are indicates as aspects directly related to the project value addedness with respect to functionality provided for the target domain of innovation exploitation and technology transfer (IETT):

- *Business agreements between brokers*. The brokers are organised into networks which gives them the ability: a) to exchange data amongst them, b) to forward the clients' requests they do not have the means to serve, to the appropriate broker's system that might be able to serve them.. This inter-broker business function gives the brokers the ability to easily configure business agreements amongst them.
- *Speed gain and cost reduction in the mediation process.* The time that a traditional mediation process requires is shorten, since:
  - Many everyday operations that were done manually by the broker are automated and
  - Great amounts of interactions between the customers and the broker are minimised
- *Easy and quick publication of the information to the clients.* Due to the fact that the time required for the mediation process is minimised, the broker has the ability to utilise the extra gained time in order to provide faster information to the clients.
- *Media neutral - drawings, presentation, etc. can be sent out.* The customer can offer information to the system with various formats, e.g simple text, more detailed technological descriptions, algorithms or pieces of code solving particular problems, 3D designs, etc; This information is layered to various levels and is associated with pricing schemes.
- *Application of billing policies.* The information the broker has is organised in various levels from abstract info to detailed specifications. Each level has its own pricing scheme, which reflects the quality and the amount of information it has encapsulated. The information that is revealed to the customer corresponds to the amount of money he is willing to pay.
- *Personalization information offer process.* The process of automatically entering information to the system by the customer is highly assisted from the system. The user is offered guidance in order to describe-insert his information in the most possible concrete and clear way so that it can be easily retrieved and organised into levels with various pricing schemes (see above)

- ***Security.*** The data returned to the customer as a result to his query will be encapsulated in an agent. The agent therefore, will be the carrier of both the data and the permission rights to them. The agent will "destroy" the data: a) after a specific time of period b) if the customer fails to "properly" authenticate himself therefore to prove that he is the authorised person to receive the data.
- ***High quality-increased relevance.*** The system strengthens the data's accuracy-thus increases the uncertainty, by means of:
  - ○ Providing personalization of the information offer process (see above)
  - ○ Scaling the information into various levels based on its depth of details and cost
  - ○ Offering guidance to the technology offer phase (see above), so that the entered information can be as complete as possible
- ***Service combinations.*** The system administrator (broker) can use the basic services offered by the system in order to form new aggregative coalition of services, reusable from all the system users.
- ***Dynamic digital design of services.*** Through the monitoring of the mediation process the broker is able to collect statistical data, to process them according to different criteria and to produce reports and graphs of the results. In this way the brokers becomes able to identify areas of interest and add new information and links, propose assistance to their clients etc.
- ***Updated information.*** The system administrators (brokers) are always alerted when new information enters the system. That way it is assured that the answers to the customers' requests contain the most recent updated information
- ***New forms of presentation.*** The broker has in his possession various kinds of information (text, video, demos, etc) and the ability to present them with ways different to the traditional ones, e.g organising virtual brokerage events.
- ***Fine filtered access schemes to info are possible.*** The information that the broker has is organised into levels, moving from the higher level to lower level the uncertainty decreases and the cost of the information increases.

SERVICES AND FUNCTIONALITY OF THE DILEMMA SYSTEM

The role of DILEMMA is realized through the provision of the following set of envisaged services:

1. Service design services
2. Information Supply services
3. Broker-to-Broker services

4.   Services Administration and Management

Each service is analyzed in terms of its target functionality, level of performance, value brought to the users at the various scenarios. It should be noted that full functionality might be missing from some of the services as it is not within the scope of the project to develop a full-blow management information system for the target process but to achieve the **target** objectives, as set in the role of DILEMMA and focused by the various use cases and scenarios.

Service Design Services

Dilemma will have to offer numerous functionality that facilitate brokers in designing their services. The most important of them are:

- **Authoring interface:** Dilemma should provide an interface allowing the organization and the design of a service based on the concept of *service sessions* and *service elements*. This interface will be menu-driven and Web-based, which means that Dilemma not only will have to produce services for the Web environment, but also to uses WWW browsers as the interface for the particularly service-building environment.
- **Pricing configuration:** When designing a service, the DILEMMA interface should provide also the ability to configure pricing schemes on the various service or data elements of a specific service in order to apply a specific pricing scheme for a specific service. In the case of data, the ability to accommodate multiple levels of data, enables also the assignment of different values and pricing to the various data components, depending also on the pricing applied by the owner of the data, the technology provider.
- **Question editor:** This editor of the Dilemma system will assist the service author in the making up of *queries* and *validations*[8]. The service author enters a query, a number of possible sources considered as acquisition repositories and a rule related to the correctness of the result, the latter linked to the particular operational policy.
- **Searchable service glossary:** The service author can create a searchable glossary of terms; links from the notes to the glossary are added automatically by the Dilemma system.
- **Service content search:** If new service elements are included in the service, Dilemma provides a page that allows the association of names and keywords with each new service element. Users can search for those service elements based on their name and keywords. Search results are presented in the form of a service page containing individualized versions of the matching "images".

Clicking on any of them presents the corresponding full results.

- **Index:** Dilemma will have to offer automatic index generation for the provided services. The service author can define a set of words that she/he would like to appear in the index. Dilemma dynamically creates an index which points to service pages containing these words. For simplicity reasons, in the context of the envisaged solution, index entries are ordered alphabetically though other presentation patterns might be added as well i.e. with respect to the particular semantical relevance, data/information source, combined semantic and price distance items, etc.

- **References and External Resources:** The service author can associate the service content with external references such as 3rd party catalogues (e.g. of Commission funded projects, articles and URLs, so that users can find supplementary information on the current topic. DILEMMA system should provide the means to transfer other data elements into DILEMMA or convert external resources to DILEMMA format. A tool to manage such data adaptation should be available.

- **Multimedia content:** Though not a part of the project demonstration objectives, Dilemma will offer support for images, audio, video and other types of data/information formats. There will be special utilities that allow the service designer to associate multimedia content to a service page. Such multimedia content will have to be accessible to the users through icons in the button-bar of the particular service page.

Dilemma service designers can use as many or as few of the previous features as their individual needs require. For example, some may choose to put just a service calendar online while others may choose to put entire service catalogues including hundreds of related service pages and so forth.

End-User & Information Supply Services

Creating & Configuring information (Edit form): The customers of the system fill in forms describing their requirements from the broker. There are two kinds of requirements:

1. The customers *seek* information from the broker
2. The customers *offer* information to the broker

Additional information about time deadlines and multiple levels of details (based also on other type of media) will need to be specified. The user should be enabled by the system to customize his offer based upon different and incremental levels of information. Each level of information could:

1. Be assigned with additional details
2. Be based on other type of information (i.e. URL, 3D design, design figure etc)
3. Be assigned a specific price
4. Be configured as confidential and linked to confidentially agreement starting point

Throughout the filling of the forms the systems "guides" the customer in order to describe his request/offer as concrete and clear as possible, in order to increase the possibility to execute a "highly relevant" matching between the customer's requirements and the system's database

Searching: It is the core function of the system: to search technology data based on specific query data. Partial searching and search refinement techniques will be used in order to increase relevance of the given answers. The search-matching is activated:

- Every time the customer submits a form
- Every time the customer refines/re-executes an already stored query
- At predefined time intervals for monitoring services
- Every time there is a new entrance/offer (which also falls to the case of filling a form) to the system for updating services

Authentication services: User name and password (necessary to provide personalized services) and to obtain credentials for accessing confidential information.

Encryption and Data protection mechanisms: Standard mechanisms for encrypting different parts of the information and defining access rights of third party users.

Information Supply: The main features for the realization of the desired functionality of information supply will be:

1. The data protection mechanisms applied to confidential data (as defined by the input and technology audit process)
2. The ability to monitor a specific area based upon timed execution of query at specific intervals. DILEMMA should provide updates to the informed user after matching them to his query. The user should any time refine his "watch" query
3. The supply of information should start from the non-detail data, which are formed in such a way that the customer can not further exploit them without

the mediation of the brokers. In case that the customer finds one or more of the results interesting/useful and wants further information, he will have the ability to move to next level of information, based upon the configuration made by the client who offers and inputs the technology to the system. Multimedia support, pricing, data privacy and confidentiality agreement support will empower the information supply process at this phase so as to bring the interested user to the best possible level of information, depending on his actual interest on the specific technology.

User pages personalization: Dilemma creates a default service "homepage" for every user subscribed to a service. The user can modify this page to suit her/his needs. To do this, as well as to facilitate creation of dynamic IE & TT service communities, Dilemma offers to the users a facility for customizing homepages. To customize her/his page the user has to select her/his name and password. Then the window will be divided into three frames. The bottom right frame provides the user with the attribute options she/he can set for the Dilemma homepage. The possible components of a Dilemma homepage include a banner, a header message, icons representing various links to service content items and tools, a footer message and a counter possibly for combined billing and pricing information. The top right frame will display the service page as the user updates it. We have to note that this tool offers users a simple authoring interface to construct personal service homepages.

Broker-to-Broker Services

- **Sharing information:** The DILEMMA should automate the interaction and multiple way communications to all the brokers asked to provide an answer on a specific end-user inquiry. Interoperability of data and services is necessary based on common data and services typology accepted.
- **Permission schemes:** Not all broker-to-broker services should be permitted. The broker should assign permission on the basic services defining who is having the right to ask for them.
- **Broker-to-broker charging services:** Some of the broker-to-broker services should be priced. The broker must have the ability not only to permit a service to one or more brokers but also to sign pricing policy upon them.

Services Administration and Management

In order to facilitate course management Dilemma offers several services, such as service participation tracking, service progress tracking and timed queries. Moreover, administrative services include all those setup, management and maintenance tasks required to operate a Dilemma service.

- **Service participation tracking:** Dilemma lets the service provider see which service pages the users are viewing and how much time they are spending on the various service pages.
- **Service progress tracking:** The Dilemma user can check confirmed service assignments and requests for new service sessions. She/he can view own requests and compare to other service summary data.
- **Timed queries:** Queries can be written by the service author and delivered online to the users. In general, there is need to support five different kinds of queries: multiple choice, true/false, matching, fill-in-the-blank and short answer. The Dilemma user is responsible for submitting her/his preferred approach linked with a time allotted for the query expires. Dilemma will automatically "grade" all types of queries except short answers. The short answer query type provides grading assistance using an approximate pattern-matching scheme to highlight words or terms in the particular user's response. Once the query is graded, automatically or manually, the Dilemma users have access to their graded query and comments online.
- **Access control:** Dilemma service authors can define access rights to their services, considered as their intellectual property. *This is an extremely innovative point of the Dilemma project that facilitates capitalisation on intangible assets such as the concept of a service or the underlying idea, though in a passive way i.e. a service may be imitated but it cannot be copied.*
- **Dilemma Administration page:** It allows the particular Dilemma site administrator to create accounts for service authors, change their passwords, initialize and delete services. The administrator does not actually configure or add any content to a service, but simply initializes a service and hands over the new "empty" service to a service author.
- **Service Administration page:** Once a Dilemma service is set up, the service author can manage the service in any way such as: add and delete user accounts, change users' passwords and create level accounts related to levels of users (i.e. as a way to organize sets of users under a specific category).

Employing Dilemma Services in the Described Usage Cases: Before and After

Use case A: Inter-IRC collaboration for joint service provision (Table 9).

   Use case B: Dealing with detailed technological profiles and confidential data (Table 10).

   Use case C: Combination of services (Table 11).

Table 9. Valuating the before and after for use case A

Before DILEMMA	Use of DILEMMA in the case
The broker who receives a inquiry has to communicate (using phones, emails, fax) with other brokers in order to utilize the extended knowledge of the broker's network.	When the inquiry is issued the system is automatically informs the broker's network about the inquiry of a client issued through his interaction with a specific broker. The results are collected and provided to the client through electronic means. The brokers are just informed about the request and the status of the results. *Broker-to-broker information services, are active in this case in order to conduct the query, check permissions and apply inter-IRC pricing where necessary.*
The broker wants to establish a business relationship with other brokers in order to provide a joint service. He is doing this by applying a specific pricing policy and by establishing a specific procedure in his every day process in order to operate this new agreement. When there are numerous such cases, there is an obvious difficulty to operate and run all business cases.	The broker is entering into DILEMMA and specifies this new service as a combined service using the resources of other brokers. *The permissions and pricing schemes are adjusted appropriately through the authoring interface utilized by the involved brokers..*
Added Value	
Easy-to-configure business agreements between brokers.	
Each broker can exploit the valuable resources which differ in terms of nature from broker to broker (i.e. other brokers have valuable funding information while other have valuable expertise, or valuable innovations in biotechnology)	
Cost and Time savings in brokerage phases.	
Extended knowledge and information easily and quickly utilized and published to the end-user.	

Use case D: Technology watch (Table 12).

A last word about the people of the DILEMMA project: though we had been a rather (over)crowded consortium with organisations from many countries all over Europe, the steam engine of the project had been the team of the Greek IRC Help-Forward. I mention three of the chief architects – all of them senior and successful consultants with years of experience and passion for their work: Dr Anastasia Constantinou, Dr Nikos Melanitis, now Professor in the Hellenic Naval Academy and Dr Vasilis Tsakalos. All of them are good friends and remained friends though DILEMMA was a torture for them as the quality of service they were receiving from the IT people of all involved organisations (mine included) was rather doubtful.

Looking now back and making each one of us his or her self criticism of what went wrong, I personally see that not much of what went wrong could have been anticipated and proactively addressed. Many mistakes have to happen in order for someone to recognise a (personal) lack of knowledge or expertise – this is why experience is useful and a scarce capacity in many cases. On the other hand, much of the criticism about the IT people was concentrated on the inability to deliver a turn key solution that would operate and at a certain degree automate existing business processes. The failure to take corrective measures on time was a serious fault – on the other hand, what I now see and am fully convinced about is that *if* we had taken all the necessary measures to improve the system, we might have converged to a better performing service *configuration* system but for sure not to a service provi-

Table 10. Valuating the before and after for use case B

Before DILEMMA	Use of DILEMMA in the case
The client requests more details and information about a specific technology through direct communication with the broker.	The system presents to the user the first level of information (which is usually for free). It then informs the client about the next (extra) levels of detailed information and their associated costs. Continuing, it asks the client whether he is interested in getting more details, by choosing one of the next levels. The client he can proceed step-by-step and he can stop at a level of information which he finds satisfactory depending on his own criteria. *Service design service: pricing configuration, question editor are active in this case since the system: helps the user to fill in a concrete technology offer and assigns specific pricing policies to it.*
The process of information exchange between the broker and the interested client is done manually and is time consuming since a huge amount of iteration in needed.	The system reveals to the client information level by level. E.g The first level exposes only the abstract of a technology offer, the second level provides a more detailed technological description, the third level contains specific algorithms, pieces of code, 3D designs etc, and the fourth level the final technical specifications. In that way the customer gets and therefore pays the information step by step, judging whether he wants to proceed to the next level. Only when he reaches a substantial depth in levels and if he is still interested, he may contact the broker to proceed to a business agreement with the technology provider. *Access control services (from the category broker-to-broker services) is active in this case, since the service authors can define access rights to their services. Also pricing configuration services are active for the charging of the various levels.*
Added Value	
High personalization of the offer. Each user with the proper guidance from the system will have the ability to choose up to which level he would like to place his information	
Enabling of pricing schemes, for the charging of the various levels of information	
Security, each level's data will be securely encapsulated in the agent that will transform them to the client	
Increased relevance, by means of reducing uncertainty, since the broker guides the client into putting his information into the system and by assessing what is more interesting to the client. Accuracy of information is also increased because the customers (with the help of the broker) can insert more "complete" information to the system	
Step-by-step obtaining technology information.	
The client can stop at a level, which he finds satisfactory and not proceed to complete details.	
User-friendly environment – time-saving and cheaper communications.	

Table 11. Valuating the before and after for use case C

Before DILEMMA	Use of DILEMMA in the case
A client contacts a broker in order to request for a specific technology. The broker assesses the customer's request and together with the answer to his request the broker with its own initiative returns to the customer hints of other pieces of information that might be useful to him, e.g funding opportunities for the requested technology. This combination of services is done ad-hoc from the broker today.	The system automatically proposes the customer to use other services as well, in order to better solve his problem. This proposition is done at 2 stages.
	1. The first time that the customer enters with a specific technological request, the system illustrates to him all the possible services he might as well be interested in using.
	2. After the client has taken an answer to his request the system proposes to him services that can possibly be combined with the results of his request.
a. In case the broker does not maintain complementary information on various funding mechanisms for TT projects he will have for each specific case to conduct a special study on the financial instruments to serve his client. An option here could be that the broker signposts the client to another broker in the financial sector. This is time-consuming both for the broker and the client, finally the client might not show up again being disappointed with the low quality of the service offered. The bottleneck in the service is the limitation of its scope – normally the IRCs end up with the organization of a bilateral meeting between the technology seeker and the technology provider, and are not involved deeply in the negotiation phase and in seeking financial resources for the client.	The Dilemma will allow for maintaining complementary information on available financial resources and schemes not only in the country of operation of the individual IRC but also in the other countries. In addition information on legal and IPR experts in the different countries will also be maintained. In such a case if a client comes to the Dilemma and asks for a technology and technological equipment for the production of plastic bottles with maximum cost of EUR 100,000 of which EUR 60,000 will be requested as a bank loan. Thanks to the Dilemma the broker will be able to track down suitable technology and equipment in the required price range, and identify several banks (or there may be only one bank providing micro-loans to SMEs in the requested range), the experts to assist the client in the development of the business plan and the preliminary repayment schedule, as well as a lawyer to advise the client in the process of TT negotiations.
b. The ideal case would be that the broker has the exact information on the relevant financial scheme. The bottleneck here is that the available information suits only one case and the next client seeking information on financial sources might need information on a different financial scheme.	
c. The broker maintains some information on financial resources but as the search for such information is time- and effort-consuming and is not a part of the standard set of IRC services the information might be irrelevant.	
Added Value	
Reusability of service combinations, the service combinations that are generated from the operation of the system (e.g. technology requests and funding opportunities) are valuable to the system. The goal is to have as many combinations as possible and to re-use them as potential solutions to similar problems	
Service combinations' accessibility, every user of the system can have access to the various services combinations that have emerged throughout the system's operation.	
More effective satisfaction of the customers' needs, by proposing to them complementary services that they might have not thought to request.	
Timesaving, effort-saving, cost-saving, greater satisfaction of the client, virtual one-stop-shop.	

Table 12. Valuating the before and after for use case D

Before DILEMMA	Use of DILEMMA in the case
The broker receives an inquiry from a client wishing to be informed of the evolutions of a technology or thematic scheme. The technology watch process is then operated in two steps, first the initiation stage and then the recurrent stage.	Once the broker has determined both the keywords (i.e. the information topics), and the sources, he/she input both data in the Dilemma system (e.g. the keywords chosen and the different information sources chosen, including external URLs), then the system will deliver to the client on a dynamic way each new relevant information (i.e. matching the keywords) when it appears somewhere in the system. The permission and pricing schemes can then be adapted to allow the client to receive the full information each time it is generated during a given time period, or propose a "pay per view"-like mode.
To initiate the technology watch service, the broker first selects (using its know-how): i. the keywords which refers to the type of technology sought ii. the information sources (other than the internal database) which he/she believes will provide relevant information (e.g. patent databases, specific URLs, ...) The broker is then performing a search into these different sources and provides the output to the client at a specific time.	
Then on a recurrent basis, in order to inform its client of any new relevant information appearing in one of the selected sources, the broker has to periodically check, this means re-perform its initial query chasing for potential new information.	
Added Value	
The range of information sources and thus the "size of the searchable system" is parametred according to the clients needs, and the know-how of the broker which mostly relies in this aspect is thus fully valorized Cost and time is saved with the automation of the search and publication (i.e. diffusion to the client) process New information is retrieved only when it is dynamically created (i.e. existing within the system), thus saving workload (no need to make a periodic search which can proved unsuccessful if no new information has been introduced in the system)	
Time for search is decreased drastically and the sources of information are richer and more easily accessible.	
User-friendly environment.	
Lower human efforts.	

sion, supply or delivery one. There is still road ahead till the experience of a service will be satisfactorily demonstrated by the system it uses for its delivery.

ENDNOTES

[1] The personalised version of the user interface is called MyDilemma versus the other generic DILEMMA information service.

[2] See the next Section.

[3] Same as above.

[4] As it is easy to identify, there is no contradiction with the categories identified in the beginning of this report.

[5] This is a quite complex issue for which demonstration may be regarded as outside the scope of the project. It concerns the "reverse" engineering of a service into a set of constituent services that should be chosen for support of an e.g. localization exercise (a global service gets localized and a set of local service points are now assigned the responsibility for running the service).

[6] We refer to the above set of user categories which – as explained in the parentheses – should be regarded as operational specialisations of the two originally introduced categories in the beginning of this report.

[7] In our context we adopt the usual definition for an application service provider as a 3rd-party service firm which deploys, manages, and remotely hosts a software application through centrally-located servers in a "rental" or lease agreement.

[8] **Queries** concern specialized questioning regarding the existence of data/information related to a specific item e.g. a particular technology, or an offer for such a particular technology. **Validations**, on the other hand, are related to the presentation of relevance between requested data/information and an unknown set of requested evidence, so that for example an innovative technology will be directed for usage in a novel field of application or utilized for a not yet tested process. In this respect, while **queries** are of *interrogative* nature, **validations** are aiming to *manifest* novel usage patterns or opportunities. In both cases, however, the risk of any service result is related to the maintenance of a fair balance between *silence* (no feedback) and *noise* (too much feedback considered of relatively low utility).

Chapter 5
Services and the Computers

In symmetry with Chapter 4, here the core subject in this chapter is the relationships between services and their implementations in computer applications and information systems. Again, the interactive space is examined that is created to link both entities – and most importantly – how computers interact to each other through services. A theoretical part of the service development framework is presented related with Information Supply Chains and is followed by an implemented test case for a manufacturing enterprise. Important part is devoted to practical concerns like configurability of a service in other or new contexts and de novo construction of a service supply chain.

I am tempted to make a risky aphorism: that the intersection of services and the computers is the empty set. Like all aphorisms, its main purpose is not only for use as a provocative statement but also to shed light to an uncomfortable truth, namely the difficult relationship between these two terms – or should I say better between these two industries?

Imagine the simple case of an 'elementary' Boolean service: a company wants

DOI: 10.4018/978-1-60566-683-9.ch005

to implement a new corporate policy of transparency, openness and accessibility: any member of the company, from the basement porters to its CEO and Chairperson shall be subject of a tracing service to let anyone else within the company (to not exaggerate by including customers in our hypothetical example) know whether this particular person is in the company building or not.

The reason of existence for this service may be extremely positive and well-intended: anyone can easily see if someone of his or her interest is there to answer a call or reply to an e-mail or appear in a physical face-to-face meeting. From an implementation point of view, one can see that it is about an Internet- and Web-based application that may have a simple text entry field: you insert the name of the person you want to check his or her presence in the company and as an answer you get a yes or a no (therefore I called this a Boolean service).

Now imagine the following situations: one can always misspell a name – or not know exactly how to write it (is it Briggs or Brigges? Schmidt or Schmitt?). Therefore, it is good to provide a graphical navigator with the corporate organisation chart so that you know you are looking for Schmidt of the HR and not Schmitt of the Sales Department. Of course, there is always the question of privacy: people sometimes don't want to be accessible to others – either for personal reasons, or because they are too busy or because they are of villain nature (even temporarily). Should we give them the ability to hide their presence from the others? This is not to be answered by the computer programmer but somehow needs to be addressed before the launch of the service.

What I want to show with the analysis above is that there is huge space for assumptions to be made during the design or even the conceptualisation of any service. These may come either from the future user of the service also known as customer as well as the professional designer who has been hired for the design of the service. In the above example we considered the case of a duet: the customer and the computer programmer hired to design the service. In many cases, it is not a duet but a triplet that includes a management consultant. And in some other cases it is a quartet that involved in addition also some regulator or a monitoring authority. As you may see the more entities are involved and the more individuals, the more chaotic becomes the control process and the less sensible are the actions of the people. Ideally one would speak about a value chain, of a team of stakeholders with different roles who can contribute unique value elements but the reality is rather banal. At the end, we all know that camel is a horse designed by a committee…

Is there any therapy for this? Or does the all time classic Latin proverb *aegrescit medendo* applies to this case? What does it mean? The disease worsens with the treatment - or else: the treatment is worse than the disease.

The therapy is simple yet difficult to recognise: lack of common sense. I elaborate on this point later in Chapter 7 about service economics. It is sad that many companies try to heal chronic corporate diseases with the introduction of a new process or a new service – in many cases these are realised by the introduction of a new computer application.

If we lived in the middle ages and I had the absolute power of an overlord, I would be tempted to publicly execute (why not through impalement?) all those irresponsible fellows who announce services that are not needed, introduce services that are not linked with the existing process grid and are expected to operate on a higher, non-existent level, or implement services without having tested or validated them with real users and for a sufficient period of time.

I think that marketing people – semi-educated and quasi-intellectual are to be attributed a great part of the pathetic reality we face in the service field: to many of them, there is a great dose of self-satisfaction when they fantasise of a service concept; they come up with some nice term, they convince some others of the strengths and pros of their idea (increase of brand identity and image recognition, differentiation from the competition and finally – what else? – more money). The same people who can exhibit extremely rare charismas and talents if they are part of a group, if they are left alone they can exhibit huge amounts of irresponsibility.

I shall not leave any room for misunderstandings here: I don't hate marketing people – quite the opposite: as said above, many of them are charismatic and highly talented individuals. The problem with them is that they charge with transcendal expectations initially the providers and finally the customers of commodities and services while the reality is lying far aside from the promised one.

Another source of problems is the false base upon which we estimate the costs or the profits of a new service. We try to hide costs and pump up the profits while the reality is more down to earth. This is not to be attributed to my usual suspects, namely the marketing people but to managers: they want to convince others with the argument of low costs and high profits. This has to do with managerial ethics and professional or individual moral values. Why should a company ground the introduction of a new service on its cost? I am sure that several of the jobs carried out by humans in the service discipline could be equally if not even better performed by trained chimpanzees. Why not staff our companies with them? For sure, many of them may see a violation of the laws against animals abuse when employing chimpanzees. On the other hand, and as a customer I have felt humiliated by other humans who were supposed to helpfully service a request for which I was paying their company for years (and I suppose human customer abuse is same much a crime as the abuse of chimpanzees).

In the future we shall experience the aggressive come back of computers in the service industry in terms of replacing the incompetent humans with some equally (in)competent but at least more reliable and consistent computer application. I feel much better when I make an internet reservation for a flight than passing my flight reservation request to some lowly paid travel agency employee who may have wrongly noted my preferences and who may forget to come back to me.

Coming back to what I characterised as an aphorism in the beginning of this chapter: the more I think about this the more I am convinced that it is correct: the intersection of computers and services is actually the empty set. It can only be bridged by humans that are appropriately skilled for this task and with processes which are relevant and capable to fill this gap.

Massimo Paolucci, a senior researcher at DoCoMo NTT Euro-Labs in Munich, Germany who conducts research in the field of automatic Web service composition and discovery, has recognized that what we more intensively experience is that the web is moving from being a collection of pages toward a collection of services that interoperate through the Internet (Paolucci et al., 2002). According to him, 'Web services provide a new model of the web in which sites exchange dynamic information on demand. This change is especially important for the e-business community, because it provides an opportunity to conduct business faster and more efficiently. Indeed, the opportunity to manage supply chains dynamically to achieve the greatest advantage on the market is expected to create great value added and increase productivity. On the other hand, automatic management of supply chain opens new challenges: first, web services and other types of intelligent service agents should be able to locate automatically other services that provide a solution to their problems, second, services should be able to interoperate to compose automatically complex services.'

In this part of our concern is the application of some service design concepts and structures in order to support highly interconnected e-service infrastructures.

As will be further described, the novelty of our approach comes to the fact that our approach for design and management of services is implemented in a distributed service infrastructure according to a *preplanned usage of a multiple service actors' scheme*. The term distributed service infrastructure is used for description of an environment with the following characteristics:

1. It consists of a number of service flows that are executed using resources of several sites simultaneously, and
2. That service flows communicate with each other by exchanging messages over a commonly agreed network of participants (in our case it is the network of all the involved parties and units involved in the provision of a service).

Our efforts may be viewed from within the perspective of building the service flow execution kernel for service management applications that may regarded as the high-end of what we are used to name Application Service Providers (ASP) market in terms of *aggregating* functionality requested by the particular differentiated users of the distributed service environment. In this respect, the approaches we employ address the following two needs:

1. From an *operational* viewpoint, it focuses on the inter-site aspects (timing and security) for remote interoperability of the participating services. Intra-site, it will focus on the dynamic adaptation of the application to changes in the environment of a single service provision (unit).
2. From a *methodological* viewpoint, it focuses on the way to capture and validate dependability requirements and validate these requirements, on the way to derive from requirements the structure of the modeling approach, and on the use of modeling to drive the development and the assessment of the proposed solutions.

The building of the proposed services is based on:

*   *Service elements* that are regarded from the service designer's perspective as these concern reusable elements that may be used for developing new services or enhancing / changing the functionality of existing (operational) ones, and
*   *Service 'pages'* that are entities upon which the service user (i.e. a casual customer or a skilled administration employee) may regard services either for carrying out customisation activities such as personalisation of the access-to-service interface e.g. for different user categories and different types of usage (data entry, retrieval of data, sophisticated query formulation and processing, etc.).

The approach taken helps in the creation of a significant competitive advantage and market knowledge and creates first-mover advantage in the addressed transition towards *service-oriented architectures*. This know-how is faster transferable from within the operational environment to those key divisions that will be acting as uptakers and adopters. Of course, a key objective has been how to get improved ideas to those who can effectively apply them. The main focus is to gain the technological capabilities and the necessary means (i.e. methods, practices and software components) so that any new services will be affordably priced for a segment of the hospital market that has been largely unable to afford such services – namely small and medium sized enterprises with fewer than e.g. 100 employees.

The access-to-service environment under implementation enables the users of the service platform to:

*   Establish an overall Service flow direction, by means of providing linkage

to a set of pre-programmed resources that are executed in the distributed (Internet) environment, such as ERP, customer relationship management and recording applications, etc.

- Acquire resources for a particular service property which may be it a Service flow, a Service element, or a Service 'page'.
- Provide "capabilities" to a Service flow by means of integrates both structural and behavioral aspects from within a single perspective, which will be utilised to instantiate the actual service delivery at the end user's point.
- Execute the Service flow by means of utilising resources to accomplish the particularly assigned service scenario.

The last may also be regarded also the "bottom-line" for the actual service delivery by a particular Service flow to support the purpose of the latter's establishment (i.e. the reason for existence of that particular Service flow in the overall corporate value chain).

Having in mind that some of the most essential problems that users, administrators, developers and vendors of information supply services in almost all disciplines, as well as in every application and service field, face today may be viewed under the common denominator of "interoperability" problems, the presented approach illustrates possible ways to address these problems. A design goal has been to provide a cohesive technological infrastructure independent of any specific implementation pathway and to contain features that are effective and easy to use in a broad range of representative networked service environments which may be subject to variable configurations. For this reason we recognize the following types and broad categories of users:

1. Platform and service vendors (may concern IT companies, content providers or - in case they exhibit competencies in any of them - as a specialization of the broker category)
2. Professional service providers (as a specialization of the broker category)
3. Service developers (as a specialization of the broker category)
4. Service administrators (as a specialization of the broker category)
5. Service End users (i.e. the customers – either public or private owned ones)
6. Information technology managers (as a specialization of the previous End user category)

These users participate in one or more of the following four stages in the development and usage of the health-based service infrastructures:

- *Establishment:* Implementing and deploying the presented service approach across the particular information "supply chain".

- *Build:* Exercising the service elements to define a baseline service flow configuration (establishing the exchange paths between known service sources and targets as well as the various filtering mechanisms involved).
- *Operation:* Operating the service flow infrastructures.
- *Maintenance:* Exercising the introduced concepts to define changes in the distributed service configuration (e.g. to cover changes as "small" as the addition of new service elements in the overall service configuration and as "large" as merger with or replacement by another configuration such as in the case of replacing a service flow with a group of supplying service flows loosely linked and using a new distributed management scheme). This is a quite complex issue for which description may be regarded as outside the scope of this book. It concerns the "reverse" engineering of a service into a set of constituent services that should be chosen for support of an e.g. localisation exercise (a global service gets localised and a set of local service points are now assigned the responsibility for running the service).

In Table 1 we present some usage scenarios that illustrate activities in the *Build* and *Maintenance* steps that clearly demonstrate the value addedness of the approach. The reader should feel familiar with the approach as it has been also applied for the case of Dilemma described in the previous Chapter.

In regard to positioning the added value of the particular service implementation in terms of linkage with the business opportunity for the company and its real applicability and potential for adoption in the considered sector within a supportive uptake environment that would favorably sustain business development in that specific area, we note that there is certain potential in coupling the work with developments in the Application Service Provider (ASP) market segment.

In our context we adopt the usual definition for an application service provider as a 3rd-party service firm which deploys, manages, and remotely hosts a both the various application and service portfolios through centrally-located servers in a "rental" or lease agreement as well as the related business model for operating them. Our work in the service implementation helps a revisit to the topic of ASPs for two main reasons: firstly we now see that there is a strong future for ASP related businesses; and secondly there is a great deal has changed on the ASP competitive landscape.

Table 1. Propositions related with the search items and the investigation procedures

User category	Stage	Foreseen Added Value to the Users		
		Problem or need	Tools and repositories	How the system promotes better service utilisation
Platform and Service vendors	Build	Must subscribe to standards for inter-vendor interconnect	Service infrastructure, Common Repository Facility, Tools for modeling, development, deployment and service management	System provides a common "backplane" for pluggable subsystems. It may be exploited as a globally usable notation for meta-service exchange protocols which enables flexible distribution of distributed services over a heterogeneous collection of information systems.
Professional Service Providers	Build	Must accumulate and reuse elements from service engagement	Third party and in-house tools that apply meta-services to concrete service-base catalogues and vice versa	Reusable, editable, and extensible meta-service should provide a first-level "asset base" that builds (new) value. This base of reusable elements starts a self-reinforcing feedback loop with continually increasing returns improved by engagement productivity for the users.
Professional Service Providers	Maintenance	Must modify Service process configuration: knowing what and where to modify; knowing dependency closure	Third party or in-house tools to manage reconfiguration editing of a service flow	System exposes the information required to modify a service flow model. Service context definition and self-describing features for the service flows are used to isolate dependency relationships.
Professional Service Providers, Dilemma Service Administrators	Maintenance	Must integrate existing tools and data which adhere to standards other than service flow model into a distributed service configuration environment.	Tools based on ability to incorporate metamodels of services and alternate service definition practices and standards.	System does or can subsume non-service representations. For example, may be elaborated in the future to contain any XML-based service model with a focus to domain-specific characteristics.
Service Administrators	Build	Must establish and manage expressions, relationships, and lineage over multiple servicebase schemata.	Tools that use built-in facilities to define schema content, relationships, and lineage.	System design is based on need to manage such information at multiple levels. The basic services will have to be designed to allow navigation of meta-services correlated to schemata.
Service Administrators	Maintenance	Must add, subtract, re-partition, reallocate, or merge service resources in deployment configuration.	Service management tools.	System consists of models of meta-services that assist in making such changes and allow impact of these changes to be assessed.

BUILDING ENTERPRISE-WIDE INFORMATION SUPPLY CHAINS BASED ON THE FRACTAL CONCEPT

In this section we present results of research work carried out in the wider context of the formation and lifecycle management of cross-enterprise networked service structures, utilizing concepts that reside within two key research areas dealing with information flow management and alteration of present function-oriented enterprises approach towards the more efficient process orientation, building upon the Information Supply Chain concept and the Fractal Company approach.

A challenge faced in the last years by a growing number of enterprises of all sizes, from the small and micro enterprise level to the large and giant corporations relates to performance improvement in an ever more competitive marketplace in a novel way.

The two key areas where the most significant improvements may be obtained are approached, namely the information management aspects and the alteration of present function-oriented approach of enterprises towards more efficient service and process orientation. For the information flow management in the enterprise world is used the Information Supply Chain concept, while the drive towards service and process orientation is tackled using the Fractal Company approach. It should be mentioned that the use of the term fractal company was made for first time by Professor Warnecke (1983) in his book *The Fractal Company: A Revolution in the Corporate Culture*. These two "pillar" concepts are described further below.

"Conventional" supply chains concern all material-management stages from the supply of raw material through to the sale of final product to the end customer. The Information Supply Chain (hence ISC), is that parallel communications route ranging from supplier through the enterprise itself to (and including) the customer consisted of nodes and links that may comprise software, hardware and/or humans. Thus the chain links the communication between those nodes. Enterprise Information Supply Chains are important entities in Fractal Companies, the performance and optimisation of which will have a very significant effect on the design and performance of the enterprises concerned (and in particular on networked organizations).

The Fractal Company is defined as a set of individual (corporate) autonomous entities, namely the fractals, which develop linkages, share knowledge and resources collaboratively to create products and services in a way that maximizes continued capabilities and allows each entity to realize its specific goals by providing integrated solutions to customers' needs. Each fractal is a dynamic, interoperable, independently acting corporate entity (e.g. single person or just a slice of his "working-time", department, division, the entire organization, or any combination of the above) whose goals, performance, interfacing points, input and output flows can be precisely described and defined.

The Fractal concept relies on the manner in which corporate entities within an Organisation tend to replicate themselves from the elementary working cell (micro) level through to the entire Organisation (macro) level via a sequence of continuous zooms. This results to an extremely increased simplification of every Fractal Company process in terms of resemblance, as well as to the schematisation of the essential Fractal features that include self-similarity, self-organization, self-optimisation, and goal and process orientation.

Because of these characteristics, the performance of a Fractal is subject of constant assessment and evaluation – and therein lays a key advantage for continuous improvement of a Fractal company.

Combining the previously described Fractal and Information Supply Chain concepts three basic organizational entities are identified for describing any procedure or operation in a business or organization environment namely:

- Processes
- Activities
- Resources

Activities are used for fulfilling processes by consuming resources necessary to them, more specifically: A *process* is a notion free from any organisational or structural dimension. It captures a functional dimension that is transverse to the organisation and which is oriented towards a production objective. In many cases, processes can be interpreted as being akin to products that is of utmost importance when considering information chains. The notion of process is not primary or final, in the sense that it can be refined within the model by sub-processes. Process interpretation and perception is thus dependent on the level of abstraction of its observer. Consequently, a process describes a means of attaining a functional objective of the business, through activities and/or sub-processes - together with the necessary resources involved in their fulfilment.

An *activity* has been identified in the relevant literature as an action which can be characterised by a verb and an object upon which the action applies. Activities are necessary in fulfilling processes. Activities consume resources necessary to their fulfilment. The notion of activity can be considered primary or final in the sense it can not be refined within the model even if activities could be further decomposed into tasks. However this level of description is not needed as tasks can be considered as attributes of an activity.

A *resource* has been identified in a very broad sense as any production factor whose consumption occurs within activities. The notion of a resource can be considered primary or final in the sense it can not be refined within the model.

Accepting that every Resource, Activity and Process operates depending on the

Figure 1. The Executor-Controller-Coordinator

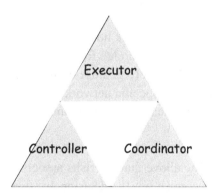

competence, authority and mission which is assigned to do, we individually describe and define each of them by means of a "triangle" consisting of three basic roles. These roles may be viewed as the primary assignments that characterize and give life to a Resource, Activity or Process and eventually to a business operation.

More specifically, each networked enterprise activity may be described in terms of an operational synthesis of the following three roles, organized in a triangle as shown in Figure 1:

- *Executor*, which is responsible for carrying out "basic" activities on the various resource types and has the ability to implement assigned jobs;
- *Controller*, which is responsible for applying performance measurements (set by the coordinator) on the executor and represents the ability of the entity (i.e. a resource, an activity or a process) to be kept in the boundaries that are defined by the coordinator;
- *Coordinator*, which is responsible for interfacing with other fractal entities and organisational components and represents the ability of the entity (resource, activity or process) to organise and regulate the assigned jobs.

The above may be viewed as task assignments to be accomplished by an ISC node – using the fractal "algebra" we describe below – to the SubComponents of a lower level node or vice versa. In this respect every process, activity and resource can be defined with the above "triangle" of executor – controller - coordinator tasks, by means of rating its characteristics.

As a result, networked enterprise structures, whether limited to the intra-enterprise context or going beyond this to include inter-enterprise value chain partners, continuously address both sides of the same dilemma, namely:

- Whether a "node" in a particular chain should be given access to information resources and any related functionalities, such as those of a decision making nature, thus empowering a network node to affect a business process;
- Or to exclude that respective "node" from access to information resources and any related functionalities (e.g. those of a decision making nature), thus reducing the impact of that specific network node on the business processes, but also keeping communication and coordination costs (and efficiency levels) lower.

It is easy to see from the above that the risks associated with a suboptimal or "inferior" structure may accompany such a decision. In other words, if a critical node for any particular business process is excluded for business or other reasons, then the decision process will work faster but its quality is likely to be doubtful. Thus an architecture whose service mechanisms are able to take account of such Info Chain trade-offs should bring valuable benefits to the enterprise concerned.

Looking closer at these two master activities to be supported by a chain component, we need to analyse their specifics and – if possible – find commonalities and overlaps. Thus, we may develop a decomposition mechanism of processes into sub-processes (or alternatively decomposition of super-processes into basic processes) - which are then, in turn, analysed into activities. The latter can then be even further analysed into the resources they consume during execution.

Taking a bottom-up view of this chain, we see that sets of different resources ("combinations" of resources) are necessary to "make up" (or realise) an activity, while sets of activities make up a process. The same also holds at this level for sub-processes that make up a higher level, complex process.

Following this path, we can regard the analysis of a business process in the following way when specific objectives must be met within specific constraints, without consuming more than some predefined level of resources:

An overall objective is set for an enterprise activity. This activity may be:

(a)   A core business activity that is:
  ◦   (a1) Either critical for the business, though only carried out once a year, or
  ◦   (a2) One that is concentrated on extremely intensive use and occurs with high frequency, or it may be
(b)   A non-core activity related to administrative issues and aspects (e.g. payroll etc.).

The set objective is initially related to a process or a sequence of processes. These may be provided as defaults which are subject to change, or as initially given fair estimates of previous good practice. The process may be decomposed to a process network, which is further decomposed in the corresponding activity network - thus at some point reaching the resources level (in fact, actually forming the leaf nodes of the process tree).

At this stage, it is straightforward to compute the demand for resources of the various categories. These may or may not lie within the present resource level. If they do not, efforts may be needed to reorganise the process tree so that individual processes get substituted with alternative ones. This results in a lower resource consumption level, which is essential, especially for small companies. Of course, a valid approach is to also try to substitute a resource category with another instance that is of lower cost.

The aforementioned mobility in the network (or tree, if we consider only hierarchical structures concerning decomposition of processes) may now very well be described using the operations of *distribution* and *integration*. We will elaborate on these two operations.

The Concept of "Distribute"

Distribution involves asking neighbouring (or not) Information Supply Chain components to participate in a process or activity. This participation may refer to the inter-enterprise level i.e. Chain components of a manufacturing enterprise participate together in a planning process with those of the company's Suppliers e.g. to handle new orders from the latter. In this case, we can consider the following scenario:

Currently (and, say, for the last 30 years), each time the Warehouse management identifies gaps in its stock, it informs the Supply department about this, and the latter proceeds to issue a new order.

This scenario has proven easy to follow, but usually resulted in sub-optimal inventory policies (or alternatively, inadequate customer service from the company). The company therefore decides to introduce changes – in order to better meet its wider objective of serving its clients with the highest quality levels.

To change effectively, the company must reconsider its Supply Chain policy, by attempting to optimise against some higher level objective. Therefore, resources and constraints must be reconsidered, as the new higher level objective affects wider "buckets of resources" and constraints.

Last but not least, it is obvious that any changes introduced will also affect the company's Suppliers, as they will now have to negotiate with their own clients – or at least exchange additional information with them.

Coming back to the *distribution* aspect, we can see that:

While in the original Information Supply Chain, it was the Warehouse management that identified stock deficiencies to the Supplies dept., and the latter had to transmit

Table 2. Comparison of current and new service situations

	Current situation	New Situation
Processes:	P_A	$P_{A'}$
Activities:	$a_{A1}\ a_{A2}\ a_{A3}\ a_{A4}\ \ldots,\ a_{AN}$	$A'_{A'1}\ a'_{A'2}\ a'_{A'3},\ a'_{A'4}\ \ldots,\ a'_{A'M}$
Resources:	$R_{aA1}\ R_{aA2}\ R_{aA3}\ R_{aA4}\ \ldots,\ R_{aAN}$	$R_{a'A'1}\ R_{a'A'2}\ R_{a'A'3}\ R_{a'A'4}\ \ldots,\ R_{a'A'M}$

a new order to the Suppliers (which might be selected sequentially or otherwise);

Within the new scenario, all Suppliers are provided with access to the company's Warehouse, thus being able to react and submit proposals for new orders. Alternatively, the company might simply provide the Suppliers with a list of required stock numbers for the new order, thus enabling the Suppliers to come back with their bids.

In any case, it is easy to envisage the changes introduced to the Information Supply Chain as being links between the Supply dept. and the Suppliers.

Cost may be equated to consumed resources (i.e. sum of the "above the line"). They could alternatively be thought of as also incorporating actual overheads required to make the transition from the current situation to the new situation.

For instance, it may be that when "opening" an internal-only process to now also include Extranet chain components, we may incur increased time delays. More people are involved and must be informed, and their feedback must be considered and taken into account, etc.

Furthermore, while an "internal" process need not be conducted formally (e.g. possibly only short memos or just a phone call), an increased need now arises to formalise the process, thereby increasing demand on resources that were previously internal-only.

The following may hold in regard to the metrics of Table 2:

- $C(P_{A'}) \gg C(P_A)$
- $E(P_{A'}) \gg C(P_A)$

where C stands for Cost and E stands for efficiency / effectiveness in meeting process objectives. Thus, one simple objective for replacing an old distribution process with a new one is to achieve improved efficiencies either in the process per se or in the wider context in which this process takes place.

It is easy to see that the E "factor" or parameter may:

- Still refer to the resources dimension – e.g. in terms of specifying efficiencies

Figure 2. Replacement of Process P_A by $P_{A'}$

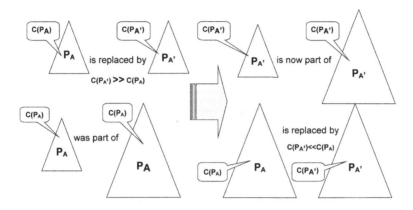

in the way that specific resources are consumed; or else
- Be related to the two further dimensions of the Space of Activities (i.e. constraints and objectives).

An example of the latter case is as follows: We suppose a process PA' replaces PA, as shown in Figure 2, so that at the activity level, collaboration is minimised. Note: This is in contrast to the situation where the change is for distributing the process constituents, so that Extranet members of the company's Supply Chain participate in its execution.

Thus, for an activity A'$_1$ to take place, we only employ a sole human employee (or, if applicable, a sole department), whereas A$_1$ required collaborations between employees as well as between departments. In this way, communication overheads may be heavily reduced, along with communication "efficiencies", as people need now no longer interact.

Clearly this was how systems operated in monolithic enterprise models based on function orientation; one may thus minimise resource utilisation and decrease overall efficiencies in order to meet some higher level objective, such as total customer satisfaction, etc.

Thus, the central point in regard to the distribution operation is the following:

How can a company process be distributed to bear (possibly) higher costs, accompanied by a measurable (and preferably predefined) set of benefits, to result in more efficient addressing of higher-order macro-processes of the company?

Figure 3. The Integration concept

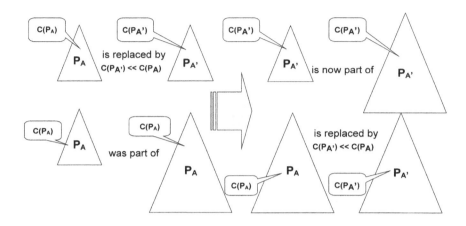

The Concept of "Integrate"

Integration occurs as a complementary pattern to *distribution*. Put simplistically –each time distribution fails, we return to employing integration (and vice versa) (see Figure 3).

More specifically, each time a company's Management identifies failure to meet its specific business process objectives, it may decide to distribute the process originally carried out by some specific Chain component to a wider set of (e.g. neighbouring) Chain components. An alternative approach is to integrate this process within another one.

For instance, let's consider the case of carrying out Product Portfolio Management operations in a manufacturing company. The company may have until now supported extended communications with Suppliers and Customers by using multiple iterations to establish customer needs and preferences for new products or upgrades. Typically, these needs would first be studied by the company's RTD dept., followed by the development of cost estimates in the Production dept. (in collaboration with Sales and Financial depts.).

Finally, the external Suppliers must be contacted to provide their estimates, etc. in order that orders for the manufacture of any externally produced parts may be placed.

The company might have been carrying out this multi-party multi-step activity for some years, but never achieved the ROIs that would justify the resources spent on it. In this respect, one can understand the Management's wish to reduce resources spent on it (actually: to rationalise expenditure). Thus, a multi-cycle Extranet info chain might have to be integrated into a single-cycle Extranet Info chain or some combined Info chain structure undertaken (e.g. multi-cycle Intranet / single-cycle Extranet).

The Reproduction Process for Information Supply Components

It is a widely known fact that fractal units can be formed using the metaphor of a Multiple Reduction Copy Machine (MRCM) (see also the work of (Peitgen et al., 1992)), which is also known as an Iterated Function System which builds, as well, on the self-similarity of each Info Chain component, and - in this respect - each Info Component may be further decomposed into other self-similar entities both at the organizational and the IT level. For a theoretical investigation of the MRCM metaphor, we can refer to the Sierpinski Gasket which explains the building of fractal oriented Components based on the above shown triangle as a starting element, a method that in principle is based on the previously stated "Distribute and Integrate" concept (see Figure 4).

In a similarly well-known diagram, namely the Feigenbaum diagram, a transition to a further level of analysis is represented by a bifurcation. The latter leads to new types of organization, by adding more (and new) types of actors into the working environment, and they usually represent a new (evolved) form of organizing existing activities or adding new activities to a pool of existing ones. In this respect, each bifurcation point represents a distribution (or integration) action; more specifically, each distribution (or integration) action takes place:

- Either for a new process, activity or resource with respect to its assignment to existing or new Info Components
- Or for a new configuration of involved Info Components in coping with existing processes / activities / resources

Having already identified the positioning and role of Info Components in the process grid of corporate (intra- and inter-enterprise) activities, we may use the triangle of executor - controller - co-ordinator for representing processes (or activities) and their evolutionary process development, starting as a single component and evolving into a network of connecting nodes in order to seamlessly integrate the fractal with the Information Supply Chain concept, going through the following steps:

1. In the lowest level processes - activities - resources are identified as the ingredients of the initial components, with the task characteristics of the executor - controller - co-ordinator

Figure 4. The reproduction Mechanism

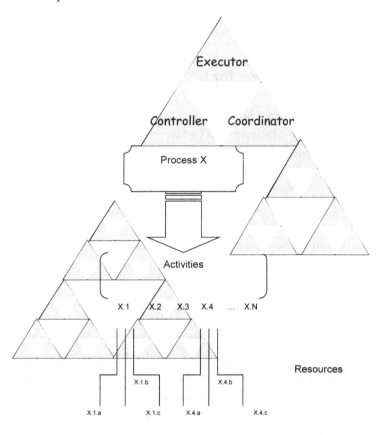

2. Information flows amongst components will be identified establishing initial connections and forming an initial info supply chain
3. By the iteration process the final info supply chain will be resulted from the initial info supply specified as primary and in which the triangles of the three tasks executor - controller - co-ordinator will be identified.

Taking into account the re-production process for generating Information Supply Components based on the Fractal theory and Distribute and Integrate concept, special attention will be concurrently paid to the establishment of a new information and communication framework for the corresponding technical systems structured according fractal guidelines.

In other words informational and communicational relations also have to be reconfigured along with the decomposition and re-synthesis of fractals. As these communicational and informational relations in modern companies and enterprises are heavily supported by means of electronic data processing (hardware, software, networks etc.) which extend from ERP systems down into the shop floor field the corresponding tools must not be rigid and strict and have also to be easily adaptable to the (new) organizational requirements.

This reconfigurability, flexibility and a number of advantages related to systems performance improvement can be realized by means of service software agents. More specifically:

- Enhanced system flexibility while the developed IT realization of the previously described theoretical background detects the most efficient and shorter route in order to distribute all the needed information and services requests.
- increase of systems flexibility by means of reconfigurability as for many kinds of new requirements only the agent has to be changed.
- Easy adaptation of the developed system to an existing network and software backbone of an enterprise when a new working group enters the network.
- Reduced network-load, thus agents evaluate data locally so that transmission of all data is not necessary and as a result instead of many remote accesses one migration and many local accesses are executed;
- In combination with Jini - technology the actual condition of the plant is always included in the agent's decisions;
- No permanent network connection is necessary, e.g. if the ERP is offline the agent still works.

Service agents are considered as autonomous, intelligent programs that move through a network, searching for and interacting with services on the user's behalf. In other words agents gather information and perform some services without the immediate presence of the user. They are adaptive, persistent, goal oriented, collaborative, flexible and proactive.

In this respect and while it is very difficult to design a conventional network that adjusts well to either changing usage patterns over short time scales or to evolving needs and circumstances over the long haul, a mobile agent based system can be reconfigured on the fly, in response to new situations or demands, and with or without human intervention.

Building upon the previously described characteristics of service agents, during the IT-realization phase of the above described theoretical background much attention was paid for achieving the materialization and implementation of an execution "kernel" for service applications, easily integratable with any existing "mainstream" ERP system, as well as with other 3rd party Business Information Systems families.

This execution "kernel" for service agent applications had also to satisfy the need for interconnection, seamless integration and interoperability by supplying different working groups with the capability of enterprise resource and service management related to Intra/Extra Enterprise Processes, and middleware linkage with third party applications.

Supply chain methodology and fractal characteristics are embodied in the developed service agent model for implementing the process oriented working groups and for providing them with the needed functionality for achieving information and service investigation of current system status.

The above theoretical approach as well as its IT realization and implementation in a real industrial environment will be clearly described and understood through the following test case.

IMPLEMENTATION IN AN INDUSTRIAL ENVIRONMENT: THE MINOS CASE

MINOS, a typical example of a Small / Medium-sized Enterprise (SME), following step by step market demands and applying modern programming, organizational and administrative methods of production, evolved its production capabilities to include a wide variety of products. So from its early years expanded its activities towards producing solar water heaters, boilers, solar collectors, kitchen hoods, kitchen air-extractors, stainless steel and synthetic sinks. The company also imports and trades in special types of kitchen hoods, water taps and acrylic bathtubs. See Figure 5 for their home page.

Having to compete with Large- and Giant European enterprises, MINOS addressed the need of developing the necessary means for achieving a desired level of agility for the coordination of corporate (human, information and technology) resources, in terms of exploring and validating novel value creation models. Those models will be based on the utilization of Information Supply Chains, as these are reflected within the context of a fractal company, to handle the rapidly changing context of a dynamic enterprise, where the different corporate value centres (which are in the case of MINOS the various company Departments) dynamically come together in response to or in anticipation of new market opportunities (see Figure 6).

And it was at that specific point that a great challenge arose concerning the realization and implementation of the theoretical Fractal Company background in a real industrial environment aiming to the establishment of an intra-enterprise context that would enable processes-orientation and promote the conversion of a function-oriented grid to a process-oriented. At the same time MINOS intra and inter enterprise navigation of business flows would be supported in a way that effective

Figure 5. MINOS Web site

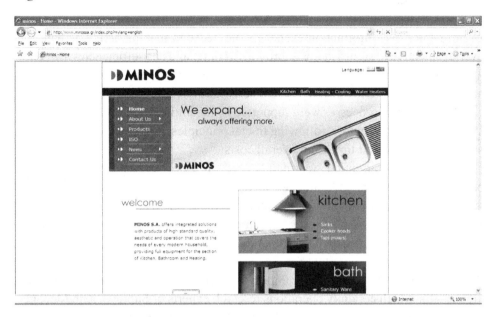

and efficient co-ordination of intra- and inter-enterprise data, information exchange, decision making and processing activities would be promoted.

Figure 6. Models of the different types of sinks available

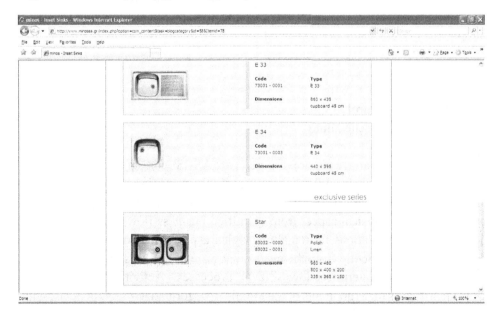

In this respect within the context of the industrial MINOS test case was developed a support system for its bidding and tendering operations that efficiently co-ordinated its intra-enterprise information exchange and decision making activities with the overall objective of significantly improving its time- and cost-efficiencies. MINOS, in the context of a restructuring or reengineering exercise, defined specific bidding processes adapted to the different characteristics of its non-standard products.

These different processes were supported by the implementation of an appropriate organizational structure, following fractal principles, and specific tools, in order to reduce process lead times and overall costs.

The focus and attention was mainly paid on a non standard product's order process, from the moment that a customer formulated a Request for a product till the creation of its Bill of Order, that resulted to the formalization of an Information Supply Chain that took place after a number of cascaded information transformations that formed the respective scale of information evolution.

Something that is important for the reader to take into account is that our team was not called by the customer for improving their supply chain management techniques – for which certainly operations research experts or Supply Chain Management specialized professionals would be needed. We were asked to improve the information supply services as a step towards the improvement of the corporate operations. As one of the early readers of the manuscript commented on this point, 'problems of supply chain are not merely from information services but just-in-time and / or zero inventories'. However, our engagement in the case was solely from the information services perspective.

In the initial state the system was implemented in way that comprised four intra-enterprise interaction cycles, each of which had the capability to communicate with Suppliers and / or Customers on a need-to-do basis, namely for:

- Financial Credit Control
- Inventory Stock Control
- Production Control
- Production Re-scheduling

In order to get the above picture (Figure 7) of "AS-IS" current enterprise's physical implementation, physical flows amongst MINOS "traditional" departments that participated in the specific process were identified (documents, invoices, e.t.c.). Then by removing the physical aspect from identified business flows and "traditional" department's constellations, the remaining logical aspect depicted what was made by the system, independently from the means that were used for its implementation.

At this stage in enterprises lowest level, Processes - Activities and Resources were identified as the ingredients of the initial "to be formalized" components, with

Figure 7. MINOS intra-enterprise interaction circles

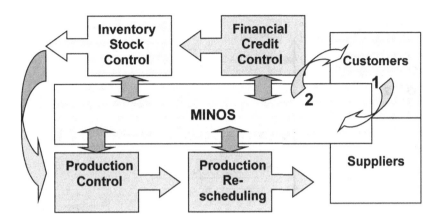

the task characteristics of the executor - controller and co-ordinator while at the same time information flows amongst those pre-components have been identified establishing the initial connections and forming an "early" info supply chain (see Figure 8).

Taking also into account the requirement's specification derived from the realized requirements analysis, as well as present system inefficiencies, next step dealt with the transformation of the current (situation as is) to the desired (situation to be) implementation by specifying, designing and realizing, in a conceptual way, information supply chains and routes, as well as, the types of navigation activities that will take place across the new organisational context and for e.g. production planning tasks.

It is at this stage that we employ the framework presented in chapter 3 by carrying out the foreseen Service Analysis using SAM and its four constituent submodels in terms of:

- Recognizing the service environment,
- Linking the envisaged service with the organizational infrastructure,
- Validating this with corporate goals and strategy and finally
- Carrying out an assessment exercise

and then proceeding to the synthesis phase and commiting to any of the two types of the new service implementation (top-down or bottom-up),

More specifically as it is shown in the following figure, by tracking down information flows amongst ISC nodes "traditional" departments constellations were

Figure 8. MINOS Information Supply Chain

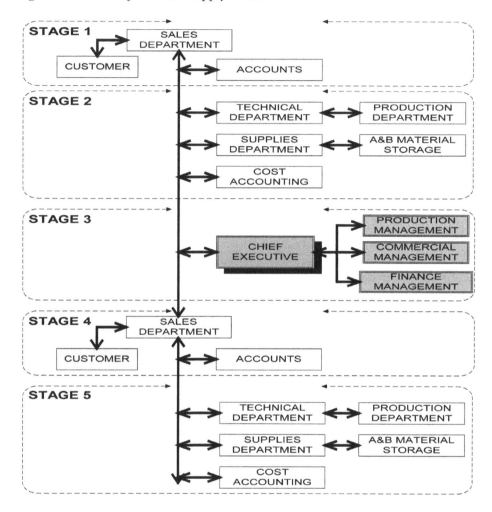

identified due to their repeated appearance. This way five processing Stages were formalized which, in turn, enclosed three bi-dimensional entities, being the MINOS ISC Components composed by Fractal Units that were reside either in the same (pre-Component A and C) or in different (pre-Component B) "traditional" organization levels mixing together structural and behavioural organizational features (see Figure 9).

This approach drove the overall process towards, via the delineation of (primary and secondary MINOS) Components within the Information Supply Chain, to the reformation of its environment establishing processorientation in the intra- and interenterprise activities.

Figure 9. MINOS Information Supply Chain Component's Identification

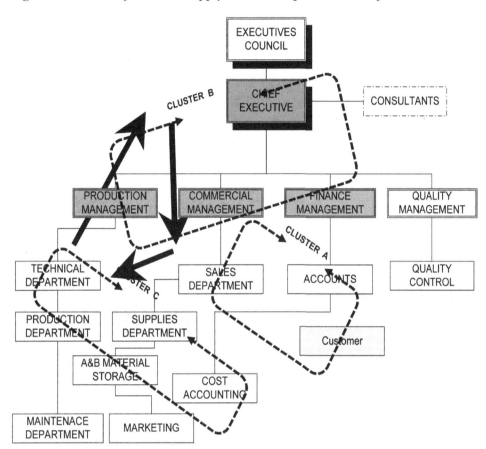

During the phase that fractal oriented Components (nodes) of the (inter and intra enterprise) Information Supply Chain were identified via the reproduction process, issues related to the dilemma of whether a "node" in a particular chain should be given (or not) access to information resources and to functionalities of decision making nature, were manipulated by the combined use of the ECC triangle and Distribute and Integrate concept (see Figure 10).

The result of this reproduction process is the schematisation of the bellow depicted structure that represents the identified MINOS Primary and Secondary Components embodying fractal characteristics, positioned within the enterprise's Information Evolution/Supply Chain, as well as, the communication pathways used for exchanged information Navigation.

Finally the IT realization of the identified framework of Fractal oriented Components that formulated MINOS Information Supply Chain, was achieved by the

Figure 10. MINOS Component-based Information Supply Chain

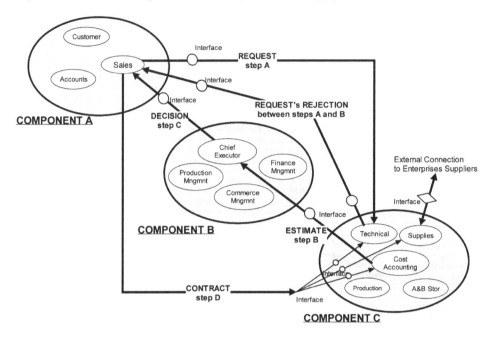

adaptation and embodiment of service agents technology in an adaptive, persistent, goal oriented, collaborative, flexible and proactive Information System.

This picture is reflected in the following qualitative aspects, regarding the *Before* and *Now* situations for the case of MINOS as well as environmental requirements and impact of it's internal structure (see Table 3).

In the world of business, changes in the working environment of enterprises are now driven by the needs of industry to respond in an agile manner to market forces, such as customer demands, increased competition and shifting patterns of global trading, etc. This also requires a clear identification and redeployment of traditional business functions; a major challenge for companies in that respect is the integration of organisation structures, advanced information and communication technology and people. There also remains a need for greater understanding of how enterprises will operate in a "shared data / information / knowledge environment", through distributed working approaches and based on the paradigm of an Information Supply Chain.

Furthermore, IT actors will need assistance to invest technologically intensive resources in the research and development of those essential building blocks that will form the new evolutionary Information Society services of the enterprise world.

More specifically, the central challenge faced by a networked enterprise is the implementation of flexible, service-oriented and time-variant co-operation models.

Table 3. The Before and Now situations for the case of MINOS

Before	Now
Demand is getting the central focus of the company	Harmonisation of the supply procedures is given priority
Info chain is mainly oriented to facilitate better / faster / etc. customer serving	Info chain is mainly oriented to facilitate enhancement in low cost / low price / low risk inflow supplies
Production and sales are treated as a 2-person game, while supplies only viewed as a operational constraints set	Production and sales take into account supplies inflow and price issues, thus being considered as a sub game of the costs of supplies minimisation game (or alternatively, supplies risk minimisation, etc.)
Tendency for single thread forwarding of information	Tendency for process parallelism through multi-thread forwarding of information
Strict distinction between synchronous and asynchronous activities	Heuristic and self adapted selection of the synchronous or asynchronous modes
Task execution bases mainly on predefined task routes at design time	Task execution bases on scenarios and practices that have been devised during run-time
Same as above	Task execution is affected by performance measures and operative metrics during run-time
Participation / involvement / role assignment in the information supply chain was strictly defined and did not change easily	Participation / involvement / role assignment in the information supply chain is loosely defined and changes as the result of quantitative yardsticks

As a result, our work in the project concerning dynamic change in the structure of info supply chains by the adoption of the fractal concept in terms of building super- and sub-structures (i.e. the various higher- and lower-level fractal info supply components). It is important for the created structures to be able to modify their formation dynamically as time goes by and as various patterns fade in or out (e.g. in the way supply chain partners are modifying their behavior, etc).

In this respect, work carried out within project's context aims to the establishment of a set of concepts enabling enterprise integration amongst distributed organizations that reside within heterogeneous IT environments resulting to the incensement of enterprises rapid responsiveness and ease in adaptation to environment's alternations. The latter will be either supported or occurred both at enterprises organizational and IT levels taking into account the related management systems of enterprise's partners (e.g., purchasing, orders, design, production, control, resources, personnel, materials, quality, etc.).

REFERENCES

Laudon & Laudon. (1997). *Management Information Systems.* Englewood Cliffs: Prentice Hall.

Nevis, E. C. (1987). *Organizational Consulting: A Gestalt Approach.* Cleveland, OH: Gestalt Institute of Cleveland Press.

Paolucci, M., Kawamura, T., Payne, T. R., & Sycara, K. (2002). Importing the Semantic Web in UDDI. In *the Proceedings of the E-Services and the Semantic Web workshop.*

Peitgen, H. O., Jurgens, H., & Saupe, D. (1992). *Chaos and Fractals: New frontiers of Science.* Berlin: Germany: Springer Verlag.

Warnecke, H. J. (1983). *The Fractal Company: A Revolution in the Corporate Culture.* Berlin: Germany Springer-Verlag.

Chapter 6
Services and the Workplace

How our workplaces are formed and shaped with respect to our conceptualization and understanding of services? How organisations can be characterized, affected and marked through their idea of services? Workplace are considered as open learning factory – open to the communities they belong to, to the markets they operate for and to the employees, customers and contractors of all types they interact with. How can all the new learning items be capitalised and transformed into knowledge assets for the companies and the employees? How can the use of a Learning Assets Management system like the CARAMBOLA concept we present be used for improvement of all aspects of service planning, implementation and operation?

The value that an organisation – or the society at large – attributes to services in general is representative of the organisation (respectively: the society) itself.

This chapter provides information that is complimentary to this of Chapter 10 regarding the culture of services. Whatever the context of a service, this does not exist in vacuo: it is provided by people who are working in an organisation to customers that are part of a more or less structured part of the society. Ethics and

DOI: 10.4018/978-1-60566-683-9.ch006

moral values that dominate in the society should be expected to affect directly any type of services under consideration.

Why should an organisation provide value-for-money or high quality services while the rest of the society is not following this path?

Even the most ambitious enterprise that treats its service portfolio as an inexpendible source of value across a long time horizon shall face the reality in terms of recruiting people for its service lines from a pool of not-well educated staff members, with low or non-existing motivations. We like to think about highly skilled service professionals who staff any position in the service sector but the reality is totally different: huge masses of lowly-skilled people who have never been checked for their competencies and capacities in providing even some basic level of a service.

One may consider this as subject of a sociological analysis but when viewing things from within a holistic perspective, this is exactly what is sought: any assumption that shall be exercised for the planning or the design of a new service needs to be grounded on the wider context of the actors and stakeholders who constitute the big picture around the service itself. Saying this, one needs to see that the same pool that provides the workers for a service line provides also the customers. If the latter are not used in receiving high quality services, then it will be easy to satisfy their needs and demands in a suboptimal way with less competent employees.

Of course, this brings us close to facing the following idiosyncrasy for services in the digital age: a company can operate in country X or region Y while having selected for providing its services to country A or region B respectively. The reason for doing this may stem from some opportunity that relates with economic efficiencies (such as lower labour costs for acquiring your personnel in country X or higher profit margins for acquiring your clientele from country).

There are numerous well known and nowadays a bit saturated examples to describe the above cases: China and India, Ireland and the countries of the Eastern Europe. The bitter reality is that although in many cases you can find cheaper personnel, this does not mean that it is equally satisfactory and shall help one's business to nourish.

Another factor that we erroneously tend to leave outside our analysis is that the societies that offer an opportunity to companies and ventures for acquiring their personnel from are transforming themselves with extremely fast pace and are less predictable and highly volatile. This means that it is becoming more difficult to establish a service line today as tomorrow most or all of the people you hired may have left to work for someone else who pays a slightly better price for their services. The equivalent for this phenomenon holds also for the customers: they may leave you for another service provider who provides something that looks better though after a closer examination may not fulfil its promises.

This means that a company faces a real dilemma: is it worth to build something that will rely on ethical values of customer and employee loyalty, when both of these parts are not exhibiting any from their side? And where should one draw the bottomline?

Wikipedia addresses the question whether the glass is half empty or half full, which is "a common expression that is used rhetorically to indicate that a particular situation could be a cause for:

- Optimism (half full),
- Pessimism (half empty),
- Realism ("that depends on whether you are pouring or drinking"),
- Functionalism (twice as large as it needs to be), or
- As a general litmus test to simply determine if an individual is an optimist or a pessimist.

The purpose of the question is to demonstrate that the situation may be seen in different ways depending on one's point of view and that there may be opportunity in the situation as well as trouble".

In our given context, any attempt to find a satisfactory answer relates to our individual perceived degree of information asymmetry.

Information asymmetry is defined as this condition in which at least some relevant information is known to some but not all parties involved in a transaction (in our case it may be the planning or the implementation of a new service) or, in general, in a business relationship. Information asymmetry is regarded as a main reason to cause markets to become inefficient, since all the market participants do not have access to the information they need for their decision making processes. The most obvious case of information asymmetry in regard to our study is this of having people of company A examining their moves with respect to company B service policy, while they have a very limited or even defective knowledge on company B actual picture.

Though in many decision-making activities information asymmetry is an inherent problem, in the service world it is highly common that participants are modelled to support at each time either the integration of a given service entity, or alternatively its distribution or provision.

Some years ago I came to the idea of a Learning Assets Management to support novel methods for corporate Intangibles Assets Accounting. As the title of the Chapter is Services and the Workplace, the reader may wonder why should the author talk about learning here? Workplace is an open learning factory – those companies that have for some reasons (due to their inherent people's culture or due diligence or both) recognised this were favourably positioned in their markets. The workplace is a 24 times 7 learning factory – produces new learning patterns, new learning products and new learning services. Unfortunately many of us lack the spiritual dexterity to capitalise on this.

Problem: Employees do learn in their organizations. Their motivation to learn largely depends on the rewards they expect to receive from their improved skills, as these result from their learning. Today these rewards are qualitatively assessed, based on human resource management principles, and not reflected in the balance sheets (value) of the organizations. But if the outcome of learning processes could be quantified, and this quantification could result in increased benefits for the employee (salary or otherwise), then the employee would be more motivated to learn, and would also target its learning towards the acquisition of skills that would ensure value to the company.

Furthermore, employee payments would be based on quantified indicators, and become more efficient. Therefore a need to quantitatively assess the outcome of inter-organizational learning processes is apparent. I envision an ICT environment that will register, monitor, and quantify the outcome of inter-organizational learning processes. The proposed system will be linked to the ERP / accounting systems of the organizations, so that the outcomes of the learning processes are reflected in the balance sheets / book value of the organization.

The aim of such an enterprise would be multifold including aspects of all the following dimensions:

- To understand and classify inter-organizational learning processes.
- To assess the outcomes of these processes and develop a matrix of processes / outcomes
- To assess the value of companies based on the outcomes of learning processes and develop a matrix of learning outcomes (processes) / company value
- To create a learning environment that is employee based (the employee in the center) which monitors, follows the progress, and assesses the outcomes of the learning process of the employee
- To link this environment to the ERP / accounting systems of the companies
- To mainstream the project results into international accounting standards

What is it about companies that make them worth many times the value of their recorded assets? What is the nature of additional value that is perceived by the market but not recorded by the company? Why do some companies have a higher market to book ratio than the others? In essence: why are some companies perceived to be more valuable than others?

Stock analysts, the most influential arbiters of corporate value, state that a very significant factor for achieving high value is the quality of investment of companies in their people, accompanied with the necessary corporate organizational and business process infrastructure to exploit their people as a whole (Klein & Hadji-michael, 2003).

The quality of the people of a company is thus an "intangible asset". Intangible assets do not have a direct market value (this is why they are called "intangibles"), but they certainly affect the overall value of the company. The better "quality" the employees of a company have, the larger the value of the company becomes.

But what affects the "quality" of the employees? It should come as no surprise that the "knowledge" of these employees, as this is embedded and utilized within the business processes of their companies, is a representative indicator of such quality. And of course learning increases this knowledge.

Within a company (like in all human settings), learning happens all the time. By definition, all business processes increase the knowledge of the people who are involved in them (at least, involvement increases "experience"). What any company would like to achieve is to understand (and exploit) how business processes create learning outcomes that become permanent and valuable knowledge assets both for the employees and for the company. To put it simply: Employees learn all the time. But what is their learning worth?

Exploring the world of services is extremely close related with learning issues – you cannot survive in the service industry without being competent. Our idea for a learning management system that will monitor the acquisition of knowledge within the company and understand how knowledge increases the competences, skills and productivity of the employees is therefore of utmost importance to support adoption of a service-friendly culture within organisations. It will then guide these employees into increasing their knowledge through the selection of the most effective learning paths, and also guide the companies into the efficient organization of their learning processes.

In the following paragraphs I present results of recent research work which I gave the code name Carambola which is the acronym for what we consider as a *C*orporate *A*ccounting *R*esearch *A*iming to the *M*anagement and *B*uilding *O*f *L*earning *A*ssets. One can ask why we chose the name Carambola for our research enterprise? There is an interesting part that deals partially with etymology and partially with the semantics of the term. The story has as follows…

Carambola (Averrhoa carambola) is actually an exotic fruit that comes from Indonesia and Malaysia. The fruit has five corners and is described as star-shaped, and commonly called the Star Fruit. I have deliberately chosen Carambola for the acronym of this research methodology, as this fruit carries several semantic and semiological parallels with the addressed field. In Table 1, I have collected most qualities of the fruit that I think fit well to the context of the presented research approach.

For those interested to learn more about the Carambola fruit you may find useful

Table 1. Fruit analogy: Carambola in its literal meaning and in the metaphorical world

Carambola (the fruit) properties	Analogies with the addressed issues in the methodological approach
Very crisp and juicy and a refreshing taste.	It aspires to bring together concerns and attempts that companies and individuals are ready to support and engage themselves with.
May be yellow to green, depending on the variety.	Not all implementations should look the same or be the same. It is normal to expect variations in the adoption styles and the relevant functioning processes.
Yellow fruit tend to be more acid in flavour, and the green ones sweeter.	Same as above with the processes, the results shall also differ as some companies will deploy Carambola for increasing their competitiveness in the markets by getting most out of their employees, while some others may use it as a leverage for trading their immaterial (intellectual) assets by means of targeted mergers or acquisitions.
It is a small tree with attractive foliage, produces large quantities of fruit and is recommended for the home orchard.	Independently on the size of an organised corporate environment, the outputs and results of the learning process can outflank stakeholders' expectations.
Young trees need protection from cold wind.	Same holds for any new attempt to create a new source of corporate or individual-level value: the environment is not always supporting or encouraging and the necessary means need to be reserved for helping the growth process.
Only light pruning is required.	Thorough supervision and cautious monitoring needs to follow each step of the learning process.
Carambola trees will flower several times a year, with a heavy crop over summer.	The fruits of intellectual and knowledge assets can flower several times and under many different circumstances.
Fruit change colour slightly when they are ready for picking, but the best check for ripeness is to eat one and see how sweet the fruit is.	No better approach than action-based learning and learning by doing,
Carambola fruits are very fragile and need to be packed carefully.	Knowledge acquired through the learning to become asset of the individual or the company is same as with the fruit, a fragile process.
Often it is picked too green and the taste suffers.	It is critical to know when a learning goal has been met and a learning objective satisfied.
Can be stored in the fridge and will keep for 1-3 weeks.	Similar to the fruit, both corporate as well as individual knowledge assets and learning capacities cannot (and should not) be accumulated but *experienced* and *consumed*.

information and pictures at: http://www.capetrib.com.au/carambola.htm.

THE CARAMBOLA APPROACH

With CARAMBOLA we aim to provide a solution that can be embedded in the business processes and human resources management systems of organizations and which could support the transformation of learning outcomes into permanent and valuable knowledge assets. The approach that we have taken and which leads the structure of the methodology and the interrelationships amongst the different activities follows the sequence:

Problem → Research → Solution → End Products

The idea is to start by proposing a set of research, development and demonstration activities towards a corporate proprietary platform that can motivate company workers to learn and disseminate their acquired knowledge within the company, creating value both for them and for the company. To get there, CARAMBOLA is driven by the discovery of established and successful learning patterns and assets in companies, and by their application in the working environment. CARAMBOLA's goal is for the employee to learn productively and the employer to harvest the learning outcomes and award the employees respectively. Thus learning is guided towards a fruitful symbiosis for both the employers and the organization.

Problem

Companies are investing in their people by motivating them to participate in training or retraining programs, as part of their other core business activities. Incentives may vary, but most companies are aware that they have to invest in their human resources to improve their business cycles and increase their capacities. However, they are not able to exhibit the existence of a traceable process for managing their investments for learning. Furthermore, it is widely accepted[1] that competition is focused not in the prices or the location of production of a product or a service but in the intellectual capital that a company possesses and the means it has organised to deploy it appropriately.

On the other hand, employees do learn in their organizations. Individual workers are aware that the value they carry for their company is not fixed but continuously under negotiation. Therefore, in order to remain attractive they have to invest in themselves and increase their learning and knowledge capital, so that they are able to keep on selling their services to their employer or seek for a new one that can better reward them for their value.

Their motivation to learn largely depends on the rewards they expect to receive from their improved skills. Learning at the workplace is often driven by employees' interest in their work and internal motivation to develop their expertise. However, rewards they expect to receive from their improved skills may also play a role. Today these rewards are qualitatively assessed, based on human resource management principles, and not reflected in the balance sheets (value) of the organizations. But if the outcome of learning processes could be quantified, and this quantification could result in increased benefits for the employee (salary or otherwise), then the employee would be more motivated to learn, and would also target its learning towards the acquisition of skills that would ensure value to the company. Furthermore, employee payments would be based on quantified indicators, and become more efficient. Therefore a need to quantitatively assess the outcome of inter-organizational learning processes is apparent.

Last but not least, an important reason that learning outcomes have not been adequately and quantitatively assessed yet is that until today learning and knowledge management related learning initiatives may have been kept apart from the corporate accounting system.

Research

Our research agenda in CARAMBOLA includes the following topics:

- *Corporate Intellectual Capital vs Individual (worker) knowledge assets:* How can a company record the knowledge assets of its workers? How can synergetic ways be developed that shall guide the interactions between what the two parts offer to each other? And how can amortization of learning investments and knowledge assets become a part of the relevant International Accounting Standards?

- *Corporate Human Resources, ERP and accounting systems vs Corporate Intangible Assets Accounting:* Corporate accounting of intangibles has been mainly treated as a set of activities related more (or solely) with patents, copyrights, trademarks and licensing agreements, and not about the people and the knowledge they carry. Such knowledge can of course be documented into patents, protected with a copyright or expressed as a trademark. CARAMBOLA aspires to provide an integrated approach (methodology + accompanying practices + application platform) to account for intangible assets such as learning and knowledge assets.

- *Interaction and interface of CARAMBOLA platform with the users and positioning within the corporate business process grid and culture:* The

Figure 1. The CARAMBOLA star. Bridging the gaps amongst the different edges of a company's assets and systems

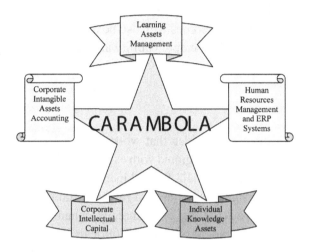

integration of the platform in the corporate culture will be at a central position in the entire endeavour. The exploitation potential of CARAMBOLA largely depends on such an integration, which will be sought by means of documenting a learning asset, configuring a learning portfolio for an individual or for a corporate business unit, etc.

- *Bridging the gaps amongst the different edges of the CARAMBOLA star:* This last item of CARAMBOLA's research agenda is going beyond the medium-term nature of the CARAMBOLA project. More specifically, it aims to put the foundations for new research in the areas that are depicted in Figure 1 at each of the CARAMBOLA star's edges. In the context of the project, this research shall provide a showcase demonstrator (i.e. fully functional for demonstration purposes but not capable for operational use) for a future Learning Assets Management system.

It must be mentioned that the above issues may apply to private, as well as public organizations. In addition, an extension of our agenda may also include learning environments per se, in which case the employees can be paralleled with the students, and the corporate environment with the learning institution. The results of CARAMBOLA are also applicable in this case, where the corporate intangible assets accounting refers to accounting of the outcome of the student learning processes (as opposed to straightforward results from exams or coursework), and these outcomes can also be transferred to the institution's own ERP or e-learning systems. In addition, various other learning assets apart from the traditional lectures and tutorials and their impact on the learning processes will also be examined. As a by-product of our research therefore, its outcomes will also be tested in learning environments per se, in order to demonstrate their applicability in these contexts alongside purely commercial environments.

Solution

CARAMBOLA is driven by the idea that work-process knowledge is generated when theoretical knowledge is integrated with experiential know-how in the course of solving problems at work (Tynjälä & Häkkinen, 2005).

The above statement signifies our area of research and the impact that the proposed work aspires to have in the area of technology-enhanced learning. To achieve this, we propose the development of a successful learning solution for the use of work organizations and by means of integrating research knowledge from different sources (see Tynjälä & Häkkinen, 2005, p. 323):

a. The theories of the learning organisation, organisational learning and learning at work, which provide a general framework for analysing the contexts and possibilities for learning in the workplace.
b. Socio-cultural theories of learning, including both institutionalised (school) learning and workplace learning, which provide conceptual tools for understanding the social nature of learning.
c. Cognitive theories of learning and studies on the development of expertise in the workplace, which enable the examination of learning processes at the level of the individual.

A novelty of our approach that forms another equally important idea of the CARAMBOLA concept is that the integration exercise to take place does not relate with a new or novel type of a learning management system but with a *learning assets management system* that organises the learning processes and monitors the transformation of the learning process outcomes into corporate and individual assets for both the companies and the individual workers.

For coping with this last research issue, we build on knowledge from a fourth area namely:

d. Accounting for Intangible Assets and Intangible Assets Management and Reporting, and current theories for hedging intellectual capital both for individual and for corporate entities.

At a practical level, the CARAMBOLA solution concerns a system that provides corporate Management with a continuous access to the formation of learning assets and with the ability to transform them into corporate knowledge assets, which – with the use of International Accounting Standards – can become an extension of existing ERP, HRM and LMS systems.

Expected End Products

The *major end product* of the entire research endeavour is a Learning Assets Management system (LAM) possibly interoperable with the following:

- Human Resources Management systems like HRnet by HRnet Software Systems and Employee Performance & Talent Management Suite by Halogen Software
- ERP systems and accounting engines (both free / open source and propriatary such as ERP5, GNU Enterprise, WebERP and PeopleSoft from Oracle, mySAP from SAP and ATLANTIS from ALTEC)
- learning management systems (both Open Source as moodle and ATutor and commercial as Saba Software and SAP Enterprise Learning).

In addition to this, one can see the need to come up with a functional methodology for organising the codification and recording of learning assets in the financial, accounting and bookkeeping operations of the companies in compliance with the participating countries legislative frameworks and the International Accounting Standards (IAS).

As third end product of the CARAMBOLA enterprise we may consider a model for integrating pedagogical and organisational approaches by means of the CARAMBOLA lifelong learning as part of the operating corporate organisational development. This model shall build on two drivers:

a. The belief that lifelong learning is used by employees to improve their current, or future, employment prospects i.e. how attractive they are for their employers and for the market in general).
b. The belief that lifelong learning is used by employers as a way of improving their organisational performance.

The focus of this model is the perspectives of people, both employers and employees, who are engaged in lifelong learning, within the European Union. Two sub-models will be put forward:

- The first will reflect employees' approaches to their own learning and self development; this is the CARAMBOLA employee model.
- The second reflects the motivations of employers in promoting lifelong learning opportunities, by engaging their employees in learning related activities and situations in order to improve the organisation's effectiveness; this is the CARAMBOLA employer model.

An extremely critical question is the following: How far is the problem we intend to address being already tackled?

The idea of linking the learning activities with the individual (employee) and corporate (employer) intangible, intellectual and knowledge assets and try to improve the means for documenting and capitalising on them is not new.

We may refer for instance, to the relatively recent (2006) work of Ladyshewsky and Ryan according to which 'the provision of e-learning opportunities is important as the 'achievement of competence…is an ongoing process…given the constant change that takes place in the workplace'. Earlier on, Macfarlane and Ottewill (2001) took the view that the one thing which employees have in common is that 'whatever their level or background is their prime motivation in studying is very probably economic.

Although we do not totally subscribe to this view, which emphasises external motivation of learning, we assume that most people desire to advance in their career and/or improve their performance in their current role, both of which will have a positive impact on their employability and earnings potential. So learning is relevant to their career course and to other factors, which are personal to each individual learner.

Furthermore, the process of knowledge transformation into an asset has already been viewed in the scientific literature as a social process where communities of practice facilitate it through learning activities: Tynjälä and Häkkinen (2005) held that 'communities of practice are informally and naturally formed of people working and interacting together.' A technology-enhanced learning environment can foster a community which, in turn, enhances the learning experience and increases individual motivation; this may even cross cultural and corporate boundaries. Whilst students are intrinsically motivated to study, they are also concerned with the value of the underlying qualification, whether they obtained it by traditional or e-learning methods, and how it will be recognised by their current, or future, employers. This is a model of learning by employees with them engaging in learning or developmental activities, to ensure their continued (and sustained) stay in the job market. It may therefore be argued that employees' intrinsic motivation is relevant to their career advancement.

Back in the mid-1990s, the pedagogical pattern project (www.pedagogicalpatterns.org) started. The goal of the project — and thereby the pedagogical patterns — has been "to capture best practice in a specific domain. Pedagogical patterns try to capture expert knowledge of the practice of teaching and learning. The intent is to capture the essence of the practice in a compact form that can be easily communicated to those who need the knowledge" (Sharp, Manns, & Ecsktein, 2003). It is obvious that a given pedagogical pattern may be useful in one community and inconceivable in another, because the pattern strives to support values accepted in the former community but not in the latter.

An extremely important and innovative point of the research approach in CARAMBOLA is that we don't only perform an analysis amongst a rich set of pedagogical patterns (listed later in this Section), but we also provide an examination of value-based ways for categorizing pedagogical patterns based on their ability to support pedagogical values.

By doing so, the underlying values of the pedagogical patterns become explicit; this is necessary if pedagogical patterns must be shareable.

In the context of CARAMBOLA we define a pedagogical value as a condition that — according to a particular pedagogical theory — stimulates learning. Bennedsen and Eriksen (2003) describe three pedagogical values. They base their position on the pedagogical ideas of Steen Larsen (1998), who has based his work on constructivism (Greeno, Collins, & Resnick, 1996). According to Larsen, effective learning processes meet the following formula: 'You learn something if and only if you work with something of your interest you are almost able to finish up'. When broken down, this formula yields three simple conditions that must be present for effective learning:

1. You have to create something in a process
2. You have to be emotionally involved in your creation
3. This process requires skills that you almost meet

These conditions provide a very simple answer to the very complex question of what is required in order to learn something, an answer that may miss some subtle details but provides good candidates for three categories of pedagogical patterns. These conditions can be regarded as *values*, in the same sense as the Agile Manifesto (Cockburn, 2001) presents four values in software development. The authors of the Agile Manifesto use the term *value* because they believe that the presence of the four agile values will yield better software development; both with respect to the quality of the systems constructed and the process for each project.

Furthermore, the values are not debatcable and are rather to be regarded as of axiomatic nature.

The three values introduced must not be interpreted too rigidly. For instance, it might be necessary to let the students listen for a while in your teaching or read articles as preparation for discussion in order to fulfil the first value. We will refer to these pedagogical values as *Work, Involvement* and *Upper Limit*.

Different pedagogical theories will most likely refer to other values, especially when considering learning as an increasingly meaningful participation in knowledgeable socio-physical contexts. One additional value type is thus *collaboration*. Formulated in the same way as the three pedagogical values mentioned above, this value becomes:

When learning, we prefer:

4.   Collaborating learners over individual working ones

We will refer to this value as *Collaboration* and this fourth value type completes the value set that we shall use in CARAMBOLA. In learning activities collaboration may occur in various forms from short 10-minute exercises built into lectures to project work on a large scale (i.e. *problem-oriented* vs *project-based*).

Several of the pedagogical patterns we promote in the project may be used in order to plan, implement and evaluate collaboration between learners. For this reason we adopt *an activity-based categorization of the selected pedagogical patterns* that should be useful for *learning communities interested in applying pedagogical patterns*.

More specifically we have chosen three categories: *Planning, Performing* and *Evaluating*:

- *Planning:* to work out the details of something in advance, including the establishment of learning goals, a schedule, evaluation criteria, and a sequence of topics.
- *Performing:* to carry through the plan, including lecturing, mentoring, supervision, etc.
- *Evaluating:* the judgement regarding the learners' performance in relation to the evaluation criteria defined in the planning.

These three activities do not necessarily need to be done in a sequential manner, but learners should normally know when they are planning, performing or evaluating. One may argue that every pattern belongs in the *Planning* category, because all activities require *Planning*; but a pattern belonging to the *Planning* category will have a significant impact on the way plans are constructed and outlined. Patterns belonging to the category *Performing* will primary affect the observable learning sessions. Finally, patterns in the *Evaluating* category help learners to assess the relative success of the executed learning activities.

Table 2. Learning phases with respect to pedagogical values

Learning phases Pedagogical value	Planning	Performing	Evaluating
Work			
Involvement			
Upper limit			
Collaboration			

We have chosen these three categories because each one contains several patterns, every pattern belongs to at least one category, and, finally, because we find them useful for practical learning purposes in corporate learning contexts (see Table 2).

The pedagogical patterns that will be available for testing and validation purposes shall be selected from a list of currently available patterns of the Pedagogical Patterns Project (PPP – www.pedagogicalpatterns.org). Such patterns can relate to participants feedback, experience level, grading, self-testing, real work situations, group works, etc.

The main concept is that *not all* pedagogical patterns are appropriate for *different* type of issues, during each of the three *different* learning phases, for *different* individuals and *different* corporate environments and cultures. While for an individual in corporate environment X the best way to acquire a knowledge asset is by having him or her exposed to learning style *Real World Situation*, for some other employee of the same company the most appropriate learning style might be this of *Groups Work*.

So far, systematic assessment of learning outcomes has been mainly carried on in formal education and training, whereas in more informal workplace learning the outcomes tend to be less predictable and more difficult to measure (Hager, 1998). Although formal learning has become more important in workplace as well, the assessment methods are still in their infancy and tailored on ad hoc basis. In the school contexts the most renowned venture of assessment of learning outcomes is the Program for International Student Achievement (PISA) by OECD.

In the venture of assessing learning outcomes at work the first step is to define what should be measured and what are the components of professional knowledge. According to Bereiter (2002) expert knowledge can be classified in the following categories:

1. *Statable knowledge* which refers to declarative knowledge that can be put into some explicit form. Le Maistre and Paré (2006) refer to this type of knowledge with the term *professional content knowledge* and Eraut (2004) with the term

encoded knowledge.

2. *Implicit understanding* which is unstated, tacit knowledge. We acquire implicit understanding through our experience, not through reading from books. That is why it remains implicit. The role of experiential tacit knowledge is very important in high level expertise (e.g., Dreyfus & Dreyfus, 1986).

3. *Episodic knowledge* including memories of different episodes, events, cases and narratives from our past. Research on expertise has shown that much of the reasoning and decisions made in occupational situations is based on repertoires of previous cases.

4. *Impressionistic knowledge* can be seen as extremely vague implicit understanding, and it is expressed in feelings or intuitions. Bereiter (2002, p. 131) refers to a line by a young stockbroker in Walker Percy's *The Movie Goer*: "I woke up that morning with a good feeling about American Motors". A prerequisite for having such feelings is a great amount of experience in the field in question.

5. *Skill* which is often described as procedural knowledge and practical know-how –being able to do things.

6. *Regulative knowledge* consists of self-regulative knowledge which involves meta-cognitive knowledge about one's own ways of doing and thinking, strengths and weaknesses, and more general knowledge involving the principles and ideals which certain professional groups pursue in order to accomplish their work.

Of these forms of knowledge statable knowledge is most easily to be assessed with traditional assessment tools such as paper-and-pencil tests and exams. In recent years, different modes of performance assessment have been developed for evaluating practical skills especially in the context of vocational education and training (e.g. Stenström & Laine, 2006; Baethege et al., 2006). In contrast, informal, implicit and tacit knowledge which we gain through our experience is more difficult to be measured. However, accounts on organisational knowledge creation (e.g. Nonaka & Takeuchi 1995; Nonaka et al, 2006) emphasise the importance of interaction and transformation of different modes of knowledge and explication of implicit knowledge. Therefore, one of the most important challenges for assessing learning outcomes at the workplace is to develop methods which make it possible to explicate and measure intangible learning outcomes. The task becomes even more challenging when we take into account the fact that in high level expertise the different types of knowledge are not separate but tightly integrated into a whole: the deeper the expertise is, the deeper the integration between the forms of knowledge becomes. This follows that assessment tools should be able not only to measure separate skills or pieces of knowledge but also the extent of the integration of different elements of expertise.

In addition to the forms of personal knowledge described above there is also socio-cultural knowledge that is embedded in the tools and practices of social communities (e.g., Bereiter, 2002; Wenger, 1998). This knowledge is often tacit but it can be explicated as well. For example, written rules of action and procedures documented in quality manuals represent explicit socio-cultural knowledge. One challenge for assessing learning outcomes is to define the relationship between the individual knowledge and socio-cultural knowledge.

In recent years, at the European level there have been attempts to analyse the components of vocational and professional competences and develop methods for assessing them. For example, the European Qualifications Framework (EQF http://ec.europa.eu/education/policies/educ/eqf/rec08_en.pdf) presents learning outcomes in three general categories: knowledge, skills and competences (in which the last one refers to the ability to use knowledge, skills and methodological abilities in work or study situations and in personal and professional development). This categorization is far too general for assessing learning outcomes at the workplace and it does not take into account the integrative nature of professional expertise.

A more promising and more detailed framework for assessing learning outcomes at work can be found in the proposal of carrying out a "VET-PISA", that is, a programme for evaluation of learning outcomes in vocational education and training (Baethege et al., 2006). It divides competence domains in three basic categories: cognitive competence, functional competence and social competence. These all can be assessed in the following areas of individual capacities: 1) attitudes, values and perceptions, 2) incentives and motivation, 3) metacognitive strategies, 4) declarative knowledge, 5) procedural knowledge, and 6) strategic knowledge. This categorisation is very close to the component model of expert knowledge by Bereiter described above and can be used as a basis for developing assessment tools for workplace learning. However, what is still missing is the notion of expertise as an integrated whole of these components, which follows that further development of the assessment model is still needed.

Today, e-learning systems provide a wide range of technologies which support learning and teaching. E-learning systems make it possible to learn and teach without respect to time and location. In the simplest case, a web site with static textual documents can be considered as an e-learning system. Users of this system can read training documents which are provided. Also multimedia-documents (for example pictures, videos or audio files) can be included in order to illustrate the training material. The next step is test-modules, which provide multiple testing techniques.

In order to demonstrate complex operations, simulation tools can be integrated in the learning material. These tools visualize the operations for the user and provide interaction possibilities. For example, if complex technologies must be explained, it's easier for the student to understand. Some e-learning systems provide presentation agents which guide the user through a course and direct the interest towards important aspects. Some e-learning systems provide simulations as games (for example business-strategy).

In order to allow the communication between users, modern e-learning systems provide a wide range of tools:

- Chat systems
- Blackboard systems
- Teleconference tools
- Desktop sharing
- Blog- and wiki-systems
- E-mail

Often, the users (students) of an e-learning system, create new content. For example they collect information from the WWW and provide a summary for other course members. In some application scenarios, also mobile clients like PDA or mobile phones can be used to access the learning material.

In most cases, e-learning systems must also provide administration tools.

- Tools for the administration of the system
- Generation of certificate documents for users who have finished a course
- Planning of resources (rooms, meetings)
- Statistical reports (how many users have finished a course, etc.)
- Evaluation of the knowledge of users
- Virtual lecture rooms.

A more structural way to treat e-learning is through learning objects. Learning objects is a concept specified by LOM (the IEEE 1484.12.1–2002 Standard for Learning Object Metadata), which defines a set of attributes of a learning object, including content types, learning object life-cycle, and pedagogical goals. LOM meta-information can be used for annotating learning objects within an e-learning system, in order to include well-structured meta-information of learning resources and (most importantly) to enable syntactic interoperability of learning objects. All the above are more or less the current state of e-learning software systems.

With the main focus of CARAMBOLA being learning in the workplace and building competences in the working environment we examined the state-of-the-art in this specific domain. There are some EU funded projects related to the ideas underlying CARAMBOLA that are worth to examine:

- APOSDLE – learn@work (FP6) http://www.aposdle.tugraz.at/. APOSDLE stands for **A**dvanced **P**rocess-**O**riented **S**elf-**D**irected **L**earning **E**nvironment and it is a software platform and tools that help you learn within the context of your current work and environment. It is based on the triad **work, learn, collaborate**, which means while you are working, APOSDLE provides you with what you need to know about your current task and position in an automated way, while give you guidance for whom you can collaborate and speak to. APOSDLE provides integrated technological support for all three roles a knowledge worker fills at the workplace: the role of the worker, the role of the learner, and the role of the expert.

- MATURE (FP7) http://mature-ip.eu/en/start. MATURE tries to tackle the problem of "…failures of organisation-driven approaches to technology-enhanced learning and learn from the success of community-driven approaches in the spirit of Web 2.0, which have shown that for that agility we need to leverage the intrinsic motivation of employees to engage in collaborative learning activities, and combine it with a new form of organisational guidance." In a few words the main agenda is to create a maturing process for the learning and knowledge assets in an organization in a collaborative way, making them continuously better over time.

- PROLIX (FP6) http://www.prolixproject.org/. The objective of PROLIX is to align learning with business processes in order to enable organisations to faster improve the competencies of their employees according to continuous changes of business requirements. The objectives are:
  a. To shorten the delay between identification of a learning need and the actual learning
  b. To target the learning material to the learner's individual learning style and behaviour
  c. Make available learning 'ad hoc'

Business processes guide the creation of "learning scenarios" (learning processes) which the learner or the organization executes, their performance is measured and feedback is provided for another round of this improvement process.

It is easy to see that there is an abundance of different definitions as to what intellectual capital and intangibles exactly are, which is both useful (one is able to find exhaustive and very limiting definitions of the term) and harmful (since there is no broad consensus what intangibles really comprise, basic definition problems arise, especially for research). The lack of a common terminology causes confusion. For several terms it is unclear whether they are arranged in a synonymous or hierarchical manner, since so far, neither literature nor practice has managed to find a common and clear differentiation. The terms usually found in literature (Schmalenbach, 2005) are:

- Intangible assets
- Intellectual assets
- Intellectual property
- Intellectual capital
- Knowledge based assets
- Knowledge capital

As Bontis (2001) states that this hindrance is due to the embryonic state the research field is still in, many researchers develop their own terminology, and no one is willing to give up one's own nomenclature. This leads to the conclusion it will take a while until the researchers are able to draw from a common terminology (Habersam & Piber, 2003). In the beginning of the major wave of intellectual capital research, many authors defined *intangibles* and *intellectual capital* according to the following equation:

intellectual capital = market value – book value (Edvinsson & Malone, 1997)

Defining the difference between market value and book value as *intellectual capital* is failing since this difference might be attributable to many other factors than "just" intellectual capital. As García-Ayuso (2003) states, there are many influental factors apart from intellectual capital, such as undervalued tangible and financial assets, intangible liabilities in stockholders' equity reflected in stock prices, but not under prudent accounting, and stock prices biased by market anomalies such as the January-effect. Due to these other factors, the "negative" definition of intellectual capital as stated above is rather misleading than helpful.

In addition to that, this definition seems also very "simple", which would not fit to the complexity of the subject of intangibles. Apart from the failed "negative" definition above, we find two ways of defining intellectual capital and intangibles in the literature:

1. Descriptions of the characteristics, or
2. Descriptions of the components of intellectual capital and intangibles.

Since there is no common *positive* delimitation so far, many authors and workgroups rely on describing the nature of intangibles by suggesting categorizations of intangibles and taxonomies, thus working *around* a definition. The question "*What are intangibles and intellectual capital?*" is often replaced by trying to answer "What *categories* of intangibles and intellectual capital are there?". This seems to miss the point since, by providing, for instance, three categories of intellectual capital like human capital and structural capital (Andriessen, 2004, p.60), one still doesn't know the characteristics of the term intellectual capital. It is like asking "What is a car?" and giving the answer "Off-roaders, limousines, lorries and vans!", one still has no idea what a car is. It seems to be more sensible trying to find a definition of the characteristics of intangibles and intellectual capital first in order to know *what* we are dealing with, and defining the various possible elements and components of the terminology afterwards.

Preliminary work has resulted to the sketching of CARAMBOLA's entities, architecture and technologies. Before proceeding we shall provide definitions regarding learning, knowledge and intangible assets.

Intellectual capital has always been present in a company's operations and strategies, but only in the last 15 years it got into focus of research and practitioners alike. The importance of information outside the balance sheet not reflected in traditional financial statements has grown for a company's performance, especially in, but not restricted to knowledge-intensive companies (Epstein & Mirza, 2005). Research and practice has taken up this notion, trying to find and apply different concepts in order to measure and manage intellectual capital internally, and then disclose relevant information about intellectual capital to the capital market in order to attract additional financial resources.

In the context of CARAMBOLA, it is interesting and quite challenging how we suggest to deal with the transformation of *learning outcomes* which are usually treated as *intangibles* into *knowledge assets which are treated as tradable corporate intangible assets.*

The thriving research in the field of intellectual capital and intangibles is manifold and shows a high level of variety, starting at the basic definition level. So far, literature and practice has developed many different attempts to define intellectual capital and intangibles, with no common result (Bontis, 2001). For the purposes of our research in the project, a common definition is needed. Apparently, definitions for intangibles overlap, depending from the viewpoint taken.

From our previous research experiences, perhaps the most successful attempt to define learning related intangibles was the one that Gerhard Kristandl[3] (2006) has made as follows.

Learning Assets:

1. Are non-financial, non-physical, monetary or non-monetary factors, that
2. Have been acquired or internally developed by an organisation or an individual through systematic or not training activities of various types
3. Are held for use in the production or supply of goods, services, rental to others, or administrative purposes
4. Have finite or infinite life

5. Are able to represent a company's combined knowledge, skills and other soft factors
6. Can be presented either as index scores, ratios, or counts
7. May or may not be sold separately
8. Are not represented in financial statements
9. Can be expected to be converted into profits and/or give the company a competitive advantage in its marketplace

If conditions 1 – 7 and 9 are met, and

10. The company has control over the learning outcome
11. The outcome is a result of past events or transactions (e.g. participation in a related research project or a training activity),
12. And the outcome has identifiable costs,

then the *learning outcome* is a *knowledge asset.*

The definition above has of course some limitations that are posed by practical implementation aspects and therefore will need elaborated reality-checks that shall take place during the lifetime of the project and as part of the work that shall lead to the delivery of a 'functional methodology for organizing the codification and recording of learning assets in the financial, accounting and bookkeeping operations of the companies in compliance with the participating countries legislative frameworks and the International Accounting Standards (IAS)'.

In every company both intangible and knowledge assets exist. These can take various forms:

- Papers (that were used as expertise to win contracts or pass proposals)
- Patents
- Trademarks
- Processes
- Services
- Products
- Knowledge, Know-How, Experience
- Capability
- Motivation
- Ability to work in a team
- Educational and Professional Level
- Creativity
- Learning Capability
- Culture

- Workflows
- Established Decision Making System or other related IT systems
- Network
- Copyrights
- Etc.

As mentioned before, in general intangibles are non-physical entities that a) bring revenue into the company and b) can be negotiable as having an established value. In order to meet its objectives, CARAMBOLA assigns a financial value through an accounting credit assignment scheme from company's profits to intangible value. Every intangible can be associated with an "ownership" mapping from the intangible to the employee(s) who participated in its creation. Thus each employee will obtain credit through this network in a process similar to stock markets (the value of the employee can rise and fall based on how much value his or her assets bring into the company over time)

On the other hand employees can create or work on several learning assets:

- Write Technical Reports, Papers, Deliverables, Manuals, Templates, Tutorials
- Make Presentations (slides, audio & video)
- Create internal Web 2.0 content (wikis, blogs, forums)
- Create content as Learning Object Modules (LOM) in a e-learning environment
- Create dummy/example Problems (for a trainee to solve)
- Create their Solutions for demonstration purposes
- Participate in Collaborations or Groups
- Have internal seminars or participate in external conferences
- Obtain certifications
- Participate or create Standardized Procedures of Learning (i.e. a trainee program)
- Create a compilation of web-links related to a certain problem or area
- etc.

The above (among others) constitute a learning assets repository for the company. Again as with intangibles a mapping can be created from the learning asset to the user who has contributed in its creation. To give incentives in order to create quality learning assets credit can also be attributed to a user who created a learning asset that was used by another employee who in turn created an intangible asset.

Both the intangible assets and the learning assets can be instantiated (i.e. an instantiation of an intangible asset is a web-service used in several products of a company and an instantiation of a learning asset is a Learning Object Metadata (in short: LOM) for *"Beginner Java Programming"*). The instantiations of both assets can be semantically annotated with tags in a fashion relevant to Web 2.0 content through an ontology related to the company and its respective environment.

In the duration of the "worklong" learning the learning assets used and rated by the user in order to create intangible assets are logged in the CARAMBOLA system. Using data mining, modeling and semantic information retrieval techniques on the logs and the assets repository we can:

- Identify successful learning processes (i.e. by recognizing pedagogical patterns)
- Identify successful learning assets
- Identify missing or incomplete learning assets
- Correlate learning assets with certain business and learning processes and provide guidance in relation to the characteristics of the employee (for example if a trainee is involved in a Java project, provide him with learning assets associated with Java)

Thus the CARAMBOLA system will be capable of:

- Providing an incentive to learn in order to create intangibles assets
- Guiding learning through exploitation of successful learning patterns
- Facilitating and giving incentives for the dissemination of know how
- Organizing learning and intangible assets (ontology, repository, GUI presentation)
- Assigning a quantitative value to each employee translated in the month salary or otherwise
- Assisting in learning in parallel with working in the company

The CARAMBOLA system architecture is depicted in Figure 2.

With CARAMBOLA we aimed to seize a unique opportunity of preparing the ground towards the standardization of the procedures and practices that shall be subject of research within the project lifetime. At a practical level, the CARAMBOLA solution concerns a system that provides corporate management with a continuous access to the formation of learning assets and with the ability to transform them into corporate knowledge assets, which – with the use of International Accounting Standards – can become an extension of existing ERP, HRM and LMS systems. Such a system will have the full support of international accounting standards organizations, such as the International Accounting Standards Board (IASB) that is an independent accounting standard-setter based in London, UK.

Figure 2. CARAMBOLA system architecture

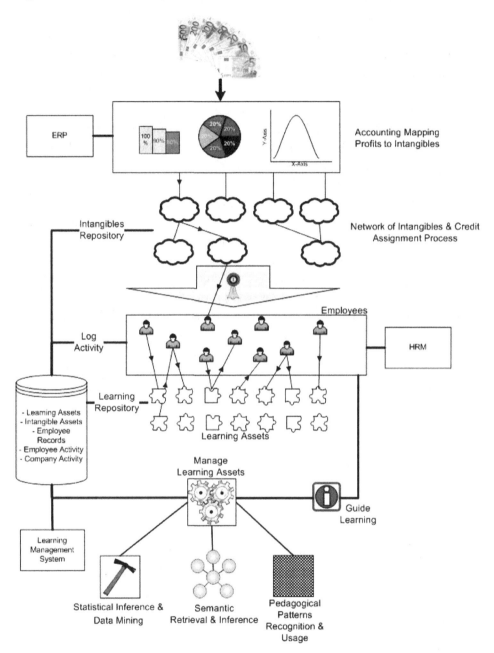

Currently the IASB is contemplating undertaking an active project on identifiable intangible assets (that is, excluding goodwill) jointly with the FASB (Financial Accounting Standards Board), the designated private sector organization in the US that establishes financial accounting and reporting standards.

A project proposal was developed and considered by the IASB at its meeting in December 2007. The Board acknowledged the importance of addressing the accounting issues relating to intangible assets, noting concerns with current requirements that lead to inconsistent treatments for particular types of intangible assets depending on how they arise. However, the Board noted that properly addressing the accounting for intangible assets would impose a large demand on the Board's limited resources. Instead, the Board expressed a desire that the research work begun and brought back when developments would enable the Board to add it to its active agenda. Consideration would be given to determine the scope and a process for continuing such research work.

Pending the outcome of further discussions about the scope for continuing the research work, there is a range of possible scopes and objectives that could be adopted for an Intangible Assets project. The scope could be one, some or all types of intangible assets. The objective could be recognition, measurement and disclosure or disclosure-only. The project proposal considered different scopes and objectives, including a comprehensive recognition-based project.

In relation to comprehensive recognition, the IASB and FASB decided that the agenda of a research proposal should address:

- The initial accounting for identifiable intangible assets other than those acquired in a business combination (with a particular focus on, but not limited to, internally generated identifiable intangible assets); and
- The subsequent accounting for all identifiable intangible assets,

both of which are part of CARAMBOLA's research agenda.

REFERENCES

Achtenhagen, F., Arends, L., Babic, E., Baethge-Kinsky, V., Weber, S., & Baethge, M. (2006). *PISA-VET. A feasibility study*. Stuttgart, Germany: Franz Steiner Verlag.

Andriessen, D. (2004). *Making sense of intellectual capital: designing a method for the valuation of intangibles*. Burlington, MA: Butterworth-Heinemann.

Baethege, M., Achtenhagen, F., Arends, L., & Babic, E. Baethge-Kinsky, & Weber, S. (2006).

Bennedsen, J., & Eriksen, O. (2003). Applying and developing patterns in teaching. In *Proceedings of the 33rd ASEE/IEEE Frontiers in Education Conference* (pp. T4A-2 – T4A-7). Champaign, IL: Stipes Publishing.

Bereiter, C. (2002). *Education and mind in the knowledge age*. Mahwah, NJ: Erlbaum.

Bontis, N. (2001). Assessing knowledge assets: a review of the models used to measure intellectual capital. International Journal of Management Reviews , 3(1), 41–60. doi:10.1111/1468-2370.00053

Cockburn, A. (2001). *Agile software development*. Boston: Addison Wesley.

Conceptual Framework For Professional Education Programs. Accessed at http://www.education.eku.edu/fact_book/PECAP/coe_ncate/conceptual_framework.htm

Dede, C. (2005). Planning for neo-millennial learning styles. EDUCAUSE Quarterly , 1, 7–12.

Dreyfus, H. L., & Dreyfus, S. E. (1986). *Mind over machine: The power of human intuition and expertise in the era of the computer*. Oxford, UK: Blackwell.

Edvinsson, L., & Malone, M. S. (1997). *Intellectual Capital: Realizing your company's true value by finding its hidden brainpower*. HarperCollins: New York.

Epstein, B. J., & Mirza, A. A. (2005). *IFRS 2005 – Interpretation and Application of International Financial Reporting Standards*. Hoboken, NJ: John Wiley & Sons, Inc.Eraut, M. (2004). Transfer of knowledge between education and workplace settings. In H. Rainbird, A. Fuller & A. Munro (Eds.), *Workplace learning in context* (pp. 201-221). London: Routledge.

Eustace, C. (2000, October). *The intangible economy impact and policy issues. Report of the European High Level Expert Group on the Intangible Economy.* Luxembourg: European Commission Report.

García-Ayuso, M. (2003). Factors explaining the inefficient valuation of intangibles. Accounting, Auditing & Accountability Journal , 16(1), 57–69. doi:10.1108/09513570310464282

Greeno, J. G., Collins, A. M., & Resnick, B. (1996). Cognition and learning. In D.C. Berliner & R.C. Calfee (Eds.), *Handbook of educational psychology* (pp. 15 – 46). New York: Prentice Hall.

Habersam, M., and M. Piber (2003). Exploring intellectual capital in hospitals: Two qualitative case studies in Italy and Austria. European Accounting Review , 12(4), 753–779. doi:10.1080/0963818030310001628455

Hager, P. (1998). Understanding workplace learning: General perspectives. In D. Boud (Ed.), *Current issues and new agendas in workplace learning* (pp. 31-46). Springfield, VA: NCVER.

Johnson, R. B., and A. J. Onwuegbuzie (2004). Mixed methods research: A research paradigm whose time has come. Educational Researcher , 33(7), 14–26. doi:10.3102/0013189X033007014

Klein, M. U., & Hadjimichael, B. (2003). *The Private Sector in Development: Entrepreneurship, Regulation, and Competitive Disciplines*. Washington, DC: World Bank Publication.

Kristandl, G. (2006). *Trying to define intellectual capital: a review of terms, definitions, and suggestions, and the attempt to find a positive definition of intellectual capital, intangibles and intangible assets.* 1st International Conference on Accounting and Finance (ICAF), 30 August – 1 September 2006, Thessaloniki, Greece.

Ladyshewsky, G., & Ryan, F. (2006). *Peer Coaching and Reflective Practice in Authentic Business Contexts: A Strategy to Enhance Competency in Post-Graduate Business Studies in Authentic Learning Environments in Higher Education.* Hershey, PA: Information Science Reference.

Larsen, S. (1998). *Den ultimative formel for effektive læreprocesser.* Hellerup, Denmark: Steen Larsens Forlag.

Le Maistre, C., & Paré, A. (2006). A typology of knowledge demonstrated by beginning professionals. In P. Tynjälä, J. Välimaa & G. Boulton-Lewis (Eds.), *Higher education and work: Collaborations, confrontations and challenges* (pp. 103-113). Amsterdam: Elsevier.

Macfarlane, B., & Ottewill, R. (Eds.). (2001). *Effective learning and teaching in Business and Management.* London: Institute for Learning and Teaching in Higher Education, Kogan Page.

Nonaka, I., & Takeuchi, H. (1995). *The knowledge-creating company: How Japanese companies create the dynamics of innovation.* New York: Oxford University Press.

Nonaka, I., G. von Krogh, and S. Voelpel (2006). Organizational knowledge creation theory: Evolutionary paths and future advances. Review paper. Organization Studies , 27(8), 1179–1208. doi:10.1177/0170840606066312

Schmalenbach, G. (2005). Working group accounting and reporting of intangible assets, 'corporate reporting on intangibles.' . Schmalenbach Business Review , 2(Special Issue), 65–100.

Sharp, H., M. L. Manns, and J. Eckstein (2003). Evolving pedagogical patterns: The work of the pedagogical patterns project. Journal of Computer Science Education , 13(4), 315–330. doi:10.1076/csed.13.4.315.17493

Sigman, M., and C. D. Gilbert (2000). Learning to find a shape. Nature Neuroscience , 3, 264–269. doi:10.1038/72979

Slavin, R. (1995). Research on cooperative learning and achievement: What we know, what we need to know. Contemporary Educational Psychology , 21(1).

Stenström, M.-L., & Laine, K. e. (2006). *Towards good practices for practice-oriented assessment in european vocational education.* Occasional Papers 30. Jyväskylä: University of Jyväskylä. Institute for Educational Reseach.

Tynjälä, P., and P. Häkkinen (2005). E-learning at work: theoretical underpinnings and pedagogical challenges.' . Journal of Workplace Learning , 17(5/6), 318. doi:10.1108/13665620510606742

Upton, W. S. (2001), *Business and Financial Reporting, Challenges from the New Economy.*, Special Report FASB.Wenger, E. (1998). *Communities of practice. Learning, meaning and identity.* Cambridge, UK: Cambridge University Press.

ENDNOTES

[1] See for instance (Ellis, 2004) as well as the (Bornemann et al., 2007) and (Nazari et al., 2007).

[2] For an exhaustive presentation of approaches defining intellectual capital by adding up its components, see (Andriessen, 2004).

[3] See also the work of G. Kristandl aiming at 'Trying to define intellectual capital: a review of terms, definitions, and suggestions, and the attempt to find a positive definition of intellectual capital, intangibles and intangible assets'.

Chapter 7
Service Economics

Here the author examines the economies of services as well as matters related to service economics. Do the same or similar laws that drive the other fields of the non-services economy also govern the service-based economy as well? How can wealth matters be addressed in the services field with application of well-know economics patterns? An improved accounting method for project management accounting is presented based on the idea of value centres next to the well-known concepts of cost centres and profit centres. The method can be of direct use for value based management purposes that is of central importance for all service-related activities (improvement / optimisation, planning, deployment, etc.).

When facing the introduction of a new service, an organisation tends to think about budgets and cost issues. It is obvious that a new service shall need money for its implementation and after its introduction a further increase in costs shall appear that relates with the people who will provide the service and the equipment that will be used for the delivery of a service.

.

DOI: 10.4018/978-1-60566-683-9.ch007

All these may form part of any syllabus in business administration departments and business schools in the world. In addition to this, sophisticated methods for accounting of services (cost-based, analytical or else) may be subject of any standard teaching plan for both undergraduate, graduate or professional development courses.

What usually lies outside the syllabus material and the courses are questions like the following:

- How much is the cost of a bad service?
- How can we ration for a service quality gradient that relates an increase (a decrease also) in the budget of a service with both qualitative and quantitative parameters?
- How better is it to not introduce or upgrade a service than do it in a maliciously suboptimal or bad way?
- What exactly defines the economy of a service?

Especially regarding the last question, we tend to think that for (what we tend to think as) a 'conventional' manufacturing company that regards its mission as the production of *tangible* goods, the existence of *intangible* services both at the internal level (e.g. from one corporate department to another) or to other third entities (like the customers or suppliers) is a burden and a clear and clean overhead. This is certainly a mistake – if not a serious delusion that does not help the company and its people at all.

But also if we focus on a 'conventional' service organisation like an insurance company, where the business is of intangible nature, again there there are big chances for a similar attitude: we sell (intangible) insurance contracts like the others sell (tangible) manufacturing goods. Period.

Any attempt to make people think out of their well-defined suffocating service boxes is difficult. How does a simplification in the clearing or reimbursement process for customers improve their sales for products to them? Or to new customers? Hmmmm. This question is received with hesitance, regarded as tangentially irrelevant or marginally contributing to (what they think as) their core business.

How easy is it to navigate their Web site and corporate portal seems as an aesthetics issue, related to the desirability of their image to the masses of innocent future victims – sorry customers, but not related to core aspects of their business such as the sales or the rationalisation of costs per customer.

Any attempt to teach a culture of connectedness amongst different issues seems to them as an unwanted ritual introduced by some uncalled shaman. Though this is exactly the bottomline of a holistic approach: to relate things that would have never been thought as useful to do so and to link the daily routine tasks that are usually suboptimally performed by the employees with the higher level mission-statement elements of the business. This is the key in creating value at the end.

To come back to the question of 'What exactly defines the economy of a service?' the answer is that there is a plethora of things that define the economy of a service – many of them may be unveiled to the providers of the service by the time they design the particular service but the majority of the elements that a single simple service defines may never be communicated to them as it shall be subject of the recipients of this service in an open ended time scale. This provides a damned good reason for people to design and implement their services in the best possible way as nobody knows how exactly their services will be used for.

On the other hand, any conscious mind should not relate the optimality element ('best possible way') in the design of a service as an increase in the costs and the budgets. Usually, bad designed services tend to be more expensive than neatly ones. But this is a long story that is not lying within the scope and aims of this book.

Let us now face the first question: How much is the cost of a bad service? With a single word: it is enormous – not in a metaphoric or poetic sense but in a literally calculated and calculating manner. Think of the following example cases: any car is shipped with a manual. I suppose this follows some regulation that enforces manufacturers to organise the functions and operative parts of their cars into some sense-making document that may help the car users in different ways: immediately after they purchase their car and want to have a quick overview of the cars capabilities and functionality, or when they will be in some special case like a breakdown that needs to be handled on site without external help.

The situation is very much the same for computer programs: again these are shipped with a manual or have one electronic help facility. Even for well established applications for e.g. word processing of big software houses it is not evident how the user shall treat their product and what type of help he or she will need. Therefore, what usually happens is that the team of the developers takes a final assignment after completing the programming job to 'write the manual'. I had found myself in the past in this position twice – and I have to be honest with the readers that this was a job that I immensely hated. What I now see is that in both cases I should not have been assigned this task: both of my supervisors at the time of the assignments were in full knowledge of my nature – and in both cases they should have avoided using me for this job. Unfortunately they both chose me exactly for the reasons that they should not have used me – or banned me from being part of the documentation team: personally I dislike using applications, I would never characterise myself as power user and for sure I would not dedicate time for scrutinising the behaviour of an application. On the other hand, I am creative, I can exhibit imagination in tasks that other people would seriously doubt whether there can exist any. In other words, I am not at all lacking on employee qualities however I am not the one who should be employed for a manual writing task. But both my ex-supervisors had appreciated the fact that I would come back to them:

- In a short period of time,
- With a fat and bulky document that would make anyone feel proud of the result (except the ones who would experience the misfortune of needing to use it as a reference),
- Without breaking their heart with complains or other valuable parts of their anatomies with problems, requests for more time to dedicate in this serious task.

To cut the long story short, the resulting cost of this bad service is simple to calculate: all the spent resources were a waste of time and money as the result was ill-performed and totally useless. We were in both cases at point zero of the service value scale. However, there is a bitter last part in this story: in both cases the need for a 'manual' had been satisfied – who cares about quality and the actual utility of a manual?

Therefore, the next time that you find yourself in front of a non satisfying service situation, with a miserable product or a manual that has been never written in order to be read, or a telephone help or hot line that is not helping at all, with incompetent support and people with a pathetic non-helpful attitude, you will be able to calculate easily the cost of this bad service – and in addition imagine the infrastructure of sick people's attitudes that maintains this cancerous infrastructure.

The next question we posed was: How can we ration for a service quality gradient that relates an increase (a decrease also) in the budget of a service with both qualitative and quantitative parameters? In other words: how can we spend resources like money and people's efforts for improving (parts of) a service in a way that can show a direct relationship of the investment with the result?

First of all the quality of service is a highly subjective issue – each service provider may define it in different ways and in areas that are unregulated as it is the doughnuts market of Pennsylvania or the hospitality market in Greek islands, this can take many different shapes according to the particular Zeitgeist and elements related not at all with the service itself.

The definition of some ad hoc indicators that we can continuously gauge is not new at all – in our case it may relate many different elements that can be objectively documented (like the salaries of support department employees) with highly subjective ones like the loyalty or the commitment, or other soft skills required by our staff.

In this respect, it is preferable to introduce some rules of thumb for our own use that will base on our observations, reflect our own experiences and our discussions with other colleagues or partners than adopt a model that has been (or has not been) introduced in some other context. For sure the risk of reinventing the wheel does exist, but at a final level of analysis all organisations need to define their own idea for the services they provide, they manage or they use.

A malservice of the academic community and the consultancy profession is that they usually provide solutions in search of problems that they usually do not want to recognise. The reason is easy to see: this lowers the costs – but their costs not the customer's or the user's. Why should a solution for a service-related problem in a Hondurian telecommunications company build on an allegedly best practice that has been conceived in a U.S. or German multinational company? And most importantly: if the reference for the success story comes from a superficial business book, then who guarantees the appropriateness of the adopted solution?

Much of the wisdom comes from common sense observations – this is what comes from my own experiences and observations. All the times that I chose to adopt easy-to-use recipes for a service problem, there was a failure in the corner waiting for me sooner or later. The main issue is that nowadays both observation and common sense are the rarest things to find in the market. And especially in the service market where people are under continuous pressure (or at least feel so), where there is an extreme emotional load amongst the parties involved in any service transaction, it is difficult to ask people for some introspection. However this is a *sine qua non* for achieving any type of improvements.

Observation and common sense are bringing us back to the bottom line of holisticity. I think that a common element that appears in highly successful people – CEOs, tycoons, entrepreneurs – is that they draw paradigms for their business from other domains. Many refer to their childhood, activities they learned to perform with their parents or grandparents and relatives. Others draw paradigms from their hobbies: be it sailing or golf, mountaineering or football, a common element is that these paradigms support introspection by means of observations these 'highly successful' people draw from other areas than their own business and an increased dose of common sense. One good question that remains to ask these people is why they don't do the simplest thing: rely on observations they shall make on their own within their own company, and instead of this they rely on reports and communications from their subordinates – many of which simply provide blue sky pictures while a much darker picture holds. This relates to a sensitive matter: the quality of the internal services and the extreme lack of reliability that these exhibit.

Another issue is now raised: how better is it to not introduce or upgrade a service than do it in a maliciously suboptimal or bad way?

For many reasons – one of which is Marketing of course … – people introduce a new service: they announce its opening, they send press releases, print pins and t-shirts, implement campaigns and several other paraphernalia which may or may not affect the quality of the service and at a great extent they may simply increase the budget at irrational levels.

In a free world, it is not a good idea to introduce a service police, taking care of who provides what type of services and whether he or she can exhibit all the necessary skills and capacities to do so. On the other hand, we all experience the many problems that have their root to an elementary failure, namely this of configuring the backbone of a service in cost efficient and economically meaningful ways.

Economics does not always have to do with money: quite the opposite, money is only a means towards several ends that can be defined from an economics theory. A basic lack in the today's service world is the lack of theory in many actions. Theory can act as the background for the existence or presence of some functionality even in a simple computer application.

For instance let's imagine a really simple word processing application that does not include any Help facility simply because there is no need for such one. This means that an entire economy of services (consultancy support, hot line and education) or products (manuals and help-guides) is left outside. The same may hold also for the case of an extremely dysfunctional word processor application: there, the designers may have consciously, purposefully and deliberately left out the Help facility for obvious reasons. Now, it is up to the market's side to either avoid use of this application, or find some ways to fill the gap: some third parties might venture for the provision of services to help users cope with the application, some other parties might decide to prepare products that aim to help access and use of the application, etc. Economy of a service relates to the big picture of that particular service. And this big picture cannot be the result of corporate tactics – it has to relate with strategy.

Increase of sales is never a strategy. It may be treated as a successful development that prepares a company for a growth in its market, or in case it happens without the necessary preparation, it may simply lead to a failure with the company going bankrupt. Same holds for the human resources that staff the service lines: there is a well-known way of treating people as an inevitable cost source, but this may lead to severe mistakes: minimising the cost of a service (while also maximising the profit margins) does not always contribute to an optimisation.

Why pay high salaries to well-trained people for addressing customer requests when one can afford to have less trained people that might get an on-the-job training and less optimally address customer demands? Many of us may think that this is a practical managerial question – though it is definitely not. This is a deep philosophical matter – and there is no simple or single answer to this.

Let's examine two discrete cases: one in which the information service is provided for free to the customers something similar to what toll-free customer lines are supposed to do, and a second case in which the customer is supposed to have a paid contract for accessing a service help-line.

Now, in a first analysis attempt the options are as follows:

- In both cases the company may use the same well- or bad-trained staff to address customer requests
- In the case of the paid line the company may use well-trained staff – the rationale for this may simply be that people pay for this service and they deserve to be treated in a more adequate way
- In the case of the toll free line the company may use ill-educated staff so that they fulfil the toll-free requirement with the minimum cost.

The key in the above analysis is the cost aspect. For sure, it is right that a company treats everything as a cost source because this is simply the truth. However, some costs are avoidable, while some others are inevitable – but for the majority of costs there is plenty of space for 'improving', 'adapting' or 'optimising'. And it is regarding these activities where the majority of management failures takes place.

Service economics can only be a rough guide for implementing your own success or failure story – and nobody can predict the result before this happens.

Having closer experiences with the domain of service business and accounting software, we have identified that in the same way that a company is using a specific model for reporting its activities and this is the same one that it uses to document its transactions with trading partners (namely this of classic double-entry accounting), there is some equal need to proceed in the identification of a system to describe decision making activities – the majority of which builds on (elementary) information management transactions.

Under "classic" double entry accounting, a transaction is a collection of two or more rows whose debits equal credits. Each row of a journal entry has attributes that everybody can agree on (date, account code, description, etc.) and a long list of other attributes that begins with everybody agreeing, and descends into progressively less consensus, around the 10th or 15th attribute. In this respect, one can come to the conclusion that classic double entry accounting is both (providing) a methodology and metadata framework capable of representing every kind of service transaction and financial state change that can exist in the service business problem space.

Collaborative business decision-making software, and all forms of supporting service management software, really may be viewed as a representation or a set of symbols, for some underlying reality. Obviously one has to consider terms like "alternative", "choice", "option" and names of certain actions throughout the system, for which meanings are not ambiguous. One also has a lot of structures representing relationships and hierarchies, which are more subtle.

Like most systems of notation and semantics, a service can never be anything but a model. It is a map to a territory, whose validity may be evaluated by reference to that underlying reality in the "real world".

A basic argument we have been facing was to reconsider the collaborative service modelling process from a new perspective. In the same way that companies have been using classic double-entry accounting as their basic mode of operation for their bookkeeping operations, which is currently facing serious limitations due to the highly networked nature of the economy in general and the business-to-business transactions amongst trading parties in particular, there is a well identified need to reconsider the foundations of the collaborative service modelling process too.

Continuing our analogy, the double-entry model is based on solid foundations mapping to the thought processes of business owners which were prevalent during the 20th century.

However, double-entry would never have happened, historically, in the presence of today's computer platforms and Internet connectivity. It is in this respect that the double-entry documentation and reporting is obsolete and could be replaced with a network-centric model. Systems for collaborative service modelling process have profoundly different requirements and (economic) drivers; because these are intrinsically shared events and data, they can be rapidly constructed in a variety of shared architectures on Internet.

An innovation we are suggesting relates to the transition from the double entry accounting paradigm that has dominated the majority of service design approaches and methodologies in the past, with a new one, namely this of collaborative service modelling processes. We can schematically say that double entry accounting is rather Newtonian: you record an asset only if you can record the related liability. By looking deeper we see that the balance sheet is intended to be a snapshot of the company's balance in the marketplace, at a point in time, where every asset or liability that has been recorded must be balanced by identifying it with the other asset or liability or equity account representing that trading partner, owner, debtor or creditor with whom a particular service related transaction is concluded.

Looking now to the accounting parts of the service management process, it is sensible to add that companies usually apply the concept of *Cost Centre* and, more recently, the concept of *Profit Centre*.

What these two terms mean is self-explicable: cost centre for a company concentrates all cost elements that relate to a specific corporate activity, while for a profit centre the idea is to conceptualise and separate all parts of the company that create profits.

The terms arc at a great extent misleading and this can be easily shown: following the above line of thought, companies would naturally like to focus on profit centres while getting rid of all cost centres. Ideally speaking, a company would consist solely of profit centres, which might be related with same – or preferably lower – number of cost centres.

This approach has become unfortunately familiar to the public sector as well: all aims to get rid of the management and ownership of hospitals or schools and the administration of several public entities has as ultimate aim the shrinkage of the giant or monstrous state apparatus.

However, this tendency to avoid costs does not lead to good results and outcomes: cutting down costs does not necessarily help bring up the profits. Why? This brings a new term on stage which we have to cautiously consider: the notion of *Value* and the related concept of a *Value Centre*.

The idea came to us from the experiences we have from international research projects. There, the notion of profit is extremely vague and doubtful for many different reasons. Therefore, one has to have an operational equivalent for counting the positive outcomes of a research activity.

Especially when considering the world of services, the idea of applying value and cost centres concepts is of utmost importance and direct utility as they can be both used for the exploration of new services as well as the management of existing and operational ones. As the reader will see, we heavily link the semantics of a service with these of a project. Actually, this idea brings only positive elements to the subject area: any service is indeed a project: spanning from the case of a short-term few-days project with a predefined deadline (e.g. the hot-line service for emergencies like the Katrina in 2006 at New Orleans) to an open-ended service within a bank which may continuously be improved or upgraded though the core elements and mission may still remain the same.

Research and development (R&D) projects are expected to reflect the way transnational multi-stakeholder consortia should move forward to seize opportunities provided by the technology they develop. Yet, the reality is that projects find that their good intentions in this respect are disabled by the Project Management procedures, which in practice are too inflexible. This is mainly due to the fact that the particular research framework patterns and practices still reflect the weaknesses of earlier approaches, from a time when the involved actors were not so fast changing, nor involved in such complex networks of alliances and partnerships, as well as linkages to other related schemes.

Furthermore, the traditional project "accounting" system and its major outward expression, the much unloved cost statements and financial reports, essentially only reflect already completed transactions (usage of resources, purchases and expenses of various categories, etc). Such a narrowly-based, backward-looking reporting mechanism is ill-suited to providing the information really needed by the project management board.

In the following paragraphs we present a novel new approach that shows all resource-related and financial reports fully expanded into comprehensive disclosures. These will portray not only the consequences of past transactions, but also a fair representation of the activities of the project participants, the obligations undertaken by them (whether executed or not), and the particular risk profile. Furthermore, our approach proposes that a project internal evaluation of the involved parties work progress is conducted, together with a financial audit.

If applied, the results of such a procedure could be communicated to the Management Boards or any other relevant party of the participating organisations. This internal project procedure should be regarded as complementary to any carried out by each individual partner's internal auditing units.

The analysis, proposals and suggestions outlined in the paper are not just aimed at preventing future sub-optimalities in projects although, considering the increase in budgets for integrated projects, such failures would pose a massive threat. More broadly and importantly, they are aimed at enhancing project effectiveness, by ensuring they are better suited to a fast growing economy, well-functioning markets, and ethical and equitable behaviour. The pursuit of these high level goals is the major purpose of this approach.

In the following we describe in more detail the means we employ to support the above principles.

Building on lessons from past projects that involved trans-European research collaboration funded by the European Commission, in which we have been actively involved either as Coordinator or as partner/ contractor, we have devised a new and more effective structure for organising and conducting work in research projects. This takes into account the structural inefficiencies that we faced in a number of such projects, that generally tended to lead to sub-optimal satisfaction of the goals originally set down. Ongoing improvement of a high level is really essential, when having in mind the costly project structures that are an inherent feature of mostly all approaches.

Within this new approach, work is organised into a set of Value Centres that are directly related to specific tangible results reflected in the particular project deliverables. Direct labour and any other costs are assigned to a set of corresponding Cost Centres, all of which are related to the aforementioned Value Centres. The Value Centres are in turn responsible for organisation of the research work and for any replanning of the project activities (see Figure 1).

Our approach also provides a two-level model for checking the project progress and the service quality:

- Checks carried out at the *first level* cover:
    - For each *Value Centre*: work carried out with respect to the Deliverables

Figure 1. Cost- and Value-Centre correspondence

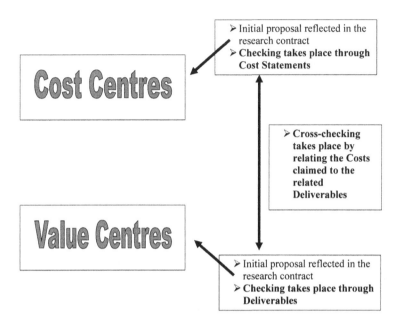

- ○ For each *Cost Centre*: project costs claimed in the cost statements, while
- • At a *second level* cross-checking occurs of the Deliverables produced against the Cost Statements provided (i.e. claimed).

This procedure enables the proper monitoring of effort (and costs) expended on the project, disabling (or at least minimising) any opportunities for ex post facto adjustment of project items.

It should be noted that the above model should not increase communication overheads; on the contrary, we firmly believe that it may increase communication efficiencies, as well as the overall project work quality. It will obviously necessitate continuous (i.e. at least monthly) monitoring of progress, based on appropriately adapted time sheets by the project participants.

The current situation is that the organisation of work within an R&D project takes place within WorkPackages. Each WorkPackage then leads to certain results, which are identifiable (and auditable) by means of Deliverables. However, slackness occurs for, amongst others, the following reasons:

- Work taking place within a WorkPackage *may* be further broken down into a set of tasks;
- These Tasks may lead to discretely identifiable Deliverables; or they may not.
- In the latter case, it may be difficult to check whether expenses (i.e. "costs") claimed against such a Task have actually been incurred and therefore whether the claim is just;
- This may, of course, be regarded as a responsibility of the Co-ordinator; or – at the final level – of the customer, who both have to audit the claimed resources for each "cost item";
- A frequent and therefore indicative example of this is the case of consortia that do not feel it necessary to allocate resources (typically in the form of person-months) to individual Tasks, thus limiting their oversight to just the overall budgets per WorkPackage. (A wise move, a cynic might add, if the entire reporting edifice lies within the sphere of virtuality.)

Currently, to the best of our knowledge, reviewing usually takes place at a high level that does not deal with such discretely identifiable "cost items". Of course there are (historical) reasons for this approach; people experienced with the idiosyncratic elements of research work per se – even where this is of the most applied nature - would argue that it is difficult to foresee the final results one or more years ahead or to firmly commit oneself to them. They would argue that at the macro level a fair balance occurs between the swings and the roundabouts of project resource consumption. But this is an insufficient argument for separating the value created within a particular WorkPackage or Task from the costs that have been claimed for its execution.

On the other hand, however, it is not difficult to provide a level of transparency that helps people work to the highest ethical standards while also encouraging them to safeguard basic principles of integrity, both at the personal and at the corporate levels.

In a relatively recent European Commission Note of February 2004 (European Commission Note "Financial collective responsibility in FP6 contracts", DG Research, Directorate A - Coordination of Community actions, Regulatory and cross-cutting matters, February 2004) it was recognised that "multi-contractor instruments apply the principle of collective technical responsibility and most such instruments also apply collective financial responsibility."

This opens the road to consortia so that "if a contractor breaches the contract and the consortium does not make good this breach by continuing to carry out the project, the Commission may, as a last resort and if all other approaches have been explored, hold the other contractors liable for the debt of that contractor under certain conditions."

There is no doubt that moral responsibility is individual by its very nature. However, in today's world, perception matters more than ever. And in these post-Enron times of meta-modern accounting, with confidence and trust having been significantly shaken, it is important that research should meet the highest integrity standards and not be hindered by the existence and operation of an old-fashioned and marginally efficient reporting system.

Paraphrasing what Baruch Lev, Professor of Accounting in the Stern School of Business at the New York University and a legendary figure in the area of Intangibles and their reporting, identified in his 2002 testimony on "the reform of corporate reporting and auditing" to the U.S. House of Representatives, one can say that currently, and in the "As-Is" situation being discussed here, we have:

- Financial reporting that is "too narrow" as it is based on already executed transactions, as reported in the periodic cost statements, and without reference to the unexecuted obligations of each party;
- Auditing that is "too cosy" as it mainly uses the same already executed transactions as its inputs for checking the validity of these claims;
- Reviewing that usually takes place in a quasi-academic and/or quasi-industrial style, and that in a majority of cases fails to address the money-for-value principle.

And though it seems transcendental, it is also a practical finding that better cost reporting shall lead to higher research results; some obvious reasons for this are that:

- If a well-defined pathway for documenting an activity is in place, and this is also traceable with the costs that this activity is incurring, people shall not (be able to) inaccurately estimate their efforts, while
- If the path is enabling tactical machinations and roundabouts, then it is only a matter of time (and not of the location) that creative or inventive accounting practices shall be grown and unfolded – which shall of course diminish the value and kill the potential of the research work.

Let's now focus on the implementation aspects of our approach. Day one of our proposed approach starts with abolition of the concept of WorkPackages as an artefact that drives the planning and organisation of work within R&D projects. This outmoded relic that reflects the sense of past times, namely the WorkPackage-centric organisation of project work and commitments, has now reached (or rather significantly bypassed) its limits.

Within this new concept, consortia shall in future develop their proposals on the basis of Value Centres. Work will be organised, reported, reviewed, and audited around these value centres. Each Value Centre shall have associated with it a corresponding Cost Centre.

In this approach, Value Centres are assigned a projected initial cost. This should be seen as a purely nominal cost for the usual corporate budgetary purposes that need not necessarily be exactly met in practice; in many cases it may be exceeded, while in others it shall not be met at all.

This approach enables re-allocation of initial project resources from value centres 'in the black' to other Value Centres that have moved into the red, based on appropriate judgements and as needed by the project. For some cases, the involved parties may decide to create a new Value Centre for some need that was not initially identified, in order to use resources for some justified activitiy that was not given sufficient importance at the beginning, or even in specific cases to not use the entire budget.

Having disposed of WorkPackages, it is possible to now focus on the Value Centres, including their outcomes, which are Deliverables. These can be either of discrete nature, notifying the completion of some task, or of continuous nature (as is usually the case for management activities).

All developments and outcomes during the entire project lifecycle will thus be traceable as a consequence of their interaction with each other. For example, it shall be possible to use a Deliverable of a Value Centre X related to User Requirements for work on a system design, that in turn devolves into some other Deliverable. We use this case as it is suitable for demonstrating why our approach is so much better than following an approach based on the structure of WorkPackages. The answer, again, comes in two parts:

- The first part relates to the existence of the capacity to cross check work done as part of a Value Centre with costs incurred as part of the corresponding Cost Centre. Is there any doubt of the necessity for this? In answer, one might consider the example where an analysis report which could be purchased for 100 Euros (overnight!) from the Internet, is submitted as the outcome by one or more partners of a WorkPackage that has allegedly cost 20 person-months and for which the remainder of a consortium has been waiting 7 months;
- The second part, which is equally important, concerns the current lack of procedures for tracing the actual give and take that occurs between the project parties, and which brings transparency to the process of results creation. (We should not forget that consortia running multi-party R&D projects derive their value solely from the existence, the volume and the quality of such

transactions: no transactions, no value; too few good quality transactions, little value, etc).

To create any type of value, one builds on his or her own existing legacies. In the case of R&D projects, these are mostly intangible assets, such as skills and tacit knowledge, corporate or organisational values and norms, technology and any other type of explicit knowledge, the particular Management Processes, and finally any other endowments that can be of use[1]. It is on these assets that core project competencies shall be improved or created within the project lifetime, and it shall also be possible to quantify the project results with respect to their particular contribution margins for each involved party and the market.

In contrast, with the current system nobody knows exactly how to measure the value created by a project. The introduction of Value Centres facilitates documentation of the initial assets within the consortium at the time of the start of the particular project, and thereafter monitoring is possible to take place in a consistent and stable way. Of course, disagreements may appear in the selection of the system to be adopted for the valuation of these resources. Our opinion is that any system should in principle be welcome, though our own recommendation is for an adaptation of that developed by Andriessen as reported in the abovementioned work.

More specifically, the central improvement – or extension – we would propose to this would be related to its use not only as a valuation tool but as a project management method. Such a valuation method would also help improve the existing templates for representing exploitation plans.

Last but not least, we propose the disassociation of the notion of project time with this of real world; it is not unusual that tasks which have been planned to consume 4 manmonths over a period of 4 months, need to expand their lifetime over two or even more additional months. This rather 'spatial quality' of project time forms an important issue that has been addressed in a highly acute way in the now for good reasons considered mythical book of Frederick Brook "The Mythical Man-Month" (Brook, 1975). We all know that in the as-is situation, projects are unnecessarilly urged to timely completion of the various tasks and WorkPackages, while a reassessment of the real time needed is not supported as it may in general cause unwished bureaucratuc overheads. Except from the ability to support predictable and foreseeable monetary inflows that stem from the processing of the corresponding cost statements, this linearity should rather make us feel uncomfortable and also feel the need to question the value that is related with respect to the associated costs.

Of course, criticism is needed for the proposed approach in respect of its capability to account for the idiosyncracies of multi-party research work, of being too commercial or realistic for actions that aim to increase innovation and competitiveness in service businesses and the service industry at large, and to contribute to greater benefits for all customers of services. We shall now seek to look at some myths that can be found in the proposed approach and some realities that may underlie it.

A first myth is that too many aspects of R&D projects are dealt with on the fly for strong controls to apply and, as time goes by, some decisions mature and get better by, inter alia, improvements in the intra-consortium communications. This implies that a chance factor necessarily exists. The proposed approach can be claimed to disable these essential characteristics of R&D. This is a myth. The approach neither disables nor enables someone to better carry out his or her research work. It merely improves all round transparency for all parties. As far as the research work in an R&D project is concerned, we face two general cases:

- These cases in which it is known what should be built but the knowledge is lacking of how to do it; for this category it is essential for the partners responsible to create new process knowledge besides the planned Deliverables. And it is also obvious that the costs will be justified not only by the final outcome but also by the means that were utilised, including also all efforts expended on documentation, exploration of possible approaches, etc.
- Those cases where it is known what should be built and where it is also known which methods should be employed to achieve this. For this, it is clear that cost claims are easier to plan in advance and commitments can be made to them with greater proximity.

For both case types, our approach only calls for a linkage of the two worlds and how reporting takes place within them.

A second myth is that the approach would be difficult to employ in view of the disparity between the accounting systems used by different actors, whether companies, organisations, or institutions. We believe this again is not a valid concern as the plethora of different methods and practices does not impact on the approach we propose. It is rather in much better semantical and operational proximity with many of the established practices in the field.

Having looked at some myths, let us now look at the unavoidable consequences of this approach.

A reality is that many projects would find that in the new approach the consortia themselves, as well as their individual participants would no longer be able to justify spending and / or costs in the several times fraudulent way they have done up to now. As the linkage to the created value will be tighter and of a more direct nature, the opportunity to support undue inflationary R&D economies will vanish. The worst that might happen (from a cynic's perspective), is that projects might cost less and produce more.

A second reality is that it shall become more difficult to use methods that are sub-optimal in terms of both the value and the cost they create. A concern we have experienced is in recognising that, by their nature, not all activities within an R&D project will be value added. It isn't reasonable to say yes; in many cases the uncertainties inherent in R&D mean that a project only partially consists of value added activities. Certainly there is need for activities of a supporting nature, or activities that are prerequisites for others that themselves create the value sought by the project. Even here, our approach aids transparency as it is now easy to make distinctions between value-added and non-value-added activities; and who would now dare to claim inflated costs for an activity that itself clearly creates no value at all?

In this way, we believe that various reporting inaccuracies of R&D projects will in future become more difficult or will lose their reason of existence. And the creation of core competencies and other types of intangible assets will become easier.

In a relatively recent article questioning whether the auditing profession can do more to identify potential problems, David Devlin, president of the Federation des Experts Comptables Europeen's (FEE), which is the umbrella body for European accountants, has recognised that "[the standard on fraud] should require [auditors] to be more sceptical of management's explanations and audit evidence. It needs to emphasise 'prove it to me' rather than 'tell me'" (Devlin, 2004).

A main postulate of our work is that by improving the system, project participants will develop their proposals and organise their work reports in a way that is closely (if not directly) linked to the actual costs of carrying out the work. Substantial improvements will also then emerge in the quality of the conducted research.

Replacing the as-is situation of WorkPackages with Value Centres, and linking the latter with Cost Centres improves the transparency of the cost claims made by consortia, while the resultant enhanced visibility makes it easier to check the quality of the conducted work with respect to the incurred costs.

This is obviously not a novelty for the business world – but it is our firm belief that it is a serious measure that will result in a drastic improvement for R&D projects.

As already seen by the reader, our approach is structured by underpinning theories and informed by key findings we accumulated over the years from the market field on the topic domain. The role of transaction cost economics to this is predominant in many respects.

It is obvious that services and e-services are affecting inter-organisational transaction patterns between companies and their customer and partners. While an understanding of the role of service related transactions and the enabling technologies is applicable, the focus has been mainly set to the enabling role of e-services in the internetworking of organisational systems in the business sector. On the other hand, we all experience suboptimalities with the given levels of quality of services we are supplied or are part of. An eclectic mix of theories, models and methods can guide the research within particular areas as deemed most appropriate. Transaction cost economics may provide perspectives to explain observed phenomena, while models such as value chain analysis provide a means of understanding the implications of service enabled processes.

Transaction cost theory is anything but new for the field of economics; though it can be safely regarded as an important theoretical development in institutional economics and may provide insight into institutional arrangements for all types of economic relationships between organisations. Furthermore, the transaction costs perspective can help design service information systems and service infrastructures appropriate to the functioning of different institutions as it provides a theory with which to select the relevant organisational phenomena, identify the information requirements and to forecast the implications of the proposed redesign. The mapping of governance structures on the dimensions of frequency of transactions and investment specificity, has been successfully applied to structure domain-related understanding and value integration.

The focus of transaction cost theory is on the conditions under which transactions would be carried out internally, in what a researcher (Williamson, in 1975 and 1991) refers to as hierarchical integration of economic activities within the firm's management structure, or in the market with external firms. In our context this means that both service providers and service customers need to choose a co-ordination mechanism in order to economise on transaction costs, which include factors such as asset specificity, uniqueness, uncertainty and complexity of the service exchange as well as opportunistic behaviour.

Williamson identifies three factors which may be expected to lead to high transaction costs:

- Asset specificity i.e. how dedicated the assets need to be to the specific task,
- Uncertainty i.e. in the service demand and supply markets, and
- Frequency presumed to be proportional to volume requirements for the services.

Transaction cost analysis also rests upon two behavioural assumptions: the bounded rationality of the decision makers cognitive process and consequent actions and the opportunism to which market arrangements may be subjected by one of the transacting parties.

In addition to this, Williamson argues that under high transaction costs firms tend to choose vertical integration to control the transaction process by closer supervision. In some cases, for example, the overheads in terms of the uncertainties and the effort needed to manage risks make it more attractive to manage the transactions internally. However, in those cases where straightforward, non-repetitive transactions involving no transaction specific investments are concerned then markets co-ordinated by the price mechanism are the optimal choice.

Ubiquity of Internet and ease of connection has of course now opened up the promise of organisations participating in different types of service network forms or in electronic service markets with previously unidentified trading partners.

The emphasis within transaction cost economics is on transactions and the costs associated with them that are deemed to determine the coordination mechanisms for economic relationships between organisations. E-services may be a key enabler in reducing transaction costs and also provide the means to overcome geographic, temporal and informational constraints thus enabling the coordination of strategies, resources and competencies between collaborating firms. Organisations may, for example, adopt e-services to reduce the costs of market search, provide effective monitoring schemes thus lowering transaction costs and improving information and service flows to facilitate improved planning and more coordinated actions to reduce uncertainty.

Organisations are seen essentially as networks of contracts that govern exchange transactions between members having only partially overlapping goals. The structural underpinning of the theory of transaction cost economics implies a rational and systematic view that is inherently limited. Nevertheless, the theory also acknowledges the importance played by human factors in terms of bounded rationality and opportunism so human decision makers are therefore considered as well the objective properties of the market. Opportunistic behaviour exists when participants act strategically by attempting to realise their own interests at others' costs and usually in the face of social norms. Trust and other non-contractual measures are therefore recognised because the feasibility of writing complex contracts may be restricted by bounded rationality in that it may be impossible to identify all future contingencies and specify appropriate actions.

REFERENCES

Andriessen, D. (2004). *Making sense of intellectual capital: designing a method for the valuation of intangibles*. Burlington, MA: Butterworth-Heinemann.

Bornemann, M., & Alwert, K. (2007). The German guideline for intellectual capital reporting: method and experiences. *Journal of Intellectual Capital*, 8(4), 563–576. doi:10.1108/14691930710830756

Brook, F. (1975). *The mythical man-month*. New York: Addison-Wesley.

Devlin D. (2004). A superior armoury for the war on fraud. *Financial Times*, February 26, 13.

Eustace, C. (2000, October). *The intangible economy impact and policy issues.* Report of the European High Level Expert Group on the Intangible Economy. Luxembourg: European Commission Report.

Williamson, O. E. (1975). *Markets and hierarchies: Analysis and antitrust implications.* New York: Free Press.

Williamson, O. E. (1991). Comparative economic organisation: The analysis of discrete structural alternatives. *Administrative Science Quarterly, 36*, 269–296. doi:10.2307/2393356

ENDNOTE

[1]   For this see also Andriessen (2004).

Chapter 8
Service Physics

When aiming towards user-centred service design, a core issue to the design of "ergonomically correct" service interfaces is their appropriateness with respect to the particular human user behaviour attributes, as they evolve during the utilisation of an interactive service and its constituent applications. The exploitation of human behaviour aspects in the service interaction techniques design process is of significant interest and is presented in this chapter. Though it has been tempting to synthesize many of the presented service design guidelines we prefer to adopt a laundry list-like approach as the materialisation of a service interface design technique heavily depends on a plethora of parameters. In many cases, for the same audience a service implementation needs to be differentiated from other similar services, while in certain other cases this is not part of the recommended actions.

Service physics – what should someone understand under this term? Similar to our high school physics, there are several terms that one can bring in mind when thinking about physics: mechanics, fluid motion, energy, electricity, and many others. Switching back to the service discipline, one can pose questions like: what

DOI: 10.4018/978-1-60566-683-9.ch008

does constitute a service? Which are its elements? Does it make sense to talk about service atoms? And which are the integral parts of a service? What is the nature of a service? Is it a static element with some type of certain 'mass' within its encompassed environment or is it a dynamic entity like a wave that flows from some point to another as part of a service flow process? Or – similar to the case of light in modern physics – is it both?

There are serious questions that may be raised by the reader: is this a serious discussion? And where does it lead? And which will be the contributions that such an approach can have?

I have been for years consuming megabytes of printed or on-screen accessed bibliography regarding service; mega-sequences of verbose prose about architectures, billing models, silver bullet solutions to address ubiquity of a service, anonymity in a service or perplexity and confusion in the mind of a service consumer. A common denominator in all them was the fact that there was a set of conceptual hypotheses which were made that lacked on coherence with each other. In other words, though our modern physics has evolved since the times of the ancient Greek philosophers who spoke each one with different words and in different terms about the nature of the materials and the laws that govern them and our lives, in the area of services we rather seem to find ourselves in the times of Pre-Socratic philosophers. This is not bad at all – quite funny is only the fact that we neglect to accept this simple reality. As a descendant of the ancient Greeks I can risk a feather-brained judgement: many of the ancient Greek philosophers despised empiricism and tended to limit their observations only into what they thought as useful for support of their own views. This is not bad at all – and is usually experienced in areas like politics and marketing, on the other hand it is totally unscientific and does not constitute a fair basis for establishing an improved system for exchange of ideas. What I remember from the lectures of philosophy in the high school is a set of postulates that were made by one or the other philosopher. When I tried to create something that nowadays one would call a conceptual map of their beliefs for facilitating memorizing the different names and their theories, the result was chaos (in any literal sense) (Potter, 2002).

Unfortunately this picture very well describes the area of services: jargons, nomenclatures, theories and approaches proliferate in a way that does not help anyone. I am sure that the same was happening in the origins of any other science – the difference is that nowadays it is more difficult to establish a new science as there is a plethora of other sciences who volunteer to help its establishment and functioning. At this point, I regret to confess that the best one can do is follow exactly what the ancient Greeks were doing with great comfort: establish a new science or domain of structured- and organised-to-be knowledge: most of the modern terms that end up with an *ology*, like zoology, or *onomy*, like astronomy, relate to an area of knowledge that has been separated from the general corpus of knowledge in order to improve its study and its interactions with other areas.

The maintenance of cords to all other sciences like computers, management, business, accounting does not let the service science to grow independently, using of course parts and elements of other sciences as well.

INTERFACE GUIDELINES FOR THE SERVICE DEVELOPMENT PROCESS

When aiming towards user-centred design, a central issue to the design of "ergonomically correct" user interfaces is their appropriateness with respect to the particular human behaviour attributes, as they evolve during the utilisation of an interactive service / application. It should be noted that while the physical characteristics of a user might be viewed as static over a limited time span, human behaviour is adaptive and, thus, it might be described as an evolving process that converges to an "equilibrium" state. This state is reached, usually, after an initial period of gradual familiarisation whose duration might vary.

In such a context, the exploitation of human behaviour aspects in the interaction techniques design process is of significant interest. More specifically, the interaction techniques to be supported by the user interface of the demonstrators should meet the interaction requirements of the end users during their gradual and evolving transition from novice users to expert and frequent ones.

According to (Rasmussen, 1981), three classes of behaviour exist, namely skill-based, rule-based and knowledge-based behaviour. The Skills-Rules-Knowledge (henceforth SRK) classification aims to the reduction of human error in the control of complex systems. Reducing human error should be viewed as a problem for the system designer, but of course the designer cannot possibly predict all possible malfunctions and states of a system. SRK suggest a way human operator variability may be viewed at the design stage and is a general description of an operator's mental activities. Above all, SRK is meant to serve as a normative function in guiding the design of displays. At the *skill-based level*, human performance is governed by stored patterns of preprogrammed instructions represented as analogue structures in a time-space domain. Errors at this level are related to the intrinsic variability of force, space, or time coordination. The *rule-based level* is applicable to undertaking familiar problems in which solutions are governed by stored rules of the type IF <STATE> THEN <DIAGNOSIS> or IF <STATE> THEN <REMEDIAL ACTION>. Here errors are typically associated with the misclassification of situations leading to the application of the wrong rule or with the incorrect recall of procedures. The *knowledge-based level* refers to novel situations for which actions must be planned on-line, using conscious analytical processes and stored knowledge. Errors at this level arise from resource limitations and incomplete or incorrect knowledge. With increasing expertise, the primary focus of control moves from the knowledge-based towards the skill-based level; but all three levels can coexist at any one time.

Skill-based behaviour consists of the performance of more or less stored patterns of behaviour, e.g. manual control. One primary characteristic of skill-based behaviour is that no interpretation of the meaning of a display is required; the display must be unambiguous with regard to the required action to take.

Skill-based behaviour refers to highly trained sequences of "automated" behaviour typical for frequently encountered tasks and is a very close coupling between the sensory input and the response action. Skill-based behaviour does not directly depend on the complexity of the task but rather on the level of training and the degree of practice in performing the task. While different factors may influence the specific behaviour of a particular individual, a group of highly trained operators would be expected to perform skill-based tasks expeditiously or even mechanistically with a minimum of mistakes. For the two other classes of behaviour (i.e. rule-based and knowledge-based) the connection between sensory input and output actions is not as direct as in skill-based behaviour.

It should be noted that the borderline between skill-based and rule-based behaviour is fuzzy at times. A keypoint is that what is rule-based for one person can be skill-based for the person who is at such a high state of practice that he can execute a sequence of actions based on a single stimulus. For instance, we classify as skill-based behaviour the performance of well-memorised and frequently rehearsed immediate emergency actions.

Rule-based behaviour denotes behaviour that requires a more conscious effort in following stored or written rules, e.g. setting up an environment (Rasmussen, 1981). The activity at the rule-based level is to coordinate and control a sequence of skilled acts, the size and complexity of which depend on the level of skill in a particular situation. Rule-based behaviour is applicable for familiar but longer and more complex work situations where conscious control of a stored or prescribed sequence of tasks is required (Komerska & Ware, 2003). Elements of the procedure can activate skill-based behaviour but the rule is predominant and must be followed in order to achieve the relevant goal. Thus rules are sequences of state-action-check tasks.

Rule-based behaviour is governed by a set of rules or associations which are known and followed. A major difference between the rule-based and the skill-based behaviours results from the degree of practice. If the rules are not well practiced the human being has to consciously recall or check each rule to be followed. Under these conditions the human response is expected to be less precise and more prone to mistakes, since additional cognitive processes must be called upon. The potential for error results from problems with memory, the lack of willingness to check each step in a procedure and failure to perform each and every step in the procedure in the proper sequence.

Knowledge-based behaviour applies to cases in which the situation is to some extent unfamiliar - that is, where considerably more cognition is involved in one's deciding what to do. Knowledge-based behaviour is necessary where skills or rules are either unavailable or inadequate so that the conscious problem solving and planning are called for in order to meet the demands of the unfamiliar situation which has arisen. In this mode, information needs to be treated as symbols which can be directly utilised and manipulated within the particular system model and structure which form the reference frame for thinking about the system (Pirolli, 2003).

The design of user interfaces should take seriously into account these three levels of human behaviour and the variations and modifications that take place within the human operator when performing a task by means of an interaction technique as time goes by, i.e. the utilisation of a specific interaction technique that initially referred to knowledge based behaviour, evolves gradually to a combination of rule based and knowledge based behaviours and finally converges to skill based behaviour. In this respect, if an interaction technique is exceptionally demanding in terms of cognitive, perceptual and motor resources for the novice user, its learning curve might have a "smooth" and "polished" slope and thus the transition from a purely knowledge-based behaviour to a skill-based one might show a significant time slow-down.

Conclusively, it should be mentioned that according to (Ivergard, 1989) there is no complete congruence between these different types of "behaviour" and the different forms of skills presented above. As a rough guide, what in (Rasmussen, 1981) is called skill-based behaviour corresponds, according to (Ivergard, 1989), to motor skill and sensorimotor skill; knowledge-based behaviour corresponds approximately to cognitive skill; there is no direct equivalent to rule-based behaviour.

According to (Carter, 1992), standards can help designers avoid errors, provide consistency, enhance usability, improve user performance and enhance the comfort and well-being of users. Additionally standards can provide a basis for evaluation.

While the distinction between Standards and Guidelines is often blurred, the former generally carry a greater weight of certainty and a method for evaluating compliance. Standards go through formalised voting and commenting procedures while guidelines are the direct product of their authors and of any reviewers that the authors care to get involved. Standards and guidelines are usually but not always platform independent as opposed to style guides which make recommendations on how to design for implementation on a specific platform. Standards are generally focused on the design of a single, fixed format interface. However it is well accepted that individual users may be more comfortable and productive with considerably different interfaces from one another. This leads to the need for standards that allow for individualisation (via customisation or adaptation) within the realm of different interfaces that each meet both a user's needs and all other applicable standards.

Complexity of Tasks

According to (Boyer et al. 1992), demographics indicate that the population in the United States and other industrialised nations is growing older and that the number of older systems users can be expected to increase substantially over the next several decades. In order to assess possible differences between age groups the mental workload experienced by older adults as compared to that experienced by younger adults was investigated. Two tasks were utilised to assess short term memory (continuous recognition) and psychomotor (first-order unstable tracking) performance (Huber & O'Reilly, 2003). The workload of each task was assessed and memory task performance measures and subjective workload ratings indicated a decrement in performance and an increase in workload for the older group relative to the younger group (Shelton & McNamara, 2001).

Implications for system design for older users are that memory-laden tasks should be supported for such users while first-order tracking psychomotor tasks require less additional support (Perry, 2003; Melcher, 2001). Tasks requiring heavy short term memory use might be enhanced with memory aiding (Hollingworth & Henderson, 2002). For example, users of systems involving computer displays might be aided through a system which retains a chain of previous commands on the display. Extrapolations of possible actions based on previous commands could also be displayed to reduce working memory load.

The increased life expectancy of the elderly may require substantial redesigning of environments in order to accommodate age related body changes. One of the most important aspects allowing the elderly to function independently is the ability to reach for items comfortably during daily activities, i.e. to perform activities of daily living (ADL). Designing for an independent elder requires knowledge of reach measurements that determines the optimal design of working / living environments. (Wright et al., 1994) provide reach capability design data of elderly people between 65 and 89 years of age.

Living independently with the ability to perform ADLs influences the continued lifestyle of the elderly without the need for an institutionalised home environment. Successful performance of ADLs depends on the capabilities of the elderly and the particular task. Based on the results and the discussion found in (Wright et al., 1994), it is possible to conclude that age has a profound effect on reach capabilities of individuals which is particularly true when individuals reach the age of 85 years. The discussion also leads us to conclude that elderly as a whole form a distinct population when compared with younger individuals. Therefore it is critical that designers consider the reaching capabilities of the elderly when designing working or living environments for them.

(Modrick, 1992a and 1992b) discuss issues related to system complexity with respect to human performance, memory and training as well as a review of concepts and approaches to complexity.

The intuitive sense of complexity is that it increases with increases in task attributes such as the number of options among which one must choose, amount of information to evaluate and filter, etc. In this context, (Modrick, 1992a) provides us with the following propositions:

- Increased complexity is associated with increased difficulty, time to perform, and trials to learn as well as decreased retention of knowledge or skill.
- Cognitive activities are more difficult and less robust than psychomotor activities.
- The cognitive and memory demands imposed on the operator/user have increased.
- In turn, performance will be degradaded.
- Performance degradation can be offset by appropriate design of user/system interfaces, performance and decision aids, and task procedures.
- Predominantly psychomotor tasks have been changed to activities that are more cognitive.

Research on complexity can be grouped into three principal lines of investigation:

- Procedural complexity, i.e. the structural organisation of the procedure for executing a skill or task,
- Cognitive complexity, i.e. the organisation of the supporting and enabling knowledge needed to learn and execute the skills of information extraction for problem solving in a given operational context, and
- Conceptual complexity, i.e. the number and connectedness of conceptual rules for combining information items into conceptual structures.

(Wisher, 1992) describes the relative effects of task complexity on the retention of a skill over prolonged periods of non use. Though the study focused on the decay of skill and knowledge of reservists called up for active duty during Operation Desert Storm, the findings are generalisable and therefore of immediate use in the case of elderly people.

Unused skills decay in a systematic fashion. Skill retention, the inverse of decay, denotes the remembrance of how a skill should be performed long after it has been initially acquired. The identified six variables that have yielded consistent data in predicting the retention of skills and knowledge are:

- *The degree of original learning*
- *The particular task characteristics*
- *The retention interval*
- *The instructional strategies*
- *The methods employed for retention*
- *The individual differences*

Typically the research on skill decay yields a decelerating function of skill loss with respect to time, where the underlying model for the retention curve is driven by the characteristics of the tasks, e.g. number of steps, built-in feedback, mental processing requirements, etc. The findings suggest a gradual decay of psychomotor skills but a relatively rapid decay of procedural skills while previous skill qualification score was the best predictor of skill decay.

(Robertson & Hix, 1994) provides a set of user interface design guidelines for the target population of mentally retarded adults. The guidelines were empirically and heuristically developed as a result of an exploratory study that examined the ability of adults diagnosed as moderately developmentally disabled to successfully use a personal computer, input devices preferred, and user interface design factors to be considered when designing or selecting applications for this population. Though computer science literature discussed advanced assistive technologies such as eye-blink technologies and speech synthesis, to help mentally retarded persons with severe physical handicaps meet specific disabling conditions, on the other hand the usability of commercially available devices has not been addressed. The guidelines have been tested using two prototype games: Shopping which was designed to teach money-handling skills, and Getting Dressed to teach a basic life skill. Follows the list of the guidelines:

- Pace of screen action should be completely under control of the participant. Sudden or unexpected movement is confusing.
- A paradigm that locks window boundaries in place is preferred to one that allows window resizing.
- Active areas need to be at least 1.5 inches from the menu bar and placed so that icons will not be dragged near the menu bar.
- Pull down menus caused both motor control and cognitive problems. Alternative means of presenting information need to be used.
- Strong visual feedback based on familiar experiences aids understanding. For

example, the concept of "put back" was not comprehended when participants clicked a button to substract an item from the accumulator. The concept was immediately understood when participants moved an item out of the shopping cart.

- Meaning of icons must be taught. Icons on the main menu were recognised correctly after a familiarisation session. A question mark for help seemed not to have meaning, probably because the help screens were text based and participants had limited reading ability. Primary users of help screens were counsellors in the group home.
- The target population is especially sensitive to screen clutter. If multiple items can be moved, a clear path through the grouping is essential for comprehension.
- The target population is more likely to accept the computer as a shared activity rather than as a stand alone computer assisted instructional program. Devices that make the screen fun for a counsellor or volunteer to use will enhance the mutual enjoyment and usability of applications.

(Czaja & Sharit, 1993) presents a study concerning the development of a methodology to evaluate stress for computer-interactive tasks as a function of both the mental workload of the task and the age of the individual.

When addressing the issue of computers and stress an important question to consider is how the influx of technology into work settings impacts on the work life of older adults. The importance of this issue is due to the fact that the number of older people in the population is increasing and the workforce is ageing. Because there are physical and psychological changes that occur with ageing which impact on task performance, it seems reasonable to assume that computer tasks may result in differential levels of stress for elderly people.

Although computer technology reduces the physical demands for performing jobs, it increases the information processing demands, which is a factor that may generate stress for older people due to the changes in cognitive functioning occurring with age.

Three tasks were designed for this study and intended to be representative of computer-interactive tasks performed across a large variety of occupations. The three tasks were:

- A data entry task
- A file modification task
- An inventory management task

The tasks differed on the number and type of decisions, control over work method, degree of repetitiveness and complexity.

The findings of the study suggest age differences in the tasks which increase in relation to the task complexity. The results identified a number of task characteristics with potentially important implications for the design of computer-interactive tasks. One of the factors to be considered when assessing the appropriateness of a task for older populations is the pacing requirements of the task per se. The cognitive complexity of the task also needs to be considered; if there is a misfit between task complexity and worker capabilities, emotional strain and worker dissatisfaction may occur. Computer tasks may also be stressful for older people because of the potential for these tasks to impose a tight external control over the way a task is performed.

The use of the appropriate interaction metaphors may facilitate interaction and increase the usability of an application / service through the reduction of the required cognitive efforts for the accomplishment of the various application tasks.

The book metaphor approach was adopted in a study reported in (Yoshimune & Ogawa, 1994) to simplify database access. The intent was to improve access speed and comfort. A book metaphor interface (BMI) was created to a set of about 300 design guidelines. However, experiments revealed that the BMI did not offer a significant improvement over the equivalent printed version of the guidelines. The BMI was more comfortable but users did not perform the task any more rapidly. The problem was that novice users did not understand the tools offered by the BMI and so failed to use them in the optimum manner. An agent was added to the BMI that monitors the user's commands and when the user deviates from the optimum procedure graphically suggests what the more correct procedure would be. Results suggest that user's efficiency is increased by the feedback system while user acceptance is at a high level too.

Menus

Research work reported in (Gibbons, 1992) presents a global definition for menu systems and proposes a domain structure in support of the provided definition. The domain of menus is divided according to the proposed definition into three areas: *(i) allowable menu system structure; (ii) identifiable menu system objects,* and *(iii) menu system sequence control aspects*.

Most of the research on menu based dialogue has been narrow in scope, centring around three specific areas:

- *The depth/breadth trade off in the menu structure*
- *The ordering of menu options*
- *The role of option designators*

The most often debated research area within menu based systems centres around determining the optimal depth (number of panels) and breadth (number of menu options per panel) in a menu system. Though structures of intermediate depth and breadth are preferred, there is also argued that breadth is the most important factor, i.e. with increased breadth and decreased depth menu selection could be optimised in execution time, search speed and accuracy could be improved and errors reduced.

As far as the menu ordering is considered, typical research in this area examines the difference between alphabetic, random, frequency and categorically organised menu panel lists.

The third area that has concentrated on the use of option designator codes for menu option selection has proceeded to a distinction between explicit (usually set apart from the menu option) and implicit (part of the menu option) menu option designator codes for all types of option designators (sequential: alphabetic, numeric; function key; mnemonic; key letter). Research results clearly identify mnemonic codes whether they are implicit or explicit as being superior to the others. A mnemonic code is one which uses the first letter or first several letters of the menu option name as the option designator code.

The adopted definition in (Gibbons, 1992) follows:

Menu dialogues are a human-computer interaction style which provides information retrieval and command control functions to the user through the selection and execution of menu option selection targets. The menu dialogue is represented within the user environment by a menu system. The menu system is the aggregate sum of menu panel organisation (Structure), menu panel elements (Objects), user and system actions (Sequence Control), and the interrelationship of these items in the presentation of a menu dialogue.

Structure: The first step in organising the menu domain is to make the global distinction between menu systems as Command interfaces and as Information retrieval interfaces. While in the former a limited number of commands available and frequent use of the menus means that the menu items are usually known and the task becomes a simple locating process, whereas in the information retrieval menu system the selection targets must be categorised under one of the menu items, these items being classes of information that can be found in the database.

Secondly, most menu systems can be organised into one of four different categories: Single menu; Linear sequence; Hierarchical structure, cyclic or acyclic; Networked. In single menu structures all menu options are placed on one menu panel. Linear sequence menus present a series of independent menus in a predefined order. Tree structured menus are hierarchically arranged semantic groupings of menu options. This is the most common structure and is used when the number of menu options is large. Networked structures provide users access to different sections of a menu system.

Objects: Menu System Objects are the portions of the menu system displayed to the user at a given point in time. There are two basic classifications of menu system objects: Menu Panel and Optional Menu Panel Objects.

Sequence Control: A wide range of sequence control characteristics exist which can make similar menu function quite differently. Different methods of sequence control exist (cursor control, point control, direct control) along with various processing stages (selection, execution and processing).

Menu Option Selection is the phase in sequence control where users indicate their selection of a desired selection target. Menu Option Execution is where users indicate execution of the selected menu option(s), verify the execution indication action and make necessary corrections. Menu Option Processing is where the menu system processes the selected menu option(s) following the execution indication action.

Older adults have evidenced a poorer ability to use grouping factors in such tasks as Embedded Figures, Incomplete Figures and partial report. Difficulties in disambiguating the findings of these studies has left unanswered the cause of this age-related difference. By taking into account age-related differences in visual short-term memory, the results of (Humphrey et al., 1994) suggest that older adults maintain the ability to capitalise on the perceptual organisation of the visual environment as a means of facilitating recall performance.

Taken together, these results suggest that older adult's recall performance is at least as sensitive as that of younger adults to the effects of grouping factors in organising the visual environment. These results suggest that grouping character strings by proximity or similarity of colour can enhance recall performance. Grouping the units of the codes or messages into groups of five will increase the likelihood that all the units of the group are recalled. Most importantly, this benefit in recall will not be able at the expense of elements that come later in the string. Grouping by proximity had the larger effect on recall performance but grouping by similarity did provide some benefit.

Electronic consumer products such as desktop laser printers, facsimiles, copiers, etc, which have a small visual display panel are ubiquitous. They are characterised by presenting only a single menu item at a time which is usually organised in a hierarchical tree structure. Since users see only a single line information on the display and use them infrequently, the optimal menu design may be different from that of an ordinary computer display. (Han & Kwahk, 1994) provides us with data based on an experimental activity that has been conducted to examine variables for designing the optimal menu on a single line display. Because users can see only a single item at a time, they often face navigation problems such as getting lost or taking an inefficient pathway while searching for a target item. The optimal menu design for these displays are expected to be different from that suggested for ordinary displays. Prior to the experiment, the user interface of desktop laser printers currently available in the market were surveyed. Most of them used a hierarchical tree structure and the average number of menu items was 45. A 16 character LCD panel was popular for the user interface. A representative example of the user interface was prototyped that consisted of the single line display, a button labelled *Menu*, a button labelled *Select*, and two *Previous* and *Next* buttons.

The search task on a single line display turned out to be more difficult than that on the ordinary display. This result may stem from the fact that the subject could see only a single item at a time and was required to make a decision on whether the menu category displayed was appropriate for the target item. On the other hand, the subject using the ordinary display was able to compare several menu items displayed simultaneously, and as a result, make a relatively easy selection of the correct category for the target item.

User experience about the menu structure appeared to be more important in designing a menu on a single line display. A post-hoc analysis showed that the search performance on the single line display was found to be seriously affected by the user experience, while it was noted on the ordinary display. When using the ordinary display, the subjects were able to model easily the menu structure since all the alternative menu items at the same level and the navigation path were diplayed simultaneously. Hence the user experience did not affect the search performance. On the contrary, when using the single line display, the subjects could see neither the menu structure nor the navigation path. Therefore, the search performance was significantly enhanced with the training provided, i.e. with the mental model of the menu structure.

The following guidelines are suggested in designing a menu on a single line display:

- Menus with depth 2 are recommended for infrequent users although menus of depth of up to 3 can be used.
- It is essential to provide the user (especially for the infrequent) with navigation aids such as a map of the menu structure.
- Menus with depth 6 or more should be avoided.
- If more than 64 items should be included in the menu, it is recommended to increase the menu breadth rather than the menu depth.
- Deeper menus (not more than 6 levels) can be used for frequent users without sacrificing search performance.

Whenever possible, it is necessary to provide feedback on the previous selections or information about the user location in the menu.

(Philipsen 1994) provides the report on a visual search experiment that was conducted to analyse the effects of highlighting on visual search performance in menu options. Highlighting is usually considered as improving information processing efficiency. A distinction is made between valid (target) highlighting and invalid highlighting (i.e. highlighting distracting information). In the context of the study, six different modes of highlighting were tested namely:

- *Brightness increase*
- *Reverse video*
- *Colour [red]*
- *Reverse colour*
- *Blue-on-yellow*
- *Red-on-green*

on a black screen background. The results show that large highlighting benefits exist where absolute performance is poor, and small highlighting benefits are accompanied by high absolute performance. It should be noted that a highlighting benefit is defined as the difference in search time and error proportions between a highlighted and a neutral condition, whereas absolute search performance gives the performance "offset" i.e. balance for the specific highlighting mode.

For example, based on overall absolute search performance, the bright white and the reverse colour resulted in good performance data. On the other hand, in the highlighting benefit these conditions were those with the smallest effect. In terms of highlighting benefit, red colour showed the largest processing improvement whereas in the absolute performance measures this condition only showed moderate performance.

Conclusively, the suitability of the different modes in most situations where highlighting is to be employed for a brightness difference or, perhaps, only for signalling critical situations, a colour highlighting can be recommended. Use of reverse colours may be effective but the effects of these conditions are most sensitive to colour deficiencies. Finally, the widely used inversion (reverse video) technique was uniformly shown to result in low absolute performance.

Manual Performance

According to (Metz et al., 1992), using common household products is often too difficult for people with movement disabilities such as neuromuscular disorders, spinal cord injury or arthritis. Therefore, there is need to better understand the capabilities of this population when designing and adapting products that are easier for them to use. In the study reported in (Metz et al. 1992) individuals with movement impairments used two experimental home control thermostats with features that allowed easier positioning and viewing. The participants employed a variety of grasping and manipulation strategies including some that were not anticipated by the designers. Participants' preferences indicated that the appearance of the product, not just effective control design, was an important factor in their judgements.

In the study, three thermostat designs were tested, namely two experimental designs and one control. The first experimental prototype used a plastic part that fits in front of the standard thermostat whose principal feature was a vertical lever for control, while the second one was a plastic ring with a coarse edge that covered the standard thermostat.

The expectation of the research and design team prior to testing was that users would prefer the lever model because it offered better leverage and a larger grasping area. However the results did not support this expectation although both designs were reasonably effective. Though the ring model offered better stability while the lever model was somewhat harder to use when the hand was braced near the device or on the wall, the preference for the ring model was also due to dissatisfaction with the lever model as an "adapted" device. This information reminds us that the physical appearance of products often communicates a message.

Previous research shows that the self-reliance of physically impaired people can be seriously jeopardised by their inability to operate controls on everyday products. In the research reported in (Schoorlemmer & Kanis, 1992) a study is described regarding the operational difficulties faced by people suffering from Parkinson's disease, from spasticism and from visual impairments. The same source reports the forces that can be exerted by these subjects, the way they actually manipulate controls and the operational difficulties the subjects experience including both the force exertion and other operational difficulties.

Subjects were asked to demonstrate the operating of controls on their own appliances that cause them difficulties, which may concern problems with:

- Understanding the function
- Reaching, contacting, operating (including exerting force)
- Feedback

The study concluded to some general recommendations including:

- The amount of force required to operate controls should be as low as possible. However, there are three drawbacks if that force is very low, namely: (i) fine-tuning may be hampered and a mark may be easily overshot, (ii) a control may be operated unintentionally depending on the position and orientation relative to the user, and (iii) sometimes partially sighted and blind people may activate controls unnecessarily before finding the right one by touch.

- No requirement of simultaneous manipulations such as pushing and rotating a control device.
- A high degree of freedom to manipulate controls.

More concrete design recommendations are:

- The avoiding of appliances being pushed away by the operation of a pushbutton (for example by reducing the ratio between the force required to operate the pushbutton and the force that pushes the appliance away),
- The avoiding of operations that require to hold a control down for some length of time,
- The provision of enough space to rest fingers or the hand in the immediate surroundings of a control for support,
- The provision of different, easily perceptible (visual and tactile) cues about the current position of controls.

Safety Related Issues

Legibility of a warning is a major issue in the labelling of various consumer products as well as devices. (Braun & Clayton Silver, 1992) examines certain variables that are associated with legibility, namely *(i) font type, (ii) font weight, (iii) point size* and *(iv) point size contrast* between the signal word and the main body of a warning statement. A sample of undergraduate students and elderly people rated labels for (i) their likelihood to read the warning, (ii) the saliency of the warning, and (iii) readability of the warning. The results indicated that:

- Participants were more likely to read the warning in Helvetica type than in Times or Goudy.
- Bold type was more likely to be read than Roman type.
- There was a greater likelihood of reading the warning when the main body was in 10-point size as compared to 8-point size.
- A 2-point size difference between the signal word and the main body of the warning produced a greater likelihood of reading the warning over a 4-point size difference. One possibility for this result is that the 4-point difference minimises the importance of the main body of the warning therefore making only the signal word salient.

There appear to be two approaches to making a product or system safe for use; firstly is to design the system in such a way that potentially dangerous features are either absent or inaccessible, and secondly is to provide an informative sign that warns the user of a hazardous feature and/or instructs the user in the safe use of the product or system.

Accident prevention signs usually consist of two elements, i.e. a signal word that indicates the level or type of hazard, e.g. DANGER, WARNING, CAUTION, and a major message that identifies the hazard and/or contains instructions to be communicated to the user, e.g. HIGH VOLTAGE, WATCH YOUR STEP. (Polzella et al., 1992) provides a study concerning the perceived effectiveness of danger signs where:

- Signs containing a hazard label and instructions were rated as least likely to be recalled at a later time; however they were rated as easiest to understand, most informative and most likely to be complied with.
- Signs containing a hazard label only were rated as least informative and most difficult to understand; however they were rated as most likely to be recalled, as depicting a high degree of danger, and also likely to be complied with.
- Signs containing instructions only were, finally, rated as generally less effective.

(Huey et al., 1994) concerns a study aimed at selection of alarm sounds with improved audible performance characteristics for older listeners over current conventional smoke detectors. Most older Americans live in private residences and are primarily responsible for their own fire safety. This population is particularly in need of the warnings provided by smoke alarms; unfortunately, current alarm features are poorly suited for them. Many current residential smoke detectors possess alarms that have their primary frequency peak in the 4000 Hz region of the audible spectrum. Additionally, many of these alarms are constant instead of providing temporal modulation of the signal.

Unfortunately, this region tends to be prone to hearing loss in the elderly caused by presbycusis. This age-related hearing impairment is not constant for all alarm frequencies. In the conducted study, features are suggested for the design of an improved smoke alarm for elderly users. These results point to sound with a primary peak at 500 Hz with a fast modulation rate to improve detection, perceived attention-getting value, and even localisation effectiveness to some degree (Card & Nation, 2002). It appears that a new alarm design incorporating lower frequency sound could help to improve detection among elderly users.

It is widely accepted that colour affects behaviour; colour influences the saliency and memory of warnings, compliance behaviour and the level of conveyed hazard.

Moreover, research has examined the connoted hazard of various colours and signal words separately. Work reported in (Braun, 1995) examines the interaction of signal words and colours. Of the colours used, red conveyed the highest level of perceived hazard followed by orange, black, green and blue. There were significant differences among the signal words which were grouped into three different hazard level categories. High hazard words conveyed significantly more hazard than moderate and low hazard words. Likewise, moderate hazard words conveyed significantly more hazard than low hazard word group.

The appropriate use of colour in safety signs and labels is addressed under a series of standards published by the American National Standards Institute (ANSI). Similar standards are outlined by other agencies such as the Society of Automotive Engineers (SAE) and Westinghouse. The variability among standards is relatively small. For instance, Westinghouse pairs the colours red, orange and yellow with the terms DANGER, WARNING and CAUTION, respectively. ANSI calls for the same colour combinations, while SAE associates yellow with WARNING and CAUTION.

The experiments indicated that the communication of hazard is a function of both the signal word and the colour in which it is printed. Although it is true that each colour examined enhanced the perception of hazard over black, it is important to note the variability among the colours. Labels depicting signal words such as DANGER might not convey the appropriate level of hazard if printed in green or black.

Iconic and Pictorial Presentation

In (Lin, 1992) a study is reported that aimed to provide the designers with a predictive tool for evaluating and modifying the icon design. Starting from a list of 14 items that have influence on icon recognition and design that are presented subsequently, the original fourteen items converged into the six important items presented in boldface (memorable was correlated with recognisable):

- **Associable**
- Unique
- Elegant
- Culture-related
- **Symbolic**
- Pictorial with referent
- Recognisable
- Representative
- **Meaningful**
- **Concise**

- **Eye-catching**
- Contemporary
- **Memorable**
- Object-related

After a factors analysis three cognitive factors were derived from the six important items:

- **Communicativeness**, composed of items Identifiable and Meaningful,
- **Design Quality**, composed of items Concise and Eye-catching,
- **Image Function**, composed of items Associable and Symbolic.

The study recommends that the six important items can be used for guiding designers to modify the proposed icons at the design stage, while the three cognitive factors could be useful to evaluate the overall quality of current icons.

Because of their relatively universal information transmission potential, pictorials have been suggested as a common means of safety communications across heterogeneous groups of users and uses. (Brelsford et al., 1994) present a study that used a training paradigm designed to enhance comprehension and retention of pharmaceutical and industrial-safety pictorials. Manipulated were (i) time of testing, (ii) content of instruction and (iii) difficulty level. The results showed substantial training effects: there was little change in scores between the test immediately after training and the test after a one week delay. Easy pictorials were comprehended (both initially and following training) better than difficult ones, although the latter showed the most dramatic increase in understandability after training. Additionally, the instruction content manipulation (by means of adding an explanatory statement to the verbal label) which had been expected to influence the degree of encoding had no effect on retention. The substantial gains in understanding the more difficult pictorials suggest that brief training as little as giving the pictorial's verbal meaning once, can have a large impact in facilitating comprehension for pictorials that would otherwise not be understood by many people.

The most important point of the research reported in (Brelsford et al. 1994) is that very brief instruction with only the associated verbal label substantially increased comprehension of difficult pictorials. This finding is important because pictorials are being created and used in a variety of contexts in which their meaning is not always readily apparent. The present results suggest that while highly understandable pictorials are the best pictorials to use when they are available, very brief training of poorly-understood pictorials appears to raise comprehensibility dramatically.

(Jordan & Moyes, 1994) provides an empirical study regarding the effects for representational type and the universal application of icons. Universal applicability might be defined as how "broad" is an icon used. For instance, if an icon is utilised for denoting all printing functions, this icon would have "universal application" in this context. However, if icon A were used for printing some objects and icon B for others, then the interface would not exhibit this type of consistency. Results indicated that for those with previous experience of an interface the guessability of tasks associated with the icons was more strongly affected by universal application than by representational type.

The same source suggests that as long as icons are standardised and applied universally, the design of the icons themselves may not be so important. However, although there might be contexts in which such a corollary would be valid, there are still many situations where the type of guessability associated with representational type will be important.

The icon combinations used produced experimental tasks of the following four types:

- Type A: Representational icons, universally applied.
- Type B: Less representational icons, universally applied.
- Type C: Representational icons, non universally applied.
- Type D: Less representational icons, non universally applied.

Of immediate interest is, in this context, the notion of guessability. As guessability the same source as above specifies the effectiveness, efficiency and satisfaction with which specified users can complete specified tasks with a particular interface for the first time.

Speech Based Interaction: Voice as Interface

Speech as a medium for communicating with computers has several potential advantages whose realisation depends on the sophistication of the employed technology as well as the appropriateness of its implementation; however, its introduction may have far reaching implications for the evolution of information technology. Additionally, the auditory channel is well suited to bringing urgent information to the attention of an operator regardless of the direction of the operator's visual focus. Moreover, the auditory modality is omnidirectional so that the effectiveness of alarms is not reduced even if the user is relatively remote from a terminal. A human factors perspective is described in (Tucker & Jones, 1991), where the predominance of visual / manual interface and the reasons for its preference over speech is investigated.

The same source provides guidelines to improve the usability of speech systems as well as criteria for the assignment of output either to the visual or to the auditory channel.

Spoken output messages are preferable if:

- The message is urgent or calls for immediate action.
- The user is unable to remain in a position where he or she can easily see displayed messages.
- The visual channel is impaired by environmental conditions or sight defects of the user.
- The visual channel is overburdened or cluttered such as when multitasking on a busy CRT screen.

On the other hand, the visual output mode is considered most appropriate when:

- The message is complex, contains technical or scientific terms, or uses terms with which the user might not be familiar.
- The message is long.
- The messages are repetitive or contain a high degree of redundancy (with the exception of redundant introductory messages presented for the purpose of attunement).
- The message needs to be referred to more than once.
- The message deals with the spatial dimension in any detail (such information is usually best presented graphically).
- The message is private or confidential to the user.
- The auditory channel is overloaded with messages, signals or sounds to which the user must pay attention such as other auditory warning signals.
- The auditory environment is too noisy for the reception of aural messages.
- Interference with the performance of external tasks such as those being carried by others who are within hearing distance must be avoided.

If speech is chosen to transmit a message, the user should be given an opportunity to listen and adjust to the speech style and quality before important information is presented.

The attention-grabbing nature of speech messages makes them appropriate for conveying warning messages. This advantage can be enhanced by using a voice that is qualitatively different from others heard in the environment. With experience of particular systems, users will require less information from the system and thus should be given the facility to interrupt or otherwise control the spoken output of messages (Cutrell et al., 2000). Conversely, inexperienced users who may have difficulty comprehending a "fleeting" speech message on the initial presentation should be given the opportunity to replay particular message segments.

If both speech and text modes are to be used for message output, Tucker and Jones (1991) propose the adoption of the following guidelines:

- Speech and text modalities should not be used to transmit separate messages simultaneously if the user is required to attend both. Rather than processing one and then the other, the user is likely to become confused, and neither will be attended to. (Bingham et al., 2001)
- Mode consistency should be maintained within defined stages of the interaction, such that one mode is not used when the other is anticipated.

Factors concerning the perception of synthesised speech fall roughly into five overlapping categories presented below:

- *The specific demands imposed by a particular task*
- *The experience and training of the human listener*
- *The linguistic structure of the message set*
- *The inherent limitations of the Human Information-Processing System*
- *The structure and quality of the speech signal*

Dialogue design forms a major component of the role that human factors research plays in the implementation of automated speech recognition technology. The following guidelines concern the assignment of a voice interface to particular functions within a complex system:

- Speech should only be used when input is required infrequently in order to avoid vocal fatigue effects.
- The choice of mode for particular components should be consistent throughout the task.
- Speech is inappropriate for certain types of information such as spatial description.
- Speech can be combined concurrently with other tasks only if they are non-verbal.
- A special command vocabulary should be designed for voice input to minimise phonetic confusion of items and be economical and natural so that users find it easier to remember and use.
- Design of command syntax should include similar considerations for meaningfulness and familiarity (Irani et al. 2001; Irani & Ware, 2003).

Though the nature of the form of feedback largely depends upon the nature of the application, the three major concerns of feedback are:

- Whether or not feedback should be explicit. The provision of explicit feedback such as the visual or auditory echoing of the input should largely eliminate the problems of substitution and insertion errors. However, it is likely for such a feedback to interfere with the particular task under carried out, thus worsening input efficiency.
- The mode of presentation of feedback. If high levels of recognition accuracy are required, some form of auditory feedback is often appropriate as it is less likely to be missed by the user than is visual feedback.
- The timing of the feedback. If explicit confirmation or rejection of each input is required, it is theoretically faster, more efficient, and less annoying to provide it at the end of a string of inputs rather than affect each utterance, although in practice such a strategy can generate its own set of human factors problems.

In (Jagacinski et al., 1992) the manual performance of older and younger adults is investigated when employing *supplementary auditory cues*. More specifically, subjects attempted to perform the same manual movement pattern on repeated trials using a visual display of error. Additionally, some subjects heard a tone that was proportional to either the position or velocity of the ideal movement pattern. With the tone, both older and younger adults demonstrated increased anticipation in the form of an increased correlation of their movement pattern with the ideal velocity pattern. The benefit of the auditory displays did not carry over after they were withdrawn.

Although older adults exhibited a longer effective time delay, the older and younger adults benefited from the additional cues to comparable degrees. While some research has indicated that older adults have greater difficulty attending to multiple, simultaneous sources of information, such an effect was not apparent in the experimental activities reported in (Jagacinski et al., 1992). Supplementary auditory cues for older adults may therefore provide one methodology bringing their performance levels closer to those of their younger counterparts. One limitation of this benefit is that it occurred only while the tones were present and did not continue when they were withdrawn. While generalisations across tasks and display formats are uncertain, there is evidence that older adults can benefit from supplementary auditory displays.

In (Smither, 1992) an experimental activity is reported that investigated the demands synthetic speech places on short term memory by comparing performance of old and young adults on an ordinary short-term memory task (Vogel et al., 2001; Wang & Milgram, 2001). Items presented were generated by a human speaker or by a text-to-speech computer synthesiser. The obtained results were consistent with the idea that the comprehension of synthetic speech imposes increased resource demands on the short term memory system. Older subjects performed significantly more poorly than younger subjects, and both groups performed more poorly with synthetic than with human speech. Findings suggest that short term memory demands imposed by the processing of synthetic speech should be investigated especially when considering the implementation of voice response systems in devices for the elderly.

Schumacher (1992) provides a rather complete discussion of the area of phone based interaction. Though the study focuses on interaction with telephone and more specifically with interactive voice response (IVR) applications, the findings and guidelines are of immediate applicability in the domain of speech based interaction generally.

IVR systems are becoming more common and are being applied to more complex problems than ever before. IVR suffers because it relies on the system "knowing" *a priori* some of the reasons why people are calling. A useful IVR system needs to meet the goals of the users. Among the strengths of Phone Based Interaction (PBI) are:

- Familiarity with / Ease of use of the telephone.
- Ubiquity - Touch tone phones are widely available.
- Speed - Sometimes services are available faster through IVRs than if users have to deal with a human operator.
- Privacy - Some users feel like they can manage their affairs more privately dealing with an IVR than with a person.
- Efficiency - There are times when it is simply more efficient to deal with a machine than with an operator.

Among the weaknesses of PBIs one could identify the following:

- The telephone provides auditory display only.
- Information is presented serially. All prompts and messages are presented to the user through the telephone handset. The serial presentation of information places heavy demands on short term memory (Xu, 2002). Thus human memory limitations put an upper bound on the length of auditory displays.
- The telephone keypad has only 12 keys. All information the user provides must be numeric or numerical codes for alphabetic information.
- User often have no supporting materials such as a manual.

Design of PBIs follow from the general principles of good design: know the users and their needs, keep the dialogue simple, provide good feedback, minimise errors, provide shortcuts for experienced users, be consistent, etc.

A set of guidelines follows, excerpted from (Schumacher, 1992).

Navigation and Control

- Users should always be able to interrupt (i.e. "dial through") system prompts and messages by pressing a key.
- Users should also be able to bypass subsequent menus (i.e. "dial ahead"). Dial ahead is conceptually similar to type ahead that is common in some screen based menu systems. For instance, in a PBI with several menus users can dial ahead by entering the option numbers before the PBI explicitly offers the menus.
- Hanging up should terminate the dialogue.

Dialogue Structure

Two different classes of PBI dialogues are identified: command based and prompted. In command based, the user generates commands without explicit prompts. For instance the user calls up and enters a mode by entering a command to an audio prompt. In prompted systems there is a resemblance of human conversation: the PBI presents an audio message or menu of options and the user presses a key to select an option from the menu.

Command Dialogues

- Command based dialogues are appropriate when the IVR is used frequently, the users are expected to be experts and the users need to change modes frequently.
- Similar functions should be assigned to the same keys across different modes.
- The number of modes should be kept at five or less.

Prompted Dialogues

- Prompted dialogues can contain both menus and data entry. A menu is a list of options that the system currently has open to the user while in data entry the system asks the user to provide information.

Orienting the User to a New Menu

- When entering a new menu, the user should be given a brief title and instruction (e.g. Fare Menu <Pause> Please make your selection from the following four choices ...).

Number and Ordering of Options

- The number of prompted options should be no more than four options per menu.
- When expecting most users to be unfamiliar with the system, tell them how many entries to expect. This cues the user not to respond too soon if there is uncertainty.
- Menu options should be ordered by frequency of use or by functional grouping.
- When the number of options cannot be hierarchically limited to five or fewer options, the less frequently selected options should be put in a catch all alternative such as "For more options press 5 now".

Wording and Numbering of Options

- The goal-action sequence should be used (To do X press Y now) rather than the action-goal sequence (Press Y now to do X) for options.
- All menu options should be numbered in a given menu consecutively in ascending order, beginning with "1". Numbering alternatives consecutively allows users to anticipate the correct keystroke and use dial through.

Phraseology

- The adopted terminology should be consistent with how user's think about the task.
- The adopted terminology should be used consistently throughout the interface.
- Passive voice and negative conditionals should be avoided.
- The term "press" should be used for prompting selections for menus (e.g. "To do X press Y now").

Feedback

- For prompted dialogues, the user expects to hear the next prompt. For example, if the user selects the option "For fare menu press 1 now" then the next thing the user should hear is "Fare Menu".
- Long data entries should be repeated back to the user for confirmation. For

instance, if the user enters his social security number, the system should respond: "you entered 335 56 0844, if that is correct press 1 now, to re-enter press 2 now".

User Guidance and Error Handling

*   Menus and prompts should be repeated after a 10 second period of inactivity or after an explicit user request.
*   When the user makes an error (e.g. presses an invalid key), he should be told what the valid choices are by repeating the prompt.
*   Phrases such as "Invalid response" and "Error" should be avoided.

Non Speech Signals and Music

*   Tones or music should be avoided when aiming to attract attention or eliciting a response except in the case of prompting to record a message.
*   No background tones or music should be used during playing of prompts.

Due to advances in technology, the use and integration of voice response systems relying on synthetic text-to-speech has grown rapidly. Such devices are used in reading aids for the deaf, computer based instruction, and are almost a ubiquitous part of multimedia platforms. Research studies have revealed that the perception and comprehension of synthetic speech may be attributed to increased processing demands in short term memory. Additionally, it has been shown that the perception of synthetic speech improves with moderate amounts of training. In (Gomez et al. 1994) a study is reported that determines if the increased perceptual effects of training for synthetic speech can be attributed to a reduction of short term memory load.

Taken together, the results of the study not only confirm increased intelligibility benefits from training with synthetic speech but also suggest cognitive processing differences for synthetic speech result due to training. Specifically it is speculated that as perceptual learning occurs, listeners begin to allocate their attentional resources more effectively thereby lessening the demand that the speech system places on the listener (Fine & Jacobs, 2000; 2002).

The integration of voice technologies into telecommunication systems allows the user comfortable and easy access to new services such as audiotex, voice mail, voice fax, automated response systems, etc. The main requirement for these services over the telephone network is that they are "usable" which also implies the possibility of using any make of telephone as well as transparent dialogue handling of service procedures. (Zajicek et al., 1994) present solutions to improving caller handling dialogues with respect to ergonomic principles and language differences. The latter are identified and a solution to the problem is explored.

The most significant design issue in voice controlled computer aided telephony (CAT) is not the particularly employed technology but rather the dialogue that takes place between the user and the machine. The most common ergonomic criteria used for evaluation in CAT are those derived from practical experience of user testing. A set of such criteria followed by their implications in CAT is listed below:

- *Feedback:* System provides immediate recognition of user's action
- *Transparency:* System provides context sensitive help
- *Controllability:* User controls the dialogue pace
- *User experience:* User chooses the dialogue mode
- *Error robustness:* System automatically corrects the user error
- *Flexibility:* User chooses the I/O device (multimodality)

A voice pager system has been examined for its German and English versions. German and English users seem to bring with them different conceptual models of the system based on cultural and technical expectations that may vastly facilitate or discourage the interaction. For instance, though the English subjects seemed to have no problems with the welcome message "Thank you for calling the voice controlled pager service", the German ones considered this as a good-bye message and tended to hang up.

An interesting study reported in (deHaemer, 1997) compared the performance of spreadsheet users in two different modes of input to the computer, namely keyboard and voice input by means of an automated speech recognition system. In general, the performance of the voice interface was below that of a keyboard. The primary reason for this lack of performance centred on the speed of the ASR system.

Two tasks were chosen to represent the general class of tasks for spreadsheet users:

- A simple data entry task requiring the subject to make 10 entries of numerical data into the appropriate spreadsheet cells in response to being handed an orderly, typed list of the data to be entered;
- The second task required completion of a predesigned but incomplete spreadsheet where the subject had to move the cursor around the spreadsheet, compose formulas, copy the numerical content or formula content from one cell to another, and execute menu commands.

Two of the hypotheses that have been tested within the study were:

- In simple data entry tasks subjects perform the task better, i.e. faster, more accurately, with more confidence, using keyboard input than speech;
- Novice spreadsheet users perform relatively better under ASR compared to keyboard input than do expert spreadsheet users.

The first hypothesis was confirmed for both experts and novice users with respect to the speed of data entry. As also expected a priori, data input by keyboard was significantly faster than by speech, thus confirming the first hypothesis. Regarding the other measures of performance - accuracy, keystroke efficiency and user confidence - there was not a significant difference between keyboard and ASR input.

Regarding the second hypothesis, the overall conclusion is that automated speech recognition at its current state of the art is not a better input mode than the keyboard for subjects who are proficient with spreadsheet tasks. Novice spreadsheet users appeared interested in using ASR and believed that their tasks would be made easier by the use of speech. Experts, however, found speech input slower and expressed dissatisfaction with it, although they did indicate that command vocabularies were adequate.

Consumer Products and Devices

Memory Aids

In (Kirkpatrick et al., 1992) a study is reported that aimed to develop a design concept for an electronic memory device to enhance medication compliance in older users where a user-oriented approach was used for the development. One hundred seniors were interviewed to identify their physical, physiological and cognitive capabilities and limitations as well as their preferences for memory aid functions. A design concept was developed for a medication device that would be easy to use, reduce the likelihood of scheduling errors and would be non-threatening to older users who might otherwise be intimidated by an electronic device.

In order to enable community-based seniors to maintain their independence it is necessary to offer interventions for to ameliorate these self-care problems that are commonly associated with old age. High technology products which are being integrated into nearly every aspect of daily living are therefore candidates for research tools for addressing these issues.

The posed objectives of the research reported in (Kirkpatrick et al., 1992) were to identify functional and interface design requirements for an electronic memory aid for medication compliance that was based entirely on the preferences, attitudes, requirements and physical and cognitive characteristics of older users. The target user profile was established through interviews. Devices for user testing were selected through assessment of the state-of-the-art in memory devices. Specifications for several products were obtained and a taxonomy of the features of these devices that included electronic diaries and medication devices was developed and implemented for device selection. Finally, six devices were selected that together encompassed all the design and functional features necessary for testing: two multifunctional electronic diaries, three medication devices and one talking calculator.

A task analysis was performed on the operating tasks for each of the selected devices to identify functional and design issues.

Currently, memory aids such as calendars, phone books, paper notes, other people and alarm clocks were used by ninety two percent of the participants. The most frequently mentioned problems reported were forgetting to look, update or use current reminders. Several had specific problems ranging from physiological problems to device design issues. The most important anticipated function of the memory aid was that of remembering appointments, after which came monitoring medication and then remembering addresses and phone numbers.

Designing a device that meets specific design criteria and that does not intimidate the older user is a challenge. Criteria were established based on the literature, interviews and user testing data. More specifically, the conducted task analysis identified critical tasks which if performed incorrectly could have life threatening effects. These were related primarily with medication schedule calculations which become increasingly complex as the number of daily prescriptions increases. The required information is not always readily available or understood by the senior. Design issues regarding labels, buttons, displays and alarms were also identified and are addressed in the following design guidelines:

- *Displays:* Displays must present information and should meet the following criteria: text should be large enough to read, layout should appear uncluttered, contrast should have a uniform acceptable level, dates and times should be presented in a standard form and consistently formatted, icons should be unambiguous and visual cues should be used to assist in the interpretation of the display.
- *Buttons and switches*: Tactile and auditory feedback should be distinct and provided with each button press. Activation should occur with a discrete single button press, spacing should be generous for increased accuracy, buttons should be guarded from accidental activation and the number of buttons should be kept to a minimum. If switches are used in place of buttons, they should also be large and easy to slide.
- *Pill compartment*: The pill compartments should be easy to open and should provide easy access without risking undue contamination or spillage of pills. They should be large enough to hold many large pills and there should be

enough compartments. The proper compartment should be identified when the alarm sounds and lastly, a means should prevent unintentional opening of the incorrect compartment.

- *Labelling*: In general, labels should be large and easy to read, and their meaning should be clear and unambiguous. Buttons should not have more than one label, and labels on buttons should be large and easy to understand.
- *Alarms*: Alarms should be designed to be heard by persons with typical age-related hearing loss and by wearers of hearing aids. All important auditory information should be provided in visual form as well. If possible, Combining an auditory alarm with a tactile alarm is an optimal solution.

The design concept had large buttons to assist users with visual deficiencies and also addressed the *ambiguity problem* that users had when the button labels were written on the panel between two buttons. The design concept had large text and icon labels directly on the buttons which assist the subjects in determining the correct association between the buttons and the labels.

Remote Controls

Remote controls are considered part of everyday life. Unfortunately the experience of using a remote is not always pleasurable. Research reported in (Logan et al., 1994) documents the process of developing multiple remote control concepts that are ergonomic and enjoyable to use. Conducted experiments suggested that an expanded definition of usability may be required for certain product categories such as consumer electronics. Central to this expanded definition are the concepts of *behavioural* and *emotional* usability. *Behavioural usability* refers to the traditional work-related definition of usability. *Emotional usability* refers to additional needs such as entertainment or enjoyment, that enhance the product usage experience.

The shape of the traditional consumer remote control is rectilinear, reflecting the shape of the circuit board. There are too many buttons that are too small, difficult to read and undifferentiated in appearance. In summary, remotes tend to be suboptimal in terms of ergonomics, usability and aesthetics even if viewed with respect to able users.

The current line of high-end TVs are sold with two remote controls: either a large "universal" remote control or a simplified TV-only remote control with six buttons. The six-buttons remote control has *power, channel-up and channel-down, volume-up and volume-down,* and *menu buttons*. The menu button calls up a bit-mapped on-screen menu system that provides access to all system features including functions that may be directly accessed from the large remote control. Navigation within the menu system is accomplished using the volume-up and volume-down, respectively. Selecting an item is accomplished by pressing the menu button when a desired item is highlighted.

While the system was found to be highly usable through internal usability testing, Thomson Consumer Electronics which conducted the research has moved to a new navigation system to provide a growth path to interactive TV and HDTV user interfaces. The new navigation system is based on a rule called "point-and-select", where pointing is accomplished using *up, down, left* and *right* navigation keys. The existing simplified remote's linear positioning of buttons was not acceptable for this type of four-direction navigation, thereby requiring a new remote control design. In addition to the usability requirement for a new remote control, the Thomson Consumer Electronics design team determined that a new aesthetic was also required.

Three non conventional design concepts were prototyped and tested for user acceptability and preferences, namely the *puck*, the *shoe* and the *ball* remote controls. The form of the first was derived from the hockey puck. The second design was created to fit the contours of the fingers, hand and wrist, while the form of the third one was derived from the geometry of a familiar, non-technology object, namely a tennis ball.

The investigation indicated a strong preference toward the shoe concept, while the ball did not fair better in the consumer preference ratings. In addition to the specific research findings, a more important issue discussed in (Logan et al., 1994) concerns the fact that traditional usability research and methodology focuses on behavioural dimensions of products. However, for certain product categories such as consumer electronics, an expanded definition of usability is required that includes emotional elements of product design.

Video Cassette Recorders (VCRs)

We are all - more or less - familiar with problems in using videocassette recorders, especially the type that permit a range of programmable functions. All too often if the functions are not easy to programme they are not used. While the likelihood that poor ergonomic design of domestic products will lead to serious injury, there is a possibility that products which are difficult to use will not be used to their full potential. Therefore an approach which describes product use in order to highlight potential problems is required.

In (Baber & Stanton, 1992) an application of task analysis is reported for error identification to investigate the problems of using of videocassette recorders. Two popular models have been examined and likely points have been indicated at which errors are expected to occur during programming of the machines.

The problems of using videocassette recorders (VCRs) are common: many people simply do not programme their VCR while errors leading to users missing the desired programme can be reported by almost all VCR owners. This inability stems as much from poor design of manuals as from the complexity of the machine. More specifically questions should be answered such as:

- *What information needs to be presented to the user?*
- *When should it be presented?*
- *How should it be presented?*
- *What actions need to be taken?*
- *When should they be taken?*
- *How should they be performed?*

Two commercially available VCRs have been examined using task analysis for error identification. Both devices gave the appearance of a logical task sequence, but the one (called here VCR A) required several activity loops which could lead to confusion. User actions have been mapped onto machine states. On VCR B feedback was provided in a display on the remote control unit, while on VCR A it was provided on the machine itself.

Programming for VCR A takes place in a poorly structured loop. After the user has set the timer to "programme", and selected "on", he then receives the prompt "CH". The user presses a "channel up/down" button to select the desired channel. Subsequently, the user selects the day a programme is to be recorded on. After selecting the desired channel and day, the user must then programme the start time. This is performed by selecting set hours and changing the time using "+" and "-" buttons. The same procedure is followed for setting the finish time. Pressing the "timer" and "record" buttons, closes the programming session. While the interaction session in VCR A is largely user initiated, it is not always clear what the user ought to be doing.

VCR B uses a different approach: the user firstly presses the "direct" event button. Once the user has selected the timer programme mode, he is guided by prompts shown in the display of the remote control unit's LCD. First the user selects the recording number. This feature allows multiple programs to be composed. Next the user has the opportunity to select a recording interval, e.g. every day of the week at the same time or each week on the same day / same time. The hours and minutes flash on the LCD and the user presses "+" and "-" buttons to adjust them. Next the user sets the recording date, again using "+" and "-" buttons. Following this, the user selects the desired channel by pressing the appropriate number. Then the user presses "timer" and the program is stored.

Although the second VCR seems easier to understand than the first, there is still the possibility that users will become confused, especially as several of the prompts concern information that will only be relevant to a small number of users.

From the analysis of VCRs reported in (Baber et al. 1994), it is concluded that designers should provide easy operation of the most commonly used actions and these should require consistent activities which are easy to perform and which make sense to the user. The aim of the work reported is not, as it is also explicitly declared by the authors, to offer optimal design solutions, but to demonstrate the lack of "common sense" usage patterns that facilitate instead of complicating and perplexing interaction patterns.

Alarm Clocks

Remaining in the domain of consumer electronics, (Voute et al., 1993) provides a study on the usage of a new clock-radio that was introduced as being easy to use. Unfortunately, indications from the field seemed to imply the opposite. The use problems concerned primarily setting and switching off the alarm. User trials have been organised that provided answers to the following questions:

- *How and in what use-conditions are clock-radios or alarm-clocks used in the bedroom?*
- *What operational difficulties occur?*
- *What factors can be identified as the cause of these difficulties?*

On the basis of the indications from the field the following aspects have been taken into account as possibly related to difficulties emerging in use:

- *The layout of the environment of the bed, in particular the position of the clock and the intensity of the ambient light,*
- *Physical characteristics of the user such as dimensions of the upper extremities,*
- *Perceptual characteristics of the user,*
- *Use-habits with other alarm-clocks or clock-radios.*

The following list of requirements is limited to evidence from the field study reported in (Voute et al., 1993). A general consideration is that it should be possible to operate a clock-radio without the necessity of having to consult written directions of use. It should be noted that the clock display is analogue.

Operation

- Current functions such as setting the alarm and setting the time, or alarm functions versus radio functions should be readily operable with one hand while lying in bed.

- While operating the alarm functions, the product should not fall over or slide away.
- Controls to activate different functions should be clearly separated.
- Frequently used controls should have prominent positions.
- Setting the alarm and adjusting the time should be possible both clockwise and anti-clockwise.

Functionality

- The clock display should be easily visible and readable for someone lying in bed.
- The clock display should indicate the time left for sleeping.
- Confusion about different display information caused by similar appearance such as pointers that look alike should be anticipated.
- The clock display should be illuminated; this illumination should be continuously adjustable between 0 and 70 lux.
- The volume of the alarm should be adjustable between 30 dB and (max.) 70 dB.
- The time interval between a repeated alarm signal should be adjustable between 4 and 9 minutes, in steps of no more than 1 minute.

Telephones

The operation of consumer products and devices can be difficult because of a mismatch between the user's expectations and product functioning. The user's expectations can be seen as being based on knowledge derived from prior product interactions and experience, however when a user is confronted with a new product the product itself offers "knowledge" on its operational aspects. The latter is likely to be combined with the users existing knowledge based on experience. To gain more insight into the role of experience concerning the operation of more complex consumer products, an experimental activity was carried out reported in (Gelderblom & Bremner, 1993) in which subjects were asked to (i) give a description of how the retrieval of a telephone number from memory in general is executed, (ii) specify their expectations towards the operation of four different models separately, (iii) retrieve a telephone number from the memory of those telephones and (iv) describe their experience regarding the telephone memory while specifying products they believe adopt a comparable operating procedure. The experimental aims were to establish the influence of experience gained prior to the experiment, and the influence of experience gained during the experiment. In addition, it was possible to see whether performance differences were related to the four different telephone designs used for evaluation.

The user should employ the following procedures for the four models:

- One key to press for direct selection of the required telephone number (BT's Relate 200),
- First a key to enter the memory mode and then a keypad number for selection of the required telephone number (PTT's Monza 10),
- Double-functioned memory buttons that require SHIFT-key to be pressed if the second telephone number associated with that button is required (BT's Converse 200),
- Memorised telephone number directory system with display feedback. Requires DIRECTORY button activation, scanning and finally selection of the required telephone number by pressing the DIAL key (BT's Relate 400).

Performance differed greatly over the four telephones. This difference was not related to the sequence in which the telephones were operated, i.e. the presentation order did not affect the subjects rate of success. The experienced users however performed best on the type of telephone they were familiar with while the inexperienced ones came up with numerous diverse expectations many of which were not suitable for any telephone.

Interaction with ATMs

Automatic depositors, cash dispensers and automatic teller machines by which the general public as end users can deposit, withdraw or transfer their money by "bypassing" teller windows, are now widely installed as tools for rationalising internal clerical work and enhancing customer service.

The most significant requirement of the ATM is that it should be capable of being operated by the general public, including the elderly with ease. The method of input to inform the ATM of the user's intention, and the quality of messages from the ATM to inform the user are considered to have particularly great impact on the usability improvement of the ATM.

In (Hatta & Iiyama, 1991) a study is reported that focused on the adaptation of computer-based communication to people at the automatic teller machines (ATMs). About the one third of the subjects that participated in the experiment were elderly users. The motion analysis of the subjects identified the deficiencies of the ATM/user interface and traced them to the following causes:

- Mismatch between the thinking sequence of the user and the operating sequence of the machine, due to confusing rules and inadequate timing;

- Lack of clarity of screen frame messages and instructions, as illustrated by lack of consideration to importance of information and ambiguity of messages connecting screen frames;
- Lack of consideration to the general public as users (elderly people in particular) who are not familiar with machine.

Subjects were limited to those people who used an ATM once or twice per month or those people who were not familiar enough with the ATM. They were asked to perform the following operations:

- Deposit money with a card alone;
- Withdraw money with both handbook and card;
- Transfer money to a specified account.

As far as the performance of the elderly users is concerned, the following have been identified:

- The elderly user takes considerable time to enter the transfer amount and telephone number,
- The time requirement varies accordingly with the ease with which the name of the transferee can be entered. More specifically, the elderly user must repeat the same operation several times.
- The user must complete 27 operation steps to complete one transfer. Whether or not the user can smoothly go through this sequence depends on the methods of making entries and correcting wrong entries. Elderly users can satisfactorily proceed to a certain stage but once they make a mistake there, they often perform abnormal operations and return to the initial frame.

The difference in operation time required between the elderly users and young users depends on the accuracy and speed with which any mistake can be corrected. The elderly are not appreciably different from the young people in the motor function but are greatly different in perceptual and information processing loads as far as difficulty in understanding instructions and operations is considered.

The problems identified during the study may be summarised as follows:

- Mismatch between thinking sequence of user and operating sequence of machine;
- Confusion in sequence rules, in addition to timing and rhythm discrepancies in entry operations

- Lack of clarity of screen frame messages and instructions;
- Absence of polite messages connecting screen frames;
- Lack of consideration to characteristics of the general public as users and elderly people in particular (case of users not familiar in interaction with machines).

(Hatta & Iiyama, 1991) provides a classified set of proposed guidelines for future design of ATMs which is excerpted and presented below.

Behaviour Pattern and Characteristics

In addition to guidelines specified for the conventional CRT screens:

- Attention to people who read screen messages by tracing them with fingertips. (There are many people who have the habit of confirming contracts and other important documents by fingertip tracing to prevent misunderstanding).
- The 2cm to 3cm edge of the CRT screen should be considered as a zone the user may inadvertently touch.
- Consider the transferrer frame and next transferee frame when a transfer is to be made. The transferee frame is almost the same as the transferrer frame in screen characters and layout, so small but important differences are likely to be overlooked. People recognise an overall outline before small details. The screen display should be designed so that differences between the frames can be noticed at a glance. One remedy is to change the image pattern from one frame to the next.

Problems with Sequence and Screen Frame Planning
Sequence Planning

- The operating sequence of the machine should basically accommodate the thinking process of the user. The user's thought process involves time, place and occasion variations, however. The user also tends to insert his handbook and card into the ATM as soon as possible, and may determine when to do so in consideration of his belongings at that time.

Human-Centred Design for Implementation of Operating Sequence

- The operating sequence is implemented by the machine when triggered by the user. The time during which the machine is working is a "do nothing" delay for the user. This delay may unsettle the user or appear overly long psychologically for the user, depending on the situation. One of the causes is that the user is not informed of what the machine is doing. The user should be visually notified of the operation being implemented by the machine. This problem can be solved by judicious selection of screen design.

Guidance Screen Planning

- One screen frame, one instruction (one sentence, one meaning). One screen frame should contain one instruction as a rule. The designer should not think that blank screen space is wasteful or that continuous steps should be displayed on one screen frame. (Spence, 2002)
- Accommodation to scanning characteristics of user. Generally, the user scans the CRT screen in a random search pattern and rule based search pattern (from upper left to upper right and then gradually below, when reading sentences). The user's eyes first stop at large characters or coloured ones. The user uses this technique as he knows that he must read the displayed instruction in a short period of time. It is not always advisable to provide screen frames with headings. (Viguier et al., 2001)
- Character selection. Messages and instructions must be plainly and accurately expressed by the smallest possible number of characters. It is not easy to observe this basic rule, however. The results of linguistic research must be applied so that intended meanings can be accurately conveyed to the user with a small number of words.

(Rogers et al., 1994) investigated the usage of Automatic Teller Machines (ATMs) by older adults. One hundred interviews with older adults were conducted where the latter were queried about their frequency of ATM usage. From the initial pool of individuals a limited set was chosen (eight frequent users and eight intermediate users) that participated in an in-depth structured interview. Detailed information was gathered about usage patterns and general ATM knowledge of older adults. Though the data are derived from a sample of older adults, it is obvious that any improvements of design, safety or training will be beneficial to the population of users as a whole.

It is generally assumed that older adults are less likely to use new technology relative to younger adults and more specifically to adopt Automatic Teller Machines. On the other hand, questions remain as to why older adults are unwilling to using new technologies and whether or not their attitudes and usage patterns can be changed. Through the study presented in (Rogers et al., 1994), the types of problems that older users experience and their suggestions for the improvement of ATMs are given.

Problems with ATMs

The same source was interested in whether subjects recalled difficulties using the ATM when they first began. It is important to qualify these results with the knowledge that all of the subjects had been using ATMs for at least 3 years. Problems concerned inserting cards the wrong way, the typing of the PIN code, etc but most of them were related to getting used with it and getting familiar with its functionalities.

When asked to describe any of the problems they have had with using an ATM, subjects mentioned problems with seeing the keys and determining which keys line up with which button. The issue of being able to see the screen well was also reported as a problem. Additionally, the issue of the ATM not providing sufficient feedback was also reported as a concern that could be addressed with design improvements.

Conclusively, improved design and the development of a training program could minimise the problems experienced by older adult users. Moreover such improvements might increase their usage and enable them to take advantage of ATM features of which they are currently unaware (it should be noted that the majority of elderly ATM users uses the ATM only for withdrawals).

Adaptive ATMs

(Burford & Baber, 1994) describes a user centred evaluation that was carried out of a simulated adaptive interface for an automatic teller machine (ATM). Most attempts to produce adaptive interfaces have tended to deal with highly complex systems with a large number of possible user goals and an even larger number of possible routes by which to achieve those goals. ATMs at least currently present a very different environment as there are few discrete user goals, achievable through a strictly defined hierarchy of menus, and interactions are very brief, with only one or two subgoals being pursued in each interaction.

The standard interface of the ATM service that has been employed for the experiment included the following options:

- *Withdraw cash*
- *Display balance*
- *Mini statement*
- *Order chequebook*
- *Exit*
- *Other services*

The latter option led to a screen of the same layout with options for print statement, deposit funds, transfer current to deposit and transfer deposit to current.

An adaptive system which aims to retain the current menu structure of the ATM dialogue should try to reduce the depth of the hierarchy through which the user has to proceed. With the present functionality of ATMs this will be little more than offering a user a specific amount of cash on the initial menu rather than the generic "Withdraw cash", but with wider functionality of bill payments, multiple accounts, etc, more significant changes could be made. A positive result of this could be a reduction in the number of options presented to the user at one time, thus reducing cognitive load and transaction time.

The study produced positive indications that the provision of an adapted interface for an ATM is a usable development. More specifically, the initial user survey indicated that there is a place for adaptation, in as much as users perceive their behaviour with ATMs to be regular and consistent, and so predictable. From the times taken to perform whole transactions, there was a definite improvement in subjects who received an adaptive interface and were forewarned of it.

Design of Devices and Controls

According to (Ivergard, 1989) where design issues of the more traditional controls are discussed as well as the design of specific controls for communication with computers, traditional control panels have the advantage that they give feedback to the operator of the manoeuvres which have been carried out.

Control devices are, in general, the means by which information on a decision made by the user is transferred to the machnine / application. The decision may for instance be taken on the basis of previously read information, or on the basis of information from other sources, or from some form of cognitive process.

Functionally, controls may be divided into the following categories:

- Switching on / off, start or stop.
- Increase and reduction (quantitative changes).
- Spatial control (e.g. continuous control upwards, downwards, to the left, or right).
- Symbol / character production (e.g. producing sound or speech).
- Multi-function (e.g. controls for communicating with a computer).

Some of the principal anatomical and anthropometric aspects of control design are discussed by the same source. More specifically, the following rules are reported in form of guidelines for the design of all types of controls:

- The maximum strength, speed, precision or body movement required to operate a control must not exceed the ability of any possible operator.

- The number of controls must be kept to a minimum.
- Control movements which are natural for the operator are the best and the least tiring.
- Control movements must be as short as possible, while still maintaining the requirement for "feel".
- The controls must have enough resistance to prevent their activation by mistake. For controls which are only used occasionally and for short periods, the resistance should be about half the maximum strength of the operator. Controls which are used for longer periods must have a much lower resistance.
- The control must be designed to cope with misuse. In panic or emergency situations very great forces are often applied, and the control must be able to withstand these.
- The control must give feedback so that the operator knows when it has been activated, even when it has been done by mistake.
- The control must be designed so that the hand / foot does not slide off or lose its grip.

In the next, design guidelines for the different types of controls are given excerpted form (Ivergard, 1989).

Press-Buttons and Keys

There are suitable for starting and stopping and for switching on or off. This type of control is also suitable forfoot control. The following recommendations apply to both hand- and foot-operated controls:

- The resistance of the pushbutton should increase gradually, and then disappear suddenly to indicate that the button has been activated.
- The top of the button should have a high coefficient of friction to stop the fingers / feet from sliding off. Where press buttons are to be activated by the fingers, the concave form is preferable.
- In order to indicate that the button has been activated, a sound should be emitted if the workplace has low light levels.

Toggle Switches

Toggle switches can be used to show two or three positions. Where there are three positions, one should be up, the middle one straight out and the other one downwards. Toggle switches take up very little room. The following recommendations also apply to toggle switches:

- A sound should be heard to indicate activation of the switch.
- If a number of switches are used, they should be placed in a horizontal row. Vertical positioning requires more space in order to avoid accidental operation.

Rotary Switches

These can be divided into two categories: cylindrical and winged. The primary difference between these is that the winged version has a pair of "wings"above the cylindrical part. The wings function both as a positional mark and as a finger grip. Rotary switches may have from 3 to 24 different positions and require a relatively large amount of space, because the whole hand has to have room to turn around the switch. However, where multiple position switches are used, they take up less space than the number of pushbuttons or toggle switches required to fulfill the same function. Rotary switches can either have a fixed scale and moving pointer, or a moving scale and fixed pointer. A variant on the moving scale is to have a window which only shows a small part of the scale. The following recommendations apply to rotary switches:

- In most applications rotary switches should have a fixed scale and moving pointer.
- There should be a detent in every position.
- The turning resistance should steadily increase and then suddenly decrease as the next position is approached.
- Cylindrical switches (knobs) should not be used if the resistance has to be high. In these cases wing knobs are preferable.
- Where only a few positions (2-5) are needed, they should be separated by 30-40 degrees.
- Where fewer than 24 positions are used the beginning and end of the scale should be separated by a greater amount than between the different positions.
- Where the workplace has low lighting levels, a sound should be made to denote that the switch has been activated. In these cases there should also be a definite stop position at the beginning of the scale, so that the positions can be counted out.
- The scale should always increase clockwise.
- The scale should not be shielded by the hand.
- The surface of the switch should have a high coefficient of friction so that the

hand does not slip.
- The distance between panel and knob should at least be 3 mm.
- The maximum amount of slope on the sides of the knob should be 5 degrees.

Levers

Levers are activated either by the whole hand or just by the fingers. In general, where fine control is required, only the fingers should be used. The following recommendations apply to levers:

- The maximum resistance (force) for push-pull movements with one hand, with the control placed centrally in front of the body is between 12-22 kg, depending on how far from the body the control is positioned.
- The maximum resistance for push-pull movements for two hands is double that for one hand.
- The maximum resistance for one hand moving in the left-right direction is about 9 kg, and is considerably lower in the opposite direction.
- The maximum resistance for two-handed movements in the left-right direction is about 13 kg.
- The lever movement should never be greater than the arm's reach without moving the body.
- Where precision is required, a supporting surface should be provided for the part of the body used; an elbow rest for large hand movements and a hand rest for finger movements.
- When levers are used for step-wise control (e.g. gear levers), the distance between positions should be one-third of the length of the lever.
- Where the lever also acts as a visual indicator, the distance between positions can be reduced. The critical distance is then the operator's ability to see the markings.
- The surface of the lever handle should have a high friction coefficient, so that the hand does not slip.

Cranks

These are suited to continuous control where there are high demands for speed. Cranks can be used for both fine and coarse control depending on the degree of gearing selected. The following recommendations apply to cranks:

- Cranks are preferable to wheels where two or more revolutions are to be made.

- For small cranks less than 8 cm in radius, the resistance should be at least 9 Newton and a maximum of 22 Newton when rapid movement is required.
- Large cranks of 12-20 cm radius should be used when precision is required (accuracy between a half to one revolution), with the resistance between 1-35 Newton.
- The handle should have a high surface friction to prevent the hand slipping.

Wheels

Wheels are used for two-handed operations. Identification of the position is very important if the wheel can be rotated through several revolutions. In addition, the following recommendations apply:

- The turning angle should not exceed +/- 60 degrees from the zero position.
- The diameter of the ring forming the outside of the wheel should be between 18-50 mm and should increase as the size of the wheel increases.
- The wheel should have a high surface friction so that the hand does not slip.

In Table 1, the relative advantages of different forms of control devices for computerised process systems for four common tasks are presented.

Keyboard with Predetermined Functions for Various Keys (Fixed-Function Keyboard)

Keyboards with predetermined functions for all keys normally have two main parts - an alphanumeric or a numeric part and a function key part. The function key part has different keys for different predetermined tasks such as staring, stopping, process A, process B, etc.

This type of keyboard is characterised by the need for a large number of keys, usually one per function. Where there are many functions and several subfunctions within every main function, problems arise with grouping the keys in the proper way and in positioning the keys in a mutually logical way which is consistent in terms of movements.

The alternative to having a large number of function keys is to have just a few of them and to use particular codes instead which can be entered numerically or alphanumerically. This type of keyboard is best when the user is spanding a large part of his working time at the keyboard, which is a relative uncommon situation in the context of the foreseen demonstrators.

Table 1. Advantages of different forms of control devices for computerised process systems for four common tasks

Control	TASK			
	1	*2*	*3*	*4*
	Numeric data	Alphabetic data	Position cursor	Graphic information
Fixed-function key-board	X	XX		–
Variable-function keyboard	XX			–
Lever	–	–	(X)	
Wheel	–	–	(X)	
Light pen			X	–
Electronic data board			–	X
Touch screen	X	X	X	(X)
Mouse	–	–	X	(X)
Joystick (Track-ball)			(X)	

(X), may be sometimes usable; *X*, usable; *XX*, very good; _, not recommended. Empty columns mean that the advantages and disadvantages of the application are not known.

Keyboard with Variable Functions for the Keys (Variable Functions Keyboard)

Keyboards where there are a variety of functions for each of the different keys are relatively uncommon but often exist as part of the more traditional keyboard (e.g. the top row of keys on the keyboard). A common form of such keyboards is to have a row of unmarked keys under the monitor screen and to have squares representing the different keys directly above them on the screen. Depending on the picture being shown on the screen text appears in different windows showing the functions that the keys have for each frame.

Depending on its design, the keyboard can be pre-programmed to lead the operator naturally through the various frames. This type of programming of the keyboard functions may be an advantage for especially important types of operation where errors could have serious consequences. A major disadvantage from the user's perspective is that they may feel their work is being too highly controlled. Another disadvantage with this type of keyboard is that it requires a lot of programming resources. However, an advantage is that the hardware does not need to be changed (e.g. re-building or extending the keyboard) to any great extent even if a major change is to be made in the function of the control and conclusively this form of control should be viewed as rather flexible.

Light Pen

The light pen is a stylus that generates information when it is pointed at the screen. The light pen contains a light detector or photocell. Light pens have either a shutter or finger-operated mechanical switch that when pressed allows light to reach the light detector. In this manner, unwished activation is avoided. Because the light pen is activated by the increase in brightness of the CRT phosphor, it may typically only be used with CRT displays.

There are two modes in which the light pen may be used: *pick* or *pointing* mode, and *tracking* mode. In *pointing* mode a character or figure may be selected by first pointing to a spot on the display and then enabling the light pen. In *tracking* mode the light pen is used to position a cursor on the display. The operator aims the light pen at the cursor and then moves the pen. As long as the image remains in the light pen's field of view, a line will be traced where the pen is moved.

The field of view of the light pen can be modified and the size and spacing of the targets may depend upon the field of view chosen. For instance, a large field of view may make it easier to select a small or dim target, but it also means that the targets must not be close together or an incorrect target may be selected. It should be noted that while the light pen may be able to select extremely small targets, the human operator may not be capable of such accuracy.

Because use of the light pen involves a natural pointing gesture, this input device is well suited to menu selection tasks. While it may also be used for drawing, it is not accurate for precise sketching needs. The light pen is not capable of tracing from hard copy since it must be in contact with the screen. Conclusively, light pens are most useful in placing and moving symbols on a display, regardless of required speed.

The light pen is the only input device beside the touch screen that uses the output display as the input interface. Since this interface provides a direct relationship between output and input, it therefore allows natural pointing and / or drawing gestures to be used to input data. The light pen may also be mounted in a device that is worn on the head, providing an input device for the motor impaired user.

Among the disadvantages of the light pen, there should be referenced the fact that the user must sit within arm's reach of the display. In addition, holding the light pen to the screen can be fatiguing over long work periods.

Touch Screen

A touch screen device produces an input signal in response to a touch or movement of the finger on the display. Touchscreens have traditionally been used with CRTs, but it is also possible to use them with other display technologies. There are two principles of touch screen operation: either an overlay senses pressure or beams projected across the screen are interrupted.

When choosing a touch screen, it is important to consider their inherent characteristics in order to provide the optimal match between the touch screen and its intended application. Characteristics important in determining touch screen performance are: resolution, parallax, durability, optical clarity, installation and design, ease of use, environmental considerations and cost.

The above list of characteristics concerns hardware dimensions that affect the performance of a touch screen in different applications. In the following, several potential design parameters are briefly discussed.

Two other factors affecting performance with touch screen keys are their size and the separation between them. Experimental activities showed that the taller keys led to better performance and the tall, wide keys were preferred. The separation between keys was not as critical, and when the keys were not large enough the separation did not affect performance. Conclusively, optimal key matrix design should provide dense vertical arrangements of tall keys and wide keys are preferred.

As far as the feedback is concerned, it is possible to provide users with feedback of both the current cursor location and of the correctness of their actions. It is also possible to modify the software to accept only certain inputs as valid. Both of these techniques may be used to improve performance by making users aware of the results of their actions and by making the effects of spurious inputs or movements negligible.

Due to the nature of the touch screen device, it is best suited to certain task types. Thus, they are recommended when working with data already displayed on the screen, while they are inefficient for inputting new graphic information or for free hand drawing. Touch screen devices are quite useful in menu selection tasks. In addition, it should be mentioned that selection or entry of single characters is slow and may be beyond the resolution capabilities of the touch screen device. In such a case, rate enhancement facilities would prove useful, e.g. word prediction.

One of the most obvious advantages of touch screen devices is that the input device is also the output device. That is, there is direct hand-eye coordination. Consequently, there is a direct relationship between the user's input and the displayed output.

A second advantage is that possible inputs are limited by what is dispalyed on the screen, thus no memorisation of commands is required and input errors are minimised. In addition, the possible inputs can change as the display changes so that the operator may be led through an appropriate sequence of inputs.

Touch screens have several disadvantages. Because the output surface is also the input medium, the user must sit within arm's reach of the display. This requirement may also constrain both the workplace design and the mobility of the operator. The user must continually lift his hand to the display and may thus experience arm fatigue; additionally, the user's finger or arm may block the screen.

Another disadvantage is that regardless of the inherent touch screen resolution, there is limited target resolution possible due to the size of the operator's finger in relation to the screen.

Electronic Data Board: Graphic (Data) Tablet

Graphic or data tablets consist of a flat panel that is placed on a table in front of the display. The surface of the tablet represents the display and movement of a finger or a stylus on the tablet provides information for cursor location (Davies et al., 1988). There are two types of graphic tablets: digitising tablets that have a special stylus or puck attached to the tablet by a cable, where the stylus produces signals indicating coordinate values for cursor positioning, and touch tablets or touch-sensitive tablets. The latter respond to a touch by a finger or pen, and they use information from the tablet instead of a stylus to calculate cursor position.

One feature of the tablet that is subject to modification is the way the cursor responds to a movement or a placement on the tablet. For example, when the individual places his finger on the tablet, the display cursor may move from its current position and appear at a position that corresponds to the location of the finger on the tablet. Movement of the finger on the tablet will produce cursor movement such that the cursor location is continuously referenced to the actual coordinates of the finger on the tablet. This method may be referred to as an *absolute* mode of cursor control.

A second possibility is that when the finger is placed anywhere on the tablet, the display cursor remains in its current position. Movement of the finger in this case leads to a corresponding cursor movement relative to this cursor location. Therefore, this method is referred to as a *relative* mode of cursor control. Relative mode may be approximated by the movement of a cursor by a trackball. The difference between the absolute and the relative modes may be described as a difference in the information provided for cursor location: in absolute mode both cursor position and movement information are provided, while only cursor movement information is given in relative mode.

The amount of movement of the display cursor in response to a movement (i.e. the *control-display gain*) on the tablet may be changed. When a tablet is used in absolute mode, the control-display gain dictates the size of the tablet. For example, a gain of 1.0 means that the tablet is the same size as the display, while a gain of 2.0 means that the tablet is half the size of the display. This is true for absolute mode because the coordinates of the tablet are directly translated into a position on the display. With relative mode, the finger can be anywhere on the tablet since the finger provides movement information only. Thus, the size of the tablet may vary when relative mode is employed.

Although the fact that graphic tablets are separate from the display means that there is an indirect relationship between the output and input devices, it also means that they are more flexible than touch screen devices. The size of the tablet may vary from one that can fit on or next to a keyboard to an entire digitising tablet. Additionally, the low profile of the tablet in comparison to a joystick or a trackball means that inadvertent activation is less likely. Also, the tablet can be made easily transportable.

In addition to allowing flexibility in sizing, the flat surface of the tablet itself may be configured in many ways. For example, for ease and correctness of positioning, a template may be placed over the tablet to correspond with positions on the display in a menu selection task. This is especially useful for a task in which menu or function positions do not change.

Due to the indirect nature of the graphic tablet, it is important to include a feedback or confirmation mechanism, especially where incorrect entries may be damaging. An audible click or tone and / or a visual confirmation can be used to signal that an entry has been recognised. Visual and auditory feedback may be especially helpful since no tactile feedback is provided by pressing the tablet. Requiring confirmation and providing feedback have two benefits: first, the operator is aware that an entry has been accepted, and second, inappropriate inputs can be avoided.

A touch tablet may typically be used with either a finger or a stylus. The advantage of using a finger is its simplicity. A stylus, however, can provide greater resolution since the area over which it applies pressure is smaller than that of the finger. It also allows an operator to make small movements without requiring the entire hand or arm to move. Moving the stylus with the fingers allows fine adjustments to be made.

Graphic tablets may be effectively used for several types of tasks. A graphic tablet is virtually the only input device useful for drafting, or hardcopy data entry and free hand sketching. Touch tablets are also appropriate when the user must select or point to an item from an array or a menu. Because of their inherent graphic nature and the fact that with many tablets all fingers may not be used at one time, alphanumeric data entry with graphic tablets is typically slow.

Graphic tablets have several advantages. First the movement required and the control-display relationship are natural to many users. Moreover, the employment of a tablet seems more "natural" since the user is not required to translate a command or a movement intro a series of key presses.

In comparison with touch screen devices, in which the user points directly at the screen to the input data, the graphic tablet provides four distinct advantages:

- Both the display and the tablet may be positioned separately according to user preference;
- The user's hand does not cover any parts of the display;
- There are no problems with parallax due to the viewing angle of the user;
- Drift/ flow in the display will not affect the input.

Among the identified disadvantages of graphic tablets, there should be noted that they do not provide high positioning accuracy and, in comparison to a touch screen, they do not provide direct hand-eye coordination.

Voice Identification

Voice input in comparison with other input technologies requires a great deal of computational power and memory and is just beginning to be economically feasible. Because it is natural, voice input is expected to be well accepted by users. However, in looking at its functional characteristics, it is seen to have a fairly narrow range of capabilities. Its strengths lie in the area of text input and applications where voice commands can be used for control functions.

The basic operation modes of a speech recogniser are either speaker dependent or speaker independent. A speaker dependent system requires that an individual user adapts or trains the system to his way of speaking, thus providing a high degree of accuracy for an individual user. In a speaker independent system, the device must recognise any user with little or no prior knowledge of their speaking characteristics.

In the context of a personal communication aid system that is characterised for its high degree of individual use, a speaker dependent system may be employed that gets training with the collaboration of the end user, the facilitator, the therapist and the supplier. Of course the adoption of a speaker independent system might drastically reduce the required resources in terms of collaboration and interaction of the above actors but since the communication aid should be considered as a very "personal" item of the impaired user, we should consider the case of adopting a speaker dependent system as a deserving and competent solution too.

A second categorisation of the recogniser is whether it is a discrete or continuous word recognition system. Discrete word recognition refers to the identification of words or phrases uttered as isolated entities with a perceptible pause between successive words. Continuous speech recognition must deal with ill defined word onset and cessations as well as coarticulation effects, which change the characteristics of the word features.

Most speech input devices currently available are trainable (i.e. speaker dependent) discrete word recognisers and are offered in a variety of forms ranging from plug-in cards for various personal computers to standalone devices with communication protocols. A number of human factors issues are implied in the specifications of these speech input devices. The vocabulary size, the need for training and the ease of system integration into an application are frequently a function of the task to be accomplished by end users, their training, and their motivation.

Trackball

A trackball is composed of a fixed housing holding a ball that can be moved freely in any directions by the fingertips. It is similar to the mouse in operation. Two classes of trackballs are: (i) mechanical trackballs that make use of potentiometers, (ii) trackballs using optics (Doran, 1985).

The diameter, mass and frictional forces of the trackball may all be adjusted. Control-display gain is an additional design parameter that must be specified. Like the mouse, the trackball is a solely *relative* mode device.

Due to inherent characteristics of the trackball, it is best suited for tasks requiring rapid cursor positioning. Trackballs are also considered as excellent input devices for moving and indicating symbols on a display, especially when high speed and accuracy are necessary.

The trackball has several advantages that have contributed to its selection in many applications for the performance of critical tasks. First, it is comfortable to use for an extended period of time if users can rest their forearm, since they can keep their hand in one place and spin the trackball, stopping it when desired. Second, it provides direct tactile feedback from the ball's rotation and speed. Third, it provides high resolution of movement. Fourth, it requires only a small and fixed amount of space and it can be installed in a keyboard.

Disadvantages of the trackball are that it cannot be used for tracing and input of hand-drawn characters.

Joystick (Multi-Position Lever)

Joysticks consist of a lever approximately 2.5 to 10 cm long, mounted vertically in a fixed base. The joystick operates using one of three basic machanisms: displacement, force or digital switches (Doran, 1985).

As with touch tablets, mice and trackballs, the gain of the joystick may be changed. It is important to incorporate a dead zone of zero velocity around the center position of a rate-control joystick so that nulling the joystick input is not difficult. Gain remains an issue in the design of rate-control joysticks. In this case, the gain specifies the cursor speed that results from a unit displacement of the displacement joystick or a unit force applied to the force joystick.

A joystick may also be designed to offer viscous resistance. In this case the application of a constant force to the joystick results in a constant rate of cursor movement. Increasing the force applied to the joystick increases the rate of displacement. Viscous damping aids in the execution of smooth control movements and is particularly appropriate if maintaining a constant rate of cursor movement or acquiring a cursor location at a particular time.

Joysticks tend to be most suited to tracking tasks or to pointing tasks that do not require a great deal of precision. A joystick may be used in absolute mode for line drawing if high accuracy and speed are not required as well as in placing and moving symbols and in menu selection.

The advantages of the joystickinclude the fact that it requires only a small fixed amount of desk space and can be made small enough to fit into a keyboard. If a palm or hand rest is provided, the joystick may be used for extended periods of time with little fatigue. Because the joystick is used in various applications, there are many models available ranging from inexpensive, typically switch-activated joysticks, to more expensive joysticks that allow the user to modify many of the features discussed earlier.

Disadvantages include low accuracy and low resolution and inability to support input of single characters.

Mouse

Mice are hand held input devices that can fit under the palm or fingertips. Movement of the mouse on a flat surface is used to generate cursor movement. Mice have from one to three buttons that may be pressed to perform such functionsas changing menus, drawing lines or confirming inputs. Movement of the mouse is detected mechanically or optically (Goy, 1988).

The mechanical technique typically involves mounting a small ball in the bottom of the mouse; essentially this device is then an upside down trackball. The optical technique uses optical sensors that emit pulses as the mouse is moved across a special grid. The number of lines in the grid are counted as the mouse crosses the grid, and XY coordinates are calculated accodingly.

As indicated previously, mice typically have one or more buttons that may be pressed to perform various functions. Two methods of button depression are:

- Multiple depressions on one button
- Depression of multiple buttons

For a task in which one item is repeatedly selected, performance is faster with multiple clicks on the same button rather than with simultaneous clicks on multiple buttons. However for tasks involving several actions, performance using multiple buttons is better than when multiple clicks of the same button are used.

As is the case with the graphic tablet, the gain of the mouse may be changed and adapted to the particular user needs. Especially in the case of a mouse emulator, e.g. a mouse plate to be used by (partially) motor impaired users, the gain may be treated relatively to the cursor speed.

Mouse as well as mouse emulators are best suited for pointing and selection tasks, while graphic tablets are more suited to drawing and design tasks. In addition, as with the touch screen devices, the mouse is not well suited for single character data entry.

Mice have become popular as computer peripheral devices for several reasons: they can work in small spaces because they can be picked up and repositioned, they are generally inexpensive in comparison to other devices such as graphic tablets, and the user can locate and move the mouse while still looking at the screen. A mouse plate, on the other hand, is neither "pickable" nor "repositionable" since these two tasks are difficult to perform by a motor impaired user.

Disadvantages include incompatibilities with many computers and / or applications, a lower resolution capability and fine control requirements as well as frequent repositioning in case of limited space (for the conventional mouse only).

Service Centre Considerations

According to (Ivergard, 1989), there are three main motives for having an operator in the control room of a service centre:

1. The operator acts as a supervisor in order to carry out certain standardised routine tasks which for various reasons have or can not been automated. He also has the job of calling for expert help when some unforeseen incident occurs.
2. The operator is himself a qualified expert with the job of carrying out production planning and optimisation tasks. Simpler, more routine and predictable types of fault are dealt with by the operator. The more serious, unforeseen faults, on the other hand, are passed on to special maintenance experts.
3. The operator is primarily a maintenance-oriented expert who gets information on the process from other sources, especially those which are economic in

character. He usually looks after safety related matters himself. The operator is expected to be able to deal with most unforeseen and difficult faults and events in the process.

In the environment of a service centre and more specifically in that of the control room, there are three main types of information devices:

- *Traditional instruments*
- *VDU screens*
- *Sound signals*

Though traditional instruments are still the most common form of information devices in the control room, more and more information is being transferred to VDUs. The design of pictures and the positioning of text within each frame on a VDU is usually a compromise between several different factors. It is usually very difficult to comply strictly to the various criteria which are set in designing different frames.

The design of frames of pictures is also determined by the length of the text as there is only a limited area available, and if the text is very long its length will determine its positioning. In such cases it may be necessary to abbreviate the text. When doing this, it is of great importance to maintain the comprehensibility of a word as far as possible, even though it is abbreviated.

Through the placing of the same information in the same position in different frames the possibility of errors by the operators is reduced drastically, together with the required search time. This is particularly true for novice users who use the terminal of the control room infrequently, e.g. in the case of employing volunteers for the shift in the service centre on a weekly basis. Consistent positioning of error messages is also very important as they must always be immediately obvious to the operator who should not have to search for them.

The most fundamental criteria by which information to be used in a frame should be analysed are:

- *Importance of the information*
- *Frequency of use*
- *Sequence of use*

It is clear that even though these criteria have importance on their own, they are very closely connected. An indicative example of this is the first information to come up on the screen which is often both the most important and frequently-used information.

Regarding the use of sound signals in the control room of a service centre, it should be mentioned that certain types of information are better transmitted as sound signals rather than visual ones. This is the case in the following situations:

- When the signal is originally acoustic;
- Warning signals. The advantage is that the operator does not need to see the signal in order to detect it; i.e. he does not need to look at an instrument or a region of the VDU constantly.
- Where the operator lacks training and experience of coded messages.
- Where two-way communication is required.
- Where the message concerns something which will occur in the future, e.g. the countdown to the start-up of a process.
- In stressful situations where there is a possibility that the operator would forget what a coded message meant.

Tones are preferable in the following situations:

- For simplicity.
- Where the operator is trained to understand coded messages.
- Where rapid action is required.
- In situations where it it difficult to hear speech (tones can be heard in situations where speech is inaudible).
- Where it is undesirable or unnecessary for others to understand the message.
- If the operator's job involves him talking constantly.
- In those cases where speech could interfere with other speech messages.

Though the work reported in (Thomas & McClelland, 1994) is not related to disabled users and their interaction problems, the findings are of immediate interest for the case of service centres. (Thomas & McClelland, 1994) discusses the successful development of a communications terminal for professional applications(police, fire, ambulance, traffic services, etc). In the project where the terminal (it is the Philips DS 3000 terminal) has been developed, the primary aim was to achieve more direct involvement of customers and operators in identifying operator requirements and evaluating design proposals. The main emphasis of the ergonomics contribution was put in the design phase.

The DS 3000 is a touch screen based terminal designed to handle a complex combination of radio and telephone communications, intercoms, alarms and auxiliary functions. The major goal for the DS3000 development team was to improve the terminal in terms of the functional capability of the system, the interaction design and the graphic design.

Human factors literature concerning the use of touch screens reports that the main advantages of touch screens include that they make use of direct eye-hand coordination, they have direct input and output relationship, all valid inputs are displayed and training is minimised. The disadvantages include that the user must sit within arm's length of the display, they can cause arm fatigue, the arm and the finger often block the line of sight to the screen, target resolution is restricted due to the size of operator's fingers and they are inappropriate for small targets.

One issue raised in the field studies reported in (Thomas & McClelland, 1994) concerned the use of numeric keypad. At five of the sites numeric keypads were represented on touch screens. Control room operators complained that when these keypads were used for dialling telephone numbers,, they were slow and error prone. An experiment was carried out to determine whether the hard keypad was sufficiently superior compared to surface acoustic wave or infra-red touch screen technologies to warrant the necessary investment in providing it. The results confirmed the initial hypothesis that the hard keypad performed better than the touch screen based ones for entering number sequences.

The following improvements were set as targets for the design of the terminal:

- Flatter dialogue structure
- Greater level of dialogue consistency
- Better use of colour coding and graphic environment
- Better screen zoning and better allocation of functions (task related).

The following graphics and interaction principles were used to guide the design:

- Give first priority to incoming calls and provide access to communications at all times.
- Avoid of high impact colours. Since the DS3000 user will be working with the touch screen for most of an eight hour work shift, the graphics designers chose a colour scheme based on soft, pastel colours to create a restful effect on operators.
- Place items used most frequently in the lower half of the screen to avoid fatigue when reaching for them.
- Ensure that immediate feedback is provided for all operator actions. Visual feedback is given every time an item is activated - a short flash or a change of colour. Audible feedback, a "click" sound, is synchronised with the visual feedback to reinforce the illusion that a button has been activated. The "click" was deliberately set low to avoid acoustic disturbance, but still enough to provide the operator with confirmation.

- Use simple interaction mechanisms. Effective use of the system is supported through use of a simple interaction paradigm: touch to activate, touch again to deactivate or change state.
- Create a "flat" system structure. Efficient use of the system is supported through minimum navigation. All functions accessible to operators can be reached within four levels. All functions required on a daily basis can be reached within two levels.
- Maintain a consistent interaction cycle. A consistent style was developed for opening, closing and interacting with dialogue boxes. The possibility to have multiple dialogue boxes open at one time was strictly limited, firstly so that the operator always has an overview of where he is in the system, and secondly to avoid the screen becoming cluttered with "unfinished business", which is a particularly undesirable state in view of the safety-critical nature of the applications (police, fire, ambulance, etc).

As far as the positioning of information and control devices in the control room of a service centre is concerned, (Ivergard, 1989) provides a coherent set of guidelines and design recommendations. More specifically, when designing the instrument panel itself, the tasks to be performed by the panel must be determined first. The functions which need to be displayed using the panel must then be determined and described. A detailed description must also be made of how the information on these functions is to be received. It is important to know, for instance, whether just a single instrument panel is needed or whether it is to be one of a repeated series of similar instrument panels, or equally, whether it will be just a segment of a panel which can be successively expanded. All these facts will then form the basis for the design of the instrument panel.

There are various methods used for designing the instrument panel and which one is chosen depends on what the panel's function is going to be. For certain applications, an instrument panel which represents a model of the process may be best while in other cases this form of panel may be wholly unsuitable and give very unsatisfactory results. It may be better to have an instrument panel on which the instruments are positioned according to one of the following models:

- ***Frequency of use***. If instrument A is read more frequently than instruments B and C, A is positioned nearest to the line of sight.
- ***Sequence of use***. If instrument A is always used before B and C, the B and C will be placed to the right of A in the line of sight.
- ***Degree of importance***. In cases where the instrument is very important, it can be placed centrally even if not used frequently.
- ***Similarity of function***. Instruments which show the same function (e.g.

temperature) or cover a particular part of the process can be positioned to-gether into a group.

The following three points apply to all the above models. All three functions are explained subsequently together with design guidelines.

Visibility

The operator must be able to see all instruments from his normal workplace with-out abnormal movements of his head or body. The following design principles for positioning with respect to the visibility of different instruments on a panel should be followed:

- *Warning signals and primary instruments.* Reading of this category of instru-ment must be possible without the operator having to change the position of the head or the eyes from the normal line of position.
- *Secondary instruments.* Reading can be performed by changing the direction of the eyes, but not the position of the head.
- *Other (infrequently used) instruments.* These instruments do not need to lie within the normal line of vision.

Identification

The operator must be able to find an instrument or a group of instruments rapidly without making mistakes. The individual instruments or groups of instruments should be separated in order to ease identification. Other ways to differentiate instruments are:

- Different colours orshading between the main and subsidiary panels.
- Lines of different colours around the instruments.
- A subsidiary panel away from the main panel.

Apart from the above, textual signs can be used. Rules governing the use of such signs are:

- Positioning must be consistent, e.g. either over or under the instrument.
- All panels, groups of instruments and individual instruments must have signs. The size of the signs (text) should increase by 25% from smallest to largest, for example single instruments smallest, then groups, and so on.
- The text must be horizontal.

- The sighns which are not related to function, manufacturer's nameplates, for example, must be positioned so that they cannot be confused with functional signs.
- Signs should not be put on curved surfaces.

Stereotyped Behaviour

Both control devices and instruments should be positioned and give the readings that people would expect. Users often have a predetermined expectation of what will happen in different situations which is based on experience. For instance, particular changes on an instrument, e.g. the clockwise movement of the pointer on a circular dial indicates an increase. Certain relationships between the movement of a pointer on an instrument and the movement of the controlling device are also expected.

Errors

(Zapf et al., 1992) presents a taxonomy of errors in human-computer interaction in office environments that differentiates four classes, namely:

- *Functionality problems*
- *Usability problems*
- *Interaction problems*
- *Inefficient behaviour*

In the context of the present document we focus on the class of usability related problems. (Zapf et al., 1992) presents a taxonomy of usability related problems. The following error classes are identified:

- ***Knowledge errors***: They occur when the user is unable to perform a task with the system because he does not know certain commands, function keys, rules, etc.
- ***Thought errors***: They occur when goals and plans are inadequately developed or when wrong decisions are made in the assignment of plans and sub-plans although the user knows all the necessary features of the system.
- ***Memory errors:*** They occur when a certain part of the plan is forgotten and not executed, although the goals and plans were initially correctly specified.
- ***Judgement errors:*** They appear when one cannot understand or interpret the computer feedback after an input.
- ***Habit errors:*** They imply that a correct action is performed in a wrong situation. This is the case when switching over from one word processing system

to another takes place and the user still uses function keys that were correct in the former but wrong in the latter.

- **Omission errors:** They happen when a person does not execute a well-known subplan which is most likely when a person is interrupted in an action plan. It is the case of forgetting to save a file before quitting an application, or of forgetting to activate the alarm, though the desired waking time has been set.
- **Recognition errors:** They appear when a well-known message is not noticed or is confused with another one.
- **Sensorimotor errors:** They are placed at the sensorimotor level. Most of the typing errors would be classified as sensorimotor errors.

(Zapf et al., 1992) proposes, conclusively, that there should be put more emphasis on error management while during training period strategies to handle errors should be taught, and not only ideal usage scenarios instructed. As far as knowledge errors are concerned, training is obviously of particular relevance; this is also suggested by the differences between novices and experts (Bartram et al., 2003). Thought errors point to the need of a higher transparency of a system. The management of memory errors is supported by systems that do not require keeping many "chunks" of information in mind. Finally, judgement errors may be avoided if system information were clear and easy to understand (DeBruijn et al., 2000).

Help Facilities

Theoretically it is possible to design services and applications that are so well designed, tested and inspected that no user assistance is ever needed. Nonetheless, we should not count on such theoretical possibilities since the understanding of events and ability to predict outcomes is imperfect. In the case of applications and facilities found either in the home environment or in the environment of a service centre we cannot always anticipatewhat users will do or how the applications will be used. Help facilities provide, thus, an "insurance policy" against less-than-perfect design.

According to (Kearsley, 1988), a help system is one or more applications designed to provide user assistance embedded in a larger application or system. Although help programs are usually completely integrated with the application system they provide help with, they may also be separate and "run" concurrently with the system.

According to the same source as above, help systems consist of two fundamental aspects: the *interface* and the *content*. The *interface* includes how the help messages are displayed, how the user accesses the help system, etc. The *content* is what the help messages say. Both aspects are equally important. If the help system is difficult to use because of poor interface design, it fails to be helpful. If the content of the help messages is unclear or inaccurate in some way, the help system also fails.

Help features may be buil into existing components of the system, as it is the case of an error-handling component of a system that is designed so that it tries to help the user determine what caused an error and what steps he can take to recover from the error.

The design of a help system is closely tied to the design of the overall system. Help displays depend upon the display capabilities of the system, as do input methods. Although help systems do not necessarily have to work the same way as the system they support does, it is usually a desirable characteristic that indicates consistency in the overall design process.

A concern that is usually raised in the development of help systems is that the same information is already available in printed documentation or training materials and courses. Assuming that people use the documentation or have attended and compelted the training provided, it still does not serve the same function as a help system, which is to provide an *immediate* answer to a specific problem. In many cases if the information is not immediately available the user tries to guess, repeat a previous sequence or, even, ignore something not understood. This effect leads regularly to further problems. In reality, documentation often is not conventionally available and training is not completed or is very general in nature. So, the help system provides the only source of information and assistance available.

The first major consideration in the design of a help system is whether the helps are static or dynamic. Static halps are independent of where the user is in his interaction with the service / application and any previous user actions, while on the other hand dynamic helps depend upon where the user is or previous actions of him including also help requests.

Dynamic helps can be either context sensitive or interactive. Context sensitive help messages are determined by the current location or function being used,while interactive help messages are responses to user questions and answers.

Static helps are usually fixed text entries that serve as an online glossary: when help is requested, users are asked either to enter their request or to select an issue from a list provided. In applications that adopt the command language dialogue style, helps are often explanations of individual commands.

One design alternative is the provision of multiple levels of help for succesive help requests. Thus the first help request prodices a general / generic assistance and successive requests produce additional or more detailed / focused assistance.

There are three principal ways for users to activate help systems:

- By typing a help command;
- By pressing a designatcd help key; or
- By selecting a help option from a menu.

Each has its advantages and disadvantages. More specifically, typed input has the advantage that a complex syntax can be implemented allowing specification of multiple terms or levels. This is, on the other hand, not the case when considering the context of HHI, since errors may take place in the input and the required effort from the side of the user is rather vast.

Help keys (e.g. using a function or control key) have the advantage that they can be activated easily and independently of typed input. A disadvantage of help keys is that they may be forgotten unless the user is reminded by a promp that is constantly displayed on the screen.

The major advantage of including help as a menu option is that it is visible and evident to users every time they look at a menu. All of the three above described methods for accessing help facilities are not exclusive and can be combined. For example, pressing a help key could produce a prompt line asking the user to type in the help request.

A differentiation should be made between system- and user-initiated helps. More specifically, system-initiated messages are presented to the user as advice or suggestions, are usually triggered by error conditions or other evidence that the user has a problem (e.g. a long lapse in using a rather frequent operation of a service / application). Users often perceive system-initiated help messages as interruption and prefer to initiate themselves any help requests. Of course this is the situation when considering interaction with able users and not with elderly anddisabled ones. In such a context, system-initiated help messages also make sense to help frequent users optimise their use of a system.

In case of adopting system-initiated help messages, it is recommended that the users are given the option of turning them off or specifying the level of message enabled (e.g. advisory, caution, warning). For instance, when considering the ALARM message to be provided in caseof a gas leak situation, the message might be criticised as being too long and verbalistic:

ALERT

A GAS leak has been detected in your backroom, open the windows,

close the gas and someone will come in a few minutes

In this context, there might only occur the fact:

ALERT

GAS leak in the backroom

ALERT

A GAS leak has been detected in your backroom

Open the windows

Close the gas

As far as the content of the delivered help information is considered, (Sukaviriya, 1991) identifies two types of help information, namley that about how to perform tasks (*operational*) and that being supportive knowledge to understand purposes of these tasks (*supportive* or *conceptual*). There seem to be slightly different but complementary opinions in the supportive information. The terms *supportive* knowledge and *conceptual* assistance are rather broad and within their scope they both include *interpretive* and *how-it-works* explanations, where interpretive information provides definitions of components and how-it-works information provides concepts about functional relationships of components in a system.

Kearsley (1988) provides a set of practical guidelines for the design and implementation of help facilities. The set is excerpted and annotated with explanations and / or indicative examples.

Make the Help System Easy to Access and Easy to Return Form

Helps must not act additively to problems or make the situation more confusing. A help system that is difficult to use or makes it difficult to return to the initial state of the application will not be considered useful. Moreover, the user should be reminded that help is available by displaying the command or function key to be used to get help. If help is not available at all places or times, a message should indicate when help is and is not available.

Make Help as Specific as Possible

When people ask for help they normally have a specific question or problem in mind and want an answer or explanation that is specific to that question or problem. Help systems that involve "surfing" through a lot of irrelevant information are not going to be perceived as very helpful. In short the more specific the help the better.

Collect Data to Determine what Help is Needed

It can not be emphasised enough that the design of good help systems is critically dependent upon careful analysis of actual user problems. Instead of trying to second guess what kinds of help will be needed, the construction and use of prototypes is in this context considered invaluable.

Give the User as Much Control of the Help System as Possible

The more control users have over the help system the more useful they will find it. Users should be in general able to:

- Initiate a help request and select the help "portion" desired
- Select the level of help, if multiple levels are available
- Add to or change existing help messages

The latter results to highly individualised help that may play also the role of "Post-it" notes for the use of the system.

Different Types of Users Need Different Help

Apart from individual differences related to the type and degree of disabilities, users will differ in their degree of experience in using such a kind of systems. The most usual categorisation of users regarding their degree of expertise is that one refer-ring to *novices*, *experts* and *casual users*. One thing to keep in mind is that people can switch categories fairly quickly, i.e. a person may change from being a novice to an expert on a particular segment of an application in a few hours or someone who was once an expert may become a casual user, or experts on one system may be novices on another.

Help Messages Must be Accurate and Complete

If the user discovers a help message that is inaccurate or misleading, the credibility of the entire help system is suspect. It is, thus, essential that all help messages are reviewed for their technical accuracy and correctness.

Do Not Use Help to Compensate for Poor Interface Design

Help systems are often used as first aid kit to "patch up" poorly designed interfaces. Instead of adding more help messages there should be tried out to redesign menus and command sequences, to improve the screen layouts and the error handling, thus reducing the dependence of the user on the help system.

REFERENCES

Baber, C., & Stanton, N. A. (1992). Defining "problem spaces" in VCR use: the application of task analysis for error identification. In E. J. Lovesey (Ed.) *Proceedings of the Ergonomics Society's 1992 Annual Conference, Birmingham, England, 7-10 April 1992, in Contemporary Ergonomics: Ergonomics for Industry.* Philadelphia: Taylor & Francis.

Bartram, L., and C. Ware (2002). Filtering and brushing with motion. Information Visualization , 1(1), 66–79. doi:10.1057/palgrave/ivs/9500005

Bartram, L., C. Ware, and T. Calvert (2003). Moticons: Detection, distraction and task. International Journal of Human-Computer Studies , 58(5), 515–545. doi:10.1016/S1071-5819(03)00021-1

Baudisch, P., N. Good, and P. Stewart (2001). Focus plus context screens: Combining display technology with visualization techniques. In [Orlando.]. Proceedings of UIST , 01, 31–34. doi:10.1145/502348.502354

Bingham, G. P., A. Bradley, M. Bailey, and R. Vinner (2001). Accommodation, occlusion, and disparity matching are used to guide reaching: A comparison of actual versus virtual environments. Journal of Experimental Psychology. Human Perception and Performance , 27(6), 1314–1334. doi:10.1037/0096-1523.27.6.1314

Boyer, D. L., Pollack, J. G., & Eggemeier, F. T. (1992). Effects of ageing on subjective workload and performance. In *Proceedings of the Human Factors Society 36th Annual Meeting,* October 12-16, Atlanta, Georgia.

Bradshaw, M. F., A. D. Parton, and A. Glennister (2000). The task-dependent use of binocular disparity and motion parallax information. Vision Research , 40(27), 3725–3734.doi:doi:10.1016/S0042-6989(00)00214-5

Braun, C. C., & Clayton Silver, N. (1992). Likelihood of reading warnings: the effect of fonts and font sizes. In *Proceedings of the Human Factors Society 36th Annual Meeting,* October 12-16, Atlanta, Georgia.

Braun, C. C., Sansing, L., & Clayton Silver, N. (1994). The interaction of signal word and colour on warning labels: Differences in perceived hazard. In *Proceedings of the Human Factors and Ergonomics Society 38th Annual Meeting,* October 24-28, Nashville, Tennessee.

Brelsford, J. W., Wogalter, M. S., & Scoggins, J. A. (1994). Enhancing comprehension and retention of safety-related pictorials. In *Proceedings of the Human Factors and Ergonomics Society 38th Annual Meeting*, October 24-28, Nashville, Tennessee.

Burford, B. C., & Baber, C. (1994). A user-centred evaluation of a simulated adaptive autoteller, in Proceedings of the Ergonomics Society's 1994 Annual Conference, University of Warwick, April 19-22. In S. A. Robertson (Ed.), *Contemporary Ergonomics 1994: Ergonomics for all*, Philadelphia: Taylor & Francis.

Card, S. K., & Nation, D. (2002). Degree-of-interest trees: A component of an attentionreactive user interface. *Proceedings of Advanced Visual Interfaces*, Trento, Italy, (pp. 231–245).

Carter, J. A. (1992). Standards, the future and designers. In *Proceedings of the Human Factors Society 36th Annual Meeting*, October 12-16, Atlanta, Georgia.

Cockburn, A., and B. McKenzie (2001). 3D or not 3D? Evaluating the effect of the third dimension in a document management system. [New York: ACM.]. Proceedings of SIGCHI , 99, 434–441.

Cutrell, E. B., Czerwinski, M., & Horvitz, E. (2000). Effects of instant messaging interruptions on computing tasks. *Proceedings of the CHI 2000 Conference on Human Factors in Computing Systems, Extended Abstracts*, (pp. 99–100). New York: ACM Press.

Czaja, S., and J. Sharit (1993). Stress reactions to computer-interactive tasks as a function of task structure and individual differences. International Journal of Human-Computer Interaction , 5(1).

Davies, T. E., Matthews, H. G., & Smith, P. D. (1988). Digitisers and Input Tablets. In S. Sherr (Ed), *Input Devices*. New York: Academic Press.

De Bruijn, O., Spence, R., & Tong, C. H. (2000). Rapid serial visual presentation: A spacetime trade-off in information presentation. Proceedings, Advance Visual Interfaces (AVI '2000), Palermo, Italy, (pp. 189–192). ACM Press: New York.

deHaemer, M. J., G. Wright, and T. W. Dillon (1994). Automated speech recognition for spreadsheet tasks: Performance effects for experts and novices. International Journal of Human-Computer Interaction , 6(3).

Dillenbourg, P., Baker, M., Blaye, A., & O'Malley, C. (1996), The Evolution of Research on Collaborative Learning. In E. Spada & P. Reiman (Eds.), *Learning in Humans and Machine: Towards an Interdisciplinary Learning Science*. New York: Elsevier.

Doran, D. (1988). Trackballs and Joysticks. In S. Sherr (ed), *Input Devices.* New York: Academic Press.

Ekman, P. (2003). *Emotions Revealed: Recognizing Faces and Feelings to Improve Communication and Emotional Life.* New York: Times Books.

Enns, J. T., E. L. Austin, V. Di Lollo, R. Rauchenberger, and S. Yantis (2001). New objects dominate luminance transients in setting attentional priority. Journal of Experimental Psychology. Human Perception and Performance, 27(6), 1287–1302. doi:10.1037/0096-1523.27.6.1287

Fine, I., and R. A. Jacobs (2000). Perceptual learning for a pattern discrimination task. Vision Research, 41, 449–461.

Fine, I., and R. A. Jacobs (2002). Comparing perceptual learning across tasks: A review. Journal of Vision (Charlottesville, Va.), 2, 190–203. doi:10.1167/2.2.5

Gelderblom, G. J., & Bremner, A. (1993). The role of experience in performance on different types of telephone memory retrieval tasks, in Proceedings of the Ergonomics Society's 1993 Annual Conference, Edinburgh, Scotland, 13-16 April. In E. J. Lovesey (Ed), *Contemporary Ergonomics 1993: Ergonomics and Energy.* Philadelphia: Taylor & Francis.

Gibbons, S. C. (1992). Organising the domain of menus. In *Proceedings of the Human Factors Society 36th Annual Meeting,* October 12-16, Atlanta, Georgia.

Gomez, C. C., Shebilske, W., & Regian, J. W. (1994). The effects of training on cognitive capacity demands for synthetic speech. In *Proceedings of the Human Factors and Ergonomics Society 38th Annual Meeting,* October 24-28, Nashville, TN.

Goodwin, C. J. (2001). *Research in Psychology: Methods and Design.* New York: Wiley.

Goy, C. (1988). Mice. In S. Sherr (Ed.), *Input Devices.* New York: Academic Press.

Han, S. H., & Kwahk, J. (1994). Design of a menu for small displays presenting a single item at a time. In *Proceedings of the Human Factors and Ergonomics Society 38th Annual Meeting,* October 24-28, Nashville, TN.

Hatta, K., and Y. Iiyama (1991). Ergonomic study of automatic teller machine operability. International Journal of Human-Computer Interaction, 3(3).

Hollingworth, A., and J. M. Henderson (2002). Accurate visual memory for previously attended objects in natural scenes. Journal of Experimental Psychology. Human Perception and Performance , 28(1), 113–136.

Huber, D. E., and R. C. O'Reilly (2003). Persistence and accommodation in short-term priming and other perceptual paradigms: Temporal segregation through synaptic depression. Cognitive Science , 27, 403–430.

Huey, R. W., Buckley, D. S., & Lerner, N. D. (1994). Audible performance of smoke alarm sounds. In *Proceedings of the Human Factors and Ergonomics Society 38th Annual Meeting*, October 24-28, Nashville, TN.

Humphrey, D. G., Kramer, A. F., & Gore, S. S. (1994). Perceptual organisation and grouping factors: Age related effects. In *Proceedings of the Human Factors and Ergonomics Society 38th Annual Meeting*, October 24-28, Nashville, TN.

Irani, P., M. Tingley, and C. Ware (2001). Using perceptual syntax to enhance semantic content in diagrams. IEEE Computer Graphics and Applications , 21(5), 76–84.doi:doi:10.1109/38.946634

Irani, P., and C. Ware (2003). Diagramming information structures using 3D perceptual primitives. ACM Transactions on Computer-Human Interaction , 10(1), 1–19. doi:10.1145/606658.606659

Ivergard, T. (1989). *Handbook of Control Room Design and Ergonomics*. Philadelphia: Taylor and Francis.

Jagacinski, R. J., Greenberg, N., Liao, M.-J., & Wang, J. (1992). Manual performance of older and younger adults with supplementary auditory cues. In *Proceedings of the Human Factors Society 36th Annual Meeting*, October 12-16, Atlanta, GA.

Johnson, S. H. (2001). Seeing two sides at once: Effects of viewpoint and object structure on recognizing three-dimensional objects. Journal of Experimental Psychology. Human Perception and Performance , 27(6), 1468–1484. doi:10.1037/0096-1523.27.6.1468

Jordan, P. W., & Moyes, J. (1994). Does icon design really matter? in Proceedings of the Ergonomics Society's 1994 Annual Conference, University of Warwick, 19-22 April. In S. A. Robertson (Ed.), *Contemporary Ergonomics 1994: Ergonomics for all*. Philadelphia: Taylor & Francis.

Kearsley, G. (1988). *On line help systems: Design and implementation*. New York: Ablex Publishing Corporation.

Kirkpatrick, M., Perse, R. M., Dutra, L. A., Creedon, M. A., & Cohen-Mansfield, J. (1992). Development of a memory aid design concept for older users. In *Proceedings of the Human Factors Society 36th Annual Meeting,* October 12-16, Atlanta, Georgia.

Komerska, R., & Ware, C. (2003). Haptic task constraints for 3D interaction. *Proceedings of IEEE Haptic Interfaces for Virtual Environments and Teleoperator Systems Symposium* (pp. 270–277).

Kosara, R., S. Miksch, and H. Hauser (2002). Focus+context taken literally. IEEE Computer Graphics and Applications , 22(1), 22–29. doi:10.1109/38.974515

Laidlaw, D. H., R. M. Kirby, J. S. Davidson, T. S. Miller, M. da Silva, W. H. Warren, and M. Tarr (2001, October). Quantitative comparative evaluation of 2D vector field visualization methods. [San Diego, CA.]. Proceedings of IEEE Visualization , 2001, 143–150.

Laramee, R. S., and C. Ware (2002). Rivalry and interference with a head-mounted display. ACM Transactions on Human-Computer Interaction , 9(3), 1–14.

Lin, R. (1992). An application of the semantic differential to icon design. In *Proceedings of the Human Factors Society 36th Annual Meeting*, October 12-16, Atlanta, GA.

Logan, R. J., Augaitis, S., & Renk, T. (1994). Design of simplified television remote controls: A case for behavioural and emotional usability. In *Proceedings of the Human Factors and Ergonomics Society 38th Annual Meeting,* October 24-28, Nashville, TN.

Melcher, D. (2001). Persistence of visual memory for scenes: A medium-term memory may help us keep track of objects during visual tasks. Nature , 412, 401. doi:10.1038/35086646

Metz, S., Misle, B., Denno, S., & Odom, J. (1992). Thermostats for individuals with movement disabilities: Design options and manipulation strategies. In *Proceedings of the Human Factors Society 36th Annual Meeting,* October 12-16, Atlanta, GA.

Modrick, J. A. (1992a). Review of concepts and approaches to complexity. In *Proceedings of the Human Factors Society 36th Annual Meeting, October 12-16, Atlanta, GA.*

Modrick, J. A. (1992b). The role of complexity in human performance, merry and training. In *Proceedings of the Human Factors Society 36th Annual Meeting, October 12-16, Atlanta, GA.*

Perry, M. (2003). Distributed cognition. In J. M. Carroll (Ed.) *HCI Models, Theories, and Frameworks: Toward a Multidisciplinary Science*, (pp. 193–223). San Francisco: Morgan Kaufmann.

Philipsen, G. (1994). Effects of six different highlighting modes on visual search performance in menu options. International Journal of Human-Computer Interaction , 6(3).

Pirolli, P. (2003). Exploring and Finding Information. In J. M. Caroll (Ed.) *HCI Models, Theories and Frameworks: Toward a Multidisciplinary Science*. San Francisco: Morgan Kaufmann.

Plumlee, M., & Ware, C. (2002). Modeling performance for zooming vs multi-window interfaces based on visual working memory. *Advanced Visual Interfaces, Trento, Italy, May Proceedings*, (pp. 59–68).

Plumlee, M., & Ware, C. (2003). An evaluation of methods for linking 3D views. *Proceedings of the ACM SIGGRAPH 2003 Symposium on Interactive 3D Graphics, Monterey, CA*, (pp. 193–201).

Polzella, D. J., Gravelle, M. D., & Klauer, K. M. (1992). Perceived effectiveness of danger signs: A multivariate analysis. *Proceedings of the Human Factors Society 36th Annual Meeting, October 12-16, Atlanta, GA*.

Potter, M. C. (2002). Recognition memory for briefly presented pictures: The time course of rapidly forgetting. Journal of Experimental Psychology. Human Perception and Performance , 28(5), 1163–1175. doi:10.1037/0096-1523.28.5.1163

Rasmussen, J. (1981). *Human errors: A taxonomy for describing human malfunction in industrial installations*. Report N. Riso-M-2304, Riso National Laboratory, Denmark.

Rensink, R. A. (2000). The dynamic representation of scenes. Visual Cognition , 7, 17–42. doi:10.1080/135062800394667

Rensink, R. A. (2002). Change detection. Annual Review of Psychology , 53, 245–277. doi:10.1146/annurev.psych.53.100901.135125

Robertson, G. L., & Hix, D. (1994). User Interface design guidelines for computer accessibility by mentally retarded users. In *Proceedings of the Human Factors and Ergonomics Society 38th Annual Meeting, October 24-28, Nashville, TN*.

Rogers, W. A., Kirsten Gilbert, D., & Fraser Cabrera, E. (1994). An in-depth analysis of automatic teller machine usage by older adults. In *Proceedings of the Human Factors and Ergonomics Society 38th Annual Meeting, October 24-28, Nashville, TN*.

Ruttkay, Z., H. Noot, and P. Hagen (2003). Emotion disc and emotion squares: Tools to explore the facial expression space. Computer Graphics Forum , 22(1), 49–53. doi:10.1111/1467-8659.t01-1-00645

Sadr, J., F. Jarudi, and P. Sinha (2003). The role of the eyebrows in face recognition. Perception , 32(3), 285–293. doi:10.1068/p5027

Schoorlemmer, W., & Kanis, H. (1992). Operation of controls on everyday products. In *Proceedings of the Human Factors Society 36th Annual Meeting, October 12-16, Atlanta, GA*.

Schumacher, R. M. (1992). Phone based interfaces: Research and guidelines. In *Proceedings of the Human Factors Society 36th Annual Meeting, October 12-16, Atlanta, GA*.

Shelton, A. L., and T. P. McNamara (2001). Systems of spatial reference in human memory. Cognitive Psychology , 43, 274–310. doi:10.1006/cogp.2001.0758

Smither, J. A.-A. (1992). The processing of synthetic speech by older and younger adults. In *Proceedings of the Human Factors Society 36th Annual Meeting, October 12-16, Atlanta, GA*.

Spence, I., and A. Efendov (2001). Target detection in scientific visualization. Journal of Experimental Psychology. Applied , 7(1), 13–26. doi:10.1037/1076-898X.7.1.13

Spence, R. (2002). Rapid, serial and visual: A presentation technique with potential. Information Visualization , 1, 13–19. doi:10.1057/palgrave/ivs/9500008

Sukaviriya P. N., (1991, September). *Multimedia help: A literature survey and a preliminary experimental design*, (GIT-GVU-91-18). Graphics, Visualisation and Usability Center, Georgia Institute of Technology, Atlanta, GA.

Thomas, B., & McClelland, I. (1994). The development of a touch screen based communications terminal. In *Proceedings of the Human Factors and Ergonomics Society 38th Annual Meeting, October 24-28, Nashville, TN*.

Tucker, P., and D. M. Jones (1991). Voice as Interface: An overview. International Journal of Human-Computer Interaction , 3(2).

Viguier, A., G. Clement, and Y. Trotter (2001). Distance perception within near visual space. Perception , 30, 115–124. doi:10.1068/p3119

Vogel, E. K., G. F. Woodman, and S. J. Luck (2001). Storage of features, conjunctions and objects in visual working memory. Journal of Experimental Psychology. Human Perception and Performance , 27(1), 92–114. doi:10.1037/0096-1523.27.1.92

Voute, C. C. C., Kanis, H., & Marinissen, A. H. (1993). User involved redesign of a clock radio, in Proceedings of the Ergonomics Society's 1993 Annual Conference, Edinburgh, Scotland, 13-16 April. In E. J. Lovesey (Ed.), *Contemporary Ergonomics 1993: Ergonomics and Energy.* Philadephia: Taylor & Francis.

Wang, W., & Milgram, P. (2001). Dynamic viewpoint tethering for navigation in large-scale virtual environments. *Proceedings of the Human Factor and Ergonomics Society*, 1862–1866.

Ware, C., Plumlee, M., Arsenault, R., Mayer, L. A., Smith, S., & House, D. (2001). GeoZui3D: Data fusion for interpreting oceanographic data. *Oceans 2001 Proceedings*, Hawaii, 1960–1964.

Ware, C., H. Purchase, L. Colpoys, and M. McGill (2002). Cognitive measurements of graph aesthetics. Information Visualization , 1, 103–110. doi:10.1057/palgrave. ivs.9500013

Weigle, C., W. Emigh, G. Liu, R. Taylor, J. Enns, and C. Healey (2000). Oriented texture slivers: A technique for local value estimation of multiple scalar fields . Proceedings of Graphics Interface , 2000, 163–170.

Wisher, R. A. (1992). The role of complexity of psychomotor and procedural skills. In *Proceedings of the Human Factors Society 36th Annual Meeting, October 12-16, Atlanta, GA.*

Wright, U., Major Kumar, G., & Mital, A. (1994). Reach design for the elderly. In *Proceedings of the Human Factors and Ergonomics Society 38th Annual Meeting, October 24-28, Nashville, TN.*

Xu, Y. (2002). Limitations of object-based features encoding in visual short-term memory. Journal of Experimental Psychology. Human Perception and Performance , 28(2), 458–468. doi:10.1037/0096-1523.28.2.458

Yoshimune, T., & Ogawa, K. (1994). Graphical feedback system to effectively support user's task. In *Proceedings of the Human Factors and Ergonomics Society 38th Annual Meeting, October 24-28, Nashville, TN.*

Zajicek, M., Brownsey, K., Muller, C., & Runge, F. (1994). Perspectives on language differences in computer aided telephony, in Proceedings of the Ergonomics Society's 1994 Annual Conference, University of Warwick, 19-22 April. In S. A. Robertson (Ed), *Contemporary Ergonomics 1994: Ergonomics for all.* Philadelphia: Taylor & Francis.

Zapf, D., F. C. Brodbeck, M. Frese, H. Peters, and J. Pruemper (1992). Errors in working with office computers: A first validation of a taxonomy for observed errors in a field setting. International Journal of Human-Computer Interaction , 4(4).

Chapter 9
Service Metaphysics

Transcendental matters of services: communities of users, service idealism, theo-
logical and existentialist perspectives on services – this chapter (in contrast to
the previous one) is the most philosophical part of the entire book though it is of
straight utility for its linkage to many service business and management topics.
Furthermore, in this chapter we present a methodology (PACE) that helps for the
valuation of intangible assets like (what else?) services. PACE is presented with
practical examples and contextually linked with project and other service related
activities. Services unequivocally constitute an area where increasing interest of
experts from the areas of intellectual capital management and valuation will be
concentrated, as they on their own possess qualities and characteristics of intangible
assets because of their immaterial nature.

I don't know what exactly you may expect to find in a Chapter entitled Service Metaphysics – what I know for sure is that the ancient Greek philosopher Aristoteles used this term for describing some of his books that were subsequent to his books about physics. Here, we can still use this convention and treat anything that was not

DOI: 10.4018/978-1-60566-683-9.ch009

part of the physics of services as belonging to the service metaphysics.

Let's look firstly at some common misconceptions in the business world of services:

- "An institution able to show a record of efficient involvement in service-related projects and activities in a specific area in the past is able to set up a similarly adequately skilled service team in any new service development project".
- "A company active in the service area addressed by a particular project with a successful record of sales (products or services) will be similarly willing to sell the products or services, resulting from the service research project it participates".
- "A company or institution participates in a research project in order to develop know-how necessary for its future service operations, to cope with future challenges and to establish strategic alliances".

In many cases, regarding the above, there is a huge discrepancy between what is put forward in a discussion for the introduction of a new service proposal or a service performance review and the daily routine of a project. In certain other cases, intentions need to be supported by actions. In all cases, the everyday financial pressure – in periods of economic uncertainties in particular – affect the initial commitment to a project, under the surging demand for cash-flow and better economic indexes of the organization.

For the needs of our investigation, we focus on the case of research projects which form an exciting case of a service structure. A research institution might, for instance, truly wish to enter a new research area, but has to operate under the tremendous pressure to bring in money – which makes researchers grasp at any opportunity that appears on the street corner. In the event of a proposal being successful, they will lose time and momentum because they will have to organize an ad hoc team – either by asking people who might be interested, or by hiring new people to get on board. This kills the potential of a good head start to a project. Or, in a similar fashion, a commercial company might truly wish to bring new products in the market, if the project infrastructures were better and stayed closer to the market realities and the actual market demands, which is a difficult task for research projects; the demand side in a market builds on and pays for tangible items – things that you can see and immediately judge their actual utility and value.

While the other side, namely the project supply-side, usually shows ambivalence towards speculative opportunism (yesterday we were selling information brokerage systems – today we sell Semantic Web – tomorrow Grids and Grid computing), it is not uncommon to have such a concept drift taking place continuously; this happens in the economy and in the market.

As the above may seem apocryphal, we list two cases that relate with real projects in which we participated.

- The first case relates with a recently completed project, where we had taken the responsibility to prepare a business plan. We collaborated closely with the project manager and from the very start we had expressed our commitment to support this plan even after the completion of the project. We organized a set of communications and contacts with external consultants and spent much time on it – most of which did not come from the project budget as it involved several people from other departments of our institutions.
- The result was not positive as the manager's interest faded after the "successful" completion of the project. To our regret, what we know is that they keep on investing in the platform they developed in that project – and they do have a longer-term research plan for their work.
- In another also recently completed project, we had taken the responsibility to prepare a business plan. We developed a fully developed draft which we circulated to the consortium, but there was no response or reaction to this. As this project has again terminated "successfully" by submitting also the forms of what is usually called Technology Implementation Plan, why bother with such things like a business plan? It is obvious that the completion of the project meant the termination of partners' interest to the subject.

What is a lesson learned from the above stories from the front line is that there is an urgent need to examine our Value Chains – those that we have and which we need to improve, and those that we don't have and therefore need to create from scratch. While in the more conventional economies of manufacturing much of what is going on can relate to the Supply Chain, in the world of services though the notion of supply is apparent (mainly for information entities) the focus is on aspects of value.

An easy way to remedy this is to make the submission of a business plan part of the contractual obligations of any research project – but we can imagine of the malpractices that could be developed if this shall became a requirement. One way to cope with this is to make the business plan and in general the exploitation work part of all Research and Development activities. Instead of the case of having them running sequentially, or in parallel, currently exploitation is rather regarded as a less important part of a project's scope; the centre of gravity lies in the development and the technical tasks – the rest is viewed as more part of the administrative and paper work.

Actually, a radical approach is to couple these two activities together – as we

Figure 1. Research and (its) exploitation are bound together

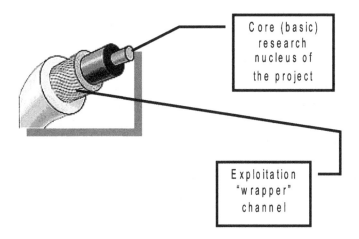

insulate a channel by a second one to form a coaxial cable. This metaphor helps us to visualize the tight coupling that should exist between the two activities. If we think of the project as a business, then a marketing working group should be established and examine from day one the business potential as well as the business paths the consortium should follow.

To achieve this, a possible approach is to connect them right from the beginning, i.e. from the proposal stage. A usual misconception regarding business plans is that they actually have to talk about a ready-to-ship product or service; this is simply not true. A research proposal is a (special type of) business plan; people prepare one in order to get funding for achieving their goals. One idiosyncratic aspect of the research proposals is that they actually form a class of meta-business plans (or business meta-plans) as they ask for funding which, if appropriately used, enables the creation of new businesses or the sustainment and improvement of existing ones (see Figure 1).

For this, members of a research consortium need to be able to answer some simple questions, including:

- What explicitly is it that we are proposing?
- *How are we going to use it? Or sell it?* For this last, we have to check whether the products we intend to use or sell really make sense from a business point of view. This has to do with issues such as not reinventing the wheel – or in the event that we are ambitious enough to introduce some new type of a wheel, we have to provide some evidence to the outside world that it will

really sell/contribute to the economy. And also:

- *Who is going to use it? Or sell it?* For this last, we have to check whether the entities to perform these tasks are actually capable of performing them or are just pretending that they are.

All three of these questions are a matter of basic common sense. They are simple questions that anyone would like to ask but would not feel comfortable to do so – and this brings us to the situation we are facing today: nobody asks for the business bottom line and nobody wants to talk on that level too. As if after several years of an unsuccessful marriage, nobody wants to open a difficult discussion.

Coming again to the area of research projects, it is easy to understand that research projects are carried out by partners operating as an extended enterprise, whose different Intellectual Assets and the value thereof need to be recognised in order to successfully prepare the ground for the completion of the project.

Taking this into account, there is a need to manage the project as a 'business' (even if this involves adopting a business attitude research), in the sense that it must be approached as a specific endeavour to achieve certain defined goals.

Based on the experience established from our involvement in several projects, there is clear evidence that a considerable majority of projects fail because they do not succeed in identifying their individual purpose in terms of the knowledge produced and excellence achieved.

This derives mainly as a result of the actual areas of research and their particular contributions being ill-defined, and the area under focus being insufficiently researched (such as who the competitors are, who the other relevant research actors are, the nature of international trends in the area).

To avoid this, an obvious remedy for any partner and therefore any project is to know at each distinct moment:

- Its assets (both tangible and intangible – especially the latter), its competitors, and (of course) the market; and
- How to express them with the most accurate figures possible.

It is not uncommon to find projects which fail to have even a fairly realistic estimation of the global situation regarding the application of the project's intended outputs in the real world and the related market conditions.

Methods for the valuation or measurement of Intellectual Assets can be characterized as 'solutions in search of a problem', and although there seems to be confusion about the distinction between valuation and measurement, the distinction is fundamental yet not fully recognized in the field (Andriessen, 2003).

The aim and the motivation of our approach is rather simple and straightforward:

to come to a quantitative overview of the monetary value of all types of intangible assets that are to be created by the project in order to be able to exploit these assets, on two levels:

- For the entire consortium cumulatively; and
- For each individual partner separately.

From the plethora of methodologies and practices which have been built variously on the schools of thought or 'communities' of – amongst others – Intellectual Capital management, Accounting, Performance measurement, and Valuation, we built our approach that we call PACE on an adapted version of the Weightless Wealth Toolkit by (Andriessen, 2004).

WHAT IS PACE?

PACE aspires to be an easy-to-use methodology that will help projects to express their assets, the ones that each one of the participating entities possess as well as the ones that are created during the project execution and which are collectively owned either by all or by more than one partners.

To this end, we made several assumptions which aimed not to support academic completeness and consistency, but rather to help for the practical presentation of key issues which tended to be neglected, though they are of utmost importance.

The name PACE comes as an acronym of the following: **P**roject **A**ssets, **C**ore competences and **E**xploitable items. As shown in Figure 2, these three concepts form the basic pillars around which our methodology is formed.

More specifically, during the lifetime of a project, and as a result of the collaborative research and development activities, it is supposed that certain *Core competences* are strengthened for each of the participating entities.

These can be related to certain intangible assets of the organisation, and an attempt to quantify their contribution margins can be made. Of course, this valuation may be highly subjective, and it is not uncommon that different people in different moments and in different contexts may valuate a certain competence or a certain intangible asset quite differently.

However, this is not an excuse for not carrying out this exercise. Even if wrongly done, at least it is worth to put figures next to core competences, as this is the first step only for revising, refining and correcting.

From any point seen, a project is judged by its outcomes; these may relate to specific Deliverables, or relate to any different type of results, synergies and achievements that have been given birth during the project execution.

Figure 2. Basic entities of the PACE toolkit

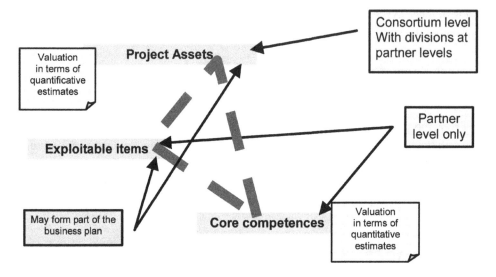

Whatever these can be, they form the ***Project Assets*** and it is these that can be traded as tangible or intangible products of the project itself. They can be collectively or equally owned or partly owned by one or more partners.

The way that this distribution will be made is not straightforward; it can either be related with the resources allocated by each of the partners involved in an achievement, or judged by quality criteria. In any case, they should be consensually agreed and accepted by all parties. Last but not least, and similarly to the case of the core competences, the Project Assets are subject to a valuation.

However, and in contrast to the case of core competences that are valuated with respect to the actual contribution margins that they can show, each assets is related with a foreseen contribution margin. i.e. while core competences are analysed with respect to how much they contribute to an organisation's existing business cycle, for the project assets the focus point is at the future and the underlying question is how much can I expect to receive from this particular asset as a contribution to my business?

Finally, there are the ***Exploitable items***. These relate to each member of the consortium and can be considered as a bridge between the overall and in many cases rather abstract project assets and the more down to earth core competences.

Exploitable items are of more tangible nature; in a basic research project that examines new types of algorithms, the exploitable item for a software company might be the improvement of a computing application that makes use of a particular algorithm. In this respect, the company may count on higher revenues, a more estab-

Figure 3. Overview for the PACE steps

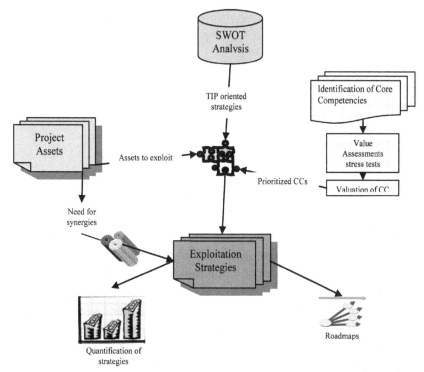

lished reputation, and an increase in sales or an appreciation by its installed base. All these latter elements can be related with figures and provide a convincing argument for the corporate Management Board to support adoption of an innovation.

Having said what PACE is, we now need to say what PACE is not: PACE is neither a business plan nor a template for some type of exploitation or commercialisation report. It aims to facilitate understanding of the approach to be employed for organising the exploitation work, and in this respect to improve the cohesion in presentation and terminology matters. Where possible, we illustrate the different parts with examples, some of which are real and others fictitious.

The approach we follow in PACE builds on a seven-step operation (see also Figure 3):

- Step 1: SWOT analysis
- Step 2: Identification of each partner's Core Competences

- Step 3: Stress tests and Valuation of Core Competences:
  - Added value test
  - Competitiveness test
  - Potentiality test
  - Sustainability test
  - Robustness test
  - Valuation of Core Competences
- Step 4: Project Assets
- Step 5: Exploitation Strategies
- Step 6: Roadmaps
- Step 7: Strategy Quantification

Going a few steps further from the original methodology of Andriessen, we have conducted a set of adaptations which are schematically presented in the paper. For example, in our approach the valuation is carried out with respect to the contribution of each particular core competence of the current and foreseen business of each partner individually.

Instead of saving on resources, which are usually scarce if not a rarity in technology-driven projects for business development, our goal was to find and apply a model that allows the estimation of the non-financial intangible assets for use in the project (i.e. in a non-accounting format), which would help us in the market valuation of different project results.

According to Baruch Lev (2001) "an intangible asset is a claim to future benefits that does not have a physical or financial (a stock or a bond) embodiment. A patent, a brand, and a unique organizational structure (for example, an Internet-based supply chain) that generate cost savings are intangible assets."

The need to evaluate the intangible assets of a project is apparent; especially in the context of the Europe Union, as since 1994 the European Commission has launched a series of studies, actions and projects which aim better to understand the knowledge economy and the importance of intangibles as competitiveness factors[1].

Though there is no standard and consistent method to evaluate intangible assets in a research project, we decided to use the Weightless Wealth method developed by Andriessen for a number of reasons:

- It is up-to-date: although this is not a virtue in itself, we believe that the method reflects current trends and concerns in the business and research community;
- It is complete, in that Andriessen took into account a set of 25 competing or competitive methods and approaches and it is with respect to this that we decided that Weightless Wealth is an appropriate method to use.

Step 1: SWOT Analysis

Our approach bases on the recognition and examination of Strengths, Weaknesses, Opportunities and Threats (SWOT), a rather all-time classic technique that aims to help at the early stages of pre-processing input to achieve the formation and classification of the set of particular project developments and results in which the project will delivered. SWOT will be performed for the project as a whole. This includes the project approach, methodology, and partners' assets. In this respect, it can be treated as a 'rough guide' to help people like corporate decision-makers and Research Directors to improve their processes and increase the value they shall be getting from the project, while it can also possibly help them to better focus on their research work items.

To give a quick inside, the Strengths category includes an **internal** list (internal: to the consortium and each partner separately, and regarding the project itself) of all the "strong" points of the subject under study (in our case this can be either the overall integrated project outcome or the particular developments which will be lead by the partner under consideration), while the Weaknesses category includes an **internal** list of all the possible "weak" points.

Respectively the Opportunities category holds an **external** list (external: to the consortium and each partner separately, and regarding the project itself) of the opportunities that might exist regarding the exploitation of the project outcomes, while the threats category includes the **external** threats that might be faced while trying to exploit the project outcomes.

For more information about SWOT analysis you can see at: http://www.amputee-coalition.org/communicator/vol2no4pg1.html

Why we do this?

- Because the SWOT analysis is a powerful but simple tool for identifying the Project's internal picture as well as the external environment.
- Because through this gathered information the partners can obtain for the first time a common view of the project's whereabouts as if this was a ready to market product.
- Because these four kinds of information will be form the basis of the exploitation strategies in the latter stages.

How to do it?

- Each partner will have to log his opinion regarding the projects approach, tools, methodology, software etc. in order to identify the strengths and weaknesses. In the same manner he has to identify the opportunities and threats

Table 1. SWOT table to be filled out by each individual partner

Strengths	Weaknesses
Opportunities	Threats

- existing in the project's market domain.
- Then the collection of all this gathered information from all partners has to be filtered in order to conclude to a common and agreed complete SWOT table (Table 1).

Step 2: Identification of Core Competencies

The second step refers to the identification of **each partner's** core competencies (CC) with respect to the project – both those that are contributed by each partner to the project and which shall affect its final outcomes, and those that are affected by the project. For each of his core competence the partner has to define which intangible assets are related with and what is the current contribution margin in a monetary fashion.

Why?

- Because we need to know the strong points (core competencies) of our business
- We need to have a clear view upon which legacy assets (intangible assets) these competencies have been build.
- And we need to have a monetary figure to quickly and adequately present the financial contribution of each of the core competence to business growth.

How?

- Firstly, the partner logs down all the strong points (core competencies) which make his organisation unique and/or viable and/or competent.
- Then for each one of this core competence we relate the intangible legacy assets which contribute to this competence or upon them the competence was build.
- As the core competence contributes to organisation's financial growth, the

Table 2. Recognition of core competences affected by the project, in relation to intangible assets and their corresponding contribution margins

Core competence	Related with intangible assets	Contribution Margin
1- Extensive Domain Know-How on Ontologies, WS, Semantic and Web Domain Knowledge	Keep up-to-date in information technology advances, new solutions and architectures	120K€
2. Expertise in ERP Systems	Corporate know how in core business domain	1.1M€

partner could obtain a figure in a monetary fashion (could be an estimation) of the core competence's contribution margin.

A special point should be made for non-commercial partners. These partners should identify the core competencies contributing to the participating project. The contribution margin of these CCs should be identified as such. i.e. if partner X participates in a project, this has been based on one or more Core Competencies that contributes to this project. The partner's income is based on his work and expertise, which in turn can be related to the core competencies owned by the partner, and offered to the project. Thus, a monetary estimation of the CCs contribution margin can be made.

At the end of this step the partner should get a complete list of the core competencies of his organisation, a clear view of his legacy intangible assets and an indication (trough the contribution margins) of the most valuable core competencies (see Table 2).

Step 3: Core Competencies Valuation

At this stage the valuation of each partner's core competencies offered and/or affected to the projected is valuated.

Valuation is carried out with respect to the contribution of each particular core competence to the current and foreseen business of each partner.

In case of failure or if partners shall face increased difficulties to organize the valuation exercise with respect to the multiple / different core competences approach, we shall choose as plan b (rather a fall-back position) the single 'aggregate' core competence scenario.

It should be noted that the stress tests described below in terms of the five checklists (Tables 3, 4, 5, 6, and 7) should be completed for *each* identified core

Table 3. Added value stress test

Added value checklist	
Added value	**Score (1=yes, 0=no)**
The core competence offers a substantial benefit for your customers or a substantial cost saving for your company.	
Customers demand this specific benefit or cost saving.	
This benefit is important for a large number of customers; it goes further than just 'nice to have'.	
Customers will continue expecting this benefit in the near future; it is not simply a passing fancy.	
Leadership in this core competence makes customers think you are different from the competition, rather than just better.	
Total score added value	

competence.

Valuation of Core Competences

An example of a valuation of two hypothetically core competencies, is shown in Table 8.

The valuation of the deployed approach shall be calculated as the result of each of the above indicators, and taking into account the relative contribution margins that this brings to the core competencies of each of the partners.

Thus, having identified that the "Expertise in ERP Systems" contributes 1.1M€, we have additionally Growth: 14, Sustainability: 5, and Robustness: 5 (100%).

Growth 14 means actually that in order to find the next year's value (t=1) we have

Table 4. Competitiveness stress test

Competitiveness checklist	
Competitiveness	**Score (1=yes, 0=no)**
Fewer than five of your competitors share this particular competence.	
You are superior to your competitors in most aspects of this particular competence.	
You invest substantially more time and money in this competence than your competitors.	
Your customers choose your products or services largely because you have this competence.	
Your leadership in this competence is generally recognized and can be illustrated by articles in trade journals, patents, and so on.	
Total score competitiveness	

Table 5. Potentiality stress test

Potential checklist	
Potential	**Score (1=yes, 0=no)**
There is an increasing demand for products / services that can be provided thanks to this core competence.	
The core competence allows the development of new products and services in the future.	
The core competence allows new markets to be entered in the future.	
There are no economic threats (customers, suppliers, competitors) that will adversely affect the use of this competence.	
There are no social threats (regulatory and social) that will adversely affect the use of this competence.	
Total score potential	

to multiply 1.1M€ with 114% and we obtain 1.254M€. in order to find the second year's estimated value we multiply the value of t=1 with again 114%.

Sustainability factor gives us the number of years to perform this calculation. In our example sustainability is 5 and therefore we can estimate for 5 years ahead.

The outcome is the total value of the listed Core Competences. This is calculated by adding the values identified for the years t=1, t=2 etc. and multiplying this total with the robustness' percentage (that is the correspondence of the robustness value with a % percentage i.e 5=100%, 4=80% etc.).

Abbreviations:

- CM stands for Contribution Margin in Euro;

Table 6. Sustainability stress test

Sustainability checklist	
Sustainability	**Score (1=yes, 0=no)**
This core competence is scarce in your branch.	
It would require considerable investments in time and / or money for competitors to master this competence.	
Patents, trademarks, and other legal measures protect components of the competence.	
This competence is a combination of a number of intangibles such as skills, knowledge, processes, and corporate culture, thus making it difficult to copy.	
This competence cannot be obtained through acquisition or from other outside sources.	
Total score sustainability	

Table 7. Robustness stress test

Robustness checklist	
Robustness	**Score (1=yes, 0=no)**
The group of people that possesses the skills and knowledge crucial for this competence is vulnerable.	
The values and norms on which this competence is built are under pressure.	
The technology and information technology systems that form part of this competence are vulnerable.	
The primary and management processes that this competence uses are unreliable.	
The endowments on which this core competence depends (like the corporate image or the installed client base) are vulnerable.	
Total = A	
Total score robustness = 5 – A	

- G stands for Growth expressed as a percentage (%) that comes as the sum of: Added Value + Competitiveness + Potential. Figures for the latter are taken from the stresstests of Tables 3-7;
- S stands for Sustainability;
- t1, t2, …: Monetary returns for year 1, year 2, …;
- R stands for Robustness expressed as a percentage (%);
- Value stands for the Gross Monetary Value of the particular intangible asset created in the project and is expressed in Euro.

Step 4: Project's Assets

At this step the consortium needs to log and agree on the project's assets. These might include everything from patents to software or methodologies etc. Also the

Table 8. Valuation table

Competence	CM	G	S	t=1	T=2	T=3	t=4	T=5	R	Value
1- Extensive Domain Know-How on Ontologies, WS, Semantic and Web Domain Knowledge	120K€	12	3	134K€	151K€	169K€	-	-	5 (100%)	454 K€
2. Expertise in ERP Systems	1.1M€	14	5	1.254M€	1.429M€	1.629M€	1.857M€	2.117M€	5 (100%)	8.286M€
Total:	1.22M€	-	-	1.388M€	1.580M€	1.798M€	1.857M€	2117M€	-	8.740M€

Table 9. Project Assets table

No.	Title of the asset	Partner(s) owning the result(s) & mainly involved in their future use
1.		
2.		
3.		
4.		
5.		
6.		
7.		
8.		

consortium has to agree on the ownership of the assets (see Table 9).

Why we do it?

- Because the consortium needs to know what are the project's assets and who owns them.
- Logging the Assets help us define the obvious synergies in our exploitation path, for example when the asset is owned by more than one partner.

How we do it?

- For each asset the owning partners are identified. An asset may belong to more than one partner. This should be clearly logged. Other assets may belong to the whole consortium.

Step 5: Exploitation Strategies

This is the most important step. Each project partner needs three sets of information for coping successfully with this step regarding exploitation strategies. The first is the **complete SWOT matrix** as this was defined in the first step, the second is the list of **core competencies with their total values** (outcome of Step 3), and the third is the list of the **defined project Assets**.

In this step, we have to identify all the distinct exploitation strategies which may relate from the previously (Step 4) identified Project Assets. This means that the framework should offer strategic alternatives that should/must fall into the following categories:

- **IMP:** Improvement or change of internal process(es)
- **NPS:** New product / service development
- **LIC:** Revenues through License agreement
- **MKT:** Revenues through Marketing agreement
- **MAN:** Revenues through Manufacturing agreement
- **JV:** Revenues through establishment of a joint enterprise or partnership
- **PPP:** Revenues through establishment of a Private-public partnership
- **FIN:** Revenues through development financing
- **VC:** Revenues through venture capital/spin-off fundraising
- **CONS:** Revenues through provision of consultancy
- **R&D:** Revenues through further research or development

The process for this Step is as follows:

1. Each partner looks at its own core competencies and prioritizes them according to their contribution margin.
2. For each one of the ***project's assets*** the partners should look at the SWOT table to try to identify elementary strategies (through the SWOT combinations) by exploiting the asset under examination.
3. Having defined the strategy/ies for the assets, the prioritized core competencies and their Contribution Margins will help us define which of the strategies need more focus and resources spent.

We should mention that PACE users are able to:

1. Build more than one exploitation strategies as part of a single project asset (1 or many partners - 1 project asset – many exploitation strategies);
2. Consensually decide to build synergies for carrying out a joint exploitation strategy for a single project asset or for more than one asset (many partners - 1 project asset – many exploitation strategies).

Step 6: Roadmaps

For each exploitation strategy defined in the previous Step 5, the partner(s) should fill out the table displayed in Table 10, which helps at formulating with the necessary documentation the particular exploitation roadmaps. Thus, they have to define the exploitable items (the core strategy's statement), the planned actions related to this strategy, the synergies (if any) with the consortium members, the synergies with partners outside the consortium, and the related milestones that need to be follow in order to accomplish the strategy.

Table 10. Table describing each of the various exploitation items

Exploitation item:	
Planned actions:	
Need for synergies or collaboration with consortium members:	
Need for synergies or collaboration with other parties (out of the consortium):	
Related milestones:	
Related with core competence:	
Related with intellectual asset:	
Related with Project Asset:	

The planned actions should refer to any short term activities (mostly at organisation level) that will prepare the way for strategy realisation. Time estimations should be provided for each one of the actions.

The milestones should be defined in a time continuous fashion, in respect to the sustainability defined in the previous step. Thus if for example sustainability for a core competence of this exploitable item, is 3, denotes that the realisation of the selected strategy should be completed in three time periods.

What we get?

- The benefit of filling this table is that each partner is quickly aware of his exploitable items. Not only this, but he can see which synergies are required, which are the core involved competencies contributing and the intellectual "intangible legacy assets", and which is the Project Asset(s) *offering* the basis for this exploitable item.

Step 7: Quantification of Strategies

This final step helps us quantify (monetarily) the exploitation strategies and to make projections in a time milestones depended roadmap fashion. Table 11 shows the calculation of this quantification.

What we get?

- At the end we have monetary estimations of the alterative strategies should follow. Organizations should start their exploitation activities from this point forth.

Table 11. Example of a filled out table describing expected values for the exploitation potential.

Sources	CM	G	S	t=1	t=2	t=3	t=4	t=5	R	Value
IMP Improvement or change of internal process(es)										
NPS New product / service development	260 KEur	12	5	291.2	326.1	365.3	409.1	458.2	90%	412.38
LIC Revenues through License agreement										
MKT Revenues through Marketing agreement	400 KEur	12	4	-	448	501.7	561.9	629.4	45%	283.23
MAN Revenues through Manufacturing agreement										
JV Revenues through establishment of a joint enterprise or partnership	1,2 MEur	9	3	-	-	1308	1425	1554	30%	466.2
PPP Revenues through establishment of a Private-public partnership										
FIN Revenues through development financing										
VC Revenues through venture capital/spin-off fundraising										
CONS Revenues through provision of consultancy										
R&D Revenues through further research or development	180 KEur	11	3	-	-	199.8	221.8	246.1	60%	147.66
Total:				291.2	774.1	2374.8	2617.8	2887.7		1309.47

It is not in the scope of the PACE method to dictate the activities beyond this point.

The table should be the input for brainstorming and risk evaluations for choosing the most appropriate exploitation paths.

How we plan our research is essential and overall resource-critical for the impact this may have on our core business. Even for universities that are not considered as 'straight money-making' entities, involvement in research activities without a plan other than gaining access to funds may seriously disorient them from their original mission.

Our experience from several projects shows that good intentions are not sufficient for ensuring the exploitation of results. Many of the existing patterns reflect an earlier situation (actually: the 80's), when research was not as strictly monitored for its short-term results and its financial (contributions to) outcomes.

Currently, and due to the implications of the recession and slow-down in the EU Member State economies, most organizations, both profit-making and non profit-making (like universities) are trying to increase their opportunities to access Community funds, while on the other hand they are putting much greater emphasis on cutting costs and limiting their investments. This, as it is currently practiced, implies less-skilled (cheaper) research personnel and an attempt to introduce economies of scale in any possible way.

REFERENCES

Andriessen, D. (2003). IC Valuation & Measurement: Why and how? *PMA IC Research Symposium, October 1-3, Cranfield School of Management, Bedford, UK.*

Andriessen, D. (2004). *Making sense of intellectual capital: designing a method for the valuation of intangibles.* Burlington. MA: Butterworth-Heinemann.

Ellis K. (2004). Value-based competition. *American Salesman, October.*

Eustace, C. (2000, October). *The intangible economy impact and policy issues.* Report of the European High Level Expert Group on the Intangible Economy. Luxembourg: European Commission Report.

Lev, B. (2001). *Intangibles Management, Measurement and Reporting.* New York: Brookings Institute.

Nazari, J. A., and I. M. Herremans (2007). Extended VAIC model: measuring intellectual capital components. Journal of Intellectual Capital , 8(4), 595–609. doi:10.1108/14691930710830774

Quinn, J. B. (1992). *The Intelligent Enterprise: A Knowledge and Service Based Paradigm for Industry.* New York: Free Press.

ENDNOTE

[1] See for instance the report of European Commission 'The intangible economy impact and policy issues', Report of the European High Level Expert Group on the Intangible Economy, October 2000.

Chapter 10
Culture of Services

How do all different types of services affect the reality and routine of the service consumer / user? What cultural effects can we recognize to the community or the individuals? What are the cultural aspects of any newly introduced service? And how these can positively or negatively affect the society at large? In this chapter the author presents results of a research exercise related with the building of services for a collaborative community environment for experiential learning in medical emergencies. Extensive use of the Living Labs methodology has been made and is reported and related with the presented framework. The final part of this chapter is devoted to configuration aspects of the collaborative service environment.

People when dressed the role of consumers are expected to be excited when facing a new offer for a product or a service. And when they find themselves in the shoes of a sales manager or a commercial director, they are excited when fantasising domination of a market through a service or a product of theirs. This is a simple, linear type of thinking: I offer a service and someone is going to pay for it. Un-

DOI: 10.4018/978-1-60566-683-9.ch010

fortunately, even a simple transactional act like this of choosing a service is much more complicated.

Marketing people – the ones that we in many occasions wrongly think as service experts – would say: you have to cultivate a need to the people so that you can later harvest their demand for this particular service you offer to them. This is not wrong at all. It only leaves out of the picture the fact that both the cultivation of the need and its consequent harvest do not exist *in vacui* but form parts of a culture.

Imagine introducing a service to a society that has been immaculate to it and its connotations – the two most expected things to happen is that either this service will fail or … it may succeed. What we expect from a professional service designer is to find some type of strategy that will lead to a success and leave the failure for the competition. In many cases, we feel that success can be leveraged through improvements of marketing and branding. This is not wrong – however, any new service can be subject to some type of explorative study before its launch.

For many years I have been personally involved in projects dealing with some new facility that improves communication of information across the supply chain of some particular industry. All these projects failed because they were born in the minds of IT professionals and were totally ungrounded on the reality of the actual members of an industrial supply chain. On the other hand, the very same projects might have faced tremendous success if they had addressed a different audience: financial brokers or bankers.

Look in the area of e-tourism and e-travel industry: there is a plethora of service offers and many brands are proud of what they provide to their highly valued customers, but at the end many of them seem to forget the most important part: what the customer really needs and how is the best way to satisfy this need.

In the area of business analytics and data warehousing the term *concept drift* is used to describe the case of changing patterns for some specific model we have created for a market or a product. Looking back in the world of services, one can speak about *service drift* for picturing a continuous changing situation related to the positioning of a service within a wider context of suppliers, providers, customers, consumers, mediators and brokers all of them operating in a similar changing market.

Culture, as a term used mainly in the humanities, is a much richer term that carries quite a lot of qualitative elements capable to describe and illustrate several dimensions of a service realisation than any other term from the area of engineering or business. For a culture, the convolution of two or more waves can result in more than one results – while as we all know, engineers understand the convolution as a very explicitly defined operation – like a numerical addition or multiplication.

An area that we all can agree is not governed by rationality is this of corporate mergings: there, it is obvious that what the people face is a clash of cultures; it is an overstatement to talk about civilisation though at the end both terms are correct in this context (though civilisation is rather to be used for a culture at large and over a macro-period of time). I have been watching how people try to impose their own view about services and processes on the others and how less space is given for dialogue and interactivity during these periods. Same is the case when a company recruits a new executive director who is expected to bring into action his or her vision about how things should go.

It is like Russian roulette: some of these people succeed in some cases while some others fail. And – most importantly – some people who succeeded in the past are now about to fail. In most cases, the reason of success or failure is attributed to the human factor: that particular (lack of) insight that makes people capable to (blind themselves for) drive a project into a success story. This is fully correct – with one exception: this mystic formula we tend to call human factor relates mainly with the existence or the absence of a specific capacity linked with the ability to understand the cultural elements of an encountered market or business situation.

Be it the improvement of a long-existing 'traditional' service or the introduction of an innovative one, in both cases there is plenty of space for different people to drive their particular projects into success or failure. A visionary may fail for the same reasons that an 'accountant' would fail: if they prefer to view the service world from their well defined gold-ivory box and close the eyes to the multiple realities that exist out there, then for sure a failure is underway.

An important point we made above is the reference to the multiple realities. Although several of the existing approaches in the academic and research literature used to support service design and development are sufficient to create an interactive space for corporate stakeholders, there is every reason to look for new approaches.

In the classic Kurosawa film *Rashomon* of 1950, various witnesses provide completely contradictory accounts of a single event. The film does not indicate which recollection is correct; each account in turn is depicted equally realistically. The sense by the end of the film is that all we have seen is unreliable, and that no account is completely true (or completely false…).

Rashomon is deliberately and pointedly inconsistent, but uses this method to make a coherent and powerful statement. This is a capability which could be of particular relevance to a decision making activity, as it is for an interactive story, if it allows the decision making process to abandon the assumption of an explicit, unifying reality in favor of competing, possibly inconsistent realities. To the extent that inconvenient consequences of the decision maker's choices could be ignored, a decision based on such a multiple reality model could provide the decision maker with more freedom.

But the logical inconsistency found in Rashomon is not the only kind of multiple reality imaginable. A more subtle 'convolution' of reality occurs when the witnesses to an event view it in ways that are simply very different rather than contradictory. Rashomon's multiple realities are subjective but pretend to be objective (in order to convince the judge); dropping this pretense would allow each subjective reality to be judged and appreciated on its own terms. The same happens when facing different information sources – many of them contradictory to each other – within a collaborative service design framework, in which a synthesis on the different views is foreseen.

How would the multiple reality model work in practice? Realities could reflect different levels of semantics, different planes of analysis, etc. Moving from reality to reality may be intrinsically interesting enough that the viewer would have no further interactive ability; in any case, even simple aspects of the product development process could be related with respect to their significance by the number of separate realities in which they appear.

There is, however, a particular challenge inherent in the use of the multiple reality model when facing multi-party decision-making tasks: For the decision path to be satisfying, a unifying force must be found to tie the pieces of the decision-making process together, the way the investigation into the contradictory accounts does in Rashomon.

The service analyst must construct the multiple realities so that they interact with each other in some way. If done effectively, this interaction will do more than just hold the decision together; it will most likely serve as the vehicle for the central message of the decision-making process. This comes back to a sad reality many high technology companies are facing nowadays: they are not lacking on human resources to take or make service-related decisions, but they are lacking all the necessary underlying constituents frequently described as *soft skills*, which can make decisions work for their organisations.

It is therefore that the notion of cultures and the ability to see many different colors and shades, tones and undertones in a picture are a prerequisite for a service analyst, in a world that is full of color blind managers that see in few happy cases graylevel and in the majority of cases only black and white.

In general, group decisions show better performances than decisions made by individuals. Advantages of group decisions are based on their higher qualitative and quantitative capacity, better possibilities for communication, interaction, and employment of methods, as well as an easier enforceability. One of our core beliefs is that the concept of service culture may act as the central metaphor around which the main individual and organisational / corporate requirements, work and management practices, profiling issues, enabling technologies, implied by the future, new and increasingly content- / media-rich working environments can be modelled, framed and validated within several service areas and business domains to support the service development process.

Figure 1 aims to visualise the interaction of the main methodological pillars situated in the picture in the form of the triangle vertices, while positioning them with respect to the application fields included in the circle, and the basic notions that acted as drivers for the service research context which are shown in the triangle sides.

COMPARISON OF A SERVICE FRAMEWORK WITH THE LIVING LABS MODELLING TECHNIQUE

A recent aim of the European Commission is to support the pan-European creation of Living Labs as new forms of cooperation between government, enterprises, citizens and academia for a successful transfer of e-Government, e-Democracy *and* e-Services as well as other state-of-the-art applications, solutions, know-how and best practices.

Quoting the European Commission, "Innovation takes place when knowing what the market wants is brought together with knowing how to do it, in a new context" (CEC, 2005).

The Living Labs concept is not new at all – the author together with a long-time partner and good friend in research projects, Dr Francesco Molinari, have been working in this area using a somewhat different code name – 'testbed Europe' was the term we were using back in 200x. Living Labs are about moving research and development activities out of laboratories and into real-life contexts. In the past years, a number of national experiences can be mentioned across Western Europe[1].

Furthermore, on November 21st, 2006, the Finnish EU Presidency has launched a European Network of Living Labs for the "co-creation of innovation in public, private and civic partnership". This has been the first step towards a new European Innovation System, entailing a major paradigm shift for the whole innovation process.

But let's look at what exactly is a Living Lab and why we compare it as a related technique to a service framework and how this has an impact on the culture of the underlying services.

A European Network of Living Labs is a collaboration of Public Private Partnerships where firms, public authorities and people work together in creating, prototyping, validating and testing new services, businesses, markets and technologies in real-life contexts, such as cities, city regions, rural areas and collaborative virtual networks between public and private players.

The real-life and everyday life contexts both stimulate and challenge research and development as public authorities and citizens do not only participate in, but also contribute to the whole innovation process.

Figure 1. Service development process (SDP) with respect to the overall organizational and corporate context, underlying pillars and the business environment

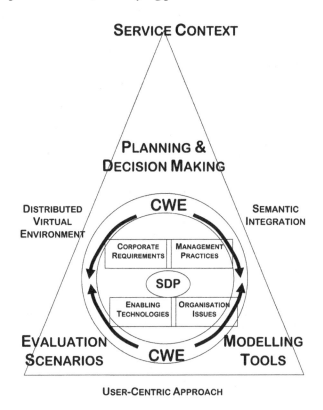

From a market and industrial perspective, Living Labs offer a research and innovation platform over different social and cultural systems, cross-regionally and cross-nationally. This is a natural move for Information and Communication Technologies (ICT), life sciences and any innovation domain that deals with human and social problem solving and people's every day lives. However, this new approach to research for innovation is a huge challenge for research methodologies, innovation process management, public-private partnership models, IPRs, open source practices, development of new leadership, governance and financial instruments.

This complexity increases remarkably with the international nature of a European Network of Living Labs, implying a set of large-scale experimentation platforms for new services, business and technology, market and industry creation within ICT environment.

The essential feature of a Living Lab is the consideration of *users feedback* and *experience* as an integral part of the testbed itself. European research has known the operational value of Living Labs methodology in 3 main areas so far:

Figure 2. Human centric systemic innovation approach (adapted from Eriksson et al, 2005)

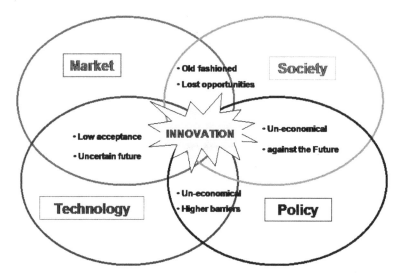

1.   Bringing laboratory based technology testbeds into real-life, user focused validation environments;
2.   Developing mobility services for citizens in a real-world early adapter community with existing and close to market technologies;
3.   Studying the collaborative working environments of the future from a pan-European perspective.

In all cases, the main focus has been on a user centred, context sensitive, multi-site and multi-stakeholder co-design or co-creation process, supported by mutual trust and implying the joint consideration of policy, market, societal and technological aspect with equal weight, as shown in Figure 2.

Following, we identify five different phases of a Living Lab configuration process (Pierson and Lievens, 2005):

a.   **Contextualisation**, meaning a prior exploration of the technological and social challenges implied by the technology or service under investigation. Applicable methods are, consequently:
   ◦   A **technological scan**, giving an overview of current and future technologies but also to map the specific functionalities and characteristics related to them;
   ◦   A **(state-of-the-art) study** in order to determine the socio-economic implications of the research focus (framework as well as topic).

b. **Selection**, meaning the identification of potential users or user groups, by means of non probabilistic or purposeful sampling. Useful criteria are, for instance:

- The **maximum variation** of underlying phenomenon (e.g. education or age);
- The search for a **significant variation** of observations (aka selective or criterion sampling);
- The **theoretical variation** of relevant concepts (according to some pre-existing study).

c. **Concretisation**, meaning a thorough description of the current characteristics, everyday behaviour and perceptions of the selected test users regarding the research focus. In this initial **measurement** we look at specific user characteristics (socio-demographic and economic) as well their relation towards the introduced technology or service. The methodology used depends on the size of the test panel: for instance, a quantitative **survey** can be integrated, depending on the sample scale, by qualitative **interviews**. The initial measurement of the sample is made before a technology or service is introduced or before the test panel becomes active in the Living Lab; it then enables to perform a second measurement and a full evaluation at the end of the project.

d. **Implementation** is actually the behavioural validation and operationally running test phase of the Living Lab. From a user-oriented and ethnographic viewpoint. We distinguish two major research methods:

- **Direct analysis**, using remote data collection techniques and strategies (like technological monitoring) and software logging tools (if applicable) on the device level (e.g. pda, mobile phone or digital television) as well as on the platform/network level;
- **Indirect analysis**, based on (thematically organised) focus groups, in-depth interviews and self-reporting techniques like diaries, all being applied to investigate the meaning and motivation for behaviour.

e. And **feedback**, consisting of two research steps:

- An **ex post measurement** based on the same techniques of the initial measurement, to check if there is any evolution in the users perception and attitude towards the introduced technology or service, to assess changes over time in everyday life in relation to technology use and to detect transitions of usage over time.
- A set of **technological recommendations** from the analysis of data, gathered during the previous implementation phase. This outcome of the feedback phase can be used as the starting point for a new research cycle within the Living Lab; in this way the iterative feature of our research cycle can be made operational.

Table 1. Comparison of the two approaches with respect to various endogenous characteristics

Endogenous characteristics	Living Labs	Service Configuration Research
user centred	√	√
context sensitive	√	√
multi-site	√	Not necessarily
multi-stakeholder	√	√
co-design or co-creation process	√	√
supported by mutual trust	√	√
implying the joint consideration of policy, market, societal and technological aspects	√	√

In Tables 1 and 2 we try to compare the Living Lab modelling technique with our proposed for coping with service modelling and configuration with respect to their characteristics and in regard to the different processes employed during their application (see respective Tables below).

Though there is only one basic difference between the two techniques, this is quite important: Living Labs are conceived as a means to support long-term activities in the areas of innovation and e-participation over a widely distributed set of participating actors. This is not the case of the Service Configuration Research concept; the latter though it mobilises different organisational actors within and outside the company (e.g. customers, suppliers or other value chain members), it uses as its fundamental cohesive element the notion of *service situations* around which the corporate service delivery or provision needs to be modelled and configured. In the Living Labs we don't organise the daily life around situations – like any living entity, e.g. the cell, a Living Lab faces different events or situations and its life is defined by them. This is on contrast to the Service Configuration Research metaphor that aims to organise principles of (organisational, business or other participants') behaviour around the concept of the situation.

From an aesthetics point of view, it should be openly accepted that the Living Labs are a very modern concept. However, this can not succeed if the actors that are organising their work as member of a Living Lab are not having the appropriate tools to organise their routine in some language that can be shared and understood with the other members. And it is at this point that Service Configuration Research may support the closing of this gap. On the other hand, Living Labs can be regarded as a very welcome add-on to the means provided by Service Configuration Research, in terms of enabling the connectivity and networking of various Service Configuration Research to formulate a new meta-entity.

Table 2. Comparison of the two approaches with respect to the application process

Endogenous characteristics	Living Labs	Service Configuration Research
contextualisation	Usually takes place through a technological scan or (state-of-the-art) study	Builds on a needs analysis or market needs; driver is empirical evidence
selection	Uses criteria like the maximum variation of underlying phenomenon (e.g. education or age), the search for a significant variation of observations (aka selective or criterion sampling) or the theoretical variation of relevant concepts (according to some pre-existing study)	Accommodates all sources of factors related to the application field, based on the participants experiences and familiarity with field practices. Encourages the use of cross-disciplinary problem solving paradigms and *ad-hoc* methods
concretisation	Methodology depends and may span from a quantitative survey to qualitative interviews	Methodology builds on the population of the three Service Configuration Research models with field data and experimentation amongst the participants with various situations
implementation	They both take place either by means of *direct analysis* using remote data collection techniques and strategies (like technological monitoring) and software tools or of *indirect analysis*, based on (thematically organised) focus groups, in-depth interviews and self-reporting techniques like diaries, all being applied to investigate the meaning and motivation for behaviour	
feedback	Combining an ex post measurement and a set of technological recommendations from the analysis of data, gathered during the previous implementation phase	Reflected in the increase or decrease of utility acquired by the Service Configuration Research, the differences in the usage patterns and the usage types, the culture that shall follow the adoption and the returns on investment

We close the analysis in this section with an indication as to how the model can be implemented and validated.

Having in mind that some of the most essential problems that users, administrators, developers and vendors of information supply services, as well as in every application and service field, face today may be viewed under the common denominator of "interoperability" problems, the presented approach illustrates possible ways to address these problems when referring to the case of Service Configuration Research implementation.

A design goal of the research was to provide a cohesive technological infrastructure independent of any specific implementation pathway and to contain features that are effective and easy to use in a broad range of representative networked service environments which may be subject to variable configurations.

For this reason we recognize the following types and broad categories of users:

1. Service platform and service vendors (may concern IT companies, content providers)
2. Professional service providers (as a specialization of the content provider category)
3. Service developers (as a specialization of the content provider category)
4. Service administrators (as a specialization of the content provider category)
5. Service End users (i.e. enterprises – either public or private owned ones)
6. Service IT managers (as a specialization of the previous End user category)

These users participate in one or more of the following four stages in the development and usage of the service infrastructures that can be separately validated with respect to performance or cost-per-benefit-related criteria:

- *Establishment:* Implementing and deploying the presented service approach across the enterprise information "supply chain" (be it in the context of an enterprise-wide case or a case limited within a specific business unit or division of the company or the organization).
- *Build:* Exercising the service elements to define a baseline service flow configuration (establishing the exchange paths between known service sources and targets as well as the various filtering mechanisms involved. For this the exploitation of previous experiences from an earlier experimentation phase can only be beneficial.).
- *Operation:* Operating the service flow infrastructures in close relationship with other enterprise processes and procedures.
- *Maintenance:* Exercising the introduced service concepts to define changes in the distributed service configuration (e.g. to cover changes as "small" as the addition of new service elements in the overall service configuration and as "large" as merger with or replacement by another configuration such as in the case of replacing a service flow with a group of supplying service flows loosely linked and using a new distributed management scheme). This is a quite complex issue for which description may be regarded as outside the scope of the research. It concerns the "reverse" engineering of a service into a set of constituent services. In Table 3 we present some usage scenarios that illustrate activities in the *Build* and *Maintenance* steps that clearly demonstrate the value addedness of the approach.

As a last remark, it should be noted that an important element of future research is the ownership of the content created within the service development process (SDP). On the one hand, there is a need to support the interests of the company that owns and operates the corporate services |as intangible assets with relatively high costs of operation and maintenance, while there are many reasons to want to support the interests of the individual participants, employees and workers; the latter are sharing within the corporate environment their most important asset namely their intellectual capacities used for recognising, analysing and assessing the various situations, while also their particular contributions to the decision-making processes and the creation of a culture within the organisation.

Though this has been outside the scope of the research, I feel that it shall concentrate the future interest of many researchers in the field. For this reason I present results of relatively recent research work which was carried out under the code name Coconut and which aimed towards the building of services for a collaborative community environment for experiential learning in medical emergencies. As Chapter 6 presented another fruit, namely the Carambola exotic fruit, Coconut, which we consider here, is another exotic fruit that goes well with the experimental nature of research in the field of services and holistic service methodologies.

ABOUT THE COCONUT CONCEPT

Although learning, in principle, could also be described as a creative destruction of old knowledge, the standard approach is to focus on it as a process of accumulation, where the outcomes of previous learning provide the starting point for acquiring further knowledge. Therefore, *learning is often described as an ongoing cycle*, like in Figure 3, where the "experiential learning model" of Kolb (1984) is represented. In this simple, yet influential model, learning occurs through a sequence of phases: first, concrete experiences generate an opportunity for observation and reflection; this, in turn, leads to the creation of new concepts and models that are then tested in novel situations; etc.

According to Kolb (1984:30), people need four different types of skills to make their learning cycle effective; more specifically, they have to:

a. Engage openly and without prejudgement in new experiences,
b. Reflect and observe their experiences from many perspectives,
c. Create concepts that integrate observations into logically sound theories, and,
d. Use these theories in decision making and problem solving.

In many important learning models, *learning starts when the person experiences a practical or a cognitive dissonance* (Tuomi 2005:21). Then routine action breaks down, the learner realizes that active sensemaking is needed, and the world needs to be reconstructed. This reconstruction may require reorganization of meaning

Table 3. Different roles in the service adoption phases

User category	Stage	Foreseen Added Value to the Users when implemented		
		Problem or need	Tools and repositories	How the system can be validated
Service Platform andService vendors	Build	Must subscribe to standards for inter-vendor interconnect	Web Service infrastructure; Common Repository (Ontology) Facility; Tools for modeling, development, deployment and service management	System provides a common "backplane" for pluggable subsystems. It may be exploited as a globally usable notation for meta-service exchange protocols which enables flexible distribution of distributed services over a heterogeneous collection of information systems (e.g. as in the case of different units that use their own ERPs to ground information within, not needing to disclose their source information to other units).
ProfessionalServiceProviders	Build	Must accumulate and reuse service elements	Third party and in-house tools that apply meta-services to concrete service-base catalogues and vice versa	Reusable, editable, and extensible meta-service should provide a first-level "asset base" that builds (new) value. This base of reusable elements starts a self-reinforcing feedback loop with continually increasing returns improved by engagement productivity for the service users.
ProfessionalServiceProviders	Maintenance	Must modify Service process configuration: knowing what and where to modify; knowing dependency closure	Third party or in-house tools to manage reconfiguration editing of a service flow	Service platform exposes the information required to modify a service flow model. Service context definition and self-describing features for the service flows are used to isolate dependency relationships.
ProfessionalServiceProviders,ServiceAdministrators	Maintenance	Must integrate existing tools and data which adhere to standards other than service flow model into a distributed service configuration environment.	Tools based on ability to incorporate metamodels of services and alternate service definition practices and standards.	Service system does or can subsume non-service representations. For example, may be elaborated in the future to contain any Web-based service model with a focus to domain-specific characteristics.
ServiceAdministrators	Build	Must establish and manage expressions, relationships, and lineage over multiple servicebase schemata.	Tools that use built-in facilities to define schema content, relationships, and lineage.	Service system design is based on need to manage such information at multiple levels. The basic Web Services will have to be designed to allow navigation of meta-services correlated to schemata.
ServiceAdministrators	Maintenance	Must add, subtract, re-partition, reallocate, or merge service resources in deployment configuration.	Service management tools.	Service system consists of models of meta-services that assist in making such changes and allow impact of these changes to be assessed.

Figure 3. Kolb's (1984) Experiential learning model

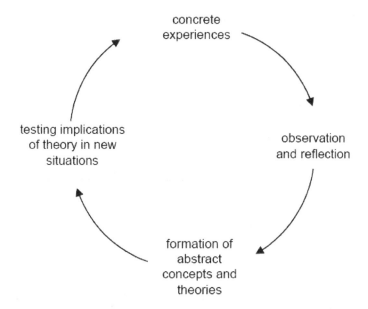

and also reconfiguration of the material environment. In classroom settings, this process can be simulated by ***problem-based learning situations***, where the student is presented with a specific construction of the world, for example using a textual description, and the dynamics of the world is shown to lead to a contradiction or a problem that needs to be solved. Students may also collaborate in solving the problem, for example, by taking different roles and presenting different interpretations of the situation.

Such problem-based learning settings can be enhanced by ***immersive information environments*** where the learner can effectively experience cognitive dissonance and where problem-solving resources are readily available (Dede 2005). ***Immersive simulation systems*** have also been widely used in several flight training and in military training applications. For instance, commercial PC-based flight simulators are commonly used to build systems that closely resemble professional multimillion-€ cockpit simulators.

Another potential example of such an immersive learning environment is the ***emergency department*** of modern hospitals (see Figure 4).

Several experiences exist in literature as well as in practice, of simulation models regarding hospital emergency departments. However, as the figure above shows, this simulation is most frequently conducted to provide the hospital's administration with managerial performance indicators such as patient waiting times, throughput

Figure 4. An emergency hospital model adapted from Takakuwa and Shiozaki (2004)

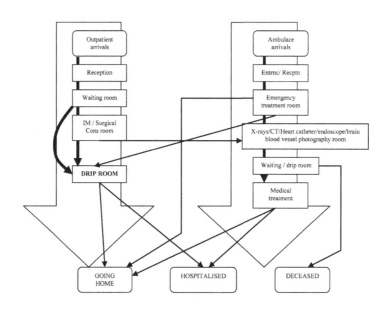

time, or various congestion indexes with respect to the existing facilities.

For the case of our Coconut implementation architecture we aimed to build an integrated, context-sensitive, adaptable and interoperable training environment for medical emergency staff, based on the concept of technology-enhanced experiential learning for competency, skills and performance enhancement.

More specifically, our research related to the professional development and upgrading of:

- Distinct professions, such as ***doctors and nurses***;
- Semi-professions, such as ***paramedics***; and
- Staff performing tasks that are not necessarily defined as professions, such as ***ambulance drivers, management and administration personnel*** and the like.

We shall later refer to the above as the Coconut ***learning community***.

From a methodology point of view, our aim was to achieve the establishment and operation of the Coconut learning community by means of employing the *Living Labs methodology*. The essential feature of a Living Lab is the consideration of user feedback and experience as an integral part of the testbed itself.

The main idea was to engage all involved actors with their respective roles across the emergency hospital "value chain", and mobilise / adapt / implement the most advanced e-learning technologies into a single immersive simulation framework that will ease the uptake of new knowledge in the field. The way we have performed this may also be considered as a "blueprint" for other areas and application topics.

The overall *criterion of success* for the Coconut approach is the extent to which the results of the implementation process will be embedded in the business processes, human resources and organisational management systems of the participating user organisations.

Training Needs of the Learning Community

Emergency medicine is one of the most challenging medical specialties and also one of the most regulated medical fields. Always on the edge of life and death, the emergency medical staff needs to know exactly what to do - doubts and medical errors in this setting are not allowed.

Our research is based on the assumption that the emergency staff have undergone the required training to carry out their functions; therefore, it does not deal with training processes up to the award of the diploma, but rather to *professional development and upgrading*.

This development is defined as an *ongoing learning process* that is carried out throughout the years, for the purpose of acquiring additional knowledge, becoming updated on innovations and developments, enhancing professional capabilities and any other action or process that contributes to the effective execution of the position holder's tasks. In this specific area, *professionals require special skills* (in addition to their routine work), such as:

- The necessity to take quick decisions under difficult conditions and to find creative solutions to similar (but never identical) problems;
- To build good teamwork skills, and the ability to work individually;
- To function well under stressful conditions;
- To be willing to work under conditions that may place themselves at risk or even endanger their lives;
- To maintain a high level of motivation; etc.

Emergency staff are also the people that arrive at a mass casualty disaster site immediately after the incident occurs or as it unfolds, and remain there for a period of several hours to several days (depending on the scale of the incident), until other bodies, such as the Red Cross, take their place. These situations usually encompass innumerable variables which cannot be fully foreseen, and therefore preparations on how to best cope with them can never be planned or designed in full. Consequently, the professional development of emergency staff is a critical element in the successful handling of mass casualty situations. This must be constructed on two levels:

1. The professional development of the individual and/or the group in the tasks they are responsible for executing and the level of leadership expected of them; and
2. The professional development of position holders to ensure effective action during an incident at the required professional level, which requires a high level of interdisciplinary planning and coordination between the various institutions and organizations taking part in the handling of the incident; if predicted scenarios (which may not necessarily occur in actuality) are not drilled in advance, this goal may not be achieved; therefore, the professional planning must be planned on both levels, implementing a ***multidisciplinary approach***.

In Europe, there are some well-established organizations and initiatives in the field. The *European Society for Emergency Medicine* (EuSEM, www.eusem.org) is a non-profit scientific organization, aiming to promote and foster the concept, philosophy and the art of Emergency Medicine throughout Europe. The ultimate objective of EuSEM is to help and support European nations to achieve the specialty of Emergency Medicine. Founded as a Society of individuals in 1994 from a multidisciplinary group of experts in Emergency Medicine (the Club of Leuven), EuSEM changed its Statutes in 2005, so that the Society now also represents Emergency Medicine national societies of as well as its members. The Society edits the *European Journal of Emergency Medicine* (EJEM).

However, the most well-known emergency medicine forum in Europe is the *European Resuscitation Council* (www.erc.edu). Additionally, there is also *The International Liaison Committee on Resuscitation* (ILCOR), also a well-known institution in this field[2].

Consensus medical documents are released periodically by all these organizations, in order to ensure ***standardized practice*** in emergency medicine. ***Emergency and trauma medicine*** comprise the few medical specialties demanding rapid integration of discrete information elements into a coherent, outcome-oriented action stream, subject to a continuous modification by the variation in the nature of the incoming patient data. Yet, studies have shown significant deficiencies in ***diagnostic techniques***, not only among internal medicine but also emergency medicine residents[3].

The *stress* of practicing emergency/trauma medicine appears to have different impact on trained vs. non-trained personnel, as shown by Alagappan et al. (1996) in a seminal study comparing the impact of a 4-week rotation on emergency medicine (EM) versus non-EM residents (www.aemj.org/cgi/content/abstract/3/12/1131). While the level of psychological distress increased significantly in the latter group, *the reverse trend characterized EM trained physicians*.

Therefore, it is evident that the most optimal form of training will encompass several *elements*, including: medical realism, appropriate medical content and context, skills appropriate to the treated disorder, stress imposed by the emergency/trauma medicine patient, and stress imposed by the environment. It is equally evident that in order to be optimal, such training must result in: mastery of manual skills appropriate to the level of medical training, mastery of appropriate diagnostic skills, ability to maintain mental overview ("mental readiness") of the medical situation despite its continuous fluidity, ability to manage intellectual and physical resources, and ability to function with the maximum efficiency despite external stressor factors.

Medical simulation is a rapidly expanding area within medical education. In 2005, the *Society for Academic Emergency Medicine Simulation Task Force* was created to ensure that the Society and its members have adequate access to information and resources regarding this new and important topic. One of the objectives of the task force is to create a research agenda for the use of simulation in emergency medical education. Recently, there was presented a consensus document from the task force regarding suggested areas for research[4]. These include opportunities to study *reflective experiential learning, behavioural and team training, procedural simulation, computer screen–based simulation*, the use of simulation for evaluation and testing, and special topics in emergency medicine. The challenges of research in the field of simulation are discussed, including the impact of simulation on patient safety.

In the Coconut context, output-based research and multidisciplinary efforts were employed to serve to advance simulation techniques and encourage their adoption. This is therefore an open-field and a modern issue in Emergency Medicine, to be exploited and developed in the years to come in order to target all these endpoints.

Some Background Ideas

The emergence of the knowledge society and knowledge-based economy poses new requirements for education and training: the knowledge-based economy requires a flexible, very well-trained workforce; and the citizens of the information society need to be continuously (re)trained in order to remain competitive within this workforce, and to fully exploit the knowledge society for their personal development.

The rapid evolution of learning technologies – exploiting the respective developments in information and communication technologies (ICT) – create numerous new opportunities for meeting these requirements: web-based learning environments (learning management systems, learning content management systems, etc.) can deliver life-long education and training applications and services to anyone, anytime, anyplace. However, most of these applications realize a learning context which is rather "traditional" in nature: it is mainly based on the delivery of digital learning material and the facilitation of communication between learners and tutors.

On the other hand, the Internet and world wide web provide the technical infrastructure for the realisation of *alternative learning settings*, which are heavily based on *collaboration and cooperation*. This is due to the fact that collaboration is widely appreciated as a key for effective learning, as this is demonstrated in a number of related studies and EU-funded IST projects[5]. However, computer-supported collaborative learning (CSCL) environments are still rather limited: collaboration is facilitated through file exchange and common workspaces, which have not proved to significantly affect the learning outcomes.

This is, for example, demonstrated by the fact that most existing CSCL systems still attempt to ensure *collaboration through motivation*: all members in the collaboration group receive the same "utility" (e.g. the same grades for students), in order to ensure, and in fact force collaboration (i.e. "strong" members coach "weaker" peers, to increase their individual and group overall competitiveness). Other issues which can affect the collaboration group performance, such as the synthesis of the team or the nature of the tasks are less well documented and manifested in the related literature.

Moreover, the *exploitation of CSCL systems at an organisational level* (embedding the results into the organisation's everyday practice) is much less investigated. Finally, related literature acknowledges the fact that *human-related aspects* constitute the deciding actor for the acceptability and success of IT systems in hospitals: many early clinical information systems failed to deliver what was expected, because healthcare professionals (doctors, nurses, etc) resisted their use. It is in this context that Coconut aimed to address a number of additional issues which affect the effectiveness of collaborative learning settings in the healthcare learning domain, including individual, organisational and managerial issues.

Modern ICT solutions recognise the importance of *learning as a social process* and offer new possibilities for interaction with the learning content and for guidance from teachers, trainers and tutors. This *learner-centric view* has put the trainee back in command, with a wealth of learning resources at her/his fingertips. Further to that, teachers and trainers play an even more essential role, besides virtual or traditional face-to-face interaction with their students, as they are no longer seen as simple users of a pre-determined training content, but as editors, authors and contributors to a *contextualised learning scenario*.

A lot of informal learning happens within these social activities, not to speak of the working environments, where tacit knowledge is exchanged and disseminated spontaneously within the so-called "communities of practice". A typical example of these are the Open Source Software circles, where people learn or become skilled in doing things because they participate in social interaction.

As it was previously mentioned, the research does not deal with the content related to the actions and behaviors required of the medical and paramedical staffs that practice medicine under emergency conditions. If necessary, we will make contact with some relevant hospital staff, who will supplement the learning content with these issues[6]. This notwithstanding, the question of the reciprocal relations between theoretical and clinical/practical knowledge is included in the various syllabi intended for this purpose. Regarding the professions addressed to in this project, the question of the relations and connections between *disciplinary and interdisciplinary knowledge* is a complex one, and worthy of careful contemplation.

To sum up, it is our vision that ICT clearly has the potential to stimulate learning networks and new forms of training organisation. However, "a *basic principle of good pedagogy* remains that *the design of the whole learning process* (possible supported by e-learning) is the decisive factor for the learner's success. Therefore, European countries' e-learning related measures should not be limited to questions of hard- and software, but rather focus on the pedagogy and e-learning in work processes".[7]

Professional development is development and cultivation of professional knowledge that is situational, contextual, deals with decision making and the ability to follow through on decisions made under changing circumstances and in unique situations that are characteristic of the profession. It includes a collection of successful experiences alongside theoretical learning, through which the professionals define their roles, become acquainted with their capabilities and arrive at a new understanding of what is important to do, and thus continuously construct their evolving and developing professional identity. This is a *continuous process* that originates in personal sources and is derived from the influences of the group of professionals to which the individuals belongs. The group activities and experiences create desired action and behavioural norms, while maintaining a freedom of action and autonomy. The *learning processes* comprise a source of professional authority that helps the individual achieve a renewed understanding of the role, and - as a source of influence on other staff members - on management personnel as well.

For the purposes of this paper, we refer to professionals whose roles involve *practice as its main component*. In these professions, it is important that practice enables empowerment, which can be achieved if the following aspects are taken into account in the professional development program (Yosifon, 1997):

- *Practical-applicational orientation*: the process will be oriented toward the professionals' real-life actuality, a task or a problem that they are required to deal with, and is applicable to their lives or is essential to them, so that they will optimally benefit from their learning on a personal level;
- **An ongoing reflective thought process (inquiry) occurs following the experience**: the concept of "reflection", as a mental activity that is critical for the professional life, occupies a central place in the definition of the professionalisation of many professions in general, and of medical and clinical professions in particular; based on this concept, the professional examines his/her knowledge from a critical perspective, as it is expressed in his/her experiences, and devotes time to thought after the activity has been completed, with the aim of understanding the activity's meanings in order to create knowledge on action;
- **A meta-practice of problem resolution is created**: the professional meetings are dedicated to a discussion on resolving problems of various kinds; the meta-practice is constructed from generalisations phrased on the basis of the discussions, with the exposure of incidents of success and lack of success contributing to the process; the meta-practice is translated into procedures together with new knowledge that is integrated into the performance of the tasks required within the framework of the role;
- **Development is defined as important when it expresses constitutive values**: professionals have a "moral voice" that conforms to the ethics and values of their profession; this is especially true in the case of medical staff;
- **Professional development is a combined process of top-down and bottom-up**: the current trend is to view the activity of these systems in a collaborative context; the activation of the systems is complex and complicated and relies on the high professional level of the staff, and not only on technical knowledge of procedures; adult learners, particularly those who are aware of what they want, need to know and understand why they must learn or be trained; therefore, it is important that the trainees will feel that the learning is not something that is forced upon them, but rather that they are, to a certain extent, partners in the program; even in programs where the content is determined in advance, it is important to allow the trainees to participate in choosing the learning strategies and methods; the right to choose is especially important to adult learners, as it exhibits respect towards them and increases their motivation to learn (Knowles et al., 1998).

This trend is compatible with the increasing demand for ***accountability***, and therefore, with growing awareness of the importance of professionalism in other important sectors of public life than the medical and emergency contexts.

The Professional Development Cycle

In this context, the proposed ***professional development model*** is a long-term, continuous process that includes three main components, as detailed in Table 4 and Figure 5.

The research literature addressing the processes related to professional development puts specific emphasis on the difficulties involved in implementing similar programs, the (usually) partial success in their realization, and especially on the difficulty that the staff face in adopting programs, particularly when they entail significant modifications in their routine functions. In research conducted on educational systems in the late 1980s (Fullan, 1993), researchers propose to base the programs on local involvement, to encourage the development of local leadership (Peltz et al, 2006) at various levels, and to include them in the decision making process.

This project approaches the topic of ***motivation*** to professional development of position holders, according to the theoretical framework of ***andragogy***[8] (Knowles et al., 1985), which assumes that adults have the motivation to learn topics that will help them in their daily lives, will support their professional development, will incorporate issues they deal with in their professional lives; or at a minimum threshold, when the material satisfies a certain need or is interesting.

The Selected Pilot Implementation Domains

In Coconut we designed a professional development model and learning platform on two specific pilot application domains that are described in more detail below[9]:

- *Cardiovascular emergencies* (Figure 6), and
- *Mass casualty situations* (Figure 7).

The scenario for e-learning in cardiovascular emergencies is depicted in Table 5.

Below we present the scenario for mass casualty situations in Figure 7 and Table 6.

Table 4. The professional development cycle: stages and description

1. Preparatory Activities	2. Real-time Activities	3. Activities Following the Incident
These activities are the most common. Their purpose is to prepare the position holders for a mass-casualty incident. Learning from these activities for professional development purposes is based on past incidents and lessons, insights and conclusions drawn from their handling, the knowledge of persons that have participated in the handling of such incidents, research and accumulated experience.	Although in real-time the staff actions are focused on saving lives, participation in incidents may also be regarded as part of the participants' professional development, due to experience acquired through their participation. In the case of real-time activities, it is recommended to document decision making and actions taken. Documentation, at a later stage, becomes part of the raw material used for professional development.	Debriefing should be performed after each mass casualty incident. It should be conducted at the small group level, as well as at the interdisciplinary system level. Knowledge and conclusions drawn from the debriefing process will serve as information, data and conclusions for preparatory activities.

CONFIGURING THE COLLABORATIVE ENVIRONMENT

Coconut was intended to be realised in various European countries and organisations; therefore, it should also allow for adaptability to reflect the professional development of emergency medical staff with respect to the culture of each country: any national and organisational citizenship should express its commitment to take appropriate action in due time.

We achieved the establishment and operation of the Coconut learning community by means of employing the Living Labs methodology. The reason is straightforward: Living Labs represent regional innovation environments focusing on ***user communities embedded within "real life"***. Even if the planning of the project is performed in a centralised manner, it will be developed such that it can be continuously adapted and validated through the interpretations and comments given by professionals. As a result of this cooperative approach, participants will acquire full or partial ownership over the planning and their motivation to implement the pilots will increase.

Additionally to the technological aspects, Living Labs allow a deep insight into the ***human dimension of technology***, which is of paramount importance for a successful societal deployment of new technologies. As a consequence of this potential, the Living Lab approach is taken as a natural candidate for the implementation of large scale evaluation, demonstration and validation activities related to ICT RTD.

A Living Lab refers to a setting that is created with specific targets and has a clear structure, but in the same time it is dealing with the uncontrollable dynamics of daily life. Therefore, its configuration holds an open character according to which technology is shaped out of specific social contexts and needs, and which

Figure 5. The professional development cycle of emergency staff

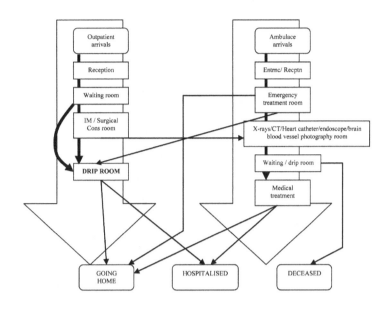

users are seen as co-producers. Researchers within Living Labs are restricted to monitoring what is going on "from the inside"; on the other hand, they are part of a Living Lab themselves, and are able to intervene in order to contribute to a better implementation of technological innovations in social practices, and deal with the unpredictable processes by reflecting upon and consequently adjusting their initial methodology.

The ***problem*** faced by current Living Labs is that, although similar services and products are usually developed, a ***coherent framework for cooperation*** inside a Living Lab is missing. Thus ***every new Living Lab has to start (almost) from scratch*** in configuring itself for the selected beneficiaries.

Within Coconut, we will build and populate our targeted experiential learning environment according to the following steps of a Living Lab configuration process as summarised in Pierson & Lievens (2005).

- ***Contextualisation***, referring to the prior exploration of the technological and social challenges implied by the technology or service under investigation;

Figure 6. Coconut use case #1 (Cardiovascular Emergencies)

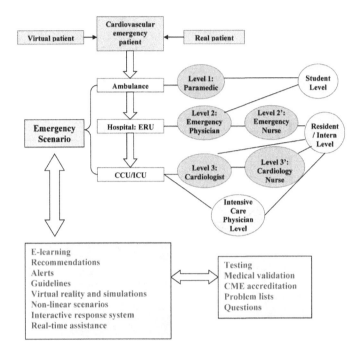

- ***Selection***, referring to the identification of potential users or user groups, by means of non-probabilistic or purposeful sampling;
- ***Concretisation***, referring to a thorough description of the current characteristics, everyday behaviour and perceptions of the selected test users regarding the research focus;
- ***Implementation*** is actually the behavioural validation and operationally running test phase of the LL, from a user-oriented and ethnographic viewpoint; and
- ***Feedback***, consisting of two research steps:
  - An ***ex post measurement*** based on the same techniques of the initial measurement, to check if there is any evolution in the users perception and attitude towards the introduced technology or service, to assess changes over time in everyday life in relation to technology use and to detect transitions of usage over time; and
  - A set of ***technological recommendations*** from the analysis of data, gathered during the previous implementation phase; this outcome of

Table 5. The scenario for e-learning in cardiovascular emergencies

Description	User logs in, selects level, selects emergency scenario from different scenarios available, runs a virtual case or introduces real case data, gets feedback in terms of recommendations/ alerts/ messages. Then completes training by doing a short multiple choice test or by listing questions, problems, conclusions.	
Actors	Expert Doctor, Doctor in training, Medical student, Nurse, Paramedic, Emergency action agent, Guideline agent, Testing agent	
Assumptions	Preconditions	Scenarios for different cardiovascular emergencies are available;
		Collection of real patient data from the EHR is possible;
		Different levels of training are pre-designed for different types of users;
		Multiple testing options are available;
		Check-up, correction and medical validation rules are established.
	Post conditions	System-generated recommendations/ alerts/ messages are confronted to the real-time situation if the case;
		When training is completed, certification of the trainee is available taking into consideration results of the testing.
Steps	a) User performs authentication and selects the required level of training;	
	b) The targeted cardiovascular emergency scenario is then selected;	
	c) Virtual case data or real-case data are loaded to the system;	
	d) Systems generates recommendations, algorithms, decisions, alerts and messages according to the selected scenario;	
	e) Short testing is provided for the user, in different modalities, to be selected by the user;	
	f) Problems list and questions list available as a feedback to the system from the trainee;	
	g) System's recommendations are applied to the current medical situation if the case.	
	h) Certification is provided to the trainee.	
Variations	Interactive options should be available to make training more efficient, like allowing the trainee to select the next steps in an algorithm or to generate his/hers own recommendations, to be thereafter assigned to a "right or wrong" message from the system.	
Non-functional requirements	1. The platform should be user friendly, with very clearly defined parameters, letting no space to confusion;	
	2. Many users should be able to use the platform in the same time, for different levels of training.	
Issues	For the real-time assistance options, speed of the system will be essential to ensure in-time recommendations to be applied to real emergencies management.	

Figure 7. Coconut use case #2 (Mass Casualty Situations)

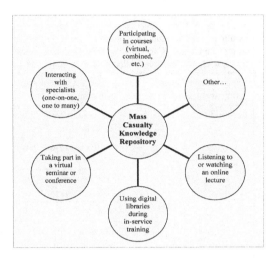

the feedback phase is used as the starting point for a new research cycle within the LL; in this way the iterative feature of research can be made operational.

To come up with ***reliable*** measures of the success of the application of the Living Labs approach in the project, we will cater for the design of commonly accepted benchmarks that will combine quantitative and qualitative aspects of the application exercise and will comply with field standards, as these stem from three well respected and accredited bodies namely the European Society for Emergency Medicine (EuSEM), the European Resuscitation Council, and the International Liaison Committee on Resuscitation (ILCOR).

The paramount purpose of the effort invested in the professional development of position holders - via a high-quality adaptable and interoperable training environ-

Table 6. The scenario for e-learning in mass casualty situations

Description	A single, multimedia knowledge repository for all information and "experiences" accumulated from natural disasters or human related catastrophes from all over the world. A learning environment for emergency staffs of various countries – something that can greatly contribute to reinforcing the sense of belonging of these staffs to the international professional community dealing with mass casualty situations. The sense of belonging supports individuals' and teams' desire and capabilities to contribute from their own knowledge and experiences, particularly when provided with audio-visual tools that help to illustrate and become familiar with situations, incidents and people.
Actors	Emergency teams, Medical centers, NGOs, Groups participating in continuing education programs, & Individuals (real-time use, during an incident, can also be envisaged).

Table 6. continued

Assumptions	Preconditions	A variety of digital libraries (DL) should be present, such as a case study DL, a DL of lessons, insights and conclusions derived from previous incidents, a DL of filmed lectures, a DL of incidents that have been filmed and documented, a DL of articles, a DL of procedures, glossaries, DL of training kits for actions and more;
		Access should be enabled to medical and other information systems, from which the users will be able to obtain reliable and up-to-date information both at the preparatory stages and for the purpose of functioning in real-life incidents;
		Access should also be enabled to a learning management system in which it will be possible to manage courses and additional learning frameworks in an effective and straightforward manner;
		Various tools should be present for synchronic and asynchronic communication among different participants, such as instant messaging, forums, video conference tools, environments for synchronic meetings and more;
		Effective and user-friendly search and information retrieval tools should allow to search for and find updated knowledge resources quickly;
		The platform is intended to serve teams from several countries already at the pilot stage. Therefore, it is important that from the beginning it operates in several languages.
	Post conditions	We recommend considering the possibility of constructing digital libraries on the basis of Wiki technology, which enables information creation and editing by the participants. The basic assumption is that over time, the databases will be expanded and enriched as a result of the experience acquired by the participants in the project, and at later stages – by other participants dealing with emergency medicine.
		Such a system will contain, among others, analytical tools used for analyzing the learners' use and learning effectiveness; therefore, it will also be able to serve the assessment process in this project.
		One of the challenges in this project will be to use information transfer and communication technologies that will operate via the different end users' diverse equipment (laptops, PDA, cellular devices, GPS handheld ultrasound equipment and more). Part of the preparatory stage will include the selection of the various technologies and devices under different conditions.
		Another conclusion of the research (Peltz et al, 2006) conducted following the tsunami disaster in Thailand emphasizes the need to transfer reliable and up-to-date information; this is seen as one of the essential conditions of a system that functions well in mass casualty situations. A crucial issue of the configuration stage will be the updating of the information and knowledge following incidents, via the synchronization of end equipment.
		One of the characterization stage priorities will be to identify the languages needed.

Table 6. continued

Methodologies used	a) Workshops
	b) Role Play
	c) Simulation
	d) Debriefing
	e) Learning from Successes
	f) Case Study
	g) Use of Visual Technology
	h) Participation in Projects or in Planning Teams

ment - is to enhance the performance of the Coconut learning community, responsible for providing medical assistance to casualties in emergency situations and/ or during terror and/or other emergency mass casualty incidents. To this purpose, we basically intend to leverage upon the ***Living Labs Methodology*** for community animation and collaboration improvement, and on Kolb's (1984) model of ***Experiential Learning*** introduced above.

The design of experiential learning systems require insights, concepts, technologies, and methodologies from a host of disciplines that often have limited dialogue with one another (Davis 2003). Researchers in computer science — in the topics e.g. of Database Interoperability, Signal Processing, Information Retrieval, HCI, CSCL and Artificial Intelligence — will have to include, understand, and mutually redefine other areas of humanistic inquiry such as Epistemology, Phenomenology, Decision Support Systems and of course Emergency Medicine. This dialogue and collaboration takes time, commitment, and considerable effort, but can ultimately result in a "***hybridized theory and practice***", capable of addressing problems that no single discipline or cluster of related disciplines can attempt alone.

Hence, the Coconut project will begin its efforts by drawing on disparate disciplines, trying to redefine their boundaries, assumptions, and methodologies, to generate a new theory and practice of e-learning systems design in the context of Emergency Medicine and in the framework of Living Labs-like cooperative environments.

We will argue that experiences as such cannot be captured, stored, or transmitted, only the data which occasion experiences in human minds can. Prior research in communications theory and the phenomenology of lived and mediated experience provide us with frameworks for understanding how to structure data so as to affect the experiences that human minds create when they encounter these structured data (Davis 2003:51). Assimilating and taking advantage of such data requires recognition of their multimedia nature, the development of semantic models across different media, the representation of complex relationships in the data (such as spatio-temporal, causal, or evolutionary), and finally, the development of paradigms to mediate user-media interactions (Singh et al. 2004). To help generate insights from multiple heterogeneous data sources, any experiential environment has to allow users apply their senses directly to observe data and manage the information related to a particular event, based on their own personal interests in the context of that event (Jain 2003).

Reflecting humans' perceptual and cognitive strengths, experiential environments involve several key features (Jain 2003:51):

- *They are direct.* An experiential environment provides a holistic view of an event without using arcane metaphors and commands. Users are in a familiar environment in which they use natural actions based on familiar operations and their anticipated results. Data is readily interpreted by users' human senses; users then interact with the dataset to produce modified datasets.
- *They provide the same query and presentation spaces.* What-you-see-is-what-you-get, or WYSIWYG.
- *They consider both user state and query context.* Ideally any system should know the state and context of its users and present user-relevant information in the given state and context. People operate best in known contexts and tend to lose focus when confronted by context switching.
- *They promote perceptual analysis and exploration.* Because users employ their senses to analyze, explore, and interact, the system becomes more compelling and understandable. Text-based systems provide abstract information in visual form. Video games and simulation systems are engaging because they provide users with powerful multimedia environments.

The innovation degree of the Coconut environment can be measured with respect to pedagogical, organisational, methodology and technology aspects. *On the pedagogical side*, we already mentioned above several innovation aspects like:

- The *interdisciplinary, system-wide approach* to professional development of position holders;
- The integration of *theory and practice* throughout the learning process;
- The use of *medical simulation* as part of an *experiential, problem-based learning*;

Here we can add the topic of *curriculum and syllabi design* for emergency medicine position holders. Preparing a curriculum and syllabi for professional development and upgrading, particularly in the area of teaching and learning, is a real challenge. It includes blended learning methods, the use of face-to-face models and virtual models - separate or combined - for designing and implementing professional development systems at various levels. This expertise should be expressed in the programs for the professional development of emergency medical staff, since there are principles, assumptions and generic models that are realized each time professional development takes place.

The preparation of syllabi should be carried out on the basis of a certain doctrine. It appears to us that in the area that our research deals with, it will be necessary to relate to professional development programs, but also to develop some of the doctrine. Our research puts a specific emphasis on the preparation of syllabi that are based on *uniform execution standards and procedures*, in order to ensure uniformity in all the EU countries. The design of the programs will have to take into account local conditions, laws and regulations, on the one hand; and determine standardization in professional development, on the other hand.

Another possible improvement lies in the *development of professional upgrade programs* with accompanying *advancement tracks* for individuals. This, of course, depends on the various professions and on the conditions existing in each country; however, it also comprises an important incentive for autonomous professional development. Professional development programs should include both compulsory programs ("must") and voluntary ones, which professionals may choose to participate in of their own free will ("nice to have").

On the organisational side, we already mentioned our focus on the embedding of training activities and results into the everyday practice of hospitals and rescue organisations. Our research aimed to the development of *a management culture with a strong awareness for Life-Long Learning* (LLL) as an expression of professional development. Based on this viewpoint, learning activities are planned and designed, both on a personal and on a group-organizational level, in order to enhance the organization's performance level. This allows for position holders to master autonomous learning skills and learn both within structured frameworks and independently. Therefore, the various methodologies include different types of professional development, starting from learning with colleagues either within or outside the organization, through synchronous and asynchronous and blended web-based learning to learning within the framework of interdisciplinary, system-wide exercises. Diverse professional development usually generates a high level of motivation and a sense of satisfaction in the workplace, and a higher capacity of self capability to implement the material that has been learned - learning in itself does not enhance capabilities.

A number of research studies have demonstrated that only professional development that is grounded on a management culture that demands implementation produces the desired results, while operating systems that are based on a bureaucratic mechanism has not led to a significant enhancement of these systems' quality. This literature emphasizes the organizational culture, the learning of organization and the learning of the individual throughout his/her professional life.

Professional learning processes should impart values concerning the importance of LLL and the autonomy of professional self-development, together with knowledge in the subject matters. Undoubtedly, in the context of globalization and the tough competition in the employment market in most European countries, it is important for the emergency staff to internalize the significance of education and learning throughout their professional lives.

To summarize, our research included activities at organisational level that build on, and enhance capacity (for those in its initial stages), empower and reinforce professionalism to a level of maximal mastery required, and ultimately, produce professionals who are experts in their respective fields. Here is where the Living Labs approach was proven to be helpful, and where the main innovation lies *on the methodology side*.

The Living Labs framework is a particular innovation approach in which *all stakeholders participate* in the development process of a product, service or application. It refers to an R&D methodology where innovation (like service, product or application enhancements) is created or validated in collaborative, multi-context, empirical real-world environments. By this approach, the individual is focused in his or her role as a citizen, user, consumer, or worker. The main difference between traditional consumer research programs and the Living Labs is this people's involvement in their every day lives, encompassing all of their societal roles. This locates the Living Lab framework, though with a set of differentiating attributes, in the area of "user centric" design and validation/evaluation methodologies, conceiving of the integration with users as the most powerful source of innovation.

REFERENCES

Bond, W. F., Lammers, R. L., Spillane, L. L., Smith-Coggins, R., Fernandez, R., Reznek, M. A., et al. (2007). The use of simulation in emergency medicine: A research agenda. *Acad Emerg Med Journal*.

CEC (2005). European Commission Staff Working Document, "Annex to the Proposal for a Decision of the European Parliament and of the Council establishing a Competitiveness and Innovation Framework Programme (2007-2013)", SEC(2005) 433 of 6th April 2005.

Crisis resource management training in emergency medicine (n.d.). Retrieved from http://www.straylightmm.com/

Darling-Hammond, L. & Wise (1992). Teacher Professionalism. In M.C. Alkin (Ed.), *Encyclopedia of Educational Research,* (6th Ed., pp. 1359 – 1366). New York: Macmillan.

Davis, M. (2003, November 7). Theoretical foundations for experiential systems design. *Proceedings of ETP, 03,* 45–52. doi:10.1145/982484.982491

Disaster Medical Assistance Teams. *A Literature Review.* (n.d.). Retrieved from http://www.health.wa.gov.au/disaster/DMAT/index/disaster%20medical%20assistance%20teams%20literature%20review%202006.pdf

Eriksson, M., Nitamo, V. P., & Kulkki, S. (2005). *State-of-the-art in utilizing Living Labs approach to user centric ICT innovation – a European approach.* Retrieved from http://www.cdt.ltu.se/main.php/SOA_LivingLabs.pdf?fileitem=2402350*European survey on training objectives in disaster medicine.* (n.d.). Retrieved from http://www.euro-emergencymed.com/pt/re/ejem/abstract.00063110-200702000-00005.htm;jsessionid=FsZBcnZ9twTGTsrK1tk91YyYTFVpGnzzhZgJh8Q7yhhn1RSpsDQy!-1412202079!-949856144!8091!-1

Fenech, J. (2005). *E-Learning: How can we achieve an effective and qualitative learning experience?* Retrieved from http://www.filternetwork.org/downloads/MSX%20paper%20Justin%20Fenech.doc

Founding Members of the International Liaison Committee on Resuscitation. (2005). The International Liaison Committee on Resuscitation (ILCOR)--Past and present. *Resuscitation, 67,* 157–161. doi:10.1016/j.resuscitation.2005.05.011

Fuchs, A. (2002) *About trainers, trainees and training.* Tel Aviv, Israel: Cherikover.

Fullan, M. G. (1993). *Change forces – probing the depth of educational reform.* London: The Falmer Press.

Jain, R. (2003). Experiential computing. *Communications of the ACM, 46*(7), 48–54. doi:10.1145/792704.792729

Johnson, R. B., & Onwuegbuzie, A. J. (2004). Mixed methods research: A research paradigm whose time has come. *Educational Researcher, 33*(7), 14–26. doi:10.3102/0013189X033007014

Knowles, M. S., et al. (1985). *Andragogy in action.* San Francisco: Jossey-Bass

Knowles, M. S., Holton, E. F., & Swanson, R. A. (1998). *The adult learner* (5ᵗʰ Ed.). Houston, TX: Gulf Pub. Co.

Kolb, D. (1984). *Experiental learning: Experience as the source of learning and development.* Englewood Cliffs, NJ: Prentice Hall.

Medical Readiness Trainer Team. (2000). An immersive virtual reality platform for medical education: Introduction to the medical readiness trainer. *Proceedings of the 33rd Hawaii International Conference on System Sciences.*

Peltz, A., Schwartz, S., Nakash, L., & Levi, G. Bar-Dayan (2006). *Disaster healthcare system management and crisis intervention leadership in Thailand – Lessons learned from the 2004 tsunami disaster.* Retrieved from http://pdm.medicine.wisc.edu/21-5%20PDFs/peltz.pdf

Pierson, J., & Lievens, B. (2005). Configuring Living Labs for a 'thick' understanding of innovation. *Proceedings of EPIC Conference, 2005,* 114–127.

Rappaport, J. (1981). In praise of paradox, A social policy of empowerment over prevention. *American Journal of Community Psychology, 9*(1), 1–25. doi:10.1007/BF00896357

Role of exercises and drills in the evaluation of public health in emergency Response (n.d.). Retrieved from http://pdm.medicine.wisc.edu/21-3 PDFs/gebbie.pdf*Disaster Planning Drills and Readiness Assessment* (n.d.). Retrieved from http://www.ahrq.gov/news/ulp/disastertele/green.ppt

Rosenfeld, Y., Sikes, Y., Weiss, C., & Talal, D. (2002). *How to convert "learning from successes" into a lever for developing in-school learning.* Jerusalem: Brookdale Institute.

Senge, P. (1990) *The fifth discipline. The art and practice of the learning organization. Currency.* Retrieved from http://leeds-faculty.colorado.edu/larsenk/learnorg/senge.html

Shkedi, A. (2003). *Qualitative research: Theory and application.* Tel Aviv, Israel: Ramot.

Singh, R., Knickmeyer, R., Gupta, P., & Jain, R. (2004) Designing experiential environments for management of personal multimedia. *Proceedings of MM'04,* October 10–16 2004, New York (pp. 496-499).

Slavin, R. (1995). Research on cooperative learning and achievement: What we know, what we need to know. *Contemporary Educational Psychology, 21*(1).

Takakuwa, S., & Shiozaki, H. (2004). Functional analysis for operating emergency department of a general hospital. In R.G. Ingalls, M. D. Rossetti, J. S. Smith, & B. A. Peters, (Eds.), *Proceedings of the 2004 Winter Simulation Conference,* (pp. 2003-2011).

Tuomi, I. (2005) *The future of learning in the knowledge society: Disruptive changes for Europe by 2020.* Background paper prepared for DG JRC/IPTS and DG EAC. Retrieved from http://www.meaningprocessing.com/personalPages/tuomi/articles/TheFutureOfLearningInTheKnowledgeSociety.pdf

W.A.D.E.M. (2004). *International standards and guidelines on education and training for the multi-disciplinary health response to major events that threaten the health status of the community.* Retrieved from http://pdm.medicine.wisc.edu/Issues.pdf

Yosifon, M. (1997). *Reshaping of patterns of teaching: A Study of the process of change in a middle school in Israel* [Hebrew]. Ph.D. dissertation, Tel Aviv University School of Education, Tel Aviv, Israel.

ENDNOTES

[1]   This idea started at MIT Boston with William Mitchell, *MediaLab* and *School of Architecture and City Planning,* with experiments spanning from the US (http://architecture.mit.edu/house_n/placelab.html or http://www.sfu.ca/livinglab or http://www.calit2.net/research/labs) to Singapore (http://www.ida.gov.sg), from Finland (http://www.sparknet.fi or http://www.mobileforum.org or http://www.helsinkivirtualvillage.fi) to Norway (http://www.fremtidshuset.com), from Sweden (http://www.testplatsbotnia.com or http://www.livinglabs.se) to Germany (http://www.mobilecity.org or http://www.fokus.gmd.de/home), from the Netherlands (http://www.research.philips.com/technologies/misc/homelab or http://www.livingtomorrow.com) to Denmark (http://www.crossroadscopenhagen.com).

[2]   Compiled by the Founding Members of the International Liaison Committee on Resuscitation (2005), The International Liaison Committee on Resuscitation (ILCOR)--Past and present. *Resuscitation* 67, 157-161.

[3]   Medical Readiness Trainer Team (2000), An Immersive Virtual Reality Platform for Medical Education: Introduction to the Medical Readiness Trainer. *Proceedings of the 33rd Hawaii International Conference on System Sciences.*

4   William F. Bond, Richard L. Lammers, Linda L. Spillane, Rebecca Smith-Coggins, Rosemarie Fernandez, Martin A. Reznek et al. The Use of Simulation in Emergency Medicine: A Research Agenda. *Acad Emerg Med* published online before print February 15, 2007.

5   We are especially aware of the CWE (Collaborative Working Environments) cluster of European Commission FP6-IST and FP7-ICT Programme research projects currently ongoing across Europe.

6   Preliminary handling of the above may be found in W.A.D.E.M (2004).

7   *Achieving the Lisbon goal: The contribution of Vocational Education and Training (VET)*, November 4, 2004 (p. 17). The highlights are ours.

8   Andragogy = Adults Pedagogy, or learning methods and techniques used to teach adults.

9   The pilots are indeed quite heterogeneous but we believe this can be an asset not a limitation for the sake of the project.

Chapter 11
Future of Services

The dominance of services in our world and the challenges that the society and the individuals are facing. About the emergence of the Service Science as an independent discipline that will be taught, studied, researched and applied. Formulation of the scientific foundations of a Service Science. Spirituality and transcendental elements in the service discipline. Novel concepts and knowledge areas: service terrorism, service anarchy, service activism, service tyrannies. The role of history and arts and the inrush of humanities in the service domain.

Services shall definitely constitute the future of our global economies – as they always did and do in all levels all the years but now the difference will be that this dominance of services shall be evident and apparent in all levels of the society and the economy. This means that the emergence of the Service Science as an independent discipline that will be taught, studied, researched and examined shall take place. For sure, this is not a novelty: management and accounting as well as computers experienced at some point of their lifetime their transformation from a profession towards a science. And of course there is still a part of the people that don't accept

DOI: 10.4018/978-1-60566-683-9.ch011

them as such – at the end it is not a matter of taste but a matter of fact what defines something as a science.

The problem that I foresee with services is the basis upon which the formation of the scientific foundations will base: engineers have all the good reason to prefer an engineering background on services; same good is the reason for economists and business and / or management science professionals. Finally accountants, computer scientists and sociologists can exhibit some grounded reasons for supplying the basis for this 'new old' science.

My opinion is sharp-cut: there should be a totally new basis that shall reflect concerns and considerations of all the aforementioned disciplines. Even more: at a great extend, I see the need for introducing an extensive degree of spirituality and transcendal elements in the service science – though the obvious remark is that this comprises an unscientific practice. The reason for this comes from observation of phenomena that dominate our daily personal and working lives: management does not refer to Taylorism but – more and more – relates to leadership, where the latter term connotes terms like an enlighted leader who – more or less – executes his or her powers in a fashion that is totally unscientific and irrational. Additionally, dramatic elements in the organisation and conduct of business processes are not an innovation at all; the same holds for the ritual aspects that can be found in numerous occasions within the modern corporate and business world. The answer to this is simple: there is a need from the people to satisfy several levels of their lives both as individuals as well as members of an organised – professional or non-professional – community and to do so there is a need to introduce transcendal elements that can address parts of the encountered situations in a satisfactory though totally unscientific way.

To know how to do this is an extremely serious and scientific aspect that shall more and more be given increased importance by service scientists and service professionals. We should not forget that religion in all its more or less sense-making realisations constitutes an extremely good case for examining service science in an extremely well-defined application area namely this of intangible spirituality. At least, when you pay for an insurance service or a financial service, there are ways to measure the success or the satisfaction of the supplied (intangible) service in terms of some types of (tangible) results. Religion, on the other hand, does constitute an area where the success of the supplied service does not have a tangible equivalent to use as a benchmark.

What one should be able to see here is all the dangers that can relate with what I expect to happen in terms of a violent and forceful attack of this new type of (should I call them holistic?) services which shall promise to fulfil expectations that are not lying at the area of the service as such. Marketing and branding can provide some good examples for what we mean by this: in the same way that a successfully branded item (whatever this can be: a cloth or a computer or a beer or a car) differentiates the buyer from others who have chosen any other different brand and *not necessarily* in terms of some criteria that can be measured or valuated objectively, we expect that more and more service cultures shall be defined and promoted solely on no(n) sense-making elements. Who could have thought of paying for psychoanalysis sessions for his dog or her cat? At the end, there seems to exist a market for such a service. Similarly, one can foresee the need for supplying such a service for non-living entities like Second-Life avatars or printers and desktop computers – why not even for some office word processor applications (Have you ever considered the drabness of a word processor application of a law company? How wonderful can be the life of word processor applications residing in the computers of business men or politicians? How can this be remedied?)

It is not a crime to sell a service that seems illogical – it is a crime to not sell the service that you promised to provide. Of course marketing shall be asked for the rescue – successfully as we all can be sure. But the next time that someone will have a negative attitude towards marketing don't forget to see the other side of the coin: marketing actually provides a basic service to both service and non-service elements of the economy in terms of supplying them with metaphysical elements that may (or may not…) reside within them.

Speaking about the future of services one may expect forecasts like global service infrastructures (that by the way already and since years exist) or elaborations for multilingual services that understand natural language even if this is spoken by a minority of humans or avatars and which can supply customised service delivery and make any of their customers or consumers happy. Again, my personal opinion is that such a future view is not difficult to predict. On the other hand, what we tend to not pay the required attention is notions like service terrorism, collapses of service economies, service anarchy, service activism, service democracies (service tyrannies as well).

The reader may understand the above terms in many different ways. History can teach us a lot – the difficult part is to show willingness for learning from its many lessons.

At a great extent, all what we refer to above as – mainly dark - future directions for the service world are partly experienced nowadays. Starting from the term of service terrorism one needs to look at two different cases: firstly, we consider the case of a reality where services are used for expanding networks and incidents of terrorism worldwide. This is again not a novelty – but currently we still think of terrorism as a non-service phenomenon when it actually is such one.

Though we think of a terrorist group as an organisation that carries out certain actions against states or individuals, we don't focus on some simple facts like the following:

- There are elements of group culture and individual knowledge that drive into certain activities
- There is a thorough and deterministic pathway for rationalising even the nastiest actions. What we all tended to think of as an irrational action driven by fanatism or madness needs to be reconsidered as an extremely consistent, purposeful and conscious activity that is part of a wider Weltanschauung from the side of the terrorist.
- Branding and capture of an identity is an extremely important part of a terrorist groups business. Much of a terrorist group success bases on this and it is for this reason that counterterrorism measures should put considerable efforts on this level.
- Efficiency and effectiveness are also a sine qua non as it is an extremely wide area of know how that needs to be acquired by the terrorist group. To close the eyes to this simple reality is like suicide.

Service terrorism may relate to the capture of key services by terrorists; it may also mean the transformation of certain service providers to terrorists (To this point, there is fertile ground for debating the issue whether a service monopoly or oligopoly does constitute some type of terrorism).

In a similar fashion, one can view phenomena like the open source and free source software communities as some form of service activisms. The underlying cult for both of them may take extremely powerful forms and drive the software and Net economies in unpredictable directions. Of course, this form of activism can exhibit links to all abovementioned terms namely the terrorism, the democracy, the anarchy, the tyranny.

All of them share the entity of the community – the difference is what they do *for* the community or *to* the community. In a democracy, we suppose that decisions are made by the people and for the people, while in a tyranny decisions for the people are not made by them but by the tyrant him or herself. Republic lies in between where the people have elected the tyrants for a predefined period of time to execute tasks for which the latter are liable to the people. Institutions that control service providers either as regulators or as auditors provide similar type of facilities – though we don't use this way to analyse their business.

Sociology and political science can provide more and better answers to all the above issues. The French philosopher Luis Althusser defined a practice as any process of transformation of a determinate product, affected by a determinate human labour, using determinate means (of production). Nowadays that we talk a lot about practices on the Net, in services or e-services, it is tragically timely how much we lack on intellectuals that will be able to transform and process service or technology problems into societal or political ones and vice versa.

A great part of future service research shall build on arts – applied or not. Design of a service shall be linked with qualities that will not be easy to find in the profiles of computer science or business school graduates. Someone who can understand the tides of the art market not in the modern times but in retrospect (who bought Caravaggio paintings at the painter's time? Who bought Renoirs? And why? How were the painters positioned with respect to each other of their competitors at their times? And how did the Zeitgeist affect the prosperity of the painters and their 'schools'? one can see in my statement only a risky speculation – however, the reader should agree that the art market does constitute an extremely well defined though not yet well studied area of intangibles assets management. This is similar if not same to the case of services. The only difference with the domain of insurance is that in the latter there is always a tangible equivalent that effectuates an insurance contract or an insurance related transaction.

One may have all good reasons to ask why I do foresee such an inrush of humanities in the service domain – the answer is simple: it is because currently there is a total absence of all of them, while we all experience an excess of engineering, computing, business, management, accounting and marketing.

About the Author

Adamantios Koumpis heads the Research Programmes Division of ALTEC S.A., which he founded at 1996 (then as independent division of Unisoft S.A.). He is author of research papers, technical reports and project deliverables in the domains of data/information management and human-computer interaction. His research interests include quantitative decision making techniques and information society economics. He successfully lead many commercial and research projects both at the European and the national level in the areas of e-commerce, public sector and business enterprise re-organisation and information logistics, concerning linking of data/information repositories with knowledge management and business engineering models. Adamantios holds a PhD degree from the University of Kingston, UK and a Bachelor degree in computer science from the University of Crete, Greece.

Index